MW00345261

The Soul of Armies

A VOLUME IN THE SERIES

Cornell Studies in Security Affairs

edited by Robert J. Art, Robert Jervis, and Stephen M. Walt

A list of titles in this series is available at www.cornellpress.cornell.edu.

The Soul of Armies

Counterinsurgency Doctrine and Military Culture in the US and UK

AUSTIN LONG

Cornell University Press

Ithaca and London

Copyright © 2016 by Cornell University

All rights reserved. Except for brief quotations in a review, this book, or parts thereof, must not be reproduced in any form without permission in writing from the publisher. For information, address Cornell University Press, Sage House, 512 East State Street, Ithaca, New York 14850.

First published 2016 by Cornell University Press

First printing, Cornell Paperbacks, 2016

Printed in the United States of America

Library of Congress Cataloging-in-Publication Data

Long, Austin G., author.
   The soul of armies : counterinsurgency doctrine and military culture in the US and UK / Austin Long.
      pages cm — (Cornell studies in security affairs)
   Includes bibliographical references and index.
   ISBN 978-0-8014-5379-3 (cloth : alk. paper)
   ISBN 978-1-5017-0319-5 (pbk : alk. paper)
1. Military doctrine—United States.   2. Military doctrine—Great Britain.   3. Counterinsurgency.   4. United States—Armed Forces—Attitudes.   5. Great Britain—Armed Forces—Attitudes.   I. Title.
II. Series: Cornell studies in security affairs.
   U21.2.L66 2016
   355.02'180941-dc23   2015032898

Cornell University Press strives to use environmentally responsible suppliers and materials to the fullest extent possible in the publishing of its books. Such materials include vegetable-based, low-VOC inks and acid-free papers that are recycled, totally chlorine-free, or partly composed of nonwood fibers. For further information, visit our website at www.cornellpress.cornell.edu.

Cloth printing   10 9 8 7 6 5 4 3 2 1
Paperback printing   10 9 8 7 6 5 4 3 2 1

Contents

Preface

The seed of this book was planted in 1992, when as a young undergraduate in physics I happened to pick up a book called *The Army and Vietnam*. The book convinced me that organizations and the ideas of organizations matter more than technology in the conduct of certain kinds of war, most notably counterinsurgency. The initial idea for the book was that some organizations are more successful than others at counterinsurgency for reasons deriving from the organization's culture—the latter defined as a set of enduring organizational ideas about war.

More than two decades later, and after spending time in the midst of counterinsurgency in both Iraq and Afghanistan, I find that the resulting book is rather different than I anticipated when I began. I conclude that organizational culture does matter a great deal in how military organizations conduct counterinsurgency operations. Indeed, I am more convinced of this than ever based on both firsthand observation and careful comparison of detailed operational records.

I am now equally convinced that these differences in operations are only a partial explanation for success or failure in counterinsurgency. This probably comes as no surprise to any serious student of counterinsurgency, or even warfare generally. The operational and tactical excellence of Hannibal did not yield strategic success against Rome, nor did the collective brilliance of the Wehrmacht against the Allies.

Yet much of the counterinsurgency literature, and certainly the literature in English, implicitly assumes that if only the right mixture of operational measures is adopted, then success is all but assured. Essentially, counterinsurgency is not much different from baking a cake. However, unlike bakers, counterinsurgents confront not only an adversary that can adapt but also a

variety of other actors, ranging from local populations to allied governments. Each of these gets a vote in determining the success of counterinsurgency.

The conclusion of this book is therefore, all things being equal, that some
military organizations are more likely to conduct counterinsurgency operations that will lead to success than others. Of course, all things are seldom
equal. So rather than being a book about why some military organizations
succeed or fail at counterinsurgency, this is a book about why military
organizations are the way they are, and how that affects the way in which
they conduct counterinsurgency. This has implications for success or failure in counterinsurgency but is not, alas for parsimonious social science,
dispositive.

Organizational culture is nonetheless important to understand, as it has
very real implications both for scholars and for policymakers. For scholars,
understanding organizational culture helps explain variations in operations
that are otherwise unexplainable. In chapter 7, for example, the variation
in U.S. Marine Corps and U.S. Army operations in the same province of
South Vietnam is very difficult to explain without reference to organizational
culture.

For policymakers it is critical to know that, at least for counterinsurgency,
different organizations will conduct operations in ways that are more or less
likely to produce success, will produce more or fewer civilian casualties, and
the like. Even if particular operational approaches cannot guarantee success,
policymakers should understand the military tools they have to work with.
Likewise, if policymakers provide resources to organizations, they should
understand how those organizations are likely to use those resources.

Whatever insight this book provides is a result of a great deal of support,
and as a result I owe a great deal to a great many people and organizations.
The Massachusetts Institute of Technology's Security Studies Program, led
first by Harvey Sapolsky and then by Barry Posen, was the intellectual home
for initial work on this project. The RAND Corporation, particularly the International Security and Defense Policy Center led by James Dobbins and
the Intelligence Policy Center led first by Kevin O'Connell and then by John
Parachini, gave me another hospitable intellectual home and the opportunity to work on a variety of projects that broadened my understanding of
military and intelligence operations generally and counterinsurgency specifically, as well as the chance to see counterinsurgency up close and personal in Iraq and Afghanistan.

Columbia University's Saltzman Institute for War and Peace Studies and
the School of International and Public Affairs have provided substantial support for further development of this work, most notably in having patience
as I would wander off to Iraq, Afghanistan, and other such fun locales.
Columbia's Harriman Institute for Russian, Eurasian, and East European
Studies also provided financial support for the research and production of

this book. The manuscript was finalized while I was an International Security and U.S. Foreign Policy Fellow at Dartmouth College's Dickey Center for International Understanding. I am deeply indebted to MIT, RAND, Columbia, and Dartmouth.

Several other organizations also provided me with opportunities and funding that either directly or indirectly influenced my thinking about the topics covered in this book. Research conducted for the Office of Net Assessment in the Office of the Secretary of Defense and for the U.S. Navy's Program Management Activity-280 (Tomahawk All Up Round) shaped my thinking about military organizations and the environments, domestic and international, in which they must operate. Finally, a World Politics and Statecraft Fellowship from the Smith Richardson Foundation provided funding for archival research as well as field work in Afghanistan and Pakistan.

All of the following have read and commented on drafts of this manuscript: Michael Beckley, Rosella Capella, Owen Coté Jr., Brendan Green, Llewelyn Hughes, Colin Jackson, Jennifer Lind, Jon Lindsay, Thomas McNaugher, Will Norris, Barry Posen, Daryl Press, Josh Rovner, Harvey Sapolsky, Paul Staniland, Caitlin Talmadge, Benjamin Valentino, and William Wohlforth. I am grateful to all of them for their time and attention, which improved many aspects of my argument.

I was fortunate in finding many friends in the U.S. military and intelligence community who provided excellent insight into the workings of military organizations as well as the conduct of modern counterinsurgency. I particularly thank Lieutenant Colonel Ray Gerber (USMC), Colonel Chris Conner (ret.) (USA), Colonel Brooks Brewington (ret.) (USMC), Brigadier General Dale Alford (USMC), Colonel Pat Stackpole (ret.) (USA), Colonel George Bristol (USMC), Colonel John Agoglia (ret.) (USA), Colonel Ray Coia (ret.) (USMC), Brigadier General Billy Don Farris (ret.) (USA), Colonel Bruce "Moose" Danskine (USAF), First Lieutenant Matt McKnight (USMC), Colonel Phil "Goldie" Haun (USAF), and Captain Van Gurley (ret.) (USN), along with others who do not wish to be individually identified. I also thank two officers of the Canadian Army, Lieutenant Colonel Harjit Sajjan and Major Harpal "Manny" Mandaher, along with Carter Malkasian of the Center for Naval Analyses, for sharing their insights on counterinsurgency. I am especially indebted to retired Central Intelligence Agency officer turned CIA historian Thomas Ahern for sharing his unique perspective and wisdom on counterinsurgency in Southeast Asia and beyond.

The records at the Texas Tech University Vietnam Archive, the National Archives of the United Kingdom, the U.S. Army's Combined Arms Research Library, and the U.S. Marine Corps' Alfred M. Gray Research Center were all important in reconstructing history. I thank the staff of each of these institutes for their diligent work in making these records available online, in hard copy, or both. I also thank the staffs of MIT's Dewey and Hayden

Libraries, Harvard University's Widener Library, and Columbia University's Lehman and Butler Libraries for their assistance over the years.

Some elements of this book appeared previously in the chapter "U.S. Counterinsurgency in Vietnam: Shirking Transformation" in Adam N. Stulberg and Michael D. Salomone with Austin G. Long, *Managing Defense Transformation: Agency, Culture, and Service Change*; the RAND Occasional Paper "Doctrine of Eternal Recurrence: The U.S. Military and Counterinsurgency Doctrine, 1960–1970 and 2003–2006"; and the RAND monograph *Locals Rule: Historical Lessons for Creating Local Defense Forces in Afghanistan and Beyond.* I thank the reviewers and publishers of those works for their advice and support.

I would be nowhere today without years of unwavering support from my mother and grandmother, Charlotte Long and the late Edna Earle Arledge. One could not ask for more. I also thank Andrea, Whitney, and Michelle, each of whom did a lot for me. Most of all I thank Sian and Maggie for love and putting up with me generally, especially during my many absences during the completion of this work.

The Soul of Armies

Military Doctrine and the Challenge of Counterinsurgency

Afghanistan and Iraq have been the preeminent wars of the early twenty-first century for the United States and the United Kingdom. After initial success in toppling the Taliban regime in Afghanistan and the Ba'athist regime in Iraq, the two allies found themselves progressively bogged down in lengthy counterinsurgency campaigns. By 2006 both U.S. and U.K. forces were in dire straits in Iraq and Afghanistan as the Taliban launched new offensives even as Iraq descended into a maelstrom of violence. The allies seemed at a loss for what to do in either country.

Yet the challenge of counterinsurgency was not new for either country or for their military organizations. The U.S. military, and especially its ground forces in the Army and Marine Corps, had faced insurgencies before, most notably in Vietnam. Likewise, the British military, particularly the Army, had also fought numerous insurgencies. It was therefore all the more puzzling that counterinsurgency was proving so difficult a challenge.

According to several popular narratives of the war in Iraq, the development of a better way of fighting counterinsurgency (combined with more resources) led to a successful outcome in Iraq.[1] The promulgation of a new U.S. Army and Marine Corps doctrinal manual for counterinsurgency in 2006 was hailed as an epiphany for these organizations. After years of drift and misunderstanding counterinsurgency in Iraq and Afghanistan, this new manual would revolutionize the conduct of those wars.

Yet a comparison with counterinsurgency doctrine written forty years earlier casts doubt on this explanation, as the doctrine was functionally the same. Compare these statements of the central problem of counterinsurgency:

> The primary objective of any counterinsurgent is to foster the development of effective governance by a legitimate government. All governments rule through a combination of consent and coercion. Governments described as

"legitimate" rule primarily with the consent of the governed, while those described as "illegitimate" tend to rely mainly or entirely on coercion.[2]

Since the essence of the counterguerrilla campaign is to win back the support of the people for the established government, the importance of civil affairs is paramount. . . . In internal defense operations, because of the importance of isolating the guerrillas from the people, civil affairs becomes one of the primary missions of the counterguerrilla force. This is because all internal defense operations plans must be based on an integrated civil-military approach designed to progressively reassert host government control and gain the trust, confidence, and active cooperation of the people.[3]

The former is from the 2006 manual and the latter is from a 1967 manual, yet both define the problem of counterinsurgency in almost identical ways. As discussed in later chapters, comparisons of British counterinsurgency doctrine from the 1950s and the first decade of the twenty-first century reveal the same kinds of similarities.

At least one popular narrative argues that the doctrine was right all along and that the problem in Vietnam was one of leadership. In this telling, an enlightened general (Creighton Abrams) took command from a lesser light (William Westmoreland) and actually tried to apply the counterinsurgency doctrine as written. The result was success but, alas, tragically too late to produce strategic success.[4]

Thus counterinsurgency becomes a just-so story about the right general at the right time with the right doctrine. In Vietnam and Iraq the doctrine was correct, but Westmoreland was replaced too late. In contrast, General David Petraeus replaced General William Casey (the alleged Westmoreland figure in the Iraq narrative) in the proverbial nick of time to save Iraq.

While these narratives are appealing, they are also deeply flawed.[5] In Vietnam, as described in chapters 6 and 7 of this book, there was much more continuity than change in operations after Abrams took command. The same is true of Iraq, as described in chapter 9, where the alleged collective epiphany of the U.S. military is, upon closer examination, much less striking. Some units conducted operations in accordance with the new doctrine even before it was promulgated, yet even after Petraeus took command many continued to conduct operations that did not conform to the doctrine.[6] Moreover, the doctrine has not produced strategic success in Iraq, which in 2015 is under dire threat from militants and the specter of renewed civil war.[7]

In Afghanistan, a similar narrative could be told about the 2009 replacement of General David McKiernan by General Stanley McChrystal. McChrystal ran into political trouble and so was then replaced by Petraeus, the hero of Iraq. Yet despite having the "right generals with the right doctrine" (along with a significant increase in resources), Afghanistan remains violent and unstable. Only by arguing that, like Abrams, McChrystal and Petraeus in

Afghanistan had a better war but one that came too late can the just-so story be saved. Chapter 10 of this book argues that, as with Iraq and Vietnam, this narrative does not reflect reality on the ground.[8] Despite the problems of these narratives, a slightly modified version of the 2006 doctrine remains in place as of 2015.[9]

The British Army has an equally troubled narrative about counterinsurgency. Based on successes in confronting insurgency during the early Cold War, the British Army has been regarded as highly capable in counterinsurgency. They have long espoused a doctrine that very much accords with the doctrine that allegedly produced success in Vietnam and Iraq. Yet in both Iraq and Afghanistan the British were beleaguered and battered by insurgents. Were the early Cold War successes flukes, or is there a more systematic explanation for British success and failure?

This book addresses these puzzling observations by providing a more systematic framework for examining the central question of why doctrine and operations remain muddled in counterinsurgency. Modern militaries have generated doctrine for counterinsurgency for more than half a century, and the basic outlines of the doctrine have not actually changed. Yet the problem remains vexing to them and has generated operational responses that vary across organizations.

This is in contrast to the steady convergence across organizations toward an effective response to higher-intensity conventional conflict that Stephen Biddle has termed "the modern system."[10] These variations are sometimes idiosyncratic to individual units, but in some cases different components of a single organization have systematically different approaches. As discussed in chapter 3, the U.S. Army Special Forces approach counterinsurgency operations in a radically different manner than the broader U.S. Army.

From a policy perspective, the continuity of counterinsurgency doctrine across decades despite at best mixed results raises important questions. First, is the doctrine embodied in past and current field manuals actually the right way to fight counterinsurgency? This requires examining whether the mixed record is the result of the doctrine itself or of the way the doctrine was applied. Second, given that organizations respond differently to the challenge of counterinsurgency, are some better suited to it than others?

This book answers these questions by examining both contemporary and historical counterinsurgency campaigns conducted by the United States and the United Kingdom. It does so by proposing four main hypotheses about military organizations and the source of military doctrine. It then tests those hypotheses against the campaigns in Vietnam, Kenya, Iraq, and Afghanistan.

The conclusion, discussed at length in the final chapter, is that some organizations are, all things being equal, better than others at counterinsurgency. Yet all things are seldom equal, and, particularly for foreign militaries conducting counterinsurgency abroad, success has much more to do with local conditions than with military doctrine and operations.[11] The principal policy lesson from both historical and contemporary counterinsurgency is that the agency of outsiders is limited.

Insurgency as Power to the People: The U.S. Civil War, *Volkskrieg*, and the Boers, 1861–98

The central feature of insurgency is the use of political and military means by nonstate or irregular forces to overthrow or resist state forces. It is generally carried out by blending in with the civilian population, from whom the irregular forces draw support (sometimes willing, sometimes via coercion, often a mix). These forces, initially inferior to state forces in conventional battle, rely on a combination of subversion and hit-and-run operations.

The concept of warfare carried out by and among the civilian population was not novel in the nineteenth century. However, just as the emergence of pervasive nationalism and the Industrial Revolution enabled conventional warfare on a new and massive scale, so too it enabled a new form of "people's war." Nationalism created a motive force that, if harnessed, was no less potent for nonstate forces than it was for the state.

Equally important, the Industrial Revolution made large numbers of highly effective weapons available to nonstate forces. Most notable in the late nineteenth century was the breech-loading rifle, which gave individuals or small groups the ability to attack at long range from concealment. Dynamite similarly provided a readily portable means to destroy fixed positions. Combined with industrial-era techniques of organization and nationalism, these new technologies made "people's war" orders of magnitude more capable.

The power of modern nonstate forces was first observed in the U.S. Civil War, as noted briefly in chapter 3. Southern irregulars were able to harass Union forces, particularly as Union supply lines grew longer. Though far from decisive, these forces were nonetheless an effective complement to the regular Southern forces.[12]

Shortly after the end of the Civil War, the power of nonstate forces would be demonstrated even more forcefully. In 1870, the Prussian Army rapidly and decisively defeated the French Army in a series of battles culminating in the Battle of Sedan in September. The French emperor, Napoleon III, was captured by the Prussians and surrendered. However, a new Government of National Defense proclaimed itself in Paris and sought to mobilize the population to continue the war.[13]

One of the most effective components of this mobilization was the so-called *franc-tireurs* ("free shooters"). Originating in civilian shooting clubs, these small groups were armed with rifles and dynamite, which they wielded with lethal effect. Surprising small parties of Prussian soldiers and blowing up key military sites (such as railroad bridges), the *franc-tireurs* proved to be a major challenge to the highly professional Prussian forces despite being relatively few in number, as even some Prussian officers noted.[14]

These two early examples of insurgency did not take place on the periphery of European empires. Instead, they took place in two modern industrialized states. In contrast, wars for empire took place against indigenous forces that lacked modern organization, nationalism, and often armaments. Rather than the difficult fights the Prussians experienced in 1870–71, most imperial wars were characterized by a few set-piece battles won by European forces, followed by a negotiated settlement.

For example, in the First Dahomey War (1889–90), the kingdom of Dahomey, relying on traditional organization and outmoded muskets, was routed by a French force armed with modern weapons and allied with enemies of Dahomey. Dahomey sued for peace after two pitched battles. The Second Dahomey War (1892–94) was likewise dominated by pitched battles, which the French also won, resulting in French imperial domination until the 1950s.[15]

Modern insurgency (and counterinsurgency) was therefore not a part of nineteenth-century imperial policing, with the exception of the Boer Wars. As noted in chapter 5, on the British Army, the Boer Wars were radically different and much more difficult than typical imperial policing. But this challenge was posed by European settlers infused with nationalist fervor and using modern weapons and organization.[16]

"Wars of National Liberation": The Diffusion of Insurgency after 1945

The easy dominance of imperial powers began to change after World War II. New communication technologies and the spread of education in imperial possessions had at last suffused native populations with nationalism. The war had also weakened imperial powers such as the French and British. At the same time, the war had created enormous quantities of armaments that were often readily available to would-be insurgents. Indeed, many nationalist insurgents had been armed and trained by belligerents in the war. Most notable in this regard were the Viet Minh in Vietnam, whom the United States supported against the Japanese.[17]

Even as World War II ended, the Cold War began and provided additional impetus to insurgency. Soviet premier Nikita Khrushchev explicitly endorsed "wars of national liberation" to throw off imperialist yokes. After the Chinese Communist victory in 1949, the Soviets and Chinese began to support insurgencies in Asia, Africa, and Latin America.

This Communist strategy posed the threat of "surrender on the installment plan" to the United States and its Western allies as ever more of the world came under Communist domination. Insurgency in the less-developed world came to be considered a grave challenge by many, prompting an intellectual effort to develop ways to defeat this new threat. The new discipline of counterinsurgency was born in this environment.[18]

The initial focus of counterinsurgency research was on the problems of modernization and economic development. Scholars observed that in developing countries the negative consequences of economic development, which the developed nations had adjusted to over the course of decades and centuries, were being experienced in the space of years. As the economic conditions underlying society began to shift, pressure built on traditional society. This in turn put pressure on governments, many of whom had only recently acquired independence from colonial empires. In many cases, governmental institutions could not keep pace with societal change, leading to disorder and instability. This instability also left societies vulnerable to external Communist influence.[19]

Insurgents could thus take advantage of this flux by promising alternatives to the existing government. The government, unable to ameliorate the problems of the population, would increasingly be isolated and weakened. The insurgents could acquire almost everything they needed from the populace, progressively undermining government authority and creating "counterinstitutions" to provide taxation, justice, and the like. Eventually, either the government would collapse, unable to separate the insurgents from the people, or the insurgents would form their own armies and defeat the government in battle. This was the essence of Mao's version of "people's war," and many Western scholars adopted the Maoist viewpoint on insurgency.[20]

It was this two-part challenge, the defeat of insurgent forces and the creation or restoration of effective political institutions in turbulent societies, that confronted the U.S. Army and Marine Corps and the British Army in the 1950s and 1960s. Insurgency would subsequently reemerge as a problem for these same militaries in the twenty-first century in Iraq and Afghanistan. It thus provides an important test for theories of military doctrine.

The most critical aspect of insurgency and counterinsurgency for doctrine and operations is the ambiguity of the environment. In contrast to conventional battle between regularly constituted armies, with clear front lines and troops in uniform, insurgents blend in with the population. Local grudges and social networks, which can affect decisions to join with the insurgency or the state, are common and nearly opaque to outsiders.[21]

Military organizations must deal with this complexity while also facing occasional larger-scale attacks from insurgents and attempting to restore the power of the state. The former attacks can often resemble more familiar operations, sometimes resembling total war. Restoration of governance, in contrast, is unfamiliar, not being a major component of professional military education. Finally, counterinsurgency is in some cases (including all those presented in the following chapters) conducted in a foreign country, with language and cultural barriers further complicating the environment. An information environment more complex and ambiguous than counterinsurgency is hard to imagine.

The Broader Question of Doctrine and Operations

Beyond the specifics of counterinsurgency, the general study of military doctrine is an important part of the field of security studies. As part of the military component of grand strategy, doctrine is important to understanding the causes, conduct, and consequences of war. Doctrine can also influence the political and economic behavior of states. Different doctrines may affect alliance formation as well as civil-military relations.

Despite its importance, the study of military doctrine was, until relatively recently, not well integrated into political science and international relations. The Cold War provided some impetus for the study of nuclear doctrine, but only in the 1980s did scholars begin to generate more general theory on the sources of military doctrine. Since then, a variety of hypotheses on the origin of doctrine have been offered. At the center of this debate is the question of explaining differences and similarities across organizations in the development of military doctrine.[22]

One set of theories on doctrine takes as its starting point the observation that all organizations resist costly changes in operations. Indeed, the purpose of organization is to create stability and continuity. Change creates uncertainty, produces winners and losers within the organization, and disrupts normal operations. Doctrine, which provides a guide for operations, should therefore remain static or nearly so absent some external force. Organizations, in this set of theories, are primarily motivated by a desire to maximize their resources, prestige, and autonomy. Change in doctrine is expected to help with this maximization and is likely to be as incrementally small as possible.[23]

The main theorists in this camp are Barry Posen and Jack Snyder. In *The Sources of Military Doctrine*, Posen analyzes the development of military doctrine between the world wars in France, Germany, and Britain. Posen argues that military organizations have certain generic propensies common to all such organizations, such as a preference for offensive operations. Doctrine is formulated to satisfy these desires. However, intervention by civilians, who pay close attention to grand strategy and the international balance of power, can play an important role in the formation of doctrine by countering these propensities. These civilians ally themselves with those in the military organization who seek to challenge the organizational status quo.[24]

In *The Ideology of the Offensive*, Jack Snyder offers a similar argument. Like Posen, he argues that militaries generically prefer offensive doctrines to minimize uncertainty and to maximize resources, autonomy, and prestige. He also argues that the functional imperative for the offensive can potentially be checked by civilian intervention. He adds a role for the synthesis of interest, bias, and belief into an organizational ideology.[25]

Deborah Avant accepts the main proposition of Posen and Snyder on the need for civilian intervention to ameliorate military parochialism, but adds a role for domestic institutions. In *Political Institutions and Military Change*, Avant argues that differences in political institutions (for example, unitary parliamentary versus divided presidential) made civilian intervention more difficult in the United States than in Britain. In a divided system, such as that in the United States, military organizations can play the legislature off against the executive to prevent effective civilian intervention by either branch of government. In a unified system, such as Britain's, this strategy is much more difficult, if not impossible, to implement. This meant that British military doctrine was more readily changeable than that of the United States.[26]

A contrasting set of theories argues that organizations are goal-seeking entities infused with values. Organizations and their members, though resistant to change generally, will accept costly alterations that help achieve the goal of the organization. In these theories, effecting change requires convincing the members of an organization that it will help them achieve this shared goal and that change is the most effective way to preserve those things the organization values.[27]

Stephen Peter Rosen presents a form of this theory in *Winning the Next War*. He notes that militaries generate change internally to help them achieve their goals when they perceive changes in the strategic environment. Senior leaders facilitate this process by generating new promotional pathways for junior officers. Doctrinal change thus often requires a lengthy gestation period before coming to fruition.[28]

Kimberly Marten goes even further than Rosen by arguing that militaries can change quickly when confronted with a threat that is likely to cause existing doctrine to fail. In *Engaging the Enemy*, she argues that the Soviet military went to great lengths to change its doctrine as evolving NATO doctrine made existing Soviet doctrine inadequate. These changes were sometimes successful and sometimes not, but the value-infused organization was ready to make them to preserve its ability to achieve its goals.[29]

Finally, Elizabeth Kier offers a theory focused on organizational culture. In *Imagining War*, Kier assesses the development of military doctrine in France and Britain between the world wars. She concludes that culture has significant influence on doctrine, though she does not argue that the other factors are irrelevant. Instead, Kier conceives of culture as an intervening variable between doctrine and the domestic environment.[30]

This book proposes a cultural theory of doctrine and then tests it by examining the response of military organizations to the challenge of counterinsurgency. It argues, as does Kier, that organizational culture is a critical intervening variable between the environment (domestic and international) and doctrine. Yet culture is not, in the formulation presented here, just a collection of biases. Instead, it serves both normative and functional ends, helping organizations make sense of a complex and ambiguous environment. It also serves to bind organizations together by providing shared values and understanding for the organization's members.

Thus culture actually improves an organization's ability to respond to some environmental challenges, tying members together and filtering useful information from a sea of ambiguity. However, culture can also cause organizations to respond poorly to other challenges, filtering out as extraneous information that is potentially important while uniting members in a flawed or incomplete understanding of the challenge.

Hypotheses on Counterinsurgency Doctrine and Operations

Drawing on the literature on military doctrine and the theory of military organizational culture more fully described in chapter 2, the following hypotheses on counterinsurgency doctrine and operations will be tested against the available evidence.

Hypothesis 1: Organizations should respond rationally to the challenge of counterinsurgency, particularly if current operations are not succeeding. Organizations do not change easily, as they are intended to produce stability and predictability across time, so change will not be instantaneous. However, efforts by the organization to grapple with the challenge of counterinsurgency should be observed. In this period, officers in the organization should be observed to be actively debating the current state of doctrine and the course of operations. New doctrine should then be produced, and operations should then begin, again with some time lag, to conform to the new doctrine.

Crucially, different military organizations should come to similar conclusions about similar threats akin to convergence on what Biddle terms the modern system. This should be no less true of the challenge of counterinsurgency. Therefore, over time there should be convergence in counterinsurgency doctrine and operations across organizations, both within the same country and across countries, especially in the same environment (for example, in the same or similar countries).[31]

> H1: Counterinsurgency doctrine and operations should converge over time across all military organizations.

Hypothesis 2: As noted above, organizations are difficult to change. Change is costly, disruptive, and potentially risky. Therefore military organizations should not be expected to change absent some external pressure. A possible source of this is the intervention of civilian leaders, who are less invested in particular organizational arrangements and doctrines and more attuned to threats from the international environment.

In the case of counterinsurgency, military organizations should resist changing to face this new challenge, but civilian leaders who perceive a threat from insurgency can enable change. When counterinsurgency is perceived to be a serious threat, civilians should seek to intervene to shape counterinsurgency doctrine and should be more successful, as military officers will themselves be more amenable. Civilians should therefore be observed to be debating among themselves about the importance of counterinsurgency and then concluding that it is an important challenge. They should then intervene by seeking similarly minded military officers, who they then promote and champion.

Other observable implications include the issuing of high-level memoranda on the subject, the creation of special commissions or panels to promote counterinsurgency, and so on. This intervention should be effective across military organizations in the same state, thus producing convergence within the military apparatus of a state on the civilians' preferred doctrine and operations. If counterinsurgency is not seen as a serious threat, this hypothesis is indeterminate. Similarly, if counterinsurgency is perceived as a threat in two different states, and civilians in both states have similar preferences in doctrine, then there should be convergence across states.[32] As noted earlier, this convergence could be on any combination of the values of the dependent variable, depending on civilian preferences.

> H2: When counterinsurgency is perceived as a significant threat to a state, statesmen should intervene to promote counterinsurgency doctrine and operations. This should result in convergence over time in doctrine and operations on civilian preferences across all of that state's military organizations. A similar convergence should be expected across states if civilians in the two states have similar perceptions about counterinsurgency.

Hypothesis 2a: This is similar to Hypothesis 2, except that civilians in a unitary government (for example, a parliamentary system) should be better able to intervene. In contrast, civilians in a divided government (for example, a presidential system) should have less success, as military organizations can pit the legislature against the executive to resist intervention. Evidence for this should be observable in testimony to the legislature or in internal documents indicating expectations of problems with the legislature. Major inquiries critical of the executive's attempt to intervene and promote counterinsurgency doctrine would be strong evidence for this hypothesis.

Convergence would be predicted within unitary systems and divergence in divided systems if evidence of military organizations playing parts of the government against one another can be found.[33]

> H2a: When civilians seek to intervene as in H2, counterinsurgency doctrine and operations should converge in unitary political systems and diverge in divided political systems, via the mechanism of military organizations playing civilians against one another.

Hypothesis 3: Military organizations should create doctrines in order to maximize autonomy, resources, and prestige for the organization or to minimize problems such as uncertainty in planning. Convergence on optimal methods for securing these goods and minimizing uncertainty should produce convergence in doctrine and operations both within states and across states. For example, if the best way to acquire additional personnel for the organization is to adopt doctrine and operations that utilize large units, then all military organizations within a country should adopt these operations. The same logic also applies to the reduction of uncertainty. If massive and relatively indiscriminate use of firepower is the best way to reduce uncertainty (by simply bombarding areas where the enemy might be), then all military organizations within a country should adopt this approach. Similarly, there should be little variation geographically within a conflict if the primary drivers of doctrine are these organizational benefits. The same logic should also hold across states facing similar counterinsurgency challenges. If choice of doctrine has little impact on these organizational benefits, then this hypothesis is indeterminate.[34]

> H3: Counterinsurgency doctrine and operations should converge over time across organizations when choice of operations minimizes uncertainty or increases resources, autonomy, or prestige.

Hypothesis 4: Military organizations should create counterinsurgency doctrines and operations consonant with the elements of their organizational culture. The exact composition and role of these elements of culture will be discussed at length in chapter 2. However, to briefly summarize, organizations develop cultures based on their foundational experience, which gives the organization certain beliefs about the nature of war and military organizations. These beliefs shape how organizations prioritize and assess information on threats, opportunities, and constraints presented by the environment. The impact of culture on operations will be maximized when the information environment is highly ambiguous and will decrease as the information environment becomes less ambiguous. Therefore doctrine and operations by organizations with different cultures should diverge (and remain divergent) when information is ambiguous and converge when it is unambiguous. Convergence is also expected across states when military organizations have similar cultures.

H4: When information is unambiguous, operations and doctrine should converge over time across organizations. When information is ambiguous, operations and doctrine should converge over time across organizations with similar cultures and remain divergent across organizations with different cultures.

Culture, Doctrine, and Military Professionalization

The use of culture as a variable has a long history in political science. Research on culture focused on its role in security studies has progressed through at least three waves since World War II.[1] Tracing the evolution of theories of culture and security studies provides a useful starting point for defining and testing culture.[2]

The explicit study of international security and culture began in the 1970s, though discussion of decision making and belief in general is far older.[3] The historian Russell Weigley introduced the concept of an "American way of war" in 1973.[4] Jack Snyder coined the term "strategic culture" in a 1977 report for the RAND Corporation, and others soon began to focus on cultural variables' impact on strategy.[5] By the early 1980s, authors such as Colin Gray began to popularize cultural theories about the effect of "national style" on strategy.[6]

These theories focused on culture at the level of the nation-state rather than the organization, which raised several problems. Nation-states and even national governments are seldom if ever monolithic. National-level cultures are at best diffuse and indeterminate indicators of both preference and behavior.

As the 1980s progressed, the second wave of culture and security studies emerged as postmodern interpretation began to come into vogue. Much of the work done in this period discussed the ambiguous role of symbol and discourse. Rather than positing causal effects for culture, this strand of the literature sought to show that language and ideas are used instrumentally to justify or rationalize behavior.[7] Culture thus had no independent effect on preference or behavior.

There were some exceptions to this general trend of purely instrumental culture, authors who sought to demonstrate the effect of the organizational culture of militaries on preference and behavior. Among those against the trend was Carl Builder, a RAND analyst who wrote on the "institutional personalities" of the three major U.S. services, and Andrew Krepinevich, an

Army major who wrote on the U.S. Army's concept of war.[8] This strand of the literature was marked by a focus on the United States and a distinctly atheoretic approach to culture.

In the 1990s, the third wave of culture and security studies began as scholars started to utilize ideas about the culture of organizations (rather than nations) to explain behavior, particularly in terms of military issues that had previously been the province of balance of power or functional organizational behavior models.[9] These authors are generally cautious about overestimating the autonomous effects of strategic culture and do not totally reject the power of other variables, such as domestic institutions or balance of power. Rather, as Max Weber described, ideas are considered critical "switchmen" in mediating material effects.[10]

With the end of the Cold War, insurgency and related concepts such as civil war became increasingly prominent in security studies. Several works appeared that sought to use organizational culture to explain variation in counterinsurgency doctrine and practice. Most notable among these are works by three U.S. Army officers. In *Learning to Eat Soup with a Knife*, John Nagl explicitly compares U.S. and British Army counterinsurgency doctrine and practice, and argues that variation is explained by cultural differences.[11] His study draws heavily on the earlier work of Richard Downie, who compared U.S. counterinsurgency performance in Vietnam and Latin America.[12] The central argument of these works is that organizational culture either facilitates learning or inhibits it. Learning in turn leads to appropriate and effective doctrine.

Robert Cassidy makes similar points about the culture of the U.S., British, and Soviet/Russian armies in three works. In two books and a monograph, he addresses the influence of culture on doctrine and practice for the three organizations in peacekeeping and counterinsurgency/counterterrorism.[13] His account of the origin of culture, particularly for the U.S. Army, accords with the account given here.

These officers' views on the effects of organizational culture on doctrine are largely consistent with the viewpoint presented here. However, Downie and Nagl suffer from a problem shared by Andrew Krepinevich's earlier *The Army in Vietnam* in that they are all but atheoretic on the origin of culture. They have little explanation for why and how culture is created or how it is transmitted. Nagl, for example, spends only one short chapter outlining British and U.S. Army culture, with virtually no discussion of how it is transmitted.[14]

This atheoretic description of culture is a useful starting point, but it is open to the charges of tautology and post hoc storytelling. Cultural explanations must include plausible hypotheses about the origin and transmission of culture. In the remainder of this chapter, I build on these works by adding a more fully developed theory of the origin of culture and its transmission mechanisms.

Challenges to Using Culture as a Variable

Use of culture as a variable faces serious challenges. The first, avoiding tautology, is perhaps paramount. A second challenge is that culture is an implicit or tacit phenomenon; it exists in the minds of people, making it hard to study directly. Finally, many proponents of cultural "theories" actually resist theorizing about culture. They argue that each culture is essentially sui generis and can at best be "thickly described."[15]

Overcoming tautology, disentangling the material from the ideational, and attempting to make generalizable arguments about culture and doctrine require answering five questions. First, what are culture and doctrine, and how do they differ? Second, where does culture come from? Third, how is it maintained and transmitted in organizations? Fourth, how is military culture different from other types of culture? Finally, what are culture's limits as an analytic tool?

WHAT IS CULTURE?

Organizational culture is defined as a set of shared beliefs about the organization and its mission. These shared beliefs shape the response of the organization and its members to challenges, opportunities, and constraints relating to their environment and mission. Some responses will be deemed correct, effective, and appropriate based on these beliefs; others will be ruled out.[16]

Culture is often characterized by security studies scholars as simply a source of irrational bias. Jack Snyder, in *The Ideology of the Offensive*, argues that "organizational ideology" (which is defined in a way similar to the way culture is defined in this chapter) is essentially the synthesis of various biases with some amount of "rational" calculation. If one observes the formation of rational doctrine, then its existence is the result of rational calculation. Deviation from rationality is the result of the biases that comprise organizational ideology.[17] In short, ideology or culture is a residual used to explain doctrine that appears irrational.

Snyder also discusses the effect of ambiguous information on the influence of ideology: "Rational calculation will weigh more heavily when the evidence is clear and decisive; it will carry less weight when environmental incentives and constraints are ambiguous."[18] Ambiguous information is the permissive condition allowing ideology to dominate rationality.

The view of culture presented here is very similar to Snyder's concept of organizational ideology. The difference lies in Snyder's argument that a clear "rational judgment" of evidence always exists and that ideology can then cause organizations to deviate from this rational judgment.[19] In contrast, this chapter argues that evidence is often ambiguous and that judgment cannot be separated from the cultural rules that shape perception. In other words, the "rational judgment" of doctrine is often possible only with extensive hindsight, if at all.

This view ascribes a positive role to culture, as it plays an important role for organizations in terms of problem solving. It provides a set of analogies and other heuristics with which to evaluate the often ambiguous information from current and future challenges. It also provides a common framework for thinking, reducing transaction costs within the organization. Instead, the organization's successful practices and values become codified as culture, providing a shared template for future problem solving.[20]

The foregoing is not to argue that military organizations always exist in some postmodern soup of ambiguity and that no judgments are ever possible. Instead, as Snyder suggests, the ambiguity of information can be viewed as a variable, ranging from highly ambiguous to almost totally unambiguous.[21] Culture filters information by helping sort what is important (from the organization's perspective) from that which is extraneous. When information is relatively unambiguous, culture plays less of a role, as what is important is clear. However, when information is ambiguous, culture is very important in filtering the information "signal" from the overall "noise" of the information environment.

For military organizations, peacetime information is probably the most ambiguous, whereas major conflict is probably the least ambiguous source of information. During peacetime the only means of gathering information is through intelligence collection along with observation of events like training and exercises. As Thomas Mahnken has observed, in this information environment organizational culture weighs heavily in sorting information, which is often patchy and inconclusive.[22]

In contrast, lengthy major conventional wars provide sustained and clear feedback to military organizations. Even individuals and military organizations that have strong beliefs (cultural or otherwise) can adjust in these information environments. For example, Saddam Hussein, a noted paranoid, systematically engineered his military and security organizations to prioritize regime security over fighting external enemies. He also selected for sycophantic advisers afraid to tell him bad news. The result was an organization and leadership that conducted operations in ways that were not effective in conventional warfare (for example, limited communication between units for fear of coup plotting). Yet over the course of the Iran-Iraq War it still became clear to Saddam that the Iranians were slowly but surely defeating his military and that he needed to adjust organization and tactics. His subsequent changes led to successful operations that resulted in a negotiated settlement.[23]

However, even in major conflicts, judged with extensive hindsight, the "rationality" of doctrine is often hard to evaluate. For example, Snyder's condemnation of German strategy and doctrine in World War I as irrational is based on an argument that the Schlieffen Plan was doomed to fail. Yet the evidence on the plan is still contested a century later.[24]

HOW DOES CULTURE VARY? THE ELEMENTS OF CULTURE

Culture performs two valuable and interrelated functions for organizations, which correspond to the logics of appropriateness and consequences identified by the decision theorist James March.[25] March identifies the logic of consequences as the rational evaluation of the consequences of an action in terms of given preferences. This rationality is seldom purely rational; instead it is frequently "bounded" in some way (by information available, by decision-maker attention, and so on). In short, the logic of consequences can be reduced to answering the question "What does taking this action do for me in terms of what I want?"

The logic of appropriateness, in contrast, is the application of socially constructed rules of behavior derived from an individual's identity. These rules of behavior separate those who belong (the in-group) from those who do not (the out-group). Most religions, for example, have explicit rules of behavior for members. This identity-based logic can also include preferences, which are inherently normative. The logic of appropriateness thus seeks the answer to the question "What should someone like me do in this situation?"

March notes that both logics are often at work in decision making. The theory of culture presented here accepts this interpretation and argues that organizational culture serves as both a means of evaluating information for the logic of consequences and as a source of preferences, values, and identity for the logic of appropriateness. More simply, culture provides both an organizational view of how the world works and an organizational view of right and wrong.

Counterinsurgency, as noted, presents a tough challenge to military organizations. It is not peacetime but neither is it total war, so counterinsurgency presents many familiar elements (violent conflict between armed units) and many unfamiliar ones (the enemy deliberately blends in with the population, who form the battlefield of a "war without fronts"). The way culture interacts with the novel and familiar elements of counterinsurgency provides insight into culture's role in the formation of doctrine.

In terms of the first function, culture provides a common set of evidentiary rules and logic of cause and effect that lead from ambiguous evidence to doctrine. As an example of this phenomenon, George Hoffmann describes how culture shaped the U.S. Army's military judgment of tank performance in the Spanish Civil War. The lesson drawn from Army observers was that antitank guns would always dominate tanks, as the emplaced, immobile antitank gun would be more accurate than tanks, which would be forced to fire on the move. Antitank guns would also be concealed in many cases, enabling them to fire first against tanks moving against them. These conclusions led the observers to recommend that the tank be subordinated to the infantry and artillery units.[26]

This misjudgment, based on the cultural beliefs of both attachés in Europe and officers at the Army schools, perpetuated a doctrine that proved wholly inadequate in World War II. The French Army, with a culture similar to that of the U.S. Army, came to similar conclusions. In contrast, German officers, coming from a different military culture, drew very different conclusions from the same conflict, which had major doctrinal implications.[27]

In terms of the second function, culture provides values and preferences for organizations. In his seminal work on bureaucratic politics, Morton Halperin describes the desire of organizations to increase resources, autonomy, and morale/prestige.[28] Yet these are not generic drivers without preferences behind them, as Halperin clearly acknowledges. There are many ways to increase budget, autonomy, and the like, and as such these drivers have little independent predictive value. Further, they cannot explain why an organization would ever choose to forego autonomy or resources, except in cases where these factors trade off with one another (for example, increased autonomy at the price of lower resources and prestige).

Halperin avoids this problem by arguing that these drivers have a set of preferences behind them, which he terms "organizational essence." He points out that the U.S. Army's essence is "ground combat by organized regular divisional units."[29] I argue that providing a generally stable organizational essence across generations of officers is the function of the normative component of culture. James Q. Wilson makes similar observations about the role of organizational culture: "People did not always have to be told what to do; they knew what to do, and what is more important, wanted to do it well."[30]

In addition to the above distinction between the logic of consequences (for brevity this will be referred to as "positivist") and the logic of appropriateness (hereafter referred to as "normative"), culture also has two basic orientations. One is outward-looking at the environment, and the other is inward-looking at the organization itself. The first can be termed "strategic culture," and the second "managerial culture."

Strategic culture embraces attitudes and conceptions of war, the enemy, the environment, and the like. For example, is war limited, akin to a form of violent bargaining, or is it a more total phenomenon? From a normative perspective, if war is total, then all elements of the enemy, from his soldiers to his industrial base to his civilian population, are more or less fair game. However, if it is limited, then certain elements are probably not fair game or at least would be counterproductive to strike. From a positivist perspective, advocates of total war would agree that the key to victory in war is to apply maximum force as quickly as possible. Advocates of limited war would argue for more finely calibrated force, in line with political goals.

Managerial culture, in contrast to strategic culture, focuses on the internal workings of the organization. For example, what is the nature of military

Table 1 Elements of culture

	Strategic culture	Managerial culture
Logic of appropriateness (Normative)	What are the normative limits of war?	What is the role of an officer?
Logic of consequences (Positivist)	How is war best prosecuted?	What is the basic unit of military action?

command? This question has both positivist and normative implications. An organization might believe in high levels of initiative at each level of command, giving officers wide latitude for decision and, correspondingly, high levels of responsibility for those decisions. Alternatively, military organizations might believe that decisions should be top-down, with junior officers given relatively little discretion or responsibility.

These elements of culture will be discussed in more detail in the chapters that follow. But table 1 should give a general sense of how culture shapes doctrine. Table 1 combines the two types of variations.

Table 1 presents general types of questions answered by elements of culture. All of these elements of culture are related to the others, so the boundaries between them are somewhat fluid. Nonetheless, by providing a more specific framework for what culture actually does and why, this characterization makes culture less amorphous.

DEFINING QUESTIONS FOR CULTURE

A list of the central questions used to define the elements of a military organization's culture follows. These eight questions are not exhaustive but provide a framework for assessing the core values and priorities of the culture:

1. Is war frequent/limited or infrequent/total? (Strategic, normative)
2. What are the acceptable targets of war? (Strategic, normative)
3. What are the optimal methods of war (attrition/firepower, maneuver/shock, etc.), and how should they be combined? (Strategic, positivist)
4. What is the relationship between one's own military and other organizations (foreign, sister services, civilians, etc.)? (Strategic, positivist)
5. What are the primary duties of an officer? (Managerial, normative)
6. What is the appropriate relationship between civil and military authority? (Managerial, normative)
7. What is the basic unit of military organization (platoon, regiment, etc.)? (Managerial, positivist)
8. How should units be controlled (staff intensive, directive control, etc.)? (Managerial, positivist)

The distinction between military doctrine and military culture is often quite blurry. Many scholars would consider the functions noted earlier to be a part of doctrine rather than culture. Before proceeding, I will more precisely delineate the distinction between culture and doctrine.

Barry Posen's definition of doctrine is more or less the standard one and is therefore worth reproducing at length:

> I use the term military doctrine for the subcomponent of grand strategy that deals explicitly with military means. Two questions are important: *What* means shall be employed and *How* shall they be employed? [emphasis in original] Priorities must be set among the various types of military forces available to the modern state. A set of prescriptions must be generated specifying how military forces should be structured and employed to respond to recognized threats and opportunities . . . Military doctrine includes the preferred mode of a group of services, a single service or subservice for fighting wars. It reflects the judgments of professional military officers, and to a lesser but important extent civilian leaders, about what is and is not militarily possible and necessary. Such judgments are based on appraisals of military technology, national geography, adversary capabilities, and the skills of one's own military organization.[31]

According to Posen, doctrine is generated both to set priorities for force structure and to codify how that force structure will fight. This second element, "the preferred mode . . . for fighting wars," is important, as it explicitly introduces the concept of *preference* into doctrine. In a later work, Posen expands on this second element as distinct from the broader concept of military doctrine, referring to it as "operational-tactical doctrine": "By operational and tactical doctrine I mean the way the French army and airforce planned to fight fights, battles and campaigns. This should be distinguished from a higher order concept that goes by many different names: national military strategy, strategic doctrine, political-military doctrine, or 'military doctrine,' (the term I have used in my past work)."[32]

This distinction is important, as it limits and specifies the dependent variable in a way that the first definition of military doctrine does not. If everything an organization does or believes is grouped under the rubric of doctrine, then it becomes an almost meaningless catchall term. By separating what organizations in the aggregate *believe* implicitly (culture) from what they *do* explicitly (doctrine), it is possible to gain better understanding of why organizations take certain actions and succeed or fail in accomplishing different missions.[33]

Posen's definition acknowledges both the role of preference in doctrine and the importance of "the judgments of professional military officers" in doctrinal formation. Yet he does not explicitly discuss the sources of these preferences and judgments; instead he subsequently discusses functional imperatives such as minimizing uncertainty and maximizing autonomy. These are not "professional judgments" per se; instead they are generic organizational desires. I argue that professional judgment requires professionalism and that culture is an inextricable part of professionalism.

Doctrine is thus a consciously articulated and agreed-upon method for conducting military operations resulting from the interaction of ambiguous evidence with culture. A key difference between the two is that doctrine is articulated and transmitted through physical means (publications, best practices lists, operations orders, and so on). Culture, which provides the framework on which doctrine is built, is not articulated and is transmitted through particular experiences and environments.

Doctrine, to be clear, changes over time in every military organization, but culture does not. So since 1945 the same U.S. Army culture described in chapter 3 has generated doctrine for major combat operations that at various points has emphasized dispersal and atomic firepower (1950s), conventional mechanized offensives supported by helicopters (1960s), conventional mechanized defense (1970s), and combined air-ground operations incorporating deep attacks (1980s).[34] Yet all of these doctrines remained consonant with the Army's culture, emphasizing firepower, large-unit operations, and mass mobilization (at least until the end of the draft in 1974).

It should finally and crucially be noted that the dependent variable is first and foremost about actual practice in the field (that is, operations conducted) rather than manuals, even though manuals are often important evidence of doctrine. While written doctrine and practiced doctrine are often very similar, there can be significant deviation between them. For example, to appease civilian leadership, a doctrine could be written that appears to comply with civilian demands. If that doctrine is then subsequently ignored or subverted systematically in combat, it would clearly have been instrumental.

HOW DOES DOCTRINE VARY? AXES OF DOCTRINE

Doctrine, like culture, can vary in many ways. However, three axes of variation in operations and doctrine are of primary importance for ground force military organizations (that is, armies, though they are not always referred to as such). These are the size of units conducting operations; the level and targeting of firepower; and the integration of operations with other organizations or groups (principally civilians or other militaries).[35]

These axes are important for two reasons. First, they have tremendous impact on the battlefield. They readily capture the difference between, for example, a hostage rescue mission (very small unit, very low firepower with very discrete targeting, close cooperation with civilian authority) and the capture of a city (very large unit, very high firepower with minimal discretion, little interaction with civilian authority). Second, these three axes can be explicitly and clearly observed. The size of units used in operations is routinely recorded, as is the firepower expended. The third axis, cooperation, is sometimes less explicit, but even it can generally be determined from available records.

The size of units can be coded in binary fashion—small units versus large units. For purposes of this study, any operation conducted by a unit of company size or smaller (platoon, squad, and so on) is considered a small-unit operation. Any operation conducted by more than one battalion (two battalions, a brigade, and so on) is considered to be a large-unit operation. Any operation falling between these two ranges (larger than a company up to a single battalion) will not be coded either way.

The reason for this coding is that a battalion in modern military organizations is the smallest unit that has a full staff and organically possesses substantial ground force capabilities (heavy weapons, indirect fire weapons, logistics, and so on). It therefore marks the border between small units with limited organic capabilities and large units that are massive agglomerations of soldiers. More than one battalion in an operation indicates that hundreds of soldiers and concomitant materiel are being employed, which in turn almost always requires coordination by a higher headquarters with an even larger staff (that is, a brigade or regiment) and a senior commander.

In contrast, a company-size or smaller operation indicates the use of few soldiers and little materiel. Command will fall heavily on very junior officers (lieutenants and captains) with minimal staff. This in turn implies a substantial reliance on senior enlisted personnel (specialists/corporals, sergeants, and staff sergeants) who assist the junior officers and lead very small tactical elements such as squads.

Level and targeting of firepower are, like size of units, easily observed in operations. Firepower takes the form of rounds of ammunition, bombs, shells, and the like expended in operations. Only weapons/munitions larger than small arms (for example, rifles and light machine guns) will be counted, both because small arms are the basic weapons of any military operation and because these are seldom recorded by operation. However, even with this limitation, firepower is less easily coded than unit size. How would one establish high versus low levels of firepower? Coding in this case will be based on both objective counts (number/tonnage of rounds) and descriptions in operational reports and by commanders but will admittedly be more subjective than the clear delineation of unit size.

Targeting is a bit easier to code. If firepower is consistently employed near or in civilian population centers or in a manner that covers a very wide area (tens of square kilometers or more) with unobserved fire, it will be coded as indiscriminate. If firepower is generally restricted around civilian popula-

Table 2 The dependent variable—Doctrine and operations

Axis of variation	Value 1	Value 2
Size of operations	Large (battalion +)	Small (company −)
Level of firepower	High (by volume)	Low (by volume)
Targeting of firepower	Indiscriminate (unobserved)	Discriminate (observed)
Integration with civilians (other agencies and locals)	Disintegrated (lack of consultation/involvement)	Integrated (consultation/involvement)

tion centers and is generally used in concentrated areas with observers, it will be coded as discriminate.

Further, the two aspects of firepower will often co-vary. High levels of firepower tend to be indiscriminate due to scale—it is difficult (though not impossible) to employ vast amounts of firepower in a very small, observed area. Similarly, low levels of firepower tend to be discriminate, as firing a few rounds into a wide area without an observer is ineffectual.

Finally, integration with civilians, locals, and other military organizations is both important and observable. Integration is important, as the conduct of modern warfare is often beyond the capacity of single military organizations. Multiple military organizations (armies and air forces, for example) may be required to cooperate to conduct effective operations. Crucial political and technical expertise, along with intelligence and administrative capability, is often resident in civilian organizations. Civilians in this case can be both from the military's home country and locals from the country where war is being fought (if the two are not the same). Integration can be coded as high or low by examining records of operations and operational planning to determine who is consulted and involved and how.

Note that merely having civilians or local forces around is not the same as having high levels of integration and consultation. A military unit that pays locals to guard an intersection but otherwise has no interaction with them would still be coded as disintegrated from the locals. Likewise, if a military unit has representatives from civilian agencies attached to it but fundamentally dominates them in terms of allocation of resources and conduct of operations, that would be coded as disintegrated.

WHAT ARE THE SOURCES OF CULTURE?

The shared beliefs that constitute culture generally emerge from the formative experiences of the organization.[36] These beliefs are built up around analogies to and extensions of these experiences.[37] The parallel to individual personality formation, also shaped by early experiences, has even been explicitly noted by some scholars.[38]

In the case of military organizations, this formative period is the professionalization of the military and particularly the officer corps. Prior to professionalization, military organizations are generally too diffuse to generate an integrated organizational culture. If shared culture exists in a preprofessional officer corps, it is likely to be based on a common class rather than a uniquely military perspective.[39] In contrast, professionalism, with its requirement of long, specialized education and training, allows for the creation of an integrated organizational culture. Further, as discussed later, this professional education becomes a major mechanism by which culture is refined and maintained. The beginning of professionalism is thus the starting point of military organizational culture.

Professionalization refers specifically to the process of transitioning a given occupation—where knowledge is gained through on-the-job training, apprenticeship, specific vocational training, or some combination of these—to a profession. In a profession, knowledge is gained through formal education in a body of abstract theory and/or specialized technical skills. This education, in turn, gives the members of the profession jurisdiction over matters dealing with their area of expertise. This jurisdiction in turn yields autonomy and authority, as its members are uniquely qualified in that sphere of knowledge.[40] For example, doctors have professional jurisdiction over medicine. Professionalization also generates values, norms, and a code of conduct. These norms describe the social roles of members, how one treats peers, and so on.[41]

One of the foundational works in the field of military sociology, Morris Janowitz's *The Professional Soldier*, provides a succinct summary of the view of professional military officer corps. Janowitz notes:

> The officer corps can also be analyzed as a professional group by means of sociological concepts. Law and medicine have been identified as the most ancient professions. The professional, as a product of prolonged training, acquires a skill which enables him to render specialized service. In this sense, the emergence of a professional army—specifically, a professional officer corps—has been a slow and gradual process with many interruptions and reversals . . . [O]ne cannot speak of the emergence of an integrated military profession until after 1800. But a profession is more than a group with specialized skill, acquired through intensive training. A professional group develops a sense of group identity and a system of internal administration. Self-administration—often supported by state intervention—implies the growth of a body of ethics and standards of performance.[42]

The two elements mentioned previously as being integral to a profession, the body of abstract theory/specialized skill and a code of conduct/self-administration, correspond to the positivist and normative elements of culture proposed here. It is therefore not an aberration that military organizations develop these elements of culture; rather, it is a *requirement* of military professionalism. The difference here is that, rather than arguing for a "military professional culture" that covers all military officers, this theory proposes that military organizations can have distinctly different cultures as the result of different processes of professionalization.[43] Conversely, similar professionalization experiences would be expected to produce similar cultures.

"THE FIRST WAR" AND PROFESSIONALIZATION

The critical formative experience for military organizations is what I term "the first war," though it need not be a single war. This is the major conflict (or conflicts) that the organization takes as its template for developing professional education, and takes place in the period leading to and during the establishment of the professional schools discussed in the next section. In many cases, this war provides much of the impetus for professionalization, so it is unsurprising that it should provide much of the basis for professional education.

For example, the Prussian/German Army's "first war" was the Wars of German Unification, though professionalization began earlier.[44] The disastrous war with Napoleonic France in 1806 provided the initial push for professionalization, with formation of a Military Reorganization Committee that introduced the beginnings of professionalism into an officer corps previously dominated by aristocrats with minimal education, military or otherwise. The next several decades would be a period of proto-professionalization, as the educated officers struggled against the dominant but ignorant aristocrats. This battle did not culminate until the latter part of the nineteenth century under the famed field marshal Helmuth von Moltke (the elder). Moltke, a pro-education aristocrat, would use the lessons from the Wars of Unification as the template for the new German Army's culture.[45]

The central lessons of this time were the need for a mass mobilization army led by a technocratic officer corps, the utility of directive command rather than detailed orders, and the importance of rapid maneuver to achieve decisive battles of encirclement and annihilation (Kesselschlacht).[46] From the 1860s to the 1940s, these concepts were critical to German Army culture and were the centerpiece of German doctrines and planning. Storm trooper tactics, the operational art of blitzkrieg, and the strategic gamble of the Schlieffen Plan were all tied to these cultural elements.

Different armies can have different early experiences, leading to different organizational cultures. Yet there are probably only a fairly small number of archetypal first war experiences, based on a state's (and therefore its army's) geostrategic position and domestic society. Each of these archetypal experiences should produce similar (though probably not identical) cultures in those armies.[47]

This idea of archetypal first wars draws upon Samuel Finer's concept of the "military format." The military format includes who serves and how (professional volunteers versus conscripts), the size and type of forces, and the social makeup of the forces. This format evolves over time as society, technology, and the economy evolve.[48]

In contrast to Finer, however, I argue that once the organizational culture derived from the first war is firmly established by the professionalization of the officer corps, little evolution takes place. Military organizations may be confronted with changing society, technology, and economy (both at home and abroad) and therefore change their doctrine, yet they will retain culture based on their formative experience. All of the organization's subsequent experience is filtered through this lens.

However, while culture is enormously "sticky," one can imagine cultural change if major shifts in the domestic or international environment take place. Shifts such as these should be rare and seldom result in total revision of culture. One example of a partial change in culture, the U.S. Army after Vietnam, is noted in chapter 9. This partial change was brought about only by the combination of two technological revolutions (the nuclear revolution combined with a conventional forces revolution) and, most critically, the elimination of conscription.

Another way to produce change in culture is to destroy or disband the existing military and its education system and start over. This was done with both the Japanese and German militaries after World War II. However, inclusion of many former officers from the old military establishment meant that at least some of the culture was carried over to the new organizations.[49]

As an example of the archetype concept, the German Army experience noted earlier could be termed the "rapid-limited war" archetype. As Posen describes, the German way of war was based on "mobility above all else."[50] The Israeli Army's foundational experience in 1948 and 1956, for reasons of similar geography, fit this archetype and, unsurprisingly, has a similar organizational culture. Both armies proved superb in wars conforming to their archetype—May 1940 and June 1967 are considered to be the preeminent examples of decisive victory through rapid offensive maneuver.

This book focuses on two of the most prominent archetypes. The first can be termed a "continental army." Over the course of the nineteenth century, a new form of warfare emerged from the interaction of the new creed of nationalism with the Industrial Revolution. This type of war, variously termed "total war" or "national-industrial war," was so potent that it became the military format for most professional armies that had neighbors who could potentially invade them (for example, great powers on the continent of Europe) and, conversely, that they might want to conquer.[51]

The tremendous national sacrifice involved in this type of war means that it is seldom fought for reasons other than national survival. Threats of this type are both extreme and relatively rare. This type of war need not be fought against an external threat; two of the most prominent examples of this archetype of war, the Russian and American civil wars, were not.

The second archetype can be termed a "maritime army." As the name suggests, this is associated with a nation where the ocean, combined with a strong navy, provides the principal defense against invasion. However, the state may nonetheless have overseas interests for which it needs an army. Two principal missions are likely for this type of army: policing an overseas empire and a contribution to coalition warfare on the continent. The former mission is perhaps self-evident, while the latter mission derives from the possibility that a continent dominated by a single hostile power might be able to sever the maritime links to empire or even invade the homeland. The mission thus must often act as an "offshore balancer," requiring a limited but important continental commitment.

In contrast to the relatively low incidence of national-industrial war, imperial policing is frequent if not continuous. The threat to national existence is minimal, which means that only minimal sacrifice may be demanded. Additionally, the domestic arrangements of maritime states are often though not always more liberal (in the classical sense of limited state power to extract resources and control citizens) than those of continental powers. This combination of factors means that policing the empire must be cheap, at least in contrast to the gain from the empire, and must not require the state to resort to unpalatable techniques such as conscription.[52]

Both manpower and capital are therefore tightly circumscribed. However, the manpower will almost always be a professional volunteer force and thus relatively high quality. This gives more confidence in the capability of small units while putting more emphasis on small-unit leadership. Further, natives of the empire are often incorporated into the policing effort in some fashion, giving additional manpower. Additionally, the empire is generally not managed by the military alone, so civilian resources and expertise (from a colonial or foreign service) are often available.

Even while conducting imperial policing, these armies must prepare for the continental commitment and offshore balancing. However, the continental commitment is always seen as a limited war. This can be contrasted with continental armies, which may sometimes do imperial policing but will always place the total war mission first. The French Army of the nineteenth and twentieth centuries is an example of this type.

The archetypal first war experience of every military organization will inevitably be tied in some fashion to the particulars of geography and society. As noted, the Israeli and German armies shared an archetype due in large part to similar geography. Yet the first war can also be surprisingly idiosyncratic. As the cases presented in the following chapters will show, the U.S and British armies should have shared a similar imperial policing archetype, as both were liberal states protected by water, with little need for massive industrial armies but a strong need for policing their commercially oriented empires.

However, the peculiar experience of the U.S. Civil War gave the U.S. Army a wholly different first war archetype, one that would be expected of a continental state such as France or Russia. Japan is similarly idiosyncratic, as the professional Japanese Army of the late nineteenth and early twentieth centuries was a continental rather than maritime archetype.[53] In tables 3 and 4, I present the general elements of these two "archetypal" cultures by answering the eight central questions presented earlier.

While I argue that culture does serve a functional purpose, it is important to point out that culture is not just a reflection of underlying function. As discussed subsequently in the section on alternative hypotheses on doctrine, some argue that culture is basically epiphenomenal, a mere reflection of what an organization does. According to this argument, changing what an organization does will change its culture, after some relatively brief period of adjustment due to organizational inertia or lag.

In contrast, I argue that because culture is rooted in an organization's formative experience and professionalization process, giving an organization a new mission will force the organization to adapt, but its adaptation will remain conditioned by elements of culture. Normatively, the organization values some tasks more than others. Functionally, it has developed a logic that serves to fulfill these tasks well, and radical change is costly if not impossible.

If culture is a mere epiphenomenon of function, then significant change over time should be observed in organizations given a new mission. In the cases under study, the organizations, confronted with the same ambiguous environment, should adopt similar operations after at most a few years of war. A somewhat arbitrary but reasonable benchmark is four years, the length of World War I. All armies in that war made substantial adjustments despite organizational inertia and adopted similar practices, so this should be long enough for other armies to adjust to new missions in other contexts if only inertia is at work. If this convergence is not observed or is observed

Table 3 Continental army archetype

	Strategic culture	Managerial culture
Normative	Q1: War is primarily about national survival and infrequent Q2: War is total; blurs distinction between enemy military and civilian targets	Q5: Officer is a "manager of violence" Q6: Civil-military spheres of competence sharply delineated
Positivist	Q3: Maximal application of firepower; maneuver secondary Q4: Other services secondary to success	Q7: Management by industrial methodology emphasizing large units Q8: Staffs central to management; supporting arms secondary but vital

Table 4 Maritime army archetype

	Strategic culture	*Managerial culture*
Normative	Q1: War is primarily about imperial maintenance and is frequent Q2: War is limited and inherently political	Q5: Officer is a "leader of professional soldiers" Q6: Civil-military spheres often complementary
Positivist	Q3: Firepower important but overall infantry-centric Q4: Dependence on other organizations (natives, sister services, allied nations) normal	Q7: Small-unit leadership paramount Q8: Staff functions and supporting arms distinctly secondary

in some areas but not others, then something more than mere organizational inertia must be at work. This important difference will be highlighted in the case studies through comparison across organizations and through observation in multiple time periods.

THE TRANSMISSION OF CULTURE

To ensure continuity, culture must be transmitted in some way to future members of the organization. A number of mechanisms can be used to transmit culture in organizations. These can be formal, such as classroom experience or a required uniform. Alternatively, they can be informal, such as shared slang, jargon, stories, or folk knowledge.[54] Shared experiences, such as being a platoon commander or staff officer in a division, also can transmit culture.

In the case of professional organizations, the most powerful mechanism of transmission is probably the formal professional education system. This is unsurprising, given that professional education is the bedrock of professional jurisdiction. For military organizations, the importance of professional education is reinforced by the monopoly on instruction in combat tasks that military organizations generally hold within a given nation-state. For example, if one wants to be a lawyer or doctor, there are usually a number of competitive schools to attend. If one wants to be a fighter pilot or infantry officer, the appropriate military service school is almost always the only provider.

This does not mean that the informal mechanisms noted earlier, such as slang and folk knowledge shared in bars, are unimportant mechanisms for transmitting culture. However, it is only in the professional schools that the same experiences are shared by all members of a given military. The other informal mechanisms are more diffuse, varying from unit to unit and from base to base. The schools provide homogenization that the other mechanisms do not.

Studying the evolution of the nature of the fundamental service schools is therefore the best way to understand the culture of a military organization. These schools are those created to foster professional military education in the early period of professionalization. Understanding who is taught at these schools over time, what they are taught, and how they are taught will provide an understanding of the dominant culture of the organization. In addition to being a transmission mechanism for culture, the service schools serve as proxy for the other mechanisms noted earlier, such as experiences on staffs or shared language. The professional schools are thus both a key transmission mechanism for culture and a useful indicator of the elements of culture.

The overall school experience rather than the exact subjects taught is most important, as culture is not transmitted explicitly.[55] For example, the U.S. Army's Combat Studies Institute conducts "staff rides" for the Command and General Staff College for twenty-four battles from the U.S. Civil War. It is not the actual conduct of those Civil War battles that matters for Army culture—it is the principles these battles embody that matter. These principles, discussed in more detail later, define both the positivist and normative elements of U.S. Army culture. In contrast, only nine total battles from the Revolutionary War and the Indian Wars are given staff rides.[56]

The professional schools rather than the service academies are viewed as the locus of professionalism. The service academies provide a more general rather than purely professional education. This is the reason, for example, that even Marine second lieutenants commissioned directly from the Naval Academy still attend the Basic School for new officers.[57] This is not to say that important cultural elements are not absorbed by those who attend the academies; rather, it argues that they are not the center of culture.

This centrality of professional military education to culture is highlighted for the U.S. Army by the profiles of the division commanders in World War II. While only about half were West Point graduates, all had been to the Command and General Staff School, the Army's central professional school. An Army study elaborates:

> Fifty-two percent were graduates of the United States Military Academy. Twenty-four percent had college degrees from other institutions, and an equal percent held no college degree. All these officers eventually became members of the combat arms: 44 percent infantry, 28 percent field artillery, and 28 percent cavalry . . . Amidst all these career variables, one finds a common element in these officers' education: all were graduates of the Command and General Staff School at Fort Leavenworth, Kansas. In addition, nine of the twenty-five attended the two-year CGS course. This course provided all the officers with basic techniques and procedures, and in a real sense, the officers shared a common military theoretical foundation.[58]

HOW IS MILITARY CULTURE DIFFERENT FROM OTHER TYPES OF CULTURE?

Modern military organizational culture, though sharing the same basic characteristics, is somewhat different from most other types of organizational culture. Military forces are organizations that possess the usual organizational characteristics of specialization, division of labor, standard operating procedure, and the like.[59] Yet military service is also a profession, with members of the service having a professional jurisdiction over war in the same way that doctors and lawyers have professional jurisdiction over medicine and the law.

This duality, noted by Samuel Huntington and others, reinforces the strength of culture within militaries in two ways.[60] First, professionals respect only other professionals' expertise as fully legitimate. This means, for example, that modern military organizations promote exclusively from within except in the most extraordinary circumstances. Only those who have been through the same basic set of professional education and experience can be promoted, ensuring a higher level of uniformity in shared beliefs. This can be contrasted with businesses and even many other governmental agencies in which external promotion, even to the highest ranks, is possible. It is thus more difficult for new ideas to be introduced through an infusion of new blood.

At the same time, the organizational demands of military action prevent them from adopting only a loose professional association model, as doctors or lawyers have. Military organizations have a rigid hierarchy of command, and individual members' autonomy is limited in many ways. This hierarchy reinforces the set of shared beliefs, as members can be directed to halt activities that do not conform to the military's preferences and beliefs, and punished if they do not comply.

Additionally, this set of beliefs is reinforced by the "total" nature of military organization. Militaries have a level of control over members that far exceeds that of virtually all other organizations. Further, this control is persistent at all times and overrides most other commitments made by members. Exit from military organizations is also usually not entirely discretionary, even for officers.[61]

This totalism is further enhanced by the unique nature of military activity. Members must be prepared to give their lives for the cause of the organization and the country it represents. This requires high levels of belief by members in some or all aspects of the organizational culture, whether this belief is in the strength of the bond between small units of soldiers or a broader ideology on the nature of the self, the military, and the enemy.[62]

THE LIMITS OF CULTURE AND THE ROLE OF SUBCULTURES

Culture, even "total" culture, is not absolute. Individuals are assimilated into culture to varying degrees depending on a multitude of factors. It would be doing a great disservice to professional military officers to suggest that all members of a given service are identical or even nearly so. While culture is pervasive within an organization and can provide significant insight into organizational behavior, it should not be considered a deterministic phenomenon.

This uneven assimilation of individuals into culture means that culture should be used with care as an analytic tool. It is best used to explain organizational behavior as an aggregate. It is less useful as a tool to analyze any given individual leader or individual unit performance, as it is too uncertain at this level of detail. However, the basic pattern of organizational culture should be readily apparent when examining the evolution of professional schools and the subsequent actions of most units of that organization on the battlefield.

Further, culture is seldom monolithic.[63] This makes the use of culture as an analytic tool more problematic. Many organizations have subcultures within the broader organizational culture. A subculture, as the name implies, is a subset of the organizational culture. It can be very similar to the organizational culture as a whole or, in some cases, quite different.

In an early work on subculture, Caren Siehl and Joanne Martin termed these two types of subcultures "orthogonal" and "counter."[64] Orthogonal subcultures are essentially minor variations on the overall (or dominant) organizational culture. Counter subcultures, in contrast, may be significantly different from the dominant culture, existing in an uneasy partnership with the larger organization.

In terms of military culture, these subcultures are generally to be found within service branches or other such functional distinctions. In the U.S. Air Force, for example, the dominant culture is pilot-centered. Nonpilots (intelligence officers, ballistic missiles officers, and so on) have their own subcultures. Within the pilot subculture, a further distinction between combat pilots and support aircraft pilots is made, with each having some level of subculture. Finally, even within the combat pilot subculture, further subculture distinctions exist between bomber and fighter pilots.[65] Similarly, the U.S. Navy is considered to have three main subcultures, each related to platform type: surface warfare, aviation, and submarine.[66]

While often orthogonal and exhibiting only a friendly rivalry, branch subcultures can sometimes be counter to the dominant culture. In this case, the tension can be either productive or destructive (possibly even both at different times). Siehl and Martin note that the counter subculture can be a way for the organization to develop new ideas, yet at the same time the dominant culture may punish members of the counter subculture.

The special operations forces of the U.S. military present a good example of counter subcultures in the military context. Often at odds with the dominant culture, the special operations forces were so out of favor with the services in the 1980s that Congress eventually took steps to shield these subcultures. The Goldwater-Nichols Defense Reorganization Act of 1986 and the subsequent Nunn-Cohen Amendment created a unified United States Special Operations Command (USSOCOM) to both promote joint operations between the various special operations subcultures and to protect the subcultures from potential punishment from the dominant service cultures.[67] While the impact of USSOCOM remains debated, the tension between many in the dominant service cultures (and their orthogonal subcultures) and the special operations subcultures remains.[68]

While important, the overall impact of subcultures on doctrine is generally limited. Counter subcultures are unlikely to have a major effect on doctrine for the dominant culture, except at the margins, as they are simply too small and isolated. In contrast, similarly sized orthogonal subcultures can often influence doctrine more significantly, yet because they are so similar the overall impact on doctrine is likely to be seen only at a relatively fine-grained level of detail. Only in rare cases will two subcultures with major differences coexist on an equal footing. The U.S. Marine Corps, as noted in chapter 4, is one of the few examples of this phenomenon.

Two other important subcultures are the U.S. Army Special Forces (SF), colloquially known as the Green Berets, and the British Army's Special Air Service (SAS). Though culturally distinct in a number of ways, SF and the SAS are more similar than different. Both focus on a mission that is generally termed "unconventional" or "irregular" warfare. This catchall includes operations behind enemy lines in support of conventional operations, the conducting of guerrilla war, foreign internal defense, and direct action missions intended to accomplish limited but important goals such as capturing an enemy leader.

The central elements of culture in special operations forces are an emphasis on individual and very small unit capabilities, a willingness to work closely with other services and civilian agencies, and frequent interaction with foreigners. As such, it shares many characteristics with the maritime archetype. In fact, the special operations forces subculture can be viewed as an amplification of this archetype, with even more focus on the intense professionalism of individuals. The special operations forces, accustomed to working in small groups in areas in which the reach of government is limited, also see less distinction between peace and war. "Peace" in many cases remains violent for the special operations community, and war often bears little resemblance to the national-industrial conception of war embodied in the world wars. Table 5 summarizes the elements of this subculture (termed unconventional). The cases in the following chapters will demonstrate that the SAS is a generally well-accepted orthogonal subculture of

Table 5 Unconventional subculture archetype

	Strategic culture	*Managerial culture*
Normative	Q1: Line between war and peace very hazy Q2: War is limited and inherently political	Q5: Officer is a "leader of professionals" Q6: Civil-military spheres often complementary
Positivist	Q3: Tactical excellence paramount Q4: Working well with other services, agencies, and foreigners is critical	Q7: Small-unit leadership is critical Q8: Staff functions and supporting arms minimal

the British Army, while the SF subculture is counter to the U.S. Army's dominant culture.

Professional military organizations need shared values and ideas about war in order to effectively respond to the numerous threats, opportunities, and constraints of the domestic and international environments. Culture, which has its origins in the organization's foundational war, provides these values and ideas, enabling military organizations to evaluate and prioritize information from an environment that is often highly ambiguous. Foundational wars are frequently dictated by geostrategic position, so there are likely a limited number of broad cultural archetypes. One is associated with total war, a phenomenon most associated with continental powers. Another is associated with limited war and imperial policing, most associated with maritime powers. However, some organizations have foundational experiences that are radically different from geostrategic position, meaning that culture is not merely endogenous to this position.

The effect of culture, a filter for reducing ambiguity, will be strongest when information is most ambiguous. Highly ambiguous environments include peacetime or counterinsurgency. Culture will be weakest when information is least ambiguous, such as four years into a major war.

"The Habits and Usages of War"

U.S. Army Professionalization, 1865–1962

The U.S. Army as a professional organization is defined by the experience of the Civil War. Prior to the Civil War the Army had taken steps toward professionalization based on a limited war model informed principally by the War of 1812 and the Mexican War. Given the United States' geostrategic position and liberal democratic government, this would be the type of professional army one would expect it to have, mirroring its fellow liberal maritime state, Great Britain.

However, the total war experience of 1861–65 shifted the Army's conception of both war and itself. This chapter details the Army's process of professionalization, which centered on the creation of a School of Application for Infantry and Cavalry at Fort Leavenworth in 1881. Leavenworth and its conception of war and military professionalism gradually became institutionalized and defined the culture of the Army's officer corps. This Army culture would prove remarkably durable, surviving from the Indian Wars to at least the third decade of the Cold War.

Early Professionalism: The Old Army, 1812–61

The War of 1812 provided the first impetus to professionalization in the U.S. Army. Despite ultimate success in the war, the Army had not performed as well as some of its officers had hoped. The response, led by officers such as West Point superintendent Major Sylvanus Thayer and civilians such as Secretary of War John Calhoun, was twofold. The first was an attempt to produce a better professional officer corps, principally by refining the curriculum at West Point. As William Skelton notes, this officer corps was quite small and oriented principally on the lessons of 1812.[1] In that war, the main opponent had been a distant European power seeking to project power ashore. The Army's chief role was to defend coastal cities such as New York, Boston, and Washington. This required extensive knowledge of artillery and fortification, which dovetailed nicely with West Point's general engineering focus. In 1824 the Army also established its first postgraduate institution, the Artillery School of Practice at Fort Monroe in Virginia, based on the lessons of the war.[2]

The second response, masterminded by Calhoun, was the concept of the "expansible army." In this view, the purpose of the small standing army was to provide a cadre for an influx of citizen volunteers in wartime. There was thus less need for professional enlisted and junior officers and more for field grade and higher officers. Calhoun's plan was not fully implemented in the aftermath of the War of 1812, but a reasonable compromise was reached. The enlisted strength of the Regular Army was cut in half (from roughly 11,000 to 5,550), but the officer corps was barely reduced (from roughly 680 to 540).[3] West Point graduates completely dominated the officer corps virtually top to bottom except for certain brief periods of expansion when civilian officers were inducted.

This new model army was a clear improvement on the almost haphazard army of 1812–15 but still left much to be desired. For one, the ability of the Army to actually recruit, train, and command volunteers was made difficult by the existence of the state militia forces that would become the National Guard. Yet the Army was reasonably effective both as a frontier constabulary and in defeating the Mexican Army in 1847 (the latter victory particularly aided by the highly trained artillerymen). It was also highly effective in preparing for future defensive war with European powers.[4]

During this period the Army introduced the first publication that could be considered doctrine, in the form of General Winfield Scott's *General Regulations for the United States Army* of 1821. However, this document was so broad in focus, incorporating all manner of regulations that had little to do with combat, that it does not meet the definition of doctrine presented earlier. Instead, as its name suggests, it was a codification of general practice in the Army.

There was also little effort to plan for the use of large combined arms units in peacetime during this period. Neither divisions nor corps in the War of 1812 had been standardized, with large variations depending on time and place. Scott's subsequent *Regulations* gave a standard definition based on a power of two (two regiments to a brigade, two brigades to a division, and so on), but between 1812 and 1847 these concepts were barely used, as nothing close to a brigade size was assembled during the period. Further, both brigade and division had only a single staff officer in the form of a chief of staff.[5]

In the period between the War of 1812 and the Mexican War, the Army principally fought various tribes of Native Americans. This proved challenging to the limited war Army, as the tribes would seldom stand and fight anything like a decisive battle. Some foretaste of the methods of the Civil

War can be found in this period, such as Colonel William Worth's successful "pacification" of the Seminole in 1841. After six years of searching for
a decisive battle and the resulting inconclusive war in Florida, Worth took
command. Worth launched a campaign against the Seminoles' homes and
crops, with the resulting devastation rapidly bringing Seminole resistance
to an end.[6] However, this response is notable for being unusual at the time;
most Army engagements with Native Americans sought to bring their
elusive forces to battle.

Following the Mexican War, some revisions to the *Regulations* were
enacted. The divisional concept was further refined and for the first time
made explicitly a combined arms force of either infantry or cavalry brigades
along with corps artillery and engineering assets. However, the proportions
were not defined, and the division staff expanded only slightly, to a handful of specialized officers (artillery, ordnance, and so on). During the war, it
had been difficult to find officers capable of commanding and staffing divisions; yet following the war no peacetime corps or division structure was
established, meaning that the problem would likely reemerge in future
conflicts.[7]

The Army in 1861 thus resembled a competent army from eighteenth-
century Europe blended with a frontier constabulary. In other words, it was
on the path to becoming a maritime army, with the imperial policing role
taking place on the American continent rather than overseas. It spent the
bulk of its time protecting settlers from Indians and trying to shore up coastal
defenses. However, the nationalist mass army experience of the Napoleonic
period had more or less bypassed it. It had little in the way of doctrine or
organization for large-scale combat, instead relying heavily on ad hoc field
solutions. It had begun to professionalize, but the process was far from complete. This nascent professionalization process would be disrupted by the
experience of the Civil War, which would radically alter the Army's conception of war.[8]

The Army Learns Total War: The Civil War, 1861–65

The Regular Army split (albeit unevenly) into the Union Army and the Confederate Army in 1861. Both armies thus had more or less the same thinking
about the war: it would be a powerful but limited struggle that would
probably be over relatively quickly (like the Mexican War). This thinking
was understandable but entirely wrong. Instead of a short, sharp, and limited war, the U.S. Civil War would herald the age of total war as the nationalism of the French Revolution was linked to the economic power of
the Industrial Revolution. This experience would have profound and permanent effects on the U.S. Army, transforming it into an organization for
total war.

The following section details the initial beliefs of the armies (principally the Union but with some reference to the Confederacy) and the transformation of those beliefs by the end of the war. It does so by defining the Army's initial answer to each of the questions for defining the elements of culture based on its period of proto-professionalization. It then illustrates how the answer to many (though not all) of these questions changed substantially over the course of the war, particularly in the minds of the most successful commanders. It was these commanders who would then shape the postwar Army and its professionalization, so the lessons they learned are of particular importance.

STRATEGIC NORMATIVE ELEMENTS OF CULTURE

The first set of beliefs deals with the strategic normative dimension of war. Put simply, was war limited or total, and what were the acceptable targets of war? Initially, the Union generals believed the war was limited and that the only acceptable targets of violence were the enemy's field forces. The central experience of previous war for most of the commanders had been the Mexican War, a conflict marked by a few successful victories in the field followed by the seizure of the Mexican capital and a general policy of treating the civilian population well. There had been only a handful of violent clashes between U.S. forces and civilians, and these were not well remembered by the bulk of the officer corps, who instead recalled the skillfully won field battle of Buena Vista.[9]

These beliefs led the leadership of the Union Army to initially pursue a policy of conciliation toward the civilian population of the South while seeking to defeat the rebel field armies. Major General George McClellan, commander of the Military District of the Potomac and subsequently the entire Army, was a major advocate of conciliation. McClellan felt that crushing military victories in the field, combined with the seizure of several key cities, would drive a wedge between the slaveholding elites of the Confederacy and the nonslaveholding majority. The corollary to this policy was that the property and lives of civilians would have to be treated with the utmost respect. This view, also held by many other officers, was in essence a classic limited war view: defeat the enemy army and limit war's effect on the population.[10]

Further, this policy appeared to have worked well for McClellan in the very earliest days of the war. His campaign in western Virginia in the summer of 1861 was a notable success for conciliation and limited war. McClellan had assembled overwhelming military force to defeat rebel field forces while at the same time assuring the population he would respect their lives and property, including slaves. His success had brought forth a loyalist government and set in motion the political process that would lead to the creation of the Unionist state of West Virginia.[11]

However, the Army was not monolithic in its views about the strategic normative aspect of war. Some advocated a different and harsher view; many of these officers began the war in the Far West, particularly Missouri. While still far from deliberate targeting of civilian life and property, the attitude of senior officers in Missouri was that the population should be held responsible for acts of sabotage. Some of these officers also advocated confiscation of Confederate property and, briefly, emancipation of slaves.[12]

By the beginning of the summer of 1862, advocates of conciliation and limited war appeared poised to triumph. The Confederacy had been beaten in a number of engagements, and McClellan's Army of the Potomac was preparing to capture Richmond. However, the dynamic Confederate general Robert E. Lee inflicted a serious reversal on McClellan, and the prospect for conciliation began to recede quickly.

One important outcome of Lee's victory was the shift eastward of several prominent Union generals from Missouri and their promotion to high positions of command. Generals Henry Halleck and John Pope in particular were given high positions, with Halleck eventually replacing McClellan as commanding general of the U.S. Army and Pope taking command of the Army of Virginia. They argued for a harsher policy toward the Confederacy, encouraging the passing of a confiscation bill in Congress and allowing the Army of Virginia to requisition supplies without compensation from the rebel population.[13]

From this point forward, the beliefs of the Union officer corps about the strategic normative aspect of war would become both increasingly monolithic and increasingly harsh. This transformation is nowhere more apparent or important than in the changing beliefs of the Union's two most important generals, Ulysses S. Grant and William T. Sherman. Both began the war as almost fervent believers in conciliation but soon turned to expedients such as foraging and requisitioning supplies.[14] Yet neither was ready to embrace truly punitive measures in 1862 except in very limited circumstances, and in this they represented the view of much of the officer corps.

However, by 1863 the views of Grant and Sherman began to change. The issuing of the Emancipation Proclamation on January 1, 1863, set the tone for this transformation; in essence the Union had declared war on the livelihood of the Southern slaveholding aristocracy. Henceforth, the property of Southern civilians would be attacked more and more routinely and in ever-increasing scale. Previous economic attacks had been limited largely to railroad and war munitions factories, but in the spring of 1863 Grant and Sherman began to destroy and confiscate nonmilitary supplies. Mississippi's capital, Jackson, was occupied not once but twice by the two generals, and the second time little was left of economic value.[15]

The view of the Union Army continued to move toward the targeting of civilian property as a deliberate strategy. For example, in February 1864, Sherman launched an offensive toward Meridian, Mississippi. En route he wrecked much of the countryside as well as what remained of Jackson. Arriving at Meridian, which had been abandoned by Confederate forces, Sherman commanded his men to take a day off and then raze the city. After they worked for five days burning and wrecking, Sherman commented, "Meridian . . . no longer exists."[16]

Grant's accession to the position of commanding general of the Union Army in March 1864 ensured that this view of war would be the one promulgated from the top. He found a number of willing subordinates besides Sherman (who replaced him as commander in the West). Major General David Hunter launched a campaign in the summer of 1864 intended to wreak destruction on the fertile Shenandoah valley. After some initial success, Hunter was repulsed by Confederate general Jubal Early. As with several Confederate leaders, Early himself had become a believer in total war, at least as a retaliatory measure. After defeating Hunter, he moved into Maryland and Pennsylvania, where he burned the town of Chambersburg.[17]

Grant replaced Hunter with Major General Philip Sheridan, who was ordered not just to defeat Early's army but also to complete the devastation of the Shenandoah. Sheridan did both with dispatch, beginning in August 1864. His forces systematically burned every barn they came across on the march. After defeating Early's forces in September, Sheridan turned to the systematic devastation of the valley. Within about a month, Sheridan reported, "I have destroyed over 2,000 barns filled with wheat, hay, and farming implements; over 70 mills, filled with flour and wheat; have driven in front of the army over 4,000 head of stock, and have killed and issued to the troops not less than 3,000 sheep." He also noted the effect on the population: "The people here are getting sick of the war."[18]

An inextricable component of the campaign against the livelihood of Southerners from Mississippi to Virginia was the effect of Southern guerrillas on the Union Army. As the Union Army's supply lines stretched further and its forces also came to provision themselves more by foraging, they grew more and more vulnerable to guerrilla attacks on both supply trains and small foraging parties. Combined with larger-scale partisan actions and conventional cavalry raids, guerrillas posed a significant threat as well as infuriating commanders such as Grant, Sherman, and Sheridan. The Southern population had to be targeted not just because it supplied the Southern war machine with men and materiel but also because its members directly attacked the Union armies out of uniform, fueling the Union's move to total war.[19]

The Shenandoah campaign brought the total war view from the Western theater to the Eastern, but it was merely a prelude to the most famous example of total war ethos in the Civil War: Sherman's burning of Atlanta and March to the Sea. Sherman successfully marched from Nashville to Atlanta, capturing the city in September 1864. He subsequently ordered all civilians out of the city. In November his forces destroyed much of the city and marched southeast to Savannah, pillaging a huge swath through the Southern heartland. After reaching Savannah, Sherman turned north and inflicted a similar treatment on both Carolinas.[20]

Sherman is particularly notable for two principal reasons. First, he was the most audacious of the Union's commanders in terms of inflicting economic ruin on the civilian population. Yet at the same time, he was one of the most troubled by the morality of his effort and spent considerable time attempting to justify it.[21] Second, as discussed subsequently, it was Sherman who relaunched the Army's process of professionalization following the war, and this process bore the indelible stamp of his experience.

STRATEGIC POSITIVIST ELEMENTS OF CULTURE

In terms of strategic positivist beliefs, the officer corps of the Union was less divided at the outset of the war. Most believed in the utility of the single decisive battle followed by political negotiations based on that battle's outcome (aided perhaps by the occupation of key territory such as an enemy capital), combined with a belief in the efficacy of firepower, particularly in the form of artillery. Both of these beliefs had been validated in the Mexican War, and there was little reason to initially question them. War was thus principally about maneuvering to a superior position, especially to employ artillery, and then concluding the decisive battle successfully. The historian Russell Weigley has termed this a "Napoleonic strategy," and it had influence over both Northern and Southern generals.[22]

This initial view proved inappropriate to the Civil War. Industrial capability combined with nationalism created armies too large to defeat in a single or even a handful of decisive battles. At the same time, the United States was too big for even these large armies to effectively occupy the bulk of the country and retain the ability to conduct offensive operations. Finally, the size of armies, combined with advances in both small arms and artillery and the adoption of entrenchment, made the tactical offensive (traditionally the bayonet rush, cavalry charge, and artillery rush) problematic.[23]

A clear example of the limits of decisive battle in the early Civil War is the Second Battle of Bull Run/Manassas in August 1862. General Lee succeeded in fixing General Pope's army in place using General Thomas "Stonewall" Jackson's forces and then delivered a crushing flank attack with General James Longstreet's corps. The result was to send Pope's army retreating to Washington after suffering sixteen thousand casualties. Lee's forces suffered a little over nine thousand but were unable to pursue and destroy Pope's army. Further, Lee's offensive had cost him almost 20 percent of his force to Pope's 13 percent. Despite achieving as decisive a result as could be hoped for in a single battle, Lee had suffered heavily and not destroyed the enemy army.[24] Weigley is equally critical of many of the Union generals, arguing: "So much did these generals regard 'the battle' as synonymous with 'the campaign' and even 'the war' that when they lost a battle they never knew what to do next and withdrew into paralysis until their replacement came along. It is difficult to believe they would have demonstrated a much clearer notion of what to do next had they ever been fortunate enough to win their battles."[25]

The solution to the strategic positivist question had three main parts. The first, discussed previously, was to alter the normative component of strategy in order to target the enemy economy and population, a "strategy of exhaustion."[26] The second was to focus on continual contact with enemy armies in order to attrite and eventually annihilate them, the "strategy of annihilation." The third, more tactical and operational, was to adapt to the increasing amount of firepower by creating a system of hasty entrenchment and field fortifications that, supported by centralized control of artillery, would allow slow and methodical advance on the offensive or an equally stout defense, while the frontal assault was to be used sparingly if at all.[27] Firepower and attrition would substitute in many instances for the decisive charge, though the charge did not disappear entirely.

As with the normative dimension of strategy, Grant and Sherman would be the principal exponents of this new positivist dimension of strategy. Grant in particular grimly prosecuted a strategy of annihilation against Lee in the East. The early months of 1864 saw Grant relentlessly press Lee's army from the Wilderness to Cold Harbor, with Grant's army sustaining more than fifty-five thousand casualties while causing more than thirty-two thousand.[28] When this proved ineffective at breaking Lee's army, Grant moved to seize Petersburg, the gateway to Richmond, in hopes of cutting Lee off from supply and reinforcement. This effort failed to cut the link to the Deep South, and the two armies settled into attritional warfare.

Ultimately, Grant accepted a grinding trench warfare east of Petersburg that would last from the summer of 1864 until the end of the war. This period saw the introduction of massive siege guns and mortars as well as the use of underground tunneling to explode a mine under enemy lines (both techniques would be used again in World War I). The resulting Battle of the Crater in July–August 1864 once again demonstrated the difficulty of assaulting troops that were heavily entrenched; it also demonstrated Grant's willingness to continue attrition warfare in the face of repeated tactical and operational defeats.[29]

Sherman was less wedded to annihilation, preferring to maneuver around enemy entrenched positions and exhaust the Confederate economy when possible. However, he would fight the grinding annihilation battle when an enemy army presented itself.[30] He also became the best of the Union generals at the methodical offensive, seizing both Atlanta and Savannah by means of skirmish lines that would move forward and entrench in bounds until they eventually reached the enemy's fortification. Backed by artillery, these entrenched infantry would attrite the enemy until they fled or surrendered.[31]

The Civil War also established the U.S. Army's view of its relations to other services. The Marine Corps was a tiny force that played almost no role in the Civil War and so did not even register with the Army. The Navy and the Army, in contrast, were both important in the war but operated almost entirely independently.[32]

MANAGERIAL NORMATIVE ELEMENTS OF CULTURE

For the U.S. Army, the Civil War also began the redefinition of an officer as a manager of large organizations rather than purely a tactical leader. The principal problem that confronted the Union Army in the early Civil War was the lack of officers capable of commanding the massive armies the war called forth. Experienced officers at the field grade (major) and below were not in plentiful supply, but, combined with an influx of volunteers, they did reasonably well. At higher levels of command, there was virtually no experience or training except for the senior commanders of the Mexican War almost fifteen years previous.

Thus the chief lesson about what made a good officer was the ability to lead large groups of men. This required an entirely different set of values than had previously been understood to be at the core of officership. Before the war, even senior officers needed to know little more than how to lead a company. However, the war soon showed that delegation and the ability to focus on broader operational and strategic questions rather than just tactics were what was required of Union colonels and generals.

This may seem obvious to the modern audience, yet in the early period of the war it was not appreciated. Russell Weigley notes that Brigadier General Irvin McDowell, the commander of the entire Army of Virginia, personally led the reconnaissance ahead of his army's march to Bull Run/Manassas in 1861. Similarly, McClellan personally sighted artillery pieces before the battle of Antietam/Sharpsburg.[33] On the Confederate side, the South's second-highest-ranking officer, General Albert Sidney Johnston, was killed while providing tactical leadership at the Battle of Shiloh in 1862. His death not only resulted in what had looked to be a Southern victory becoming a defeat but also brought the Union victors, Grant and Sherman, to prominence.[34]

In contrast to this type of leader, Grant was bottom of his West Point class in tactics. However, this lack of tactical focus allowed Grant to develop his capacity for operational and later strategic leadership and management.[35] He ordered his staff officers (whose number he expanded as needed) to not only go to the front to observe and report back to him, but also to urge commanders at the front to take action if it was urgently needed and there was not time to report back to Grant.[36]

Sherman was not as skilled at delegation as Grant, yet he too was a ferociously capable organizer. His effort to prepare three armies for the march from Nashville to Atlanta in 1864 was an epic of organization, and he showed consistent ability to effectively direct these armies (a total of about one hundred thousand soldiers). His ability to combine massive foraging with efficient logistics made both the march to Atlanta and the subsequent March to the Sea possible.[37]

This ability to delegate and manage rather than provide tactical leadership would eventually be selected for across the Union's senior leadership. Generals such as Philip Sheridan, George Meade, John Schofield, James McPherson, and George Thomas showed anywhere from fair to excellent leadership at the corps and army levels, and they were aided by a number of able division commanders. It had taken nearly three years of war and a host of mistakes to select for these commanders, but the proper role of an officer in the era of total war was now clear to the U.S. Army.

Equally clear was the preferred relationship between the civil and military spheres of authority. The two spheres should be as separate as possible, with the military left to tend its responsibilities with minimal interference. Certainly most officers respected the idea of civilian supremacy over the military, but they were unhappy with what they saw as meddling in their area of professional competence.

McClellan's well-documented clashes with Lincoln over policy in the early part of the war were the high point of civil-military tension. In essence, McClellan refused to obey direct orders from the president when he felt they conflicted with his professional judgment. Following McClellan's relief (and subsequent run for president in 1864), Lincoln's relations with senior commanders such as Halleck and Grant were considerably better, and civil-military questions were muted. Lincoln and Grant more or less agreed on policy, and Lincoln trusted Grant enough to give him appropriate autonomy in conducting the war.

However, in the immediate aftermath of the war, civil-military dispute would again become an issue. Following Lincoln's assassination, Vice President Andrew Johnson assumed the presidency and issued orders that began the reconstruction of the South on relatively generous terms. These terms were too generous for Grant and Lincoln's secretary of war, Edward Stanton, who felt that Johnson was not doing enough to punish and limit the powers of former rebel elites and was doing far too little to protect Union soldiers in the South. Over the course of the next three years Grant and Stanton would revolt against Johnson with the help of radicals in Congress.[38]

Ultimately Congress would in effect split the U.S. Army in two: one part would guard the borders and fight Indians on the frontier while the other maintained a harsher version of Reconstruction in the South. The command of this latter portion of the Army was removed from Johnson's purview. His subsequent attempt to remove Stanton from power led to Congress attempting to impeach him.

Even as Grant helped lead a revolt intended to carve out significant autonomy for one part of the Army, Sherman took a different approach.

Sherman detested both politics and politicians and so sought command in the Far West. This part of the Army was hardly touched by the storm over Reconstruction, and its physical distance helped isolate it further from the machinations of politics.

These responses to major disagreements with civilian leadership would set the future tone for Army civil-military relations. Sherman's response, the rejection of politics, would be the dominant one, as he set up the Army's post–Civil War professional education system. However, Grant's experience of quiet defiance of the president helped further solidify the belief among officers that while civilians might ultimately be supreme, they were not to be allowed to interfere in the military profession's areas of competence.

MANAGERIAL POSITIVIST ELEMENTS OF CULTURE

The final set of cultural values the Army derived from the Civil War are those concerning the best practices for the management of military organizations. These positivist managerial values are tied directly to the successful but often problematic experience of the Union Army during the war. Large-unit management was what mattered, and the central importance of both staff work and combat support was well demonstrated in the war.

As noted, the principal difficulty faced by the Union was commanding large units, yet at the same time total warfare had made those units the principal building blocks of armies. Tactical success or failure by company or regimental commanders would seldom decide a single battle, much less the drawn-out campaigns needed for operational and strategic success. Further, even brigade-sized units at the time were not combined arms units; instead they were pure cavalry or infantry (later artillery brigades as well).

The division was initially the lowest level of organization to contain all arms. This made the division the basic unit of action for the Army, and the building block for the corps- and army-level formations that Grant and Sherman wielded so adroitly. By 1863, however, further reorganization was needed; the cavalry was reconstituted as an independent corps in the Army of the Potomac, and artillery was reconstituted as brigades under the corps headquarters. Following the war, War Department regulations made the division the central element of Army organization, calling it "the fundamental element and basis of organization of every active army."[39] After significant experimentation with various organizations, the final shift in federal organization of large units took place in 1864 after Grant took command in the East. He established the Army of the Potomac as a force of three corps, each with roughly three divisions totaling around twenty-six thousand men per corps.

Running such large units was more than enough to overwhelm any single man, so staffs expanded significantly over the course of the war. At all levels from regiment to corps there were increases in the number of staff officers to oversee muster (personnel), subsistence, ordnance, and the like.[40] This expansion and the use to which the staff was put varied from commander to commander; however, it was Grant's system of careful organization of the staff and investing it with considerable authority that proved most successful.

This staff expansion had visible effect on both sides at the corps level as well.[41] James Longstreet on the Confederate side spent much effort organizing his staff and gave them considerable authority. Longstreet is widely regarded as perhaps the best corps commander of the war, and his success was in large part due to this able staff.[42]

Additionally, the Union Army came to appreciate the vital role played by supporting arms. In the Civil War these were principally the various independent War Department bureaus and departments such as the Commissary General, the Surgeon General, the Chief of Engineers, the United States Military Railroad Construction Corps, and the like. Of critical importance was the Quartermaster Department under Brigadier General Montgomery Meigs, who provided for centralized procurement and auditing as well as providing advice and support to logisticians in the field.[43]

Sherman in particular recognized the importance of these organizations. Writing to Meigs while in Georgia in 1864, he noted, "I beg to assure you that all my armies have been admirably supplied by your Department, and I am sometimes amazed at the magnitude of its operations . . . And you may always rely upon my cordially cooperating with any system you may establish."[44] He gave similar credit for his success in marching on Atlanta to the Railroad Construction Corps: "The Atlanta campaign would simply have been impossible without the use of the railroads."[45] Sherman's appreciation for Grant's staff system and his own understanding of the vital nature of combat support would both be incorporated into Army culture.

Preserving the Lessons of Total War: Professional Education, 1865–98

In the period after the Civil War, the Army was in turmoil. As noted earlier, Grant became deeply involved in politics as commanding general, and Sherman went to the West. In 1868 Grant was elected president and named his old friend Sherman to be commanding general of the U.S. Army. Sherman would oversee the foundation of the Army's professional education system after the Civil War, and it would preserve and refine the lessons he had drawn from the Civil War and subsequent consideration of the war.

From 1869 to 1876, Sherman and his close subordinates such as Sheridan and protégé Emory Upton studied the armies and conflicts of Europe while considering ways to preserve what Sherman termed "the habits and usages of war." However, little could be done in this period, as Sherman and Grant had a substantial falling out, with Grant siding with his secretary of war, William Belknap. Moreover, the commanding general had no authority over many elements of the Army bureaucracy, which instead reported directly to the secretary of war. Sherman, always considering politics anathema, had little conception of the political elements of senior command and so did little to help himself in this regard. The situation became bad enough that Sherman once again fled west, moving his command to St. Louis in 1874.

During this period, Sherman wrote his memoirs, which were published in 1875. In the concluding section, "Military Lessons of the War," Sherman disseminates many of the lessons he had drawn from the Civil War. In it, for example, he describes the Army corps: "The corps is the true unit for grand campaigns and battle, should have a full and perfect staff, and every thing requisite for a separate action, ready at all time[s] to be detached and sent off for any nature of service. The general in command should have the rank of lieutenant-general, and should be, by experience and education, equal to anything in war." He further calls the division "the unit of administration." In contrast, he remarks little on the smaller subunits, noting only that the company "is the true unit of discipline."[46] The Army as Sherman envisioned it was one prepared to fight total war again, despite knowing and proclaiming that the Army would not be able to assemble a full unit of regimental size during peacetime.[47]

In addition to his vision of an Army prepared again for total war, Sherman noted the importance of military education. In addition to his admonition to preserve the habits and usages of war, he noted, "At the close of our civil war, lasting four years, some of our best corps and division generals, as well as staff-officers, were from civil life; but I cannot recall any of the most successful who did not express a regret that he had not received in early life instruction in the elementary principles of the art of war, instead of being forced to acquire this knowledge in the dangerous and expensive school of actual war."[48] Sherman clearly wanted to ensure that future officers would have more opportunity to learn before fighting.

Belknap's resignation in 1876 prompted Sherman to return to Washington and enabled him and similarly minded officers to begin establishing professional reforms. These included the formation of a new professional association and journal, moving reformers into key positions such as superintendent of West Point and of the Artillery School, and rewriting Army regulations.[49] In 1881 this reform movement culminated in the establishment of the School of Application for Infantry and Cavalry at Fort Leavenworth, Kansas. The school would, over time, become the bedrock of Army professionalism. From the beginning, Sherman explicitly wanted the school to be the training ground for the officers prepared to lead an army similar to Calhoun's expansible army. He felt that this was the only system that the American economy and political system would support that would also allow for the creation of armies on the scale of those in the Civil War.[50]

Initially, the school trained lieutenants in the most basic elements of the military profession. In the early years, there were in fact two courses. The first taught tactics and organization, while the second was almost purely remedial, teaching things as basic as history, math, and literacy. The school faced resource shortages, shortfalls of instructors, and an extremely uneven quality of students.

However, over time the commandants of the school were able to improve the instruction. They were supported in this by Sherman and his successors as commanding general, Philip Sheridan and John Schofield. Most notably, Commandant Alexander McCook worked with General Sheridan to create a code of regulations for the school in 1888. This marked the end of what Leavenworth historian Timothy Nenninger referred to as "the kindergarten era."[51] The school continued to train lieutenants but of a much higher caliber.

The school in 1898 was still short of Sherman's initial vision. Its curriculum now helped prepare students for both command and staff responsibilities and provided a broad base of military knowledge, as Sherman had hoped it would. Yet at the same time, it was not fully accepted by the Army; when war broke out in 1898, Leavenworth graduates were not given any additional consideration when assignments were made. Further, the classes were still principally made up of lieutenants who would have little opportunity to make practical use of their broad studies at the school.

In addition to the creation of an overall Army culture, the period after the Civil War saw the solidification of the three dominant subcultures of the Army. These subcultures were, perhaps unsurprisingly, the three main combat branches of the Army. As the actual fighting components of an organization devoted to war, it was almost inevitable that these would be dominant over other communities. Further, given their dependence on one another for overall success in war, it is not surprising that the three branches would share dominance over the organization. Finally, this shared dominance was mirrored by very similar thinking about the nature of war and officership. In the language of organizational sociology, these were orthogonal subcultures.

However, orthogonal does not mean identical. Further, the lack of a chief of staff and a general staff in this period gave the head of each of the branches considerable autonomy. The branches also developed (or further developed) their own schools, which further helped impart branch-specific distinctions. Thus, even within the overall Army culture, different subcultures could view the same information in somewhat different ways.

Total War on the Frontier, 1865–86

As Sherman and his successors sought to use education to preserve what they learned in the Civil War, they were applying many of these precepts continuously, albeit on a much smaller scale. The post–Civil War Indian Wars were not, as some have argued, an entirely different experience than the Civil War, casting the Army as a purely constabulary force. Instead, the Army, now shrunk to a peacetime force of only twenty-five thousand, sought to permanently defeat the Indians in the same way that they had defeated the Confederacy—through total war.

Though some significant military action (led by early advocate of total war General Pope) took place before the Civil War had officially ended, the clear beginning of the Army's war against the Indians was December 1866. In that month, Sioux warriors under the war leader Red Cloud lured nearly a hundred soldiers into an ambush near Fort Phil Kearny (in what is now Wyoming), killing them all. This shocked the nation and invoked the fury of General Sherman, who declared, "We must act with vindictive earnestness against the Sioux, even to the extermination of men, women and children."[52] Though there was a degree of hyperbole in Sherman's statement, it was not mere idle talk.

Sherman and his subordinates began planning for summer operations against the Sioux even as many civilians sought peaceful solutions to the problem. Elsewhere in the West, Sherman allowed General Winfield Scott Hancock to engage in a demonstration of force intended to awe the Cheyenne and Sioux of Kansas. This demonstration, beginning near a large village on the Pawnee Fork, quickly escalated. The Indians fled, and then apparently went on a rampage along the road to Denver. In retaliation, General Hancock burned the village despite having no real evidence that the marauding Indians were indeed the ones from Pawnee Fork.[53] This would be the first of many attacks on the dwellings of the Indians, a direct reflection of the lessons Sherman and others had learned in the Civil War.

After this brief skirmish, a number of peace initiatives sponsored by Congress and the Department of the Interior prevented further significant Army action for two years. Sherman was appointed to serve on a peace commission, which he reluctantly did. Sherman proved a reasonable negotiator and, in concert with the other members of the commission, signed several treaties. At the same time, Sherman encouraged Congress to make Indian affairs the responsibility of the Department of War rather than the Department of the Interior. In 1868 his wish was indirectly granted when Congress decreed that all money spent implementing the peace treaties be overseen by Sherman.[54]

As these events took place, skirmishing and pursuits between small Army units and various tribal raiders took place across the West. Even as Sherman was winding up his involvement with the peace commission and assuming fiscal responsibility for the Indians, a group of disgruntled Cheyenne youths raided white settlements in Kansas. Sherman immediately ordered a response to be headed by General Sheridan.[55]

Sheridan launched a winter campaign against the Indian camps in October 1868, beginning a pattern that would be repeated in future operations against the Indians. The Indians were hard to bring to battle in the summer, as they had superior mobility. But in winter they set up camps that would be static for a lengthy period and that would be hard to abandon, as the alternative would likely be starvation. Further, these camps concentrated not only the warriors of the tribe but also the women, children, and old men, making them rich targets for total war methods.[56]

A prototypical example from Sheridan's 1868–69 winter campaign was the attack by cavalry under George Custer against the village of Cheyenne chief Black Kettle in November. Black Kettle was actually a proponent of peace between whites and Indians, but both he and his wife were killed in the attack. The village was burned, animals taken or slaughtered, winter supplies ruined, and over a hundred men, women, and children killed.[57]

In addition to direct attacks on the Indian population, the Army also launched a more indirect campaign against the Indians' supplies reminiscent of the strategy of exhaustion. Principal among these supplies were the herds of buffalo that provided much of the Indian livelihood. Writing to Sheridan in May 1868, Sherman noted the link between the presence of buffalo and the presence of Indians in the central plains: "As long as Buffalo are up on the Republican the Indians will go there. I think it would be wise to invite all the sportsmen of England and America there this fall for a Grand Buffalo hint [sic], and make one grand sweep of them all."[58] This was no joke, as Army policy subsequently became not only to exterminate the buffalo themselves but also to enable others to do so. As David Smits notes, numerous analogies were made by the Army comparing the killing of the buffalo to Sheridan's devastation of the Shenandoah.[59]

The election of Ulysses Grant, somewhat unexpectedly, led to moves toward conciliation with the Indians and a limitation in the Army's total war. The reasons for Grant's so-called Peace Policy are complex but appear to have had more to do with domestic politics (such as Quaker lobbying) than with any conviction of Grant's. Nonetheless, even during the time of the Peace Policy, numerous anti-Indian campaigns took place.[60]

One prominent example is Sheridan's campaigning in the so-called Red River War of 1874–75. He sent multiple columns to converge on the area near the Red River in the Texas Panhandle where Indians of several tribes were causing trouble. Beginning in the late summer, these columns pursued the bands through the fall with only modest success, but as winter drew near many Indians, fearful of being caught in winter camp, surrendered and returned to the reservation. By the spring all of these bands had surrendered.[61]

The campaign against the buffalo continued in this period as well. In the period 1871–73, buffalo hunters eager to sell hides to the booming leather industry decimated the buffalo herd in the Kansas region. They did so with the protection and support of most if not all of the Army officers in the region. Some officers were even willing to allow buffalo hunting on Indian reservations, a clear treaty violation, in order to further deplete this vital resource of potentially violent Indians.[62]

The combination of total war on the winter camps of rebels and the rapid extermination of the buffalo herds worked slowly, as the expanses of the American West are vast and the numbers of soldiers small, but worked incredibly well. By the 1880s, only a very small number of tribes refused to submit to permanent life on the reservation. The last holdouts, Apaches led by Geronimo, surrendered in 1886.

This experience, though fought against irregular rather than regular opponents, helped confirm the elements of culture of senior Army leaders such as Sherman and Sheridan. Though the Army continued to plan for war against regular opponents—and it was with this in mind that the School of Application was established—the Indian Wars showed that even hardy irregular opponents could be defeated with total war methods. This experience would thus not only help validate the Army's culture generally; it was also thought to show how well it applied to war against irregulars. However, after over a decade at peace, the Spanish-American War would equally show that the Army was not as well prepared for total war as it had hoped.

A Real War at Last: The Army and the Spanish-American War

In 1898 the Army finally got a chance to fight a regular army for the first time since the Civil War when the United States' disputes with Spain escalated. The Spanish-American War was marked by a number of mobilization challenges that well illustrated that the Army had not fully achieved Sherman's goal of being an effective cadre for expansion. One of the major mobilization problems for the Army in terms of expansion was the National Guard. The Guard elected its own officers, frustrating the Leavenworth graduates, who believed that Guardsmen should instead be incorporated into units led by professional officers. The Army had sought to bring all enlistees directly into its ranks. Instead, it had to rely heavily on the National Guard units led by nonprofessionals. This arrangement, anathema to the Leavenworth graduates, was not particularly successful.[63]

The Regular Army was itself unprepared for the logistics of rapid expansion. This was particularly true of the various staff departments, such as the Commissary, which remained independent of any central direction below the level of the secretary of war. These departments were not well coordinated in their actions and often felt little pressure to change or expedite their peacetime procedures. This pattern combined with the decision to concentrate many of both the Regular and National Guard troops at camps in the South (where transportation networks were underdeveloped) to make mobilization incredibly slow and haphazard.[64]

Fortunately for the Army, its opponent was perhaps even less competent and was farther from the fields of battle in Cuba and the Philippines than the United States. The mobilization problems thus did not impede a fairly quick victory, aided in no small part by the U.S. Navy's successes. The bulk of the fighting in Cuba was done by a relatively small number of Regular Army troops aided by volunteers. Though mobilization had called for the creation of eight corps, the V Corps was the only one sent to Cuba.[65]

However, it was readily apparent that a more capable opponent would have caused the Army vastly greater difficulty. The response, aided by a general trend of progressivism in the country as a whole, was to rationalize Army organization. This rationalization enabled the Army to at last organize and prepare for total war effectively during peacetime.

The Root Reforms and After: Professional Education, 1898–1918

In response to the mobilization failure of 1898, Secretary of War Elihu Root sought to federalize the militia system as well as to create a true general staff system. The passage of the Militia Act in 1903 confirmed Root's success, incorporating the National Guard into the professional Army. The Army General Staff was also created in the same year. The idea of central control of citizen-soldiers by a professional officer corps and general staff was now institutionalized, though far from perfected.[66]

Root also sought to further reform the Army's education system. Though Leavenworth had briefly closed with the outbreak of war, it was critical that Army education be restarted quickly. The new system would have three tiers. The lowest tier was to be conducted by senior captains at Army posts; the students would be junior captains and lieutenants. The top tier was to be the new Army War College. The critical middle tier was occupied by the branch schools (such as the Artillery School) and the School of Application at Leavenworth, renamed the General Service and Staff College. It was to provide a general education to branch school graduates as well as the best graduates of the lower tier. The intent was that the General Service and Staff College would provide professional education to company and field grade commanders and staff officers.[67]

Brigadier General J. Franklin Bell would guide the General Service and Staff College (hereafter the College) through this period. Bell was a telling choice; a former adjutant of the Cavalry and Light Artillery School at Fort Riley, he had respect for military education. He was also a soldier cut from the same cloth as Sherman. As discussed in more detail later in this chapter, in the Philippines his response to guerrilla warfare was to "make the people want peace, and want it badly."[68]

Bell was a vigorous commandant and reformer of the college. He personally encouraged promising officers to attend the college. The college was split into two one-year schools under Bell: the first-year Infantry and Cavalry School and the second-year Army Staff College for high-quality graduates of the first year. Bell worked hard to improve the quality of the students, making the process of selection to both schools competitive.[69]

Bell also worked hard to make this kind of education respectable to the Army. Sherman and Grant, though great heroes of the Civil War, were somewhat anomalous in valuing education. Even after the Civil War, many of the senior leaders of the Army of the early twentieth century had been the nonprofessional regimental officers of the Civil War. Bell worked hard to change this, in conjunction with the Army's second Chief of Staff, General Adna Chaffee (who had taught at Leavenworth and was commandant of the Cavalry School at Riley). Bell would leave Leavenworth in 1906 to become the Army's fourth Chief of Staff and from that position would continue to encourage the development of Army professional education.

The peacetime nature of the Army during this period meant that the spread of "Leavenworth men" to senior positions took place very slowly. Further, the concept of an expansible army was not put to the test; given that Leavenworth was intended to prepare officers for this eventuality, it was hard to demonstrate the college's utility. Yet little by little it made its influence felt. Most importantly, it began to homogenize an Army that had been widely scattered geographically, intellectually, and bureaucratically. Line and staff officers got to know each other's jobs; artillery, cavalry, and artillery officers gained appreciation for the importance of the other branches to combined arms warfare.[70]

Almost as importantly, beginning in this period Leavenworth came to be central to the production of doctrine, initially in the form of *Field Service Regulations*. As the producer of doctrine, Leavenworth was able to ensure that its version of Army culture would at least be given a wide audience even among nongraduates. The doctrine it produced was entirely a product of total war culture, even though almost all officers' experience in this period had been either the Indian Wars or imperial policing, as discussed in the next section.

For example, in terms of organization, the 1908 version of *Field Service Regulations* clearly states: "The division forms the basis for army organization." It details the composition of a division (most importantly, its combined arms components of three infantry brigades, a cavalry regiment, and an artillery brigade) and the division staff (normally at least thirteen officers). More significantly, these regulations hammer home the importance of staffs and particularly chiefs of staff.[71]

Yet this doctrine was not particularly well integrated with U.S. grand strategy during the period between the Spanish-American War and World War I. The country, protected by its Navy and having weak neighbors, required an Army and a doctrine for imperial policing. The Army was forced into this role yet did not produce doctrine for this mission.

Total War and Policing at the Beginning of Empire, 1898–1918

Between 1848 and 1918, the U.S. Army was involved in two principal conflicts, the first being the policing of the Philippines. The Philippine conflict came as a direct result of the successful defeat of the Spanish. Filipinos under Emilio Aguinaldo were already in revolt against the Spanish, and, after initial cordial relations, many rose against the United States. From 1899 to 1902, the Army was forced to confront this insurrection.

Army officers, with no operational doctrine, were left to their own devices in responding to this challenge. As a result, doctrine varied from commander to commander but generally had two components. The first was to establish effective if rudimentary government, as the Army had done in Reconstruction or at various points during its frontier experience. The second was to apply the total war methods of Sherman and his successors. Yet at this point Army culture as embodied in Leavenworth had yet to fully dominate the Army, and many officers were National Guardsmen who had barely heard of Leavenworth, so there was significant variation across the officer corps in balancing these two components of policy. Some officers, already deeply schooled in Sherman's Army culture, were quite willing to fully apply total war. Other officers attempted to limit the amount of violence and in some cases placed emphasis on governance.

Two officers in particular show the wide range of variance in Army practice in the field during this period. The first was Frederick Funston, a volunteer officer who rose to the rank of brigadier general and command of a Philippine district. Funston had been rejected from West Point before going to the University of Kansas. He then held a variety of nonmilitary jobs until joining the Cuban Revolutionary Army in 1896. Returning to the United States in 1898, he was commissioned a colonel in the Kansas Volunteers and went to the Philippines with them.

In the Philippines, Funston focused on intelligence, scouting, and patrolling as the key to defeating the insurrection. At the same time, he used his charisma to build very strong relations with local elites and ethnic minorities. Initially somewhat harsh in response to guerrilla provocation, Funston quickly became a believer in amnesty and reintegration of surrendered guerrillas. He limited the reprisal actions of many of his own troops, such as the burning of houses, though some incidents did happen. His methods were sufficiently successful (and unorthodox compared to those of the professional Army) that it was Funston who succeeded in capturing supreme guerrilla commander Aguinaldo.[72]

Funston is emblematic of the limits of Army professionalism in this period. It would later be all but inconceivable to imagine any civilian being inducted into the Army at the initial rank of colonel. At the same time, his practices were successful despite their deviation from Army culture as embodied at Leavenworth.

In contrast to the civilian Funston, Brigadier General J. Franklin Bell was a true disciple of the Leavenworth culture. He had spent time fighting the Indian Wars with the Seventh Cavalry before joining the faculty at the new Cavalry and Light Artillery School at its founding in 1892. Bell took command of a volunteer regiment soon after the outbreak of the Spanish-American War and then became commander of a district in the Philippines.

Bell, like Sherman, felt that defeating the insurrection would require war on the economic and population bases of the enemy, and to that end launched operations to "reconcentrate" the population into camps as well as harshly punishing suspected collaborators.[73] Further, he directly attacked enemy food supplies exactly as Sherman would have, sending troops into enemy territory to conduct operations "having for a common object the complete clearing out of every vestige of animal life and every particle of food supply found within the region."[74]

Bell's methods fit in well with the Army's total war culture, though he was not the most extreme in applying the hard hand of war. General Jacob Smith simply told his subordinates to turn his area of command into "a howling wilderness," which some of them took literally.[75] Bell's methods were not quite so extreme and were more successful. He would be rewarded for his efforts by being made the commander of the reconfigured Leavenworth schools and then Chief of Staff of the Army.

The second mission that the Army undertook immediately prior to entry into World War I was involvement in the Mexican Revolution, which had begun in 1911. This revolution immediately south of the United States concerned then president Woodrow Wilson, and he ultimately decided to intervene in 1916. General Funston brought the Fifth Brigade of the Second Division to occupy Vera Cruz following a naval skirmish and subsequent landing.[76]

U.S. action at Vera Cruz provoked a raid on New Mexico by Francisco "Pancho" Villa, one of the contenders for power in Mexico. In response, Wilson directed a punitive expedition into Mexico under the command of General John Pershing. The expedition lasted nearly a year and was entirely unsuccessful in capturing Villa. It was more successful in engaging in skirmishes with forces loyal to Venustiano Carranza, who was unfortunately recognized by the U.S. government as the rightful head of the Mexican government. Pershing's expedition left Mexico in early 1917 even as another, greater expedition loomed. To the extent that this experience of imperial policing affected Army doctrine, it was only in showing some important aspects of new technology such as the truck.

Almost as soon as Pershing returned from Mexico, the United States entered World War I as a combatant. Leavenworth would prove its utility with the introduction of the American Expeditionary Force (AEF) to Europe in 1917. The Army performance was not stellar but given the already battered state of the enemy was sufficient to ensure victory. Further, it would not have been possible without the staff and command work of Leavenworth graduates. As AEF commander, General Pershing, though not a graduate himself, relied heavily on the expertise of graduates.[77]

Army Culture Consolidated, 1918–61

The experience of the Great War served to reinforce the values derived from the Civil War experience that Sherman had created Leavenworth to preserve.[78] First, the possibility of fighting a great power war, which had often seemed highly unlikely, had actually come about. This war had looked a great deal like the Civil War, though with newer technology. Second, the idea of centralized and industrial-scale management was firmly entrenched. The mobilization of the entire country for war required central control over military and economic issues.[79] Third, the Army had been relatively free from civilian interference once overseas, though Pershing would still cause controversy by sending a letter to the Allied high command demanding that the Germans not be given an armistice.

Even with its culture consolidated after the war, the Army was uncertain during the 1920s and 1930s about where it would fight the next great power war. The most likely candidate seemed to be Japan, and much of national (as opposed to Army) war planning was done on that basis. War plans were color-coded by country, and the plan for war with Japan was known as Plan Orange. Orange was to be primarily a naval war, with the Army's role limited mostly to the defense of the Philippines. Despite being the most likely scenario for future war, Orange would not be the Army's planning focus.[80]

Instead, the Army continued to plan for a primary mission of large army warfare. The scenarios centered on the Western Hemisphere or Europe, though both were highly implausible in the 1920s. Training at Leavenworth (now known as the Command and General Staff School or CGSS) continued to focus on the application of mass combat power and to ensure that "the average middle" of officers could manage large armies of citizen-soldiers. The classes were made up of more senior officers than in the early days of the School of Application, mostly captains and majors.[81] CGSS sought to produce officers "able to perform duties in either command or staff billets two to three grades above their present ranks, a likely possibility with the expansion of the Army during any mobilization."[82]

The small size of the Regular Army made this mobilization a requirement for any great power war and almost any minor conflict. The Regular Army fluctuated, numbering around one hundred ten thousand men total during the 1920s.[83] This was only marginally larger than the treaty-bound German Reichswehr, which was widely considered an almost useless force.[84]

During the interwar period, the Army also followed the Spanish Civil War with interest as a possible model for a future war in Europe. Unfortunately, it did not accurately assess events in Spain, leading to underestimation of the potential of armored warfare.[85] This faulty assessment of armored war was in large part due to the desire of the subcultures to maintain the status quo, combined with the ambiguity of information gathered from a foreign war fought on a relatively small scale.[86]

Despite being somewhat unprepared for armored warfare in the early part of World War II, the Army was well prepared overall for massive expansion and the application of this force to offensive operations. The experience of World War II was the high point of the Army as a total war organization. Fighting on two overseas fronts, the Army brought the war to a close in less than four years after the entry of the United States. It was decided by the mobilization of the entire country toward war and the application of the resulting combat power in offensive operations.[87] The U.S. Army expanded from the tiny force of the 1920s to almost nine million men by the end of the war, an amazing feat of mobilization management.

World War II also demonstrated the centrality of CGSC to Army culture. One survey of twenty-five division commanders in the war found that while only half were graduates of West Point, all were graduates of CGSC. As the Army historian Gary Wade notes, CGSC helped ensure that "in a real sense, the officers shared a common military theoretical foundation."[88]

In addition, firepower, particularly air power, was used lavishly against both military and civilian targets. Both the strategic bombing of German industry and the tactical use of airpower to support troops were quintessential Army applications of firepower.[89] In terms of indirect fire, an unnamed captain of the Twelfth Infantry Division provides the best summary of the Army culture: "We let the arty [artillery] fight the war as much as possible."[90]

The 1950s provided a number of threats, constraints, and opportunities for the Army. Even as the Army prepared for war in Europe, the war in Korea resulted in less than total mobilization and an unwelcome stalemate.[91] Following his election in 1952, President Dwight D. Eisenhower began advocating a national policy that marginalized the Army, relying instead on nuclear superiority embodied in the Air Force (previously the Army Air Corps) and its Strategic Air Command.[92]

The Army protested as loudly as it was capable of doing, for reasons of both organizational interest and organizational culture. Former generals lambasted the Eisenhower policy of "Massive Retaliation" even as the Army sought to develop a force for fighting on the nuclear battlefield. This included the development of tactical nuclear weapons and helicopter-borne airmobile forces.[93]

The Army also altered its divisional structure to better cope with a nuclear battlefield. The so-called Pentomic Division was built around the concept of using tactical nuclear weapons as a source of firepower to substitute for manpower. Though it was somewhat smaller than previous divisions, the Pentomic Division nonetheless remained a division in terms of most organizational elements.[94]

Even as it sought to develop a doctrine for the nuclear battlefield, the Army continued to protest against what it felt was the inordinate emphasis of national strategy on strategic nuclear war. The Army received a boost for its position when President John Kennedy, influenced by former Chief of Staff Maxwell Taylor, adopted a policy of "Flexible Response" in 1960.[95] Yet Flexible Response meant different things to Kennedy and the Army. Both agreed on the need for greater conventional forces for "limited war." Kennedy believed, however, that limited war included fighting guerrillas in "brushfire wars," while the Army felt that limited war would be a conflict with a great power army (presumably that of either the Soviet Union or China).[96]

The Army's focus is evident in the Reorganization Objective Army Division (ROAD) structure it adopted during the early 1960s. The division remained the central organization of the Army, but under ROAD it moved away from the austere Pentomic model back to something resembling the Army division of the world wars and Korea. ROAD divisions retained tactical nuclear capability but with increased conventional firepower as well. ROAD was thus well suited for the Army's concept of limited war, which had nothing to do with fighting guerrillas, despite the Kennedy administration's emphasis on that mission.

Kennedy did promote a new subculture within the Army: the Special Forces. However, the domination of the existing subcultures continued. Special Forces became an institutional orphan, never well integrated into Army doctrine.[97]

Special Forces: The Unloved Subculture

The U.S. Army Special Forces are a stark contrast to the Army of which they are a part. While the regular Army began a professionalization process after the Civil War that was essentially complete by World War II, the Special Forces came into existence only after World War II. Further, the Special Forces have always had more intimate involvement with civilians by virtue of the missions they undertake.

During World War II, missions behind enemy lines and other covert actions were conducted by a civilian agency, the Office of Strategic Services (OSS). OSS would draw on some Army resources and personnel but never fell under Army control. OSS was tiny compared to the massive Army effort, so there was no bureaucratic concern from the Army about supplying these special operators. After the war OSS was disbanded, and then reborn as the Central Intelligence Agency (CIA). CIA was given responsibility for all paramilitary and covert actions, a position the Army supported, as this relieved it of any need to maintain such a capability.[98]

This initial support for CIA having all special warfare capability would soon change, for two reasons. The first was the Korean War, where the Army realized that special warfare could be a useful adjunct to conventional warfare, especially under conditions of limited war. However, CIA had different perspectives on such operations and was not under the control of the Army.[99]

The second reason was a belief held by some in the Army as well as senior civilians that such special warfare would be useful in a conflict with the Soviets in Europe. Both sabotage behind Soviet lines and the raising of anti-Soviet partisans in Eastern Europe seemed useful to an Army confronted by the massive conventional forces of the Warsaw Pact. Yet CIA again had its own goals for Eastern Europe and was still not under Army control.[100]

The Army's response was to create the Tenth Special Forces Group and the Psychological Warfare Center at Fort Bragg in 1951–52. The deliberate admixture of Psychological Operations, which had organizational standing in the Army, with Special Forces, which did not, may have been a deliberate attempt to link the Special Forces more closely to the Army. However, this does not appear to have been overly successful. Despite the perception of some that Special Forces would be useful in conventional conflict, the Tenth Group was not well accepted and had trouble recruiting.

Moreover, Tenth Group was a radical departure from Army managerial culture, being a wholly new entity with a radically different mission and training. As one history of the Special Forces sums up: "In short, the Special Forces Group was not designed to be employed as a tactical entity—as, for instance, a conventional division or brigade might be—but rather was constructed around a cellular concept in which each area, district, and regimental detachment was viewed as a separate and distinct operating unit . . . Based primarily on the wartime experiences of a few former OSS officers in the unit, the 10th Special Forces Group developed a training program that was entirely new to the Army."[101] This odd structure meant that the colonel who commanded the group did not so much manage and command his subordinate units as parcel them out to regions where they then had considerable (if not total) autonomy. This required very lean and decentralized management that was anathema to the Army. Further, it meant that both officers and enlisted men would be highly trained specialists in small-unit actions, a far cry from the Army's normal scheme of homogeneous mass units.

The very nature of unconventional warfare was also at odds with Army strategic culture. Far from being able to treat civilians as mere targets or clutter, Special Forces had to live among and understand the populace. In many instances, failure to do so would mean capture or death for the team operating behind enemy lines.

Special Forces officers were very clearly a breed apart from the outset. As one historian notes: "Career management advisors in Washington steered ambitious youngsters away, and still do today . . . So Special Forces in the early days got a few castoffs and less than a normal percentage of quality career officers. It also got some freethinkers who had never adapted to the spit and polish of the peacetime, palace-guard, 82nd Airborne Division. It got the innovators and imaginative people who wanted to try something new and challenging, who chafed at rigid discipline, and who didn't care what the career managers at the Pentagon believed or said."[102] Even officers who made the decision to join Special Forces were encouraged to rotate through conventional Army units "in order to be accepted and respected by the other line and staff officers with who he has to deal."[103]

The Special Forces grew in the period 1952–56 but still remained a relative backwater in an Army preparing for war in Europe. In 1957, the First Special Forces Group was created in Okinawa to support the growing U.S. involvement in South Vietnam. That year, the First Group went to Vietnam and began training Vietnamese Special Forces under the auspices of the U.S. Military Assistance Advisory Group (MAAG).[104] Thus almost from its inception Special Forces was involved in counterinsurgency, even though it had not been originally created for that purpose.

In addition to being prepared to operate alongside locals, Special Forces also required an ability to work with civilian agencies. CIA, the State Department, and the U.S. Agency for International Development (USAID) were all frequent partners of Special Forces. In Laos, for example, Special Forces would work closely with CIA from 1959 to 1962 to train Laotian irregulars. Special Forces soldiers also frequently went to work for USAID or CIA after they left the Army, further strengthening the ties to those civilian organizations.[105]

A School for Special Forces: The Special Warfare Center and Q Course

The Special Forces established their professional school at Fort Bragg, North Carolina, in 1952. Initially called the Psychological Warfare Center, it was also nonetheless clearly dedicated in its initial mission statement to preparing Special Forces and was subsequently renamed the Special Warfare Center.[106] This center would thereafter remain the center of Special Forces professional education.

In 1961 the First Special Warfare Training Group (Airborne) was founded to oversee the ongoing expansion of the Special Forces. This group would be responsible for what would henceforth be the central professional school of the Special Forces. This was the Special Forces Qualification Course, routinely referred to simply as the Q Course.

The Q Course is the antithesis of the Command and General Staff College. It includes both officers and enlisted men, and focuses entirely on physical and mental preparation for operating in a twelve-man unit known as an Operational Detachment Alpha (ODA). One graduate of the course in the 1980s describes the first portion of the course as "focused on land navigation, survival, and patrolling—the basic skills needed to survive as a member of a small team operating behind enemy lines."[107] The second portion was "like being enrolled in a very bizarre university: we majored in guerrilla war."[108]

The culmination of the Q Course since 1974 has been a field exercise in which the students practice meeting guerrillas, living among a population (played by civilians), and conducting operations against an opposing army. This exercise, known as Robin Sage, takes place in the Unwharrie National Forest of North Carolina, dubbed the "Republic of Pineland" for the exercise. It strives for maximum realism, forcing Special Forces officers to meet and establish bonds with local guerrillas whom they must then convert into an effective irregular force.[109]

It is at the Q Course that Special Forces culture is transmitted. Like the Marine Basic School, it focuses on preparing officers to lead a small unit. However, there are three key differences. First, an ODA is a much smaller unit than a Marine platoon. Second, the soldiers who make up an ODA are even more carefully selected professionals. All are airborne qualified and therefore have made it through the rigors of jump school. They are also more mature, both officers and enlisted men generally having served several years in the Army (officers usually being at least captains at this point).[110] Third, the Q Course explicitly focuses on unconventional warfare, while the Basic School is more general preparation for leading a platoon.

The U.S. Army as a modern professional military organization emerged from the ashes of the Civil War. This first war experience crucially shaped Army culture into the mold of a continental power prepared for total war even though the United States is functionally a maritime power. As demonstrated by CGSC, the Army prepared officers to lead large conscript forces armed lavishly with industrial firepower. Other agencies and the indigenous population were at best secondary considerations.

While Army culture made it highly effective in both world wars, it would cause problems when the Army subsequently confronted the challenge of counterinsurgency. The avowed U.S. national doctrine for counterinsurgency would ultimately be very different than the sort of operations conducted in the Civil War or World War II. Army Special Forces, in contrast, were culturally opposite of the broader Army, which had a substantial effect on Special Forces operations in counterinsurgency.

CHAPTER 4

From the Halls of Montezuma

Marine Corps Professionalization, 1865–1960

The U.S. Marine Corps is a military anomaly. While many other countries have marines and other amphibious forces, none has them constituted as a separate military service that is functionally a second army and a third air force. It has maintained this separate status in large part because of U.S. domestic politics, where an abhorrence of a standing army collided with the need for ground forces to police a nascent empire. This chapter traces the evolution of this anomaly and its limited war–imperial policing cultural archetype.

The Marine Corps by tradition dates its birth to November 10, 1775, when the Continental Marines were established. However, much of the next century was marked by a tenuous existence as shipboard police for rowdy sailors and occasional high-profile expeditions, such as those against the Barbary pirates and into Mexico. The Corps did manage to fend off disestablishment by President (and former Army officer) Andrew Jackson, the first of many attempts to fold it into the Army. An 1834 act of Congress established the Marine Corps as part of the Department of the Navy, ensuring its continued independence.[1]

New Navy, New Marine Corps: The Beginnings of Professionalism, 1880–98

In contrast to the Army, the Marine Corps played almost no role in the Civil War. The overwhelming naval superiority of the Union limited ship-to-ship combat (with a few exceptions), and there was little expeditionary landing. The Marines' main role through the Civil War period was to serve as shipboard police and aid in blockade enforcement. This early experience of total war, which so deeply shaped Army culture, made little impression on the Marine Corps.[2]

Beginning in the 1880s, as the drive to modernize and professionalize the U.S. Navy took place, the shipboard policing role became superfluous, and the Marine Corps found itself without a mission.[3] The Marine Corps began to professionalize in response, albeit haltingly. Colonel Charles McCawley, whose fifteen-year tenure as Marine Commandant spanned the entire decade of the 1880s, sought to make the Marine Corps "an elite guard of the Navy."[4] He particularly emphasized improving unit performance through standardizing drill and, crucially, more selective enlisted recruitment from a wider base. He increased standards to ensure that all recruits were literate and could speak English, a high bar for the time.[5]

Even as he sought to improve the enlisted ranks, McCawley began the process of professionalizing the officer corps. He was aided in this by congressional efforts to rationalize the Navy, embodied in the Naval Appropriations Act of 1882, which limited the induction of new officers. This produced a surfeit of Naval Academy graduates unable to find billets in the Navy, and some turned to the Marine Corps.[6]

Luckily for the Marine Corps, the United States increasingly took an interest in Latin America and the Caribbean. In 1885 the U.S. intervened in Panama in the wake of revolutionary violence.[7] Hundreds of Marines (out of a force of only a few thousand) were immediately dispatched to Panama, which was then still a part of Colombia.

While nothing particularly new to the Marines, who had been to the Isthmus of Panama on a small scale several times since 1848, it was the size of the operation that was important. It was the largest U.S. foreign military activity since the Mexican War almost forty years earlier. By the time the operation was over, a third of the Marine Corps had been dispatched.[8]

The operation illustrated some of the same lessons about modern war at the tactical level that the Army had learned in the Civil War. Commander Bowman McCalla, the Navy commander of the operation, noted, "While the Marine Corps is highly efficient and admirably disciplined . . . their tactics are of a bygone day."[9] In a report to the Secretary of the Navy, McCalla called for a reformation of the Marine Corps as an expeditionary force that would routinely train for such operations with the Navy. While Commandant Mc-Cawley rejected this idea, McCalla's report publicly made the case for the Marine Corps to become an expeditionary force.[10]

U.S. foreign policy continued on its more assertive trajectory. The publication of Navy Captain Alfred Thayer Mahan's *The Influence of Seapower upon History, 1660–1783* in 1890 was both a sign of this increasingly ambitious foreign policy and a spur to naval buildup. Of particular importance was the fact that Mahan was called upon that same year to draw up the United States' first contingency plan for war with a European power. Mahan's plan made specific reference to the Marine Corps as a landing force for the Navy, calling it "the backbone" of any landing force.[11]

Other naval officers noted the importance of the Marine Corps to the Navy's future concept of war. One Navy officer writing in 1890 noted, "The [Marine] corps would be invaluable as a highly trained, homogenous, and permanently organized body of infantry, ready at all times to embark and co-operate with the navy in service like that at Panama a few years ago." This officer, Lieutenant William Fullam, would be the leader of the Navy push to make the Marine Corps a professional expeditionary force.[12]

As the discussion in chapter 3 demonstrated, the idea of a highly trained standing force was the antithesis of the far-flung and draft-based mobilization Army of the time. Further, a Marine Corps focused on the landing mission would relieve Navy sailors of participating in such operations. This was important, because while sailors in the preprofessional Navy could be used in landing parties, the sailors of the new Navy were too important to the functioning of modern warships to be wasted in such a fashion.

Even as the Navy prodded the Marine Corps on its mission, some Marine officers sought to improve the overall professionalism of the Corps. Most notable were Lieutenant Colonel Charles Heywood, who commanded the Washington barracks, and one of his staff, Captain Daniel Pratt Mannix. As Commandant McCawley's health began to fail in 1889, Heywood and Mannix increasingly took responsibility for the administration of the Corps. Mannix was a zealous advocate of Marine professionalization, calling for the establishment of a Marine school of application and declaring that the Marine Corps should rouse itself to do more than "hanging on to the skirts of the Army or Navy."[13]

In 1891 Colonel Heywood became Commandant of the Marine Corps, and his first general order was to establish the Marine School of Application, which opened in Washington, D.C., in 1891.[14] The school was directly under him as Commandant, though its day-to-day affairs would be run by the director of instruction, a post he gave to Mannix.[15] Heywood and Mannix also instituted promotion boards that emphasized examinations as a further spur to professionalize the officer corps.

The Marine School of Application drew heavily on the professional experience of its founder. Heywood had been the commander of the Marine brigade that entered Panama in 1885, so his ideas on the lessons of this conflict were fresh in his mind. The school initially taught both officers and enlisted a variety of practical skills such as tactics and gunnery. A specific set of instructions that stands out is on "landing and campaigning with the Naval Brigade and the best formation for fighting against superior numbers armed with inferior weapons."[16] Even as he acknowledged the Marine role in expeditionary wars such as the one he had been part of, Heywood also felt that a major future mission for the Corps should be to man the secondary batteries on the Navy's new steel battleships. This would allow the Corps to expand in tandem with the fleet.

The Navy, in contrast, was not interested in this mission for the Marines and continued to emphasize the importance of amphibious operations. In early 1892, a war scare with Chile underscored this importance, as the Navy felt that a Chilean port would have to be seized in order to provide a base for blockade. Another war scare in 1895 again raised the issue of seizing bases, this time a diplomatic dispute with Britain that saw war games including a potential seizure of Halifax, Nova Scotia.[17]

Managerial Culture Develops in the 1890s

Even as the Marine Corps' mission remained in question, Heywood and Mannix worked to make the officer corps more professional. The School of Application was the locus for this effort, though Mannix died of stomach cancer in early 1894 and was replaced by Captain Paul St. Clair Murphy. Murphy proposed extending the length of time spent at the school as well as adding additional practical study in subjects such as ordnance, which was approved in 1896.[18]

By 1897 the Marine Corps had made some progress in developing professionalism along the managerial (that is, inward-looking) axis of culture as competitive examinations and professional education (positivist) became routine for officers along with a code of conduct (normative). However, the strategic (that is, outward-looking) culture was still undefined, as the Navy simply did not want a Marine Corps that manned its secondary weapons systems. The Spanish-American War would create a shared strategic mission for the Marine Corps, yet one that was ambiguous enough to create two subcultures oriented around variations of this mission.

Shock Troops and Police Actions: Two Sides of the Same Corps, 1898–1914

The February 1898 sinking of the USS *Maine* and subsequent diplomatic escalation meant that by March planning for war with Spain was taking place in earnest. The Army and Navy were both mobilizing for war, but the Marine role was undefined until early April, when the commander of the Navy's North Atlantic squadron requested two battalions of Marines for service with the fleet. This required creating battalions, since the Marine Corps at the time did not normally maintain these formations.[19]

Fortunately, Heywood had commanded the last major Marine expedition and, with supplemental funds and aid from the commander of the New York barracks, had a battalion assembled within a week. The Navy Department decided to cancel formation of the second battalion, instead supplementing the manpower of the new First Battalion of Marines. On April 22, it embarked for service with the fleet.[20]

As noted in chapter 3, the U.S. Army's mobilization was not nearly so rapid. The Marine battalion spent two months at Hampton Roads, Virginia, and then Key West, Florida, waiting for the Army and Navy to prepare for operations. In the meantime, the U.S. Navy's Asiatic squadron under Commodore George Dewey scored a crushing victory against the Spanish fleet at Manila but lacked the men to control the Philippines. A detachment of Marines occupied a Spanish naval station to give the Asiatic squadron a base, but no more could be done pending reinforcements.[21]

In June the Marine battalion was given a mission at last: seize and hold Guantánamo Bay, Cuba, as a coaling station for the U.S. Navy. This was quickly accomplished, and the Marines linked up with local Cuban rebels, who provided intelligence and additional manpower. After a few days of skirmishing, the Marines essentially held Guantánamo for the remainder of the brief war.[22]

The Army and Navy, however, were still at odds. It would not be until July that the Army would engage the Spanish, and even then the Army and Navy disagreed over strategy. The Navy's primary goal was to destroy the Spanish fleet, whereas the Army was focused on seizing the city of Santiago. Fortunately, the Spanish capitulated rather quickly, but the contentious Army-Navy relationship was uppermost in the minds of many naval officers as the war ended.[23]

At the same time, the Spanish-American War cemented the U.S. position as a rising imperial power, as it now had overseas possessions, including the Philippines. Though Commandant Heywood still believed manning the Navy's secondary batteries was the primary role of the Marine Corps, he also realized that the burgeoning empire would need policing. In December 1898 he wrote Secretary of the Navy John D. Long, noting that many in the Navy felt that "there should be a force of 20,000 well drilled and equipped Marines who could be . . . sent to any of the many possessions recently captured by the Navy without the necessity for calling on the Army."[24]

Secretary Long agreed with Heywood's plan for expansion (initially to six thousand enlisted Marines), and Congress rapidly approved the plan. The expansion increased the size of the officer corps and authorized more senior officer billets for the Marines, including the rank of brigadier general for the commandant. The plan was signed into law in March 1899, and shortly thereafter Commandant Heywood recommended the institution of an examination for all those aspiring to receive a commission in the growing Marine officer corps. Secretary Long concurred and issued a Navy circular mandating this examination.[25]

In 1900 the Navy once again pressed the Marine Corps to focus on expeditionary warfare rather than naval gunnery. The Navy was looking to both the Pacific and the Caribbean, and its officers saw a need for Marines in defending or seizing bases in both theaters. Commandant Heywood cautiously agreed, formalizing a shift in the mission of the Marine Corps to expeditionary warfare rather than naval gunfire.[26]

Yet expeditionary warfare was a broad concept, which had two distinct missions within it. The first was the seizing and defending of advanced bases for the Navy, which appropriately came to be called the advanced base or amphibious mission. The second was imperial policing, which came to be called the small wars mission. Over the next three decades, two Marine subcultures would form around these differing perceptions of organizational mission. On one side were the amphibious advocates. They sought to make the Marine Corps into the shock troops of the Navy, seizing heavily defended beaches and islands. In contrast, the small wars advocates sought to make the Marine Corps a rapidly deployable intervention force for the execution of U.S. foreign policy.[27]

These two subcultures present a twist on the Siehl and Martin distinction (discussed in chapter 2) between orthogonal and counter subcultures. The two subcultures differed on the primary mission of the organization, yet agreed on many elements of organizational culture. They were thus simultaneously orthogonal and counter.

The two were highly orthogonal, tightly bound by common managerial culture, that is, what it meant to be a Marine officer. Central to this managerial culture was the infantry ethos embodied in the unofficial Marine Corps motto, "Every man a rifleman." No matter what other specialty he might have, every Marine was expected to be a proficient infantryman.

In marked contrast to Army managerial culture, the Marine Corps did not focus on the large units (above battalion) of infantry as the locus of professionalism. A standing Marine battalion was not formed until after the Spanish-American War. The First Marine Division was not formed until 1941, and even its constituent regiments (the First, Fifth, and Eleventh) had been formed only in the second decade of the twentieth century.[28] As noted earlier, the Army of the 1870s, despite being about the size of the Marine Corps of the 1920s, had adopted the division as its central organization.

The corollary to this focus on small units was a lack of concern about staff functions. This is not to argue that the Marine Corps did not teach staff functions. However, it did not consider staff capability the core of professionalism in the Marine Corps.[29] This lack of concern about staff functions was further strengthened by the Marine Corps' relationship with the Navy, which took care of much of the mundane but important work done by staff officers.[30] This relative lack of concern about staff work is also evident in the title and headquarters of the senior leader of each service. The Army, after 1903, has been led by a chief of staff. In contrast, the Marine Corps has been led by a commandant. While a seemingly minor semantic distinction, it is indicative of what the two services value in terms of professionalism.

Another related aspect of Marine culture that contrasts with Army culture is the relationship between the regulars and the reserves. While the Army, as noted, spent considerable time and effort grappling with the National Guard and trying to acquire a federal reserve, the Marines were unconcerned with the issue. In fact, until just before the outbreak of World War I, the Marines had no reserve component—every Marine, enlisted or officer, was a full-time professional. When the U.S. finally entered the war, only three officers and thirty-three enlisted comprised the entire Marine reserve.

Even after the Marine Corps developed a reserve, it was small and played a minimal role for decades. In 1921, after both services had undergone war-time expansion and a permanent increase in peacetime strength, the Marine Corps had fewer than five hundred reserve officers, while the Army had sixty-six thousand. Even considering the size disparity between the two organizations at the time, the Army having about one hundred ten thousand men while the Marine Corps had around twenty thousand, this is a striking contrast. Further, the Marine Corps never had to confront an equivalent of the National Guard.[31]

The Marine Corps managerial culture was thus one of professional, full-time enlisted men being led by highly skilled junior officers in small units. The overarching infantry ethos also meant that the Marine culture was very homogeneous in the sense that it lacked the platform or branch distinctions of the Army, or later, the Navy and Air Force. For example, historically, Marines do not generally acknowledge branch distinctions in the same way as the Army.[32]

Despite the shared managerial culture, the two subcultures were also counter to one another in terms of strategic culture. The amphibious subculture sought a tight relationship with the Navy while preparing for medium- and large-scale (that is, conventional) wars. The small wars subculture, in contrast, did not seek as close a relationship with the Navy, which would be less involved (except to ferry the Marine Corps to and from interventions) in the type of conflicts they believed the Corps should prepare for. The decades between the Spanish-American War and World War I would see continual struggle between the two subcultures, with each dominating in turn even as the Marine education system evolved and cemented the Corps' managerial culture.

Note too that the two counter subcultures also agreed on the critical importance of domestic politics to the well-being of the Corps. As discussed later, the Corps was institutionally somewhat insecure, sometimes being threatened with dissolution or absorption into the Army. This insecurity meant that the Corps was attuned to the importance of relations with Congress (the legislature controlling the purse and thus the number of Marines) and of public relations generally. This is particularly striking in comparison to the Army.[33]

From 1900 to 1903, the Marine School of Application was in a state of flux as the Marine officer corps expanded while simultaneously undertaking new duties in the Pacific. The Marine Corps continued to grow in both the officer and enlisted ranks, with Commandant Heywood promoted to major general in 1902 and a further expansion in personnel authorized in March 1903. By the time Commandant Heywood retired in late 1903, the Marine Corps had 255 officers (from a base of 76 five years earlier) and over 7,000 enlisted men.[34]

Partly in response to the increasing flow of junior officers, the School of Application was relocated to Annapolis in May 1903. Over the next two years its course of instruction was standardized at one year in subjects including infantry operations, small-unit tactics, regulations of the service, and gunnery. However, disruptions persisted, as the Marine Corps was involved in several ongoing conflicts, which continually pulled junior officers out to the field.[35]

The most prominent of these conflicts was the Philippine Insurrection, which saw the deployment of a brigade's worth of Marines. The Marine Corps in the Philippines was subordinated to the Army, and Marine officers followed the orders of their Army superiors. Most famously, Marine major Littleton Waller followed the orders of Army general Jacob Smith (discussed previously) to make a "howling wilderness" of the island of Samar. Waller was subsequently accused of war crimes but was acquitted by an Army court-martial.[36]

Waller, probably the preeminent Marine commander of the early twentieth century, was also prominently involved in three other Marine operations in the decade after the Spanish-American War. First, he commanded a Marine battalion in the joint Army-Navy expedition to quell the Boxer Rebellion in China in 1900. During this expedition, Waller operated closely with forces from the other seven nations working against the Boxers, most notably the Russian Army.[37]

More significantly in terms of small wars, Waller also commanded the Provisional Marine Regiment stationed in Panama in 1904. This unit was deployed in late 1903 to support the breakaway of Panama from Colombia (an echo of the 1885 Panama intervention by the Marines). Both U.S. president Theodore Roosevelt and the inhabitants of the region proposed for the canal had been frustrated by the collapse of talks with Colombia. The Panamanians revolted, and the United States quickly recognized the new state and deployed a Marine battalion under Major John Lejeune almost immediately to protect U.S. interests and deter Colombian invasion. By early 1904 the Marine force had grown to the Provisional Brigade (composed of two regiments), which was commanded by Major General Heywood's successor as commandant, Brigadier General George Elliot.[38]

Relations between the United States and Colombia improved soon after, so that one regiment was quickly withdrawn. Brigadier General Elliot returned to Washington in February, and Waller (promoted to lieutenant colonel in 1903) assumed command of the remaining Provisional Regiment. The regiment was reduced to a battalion by the end of the year, but crucially a Marine battalion would remain in Panama until 1914.[39]

This battalion protected the construction of the canal but also provided the enforcement mechanism for U.S. interests in its new client state. In 1906 the battalion, augmented by additional Marines, was called upon to prepare to ensure that public order was maintained during Panamanian elections for the National Assembly. The U.S. right to intervene to restore order had been established in the Panamanian Constitution, but there was also an ulterior motive. The United States was supporting the political status quo under the Conservative Party against the Liberal Party, so the Marine battalion served as an overt indicator of U.S. support and as a deterrent to insurrection by the Liberal Party. Most notably, when requested by the Conservative president, the battalion moved from the Canal Zone to the edge of Panama City in a very visible show of force. The result was an overwhelming Conservative victory.[40]

The actual order to move the Marines in this case came from Charles Magoon, a civilian who was both governor of the Canal Zone (a U.S. territory) and the U.S. envoy to Panama. The Marine battalion was thus subordinate to a civilian, functioning as his political enforcer. This pattern of political enforcement on behalf of civilian authority would continue throughout the rest of the battalion's time in Panama, with the Marines involved in overseeing the presidential elections in 1908 and 1912.[41]

Lieutenant Colonel Waller was dispatched for the third major intervention of this period, the pacification of Cuba in 1906. Civil unrest had erupted there, and the Platt Amendment authorized the United States to intervene to restore order. Like the Philippines and Boxer expeditions, this was another joint Army-Navy operation. However, the Marines played a larger role than in those prior expeditions. The Marines were the first units ashore in Cuba and, from an initial improvised battalion landing on September 12, expanded to an entire regiment within two weeks. Waller and another regiment arrived by October 1, and Waller took command of a Provisional Brigade composed of the two regiments. The brigade comprised nearly one hundred officers and almost twenty-eight hundred enlisted men, over a third of the entire Corps deployed in the space of a month.[42]

The Marines were not faced with a dedicated military opposition, as both sides of the civil conflict had reasons to welcome U.S. intervention. Moreover, the rebels were not geographically unified, essentially having a separate eastern and western command. The Marines nonetheless quickly acted to secure and patrol large areas of the country. The Army finally began arriving on October 10, and the Marine brigade was dissolved at the beginning of November. Waller returned to the United States, leaving behind a

Marine battalion subordinated to Army command. This battalion would remain in Cuba until 1909.[43]

These operations clearly provided impetus to the evolving small wars strategic subculture. Most of the junior officers inducted into the Marine Corps served in at least one of them. However, the operations continued to disrupt the functioning of the School of Application, which had only ten candidates available for 1906; no class was held for 1907.[44]

These frequent and persistent interventions did provide an excellent rationale for continued expansion of the Corps. In May 1908, Commandant Elliot received authorization for another forty-five officers. In the same year, the Marine Corps acquired the former Naval Station at Port Royal, South Carolina, and the school was relocated there in anticipation of at last being able to routinely serve its function of junior officer training.[45]

Interventions continued, a preeminent example being Nicaragua in 1910. Here the Marine Corps was called on to intervene rather subtly in a primarily political rather than military role and did so from an existing colonial possession, the Panama Canal Zone. A war between an anti-U.S. government and more pro-U.S. rebels was under way in Nicaragua, and the Taft administration sought some way to tip the balance toward the rebels.[46]

One of the Marine officers in this intervention was Smedley Butler, a paragon of his generation of officers and a future Marine icon who would win not one but two Medals of Honor. Though later becoming a populist and antimilitarist apostate, Butler in the early twentieth century exemplified the small wars subculture. The Marine officer and historian Merrill Bartlett sums up this period: "A generation of Marine Corps officers, typified by the frenetic and ambitious Smedley Butler, became convinced increasingly that the small wars environment . . . had become the raison d'être for the smaller of the naval services."[47]

Yet even as the Corps policed the empire, the amphibious mission had not disappeared. The U.S. Navy continued to press for the development of forces to seize and defend the advanced bases it would need for naval warfare, a mission some in the Corps welcomed. Most notable was an early graduate of the School of Application, Captain Dion Williams. Williams commanded a company in the first amphibious exercise, held in 1903 at the Puerto Rican island of Culebra.[48]

This exercise demonstrated that the concept of the mission was still not fully developed in either the Marine Corps or the Navy. The amphibious mission differed from previous experience in that it would necessitate being able to attack from the sea. In contrast, most previous Navy/Marine landings were essentially unopposed (as at Guantánamo in 1898). Numerous problems emerged, and disagreements between Navy and Marine officers in the exercise were common.[49]

The utility of both small wars and advanced base operations to justify the Marine Corps' size helped to unify the two subcultures. Even if members of one subculture felt that the other subculture was not consonant with their vision of the Marine Corps, it was still recognized as a selling point of the Corps as a whole. Sensitivity to domestic political forces would become a hallmark of Marine culture.

In 1907 a war scare with Japan, ostensibly over anti-Japanese actions in the United States, gave fresh impetus to the amphibious mission both within and outside the Corps. The Marines in the Philippines conducted ten weeks of exercises that doubled as preparation to defend the naval base at Subic Bay. Williams (now a major) referred to the 1907 exercise when drawing up requirements for an amphibious force ready for instant deployment.[50]

The war scare also galvanized the Navy. Naval officers including Spanish-American War hero Admiral George Dewey and the longtime Navy advocate of Marine reform Commander William Fullam sought to further pressure the Corps to develop the advance base force. In 1908 these reformers successfully argued to President Roosevelt that Marine guards on Navy ships were vestigial and that the Marines detailed for that duty could be withdrawn to form an amphibious force.[51]

This infuriated the senior leadership of the Marine Corps, who successfully lobbied Congress to overturn this ruling in 1909. Roosevelt's decision to remove Marine guards was only his latest step against the Corps; he had previously attempted to merge it with the Army.[52] These experiences with capricious executive authority further sensitized the Marine officer corps to the importance of good congressional and public relations.

Despite the victory in returning Marines to Navy ships, Commandant Elliot responded to the internal and external pressure to do more with the amphibious mission. In 1910, in one of his last acts as commandant, he established the Advanced Base School at New London, Connecticut (later moved to the Marine barracks in Philadelphia). This school would train units to perform the mission, as well as deflecting criticism of the Corps.[53]

While useful for the former purpose, the school bought only a brief respite from the Navy. Another war scare with Japan in 1913 gave the Navy's Fullam (now a captain and a naval inspector) another opening, as an inspection at the time found the Marine Corps still unready to perform the mission adequately. Fullam castigated the Corps over this failure, prompting the Corps to blame the Navy for failing to provide adequate materiel, including transports. The Navy's General Board and Secretary of the Navy Josephus Daniels intervened to mediate the dispute.[54]

The result was that Elliot's successor as Commandant, Major General William Biddle, established the Advanced Base Force as a standing entity in late 1913. In January 1914, two hastily formed and trained regiments, led by Lieutenant Colonel John Lejeune and Colonel Charles Long, respectively, formed a brigade under Colonel George Barnett, the Advanced Base School commander. This brigade then took part in a major exercise on Culebra in which it successfully defended the island from an attacking force.[55]

Less than three months after the completion of the exercise, the new amphibious regiments would be called on for war. Following disputes with the Mexican government of Victoriano Huerta, President Woodrow Wilson ordered the Navy and the Marine Corps to seize the port of Vera Cruz. Initial landings took place on April 21, and by April 24 the Marines had secured the city.[56]

Thus by 1914 the Marine Corps had seen development and experience in both small wars and amphibious missions. Overall, the Roosevelt Corollary to the Monroe Doctrine and the absence of major war in the Pacific pushed the Marine Corps as a whole toward the small war subculture. By the time the United States entered World War I, the Marines had had numerous deployments to Panama, Nicaragua, Cuba, Haiti, and the Dominican Republic, known as the "banana wars"; many Marines grew very comfortable with their role as de facto imperial police force.[57]

However, neither subculture dominated the Corps. Marines in the small officer corps were frequently called on to perform each mission, often in rapid succession. Colonel Waller, for example, was most associated with small wars, yet he was the overall brigade commander at Vera Cruz. Conversely, Captain Williams, the early advocate of amphibious missions, had participated in one of the many Panama interventions.[58]

Moreover, the managerial culture remained homogenous, with the school system continuing to emphasize small-unit leadership. Practical exercises in minor tactics and topography were among the highlights of the school in 1911–12. Some administrative instruction, such as basic bookkeeping, was introduced in this period, but the focus overwhelmingly remained on preparing officers to lead small groups of men into combat.[59]

Major Interventions and World War Interlude, 1915–31

The outbreak of World War I shortly after the Vera Cruz landing operation highlighted a type of war for which neither the small wars nor amphibious subculture had prepared the military. As a result, the Marine Corps paid relatively little attention to the war from 1914 to 1916. Instead, it was called on for imperial policing missions, most notably in Haiti and the Dominican Republic.

The intervention in Haiti began in 1915 following an outbreak of civil violence threatening to American interests. Colonel Waller was once again commander of the First Provisional Marine Brigade, formed from the newly created standing Marine regiments, the First and Second. Waller was assisted by Major Smedley Butler, whose actions at Vera Cruz the previous year would win him his first Medal of Honor. After an initial period of restoring calm and of negotiations in Port au Prince, it became apparent that one side in the conflict, the so-called cacos of Rosalvo Bonabo, would have to be suppressed.[60]

Waller's campaign was marked by both the small-unit managerial ethos and the developing small wars strategic subculture of the Marine Corps. He dispersed companies into the rebel-dominated areas of northern Haiti, where they established district-level bases. Each company then subdivided the district into regions controlled by a post of six to nine men. From these posts, patrols were sent out frequently to secure the area and to gather critical intelligence. Manpower was insufficient to cover an entire district with these posts, so the Marines would garrison half the district first, remaining until it was pacified. They would then shift posts to an unpacified area.[61] Butler was at the forefront of operations and would win his second Medal of Honor in Haiti.[62]

However, as overall commander Waller was not focused on simply killing the cacos. As the Marine historian Allan Millett describes, he "saw the campaign as a combination of arms-buying, amnesty-granting, and selective attacks against only the most militant leaders and their bands." This policy combined the carrot of payments and amnesty with the stick of military force in an effective political strategy. When faced with military action, most caco leaders accepted amnesty and payments to disband their groups. In December 1915, Marines recorded a total of only six engagements with small groups of rebels.[63]

Waller also realized the importance of working with the locals to provide security, as his manpower, however professional and effective, was limited. Plans to form a Haitian constabulary were drafted in September, and Butler was placed in charge of the effort in December. Butler enthusiastically embraced his new command (claiming the Haitian rank of major general), and the constabulary quickly expanded. Officered by 120 Marines (a mix of both officers and NCOs), the enlisted ranks reached twenty-six hundred, a force larger than the Marine brigade. As the constabulary grew in size and skill, it began to take over the manning of Marine posts and patrols.[64]

Butler would remain in command until 1918, when he left Haiti, but the Marines would remain for nearly two decades. Their principal function was running the constabulary, which became Haiti's shadow government. While the size of Marine forces in country shrank over this period, many Marines rotated through the country, ensuring considerable exposure to small wars within the Corps. The Haitian intervention was a critical component in the evolution of the small wars subculture, one of the "first wars" of the Marine Corps.[65]

A similar if less lengthy operation began in the Dominican Republic in May 1916 in response to fighting between factions of the Dominican government. The Second Provisional Marine Brigade, commanded by Colonel Joseph Pendleton, landed and followed the same pattern as in Haiti, attempting to negotiate a solution before launching a military campaign. The measures used in the Dominican Republic were also similar to those in Haiti, with companies being used to garrison and run districts and form a constabulary officered by Americans. The Dominican intervention ended in 1921, again after many Marine officers had rotated through the troubled country.[66]

Significantly, the U.S. Army did not play a role in either Haiti or the Dominican Republic. These two long-term colonial occupations were commanded exclusively by Marines working closely with the State Department and the Navy. Overall policy guidance in both interventions, for example, came from the State Department and Navy admirals (the Marines still having a dearth of general officers), though the details of implementing policy went to the Marines on the ground.[67]

Both missions were also disrupted by the U.S. entry into World War I in 1917. The Marines were dispatched as a component of the American Expeditionary Force (AEF), hastily sent to Europe by the United States, and many of those sent were pulled away from Haiti and the Dominican Republic. In Europe, Marines essentially acted as regular infantry. They won considerable fame at the Battle of Belleau Woods for their bravery, though this was due at least in part to somewhat skewed journalistic coverage abetted by the public affairs–conscious Marine Corps. It also spurred an attempt to create a provisional Marine division in the AEF (quashed by AEF Commander General John J. Pershing). Yet the Marines never subsequently evinced any serious interest in preparing for total war.[68]

The war predictably disrupted the education system. A huge surge in the officer ranks of the Marine Corps was approved and hastily trained before dispatch to Europe. The school was relocated to Quantico from Norfolk during the war and would remain there afterward.[69]

By 1920 the school had regained equilibrium and was more important than ever for two reasons. First was the expansion of the Marine officer corps, which had gone from about 350 in early 1916 to a peak of nearly 2,300 in 1919 before stabilizing at around 1,100–1,200 for the next decade.[70] Second, the Marines also had to pass the lessons of modern tactical warfare learned in Europe to the officer corps as a whole. These lessons did not change Marine emphasis on small-unit leadership but did require updating for the era of ubiquitous automatic weapons and high-explosive weapons such as grenades, mortars, and artillery.[71]

The school itself was renamed the Marine Officer School in 1920 and began to teach three separate courses: the basic course, a company commander course, and a field grade officer course. The emphasis remained on small-unit operations in the first two courses, with only the third teaching some headquarters staff functions. Even in the field grade course the focus remained on operations of battalion size.[72]

The basic course was separated and relocated to Philadelphia in 1924. Renamed the Basic School, it trained twenty to thirty junior lieutenants per year in courses of four to eight months' duration for the remainder of the decade. The major disruption to its function in this decade was another major intervention, this time in Nicaragua.[73]

In April 1927, the Second Provisional Marine Brigade, numbering almost three thousand men, was dispatched to Nicaragua to settle a civil conflict arising from disputes over the 1926 election. The Marines were specifically in support of the efforts of a civilian, former secretary of war Henry Stimson, to negotiate a settlement. Initially, Stimson was successful, but a member of one faction refused to lay down arms: Augusto Sandino.[74]

Sandino and his followers, the Sandinistas, established a base in northern Nicaragua, but neither side took any offensive action. The Marines, again including Smedley Butler, immediately began constructing a Nicaraguan constabulary and by July felt that the situation was in hand. Marines began to withdraw, but Sandino then began launching attacks against the Marines and the constabulary. Sandino's men enjoyed the advantage of significantly better training and equipment than rebels in Haiti or the Dominican Republic. However, the Marines had added airpower to their arsenal, providing a partially offsetting reconnaissance and attack capability.[75]

The overall Marine response to Sandino's attacks followed the familiar pattern derived from the small-unit managerial culture and small wars strategic subculture. Patrolling, intelligence collection, small garrisons in villages and key points, an offer of amnesty, the constabulary, and assaults on key Sandino bases were all combined into a political strategy like that seen in Haiti and the Dominican Republic. The result was that within little more than a year the Marines had significantly weakened the rebellion. In May 1928 over a thousand guerrillas accepted amnesty and surrendered themselves along with thousands of weapons.[76]

Following successful supervision of a national election in 1928, the Marines began to reduce force levels, shifting the burden to the Marine-officered constabulary. By the end of 1931, following a major offensive by the rebels and a counteroffensive led by the constabulary, the rebellion was over. Sandino surrendered the following year after the last Marine combat forces left Nicaragua.[77]

Advance Base Progress and Stagnation, 1915–31

The waxing of the small wars subculture in the years before World War I was matched by a waning in the amphibious mission. The progress made earlier, with the formation of a school and a standing force, stalled. By the end of World War I, the subculture was in danger of disappearing entirely, as the Marine officer corps was extensively utilized in Haiti and the Dominican Republic as well as other smaller interventions.

However, the changes in the balance of naval power after World War I created an opportunity for the amphibious subculture. After World War I, only three global naval powers remained: Great Britain, the United States, and

Japan. The U.S. Navy assessed that war with Britain was unlikely (though not impossible). Japan seemed a much more likely opponent, given its expansionist aims and the previous war scares. The Navy therefore decided to focus its planning and force structure almost entirely around war with Japan, code-named War Plan Orange.[78]

The size of the Pacific meant that both the United States and Japan would need to seize and/or hold island bases. In 1920 the chief of naval operations asked Commandant of the Marine Corps George Barnett to establish the capability to launch a force of some six to eight thousand men within two days for a campaign in the central Pacific. The Joint Army and Navy Board, at this point a sort of proto–Joint Chiefs of Staff, approved the mission as well.[79]

The amphibious subculture was given a further boost in 1920 when John Lejeune became Commandant. Lejeune had commanded a regiment in the Vera Cruz landing and then subsequently commanded first the Marine brigade and then an Army–Marine Corps composite division in France. The sum of his experiences had made him an adherent of the amphibious subculture even if he was not among its intellectual progenitors. He served as a patron to many of those progenitors, most notably Earl Ellis, whom he immediately assigned to study the problem of war with Japan (already a subject of near-maniacal interest to Ellis) from the Marine perspective.[80]

In 1921 Ellis produced Operation Plan 712, "Advance Base Force Operations in Micronesia." Lejeune approved it as the guiding document for Marine planning and force structure. Ellis died in 1923 under mysterious circumstances while on leave from the Corps, conducting "officially unofficial" reconnaissance in the islands of Micronesia. His plan, however, lived on and guided the Marine Corps amphibious mission for the next several years.[81]

The Marines conducted amphibious exercises of increasingly greater size and complexity in the 1920s. In 1922 the first postwar amphibious exercise took place at Culebra and Guantánamo Bay using only two companies. In 1924 a major exercise took place in the Canal Zone and Culebra, commanded by amphibious pioneers Dion Williams and Eli Cole. In 1925 another large exercise took place, this time on the Hawaiian island of Oahu.[82]

Lejeune continued to promote the amphibious mission and its intellectual exponents for the remainder of his nine-year tenure as commandant. He made Dion Williams, now a brigadier general, his assistant in 1928 along with Ben Hebard Fuller. Fuller had spent considerable time working on War Plan Orange with the Navy.[83]

Lejeune was replaced as Commandant by Wendell Neville, a Medal of Honor recipient and veteran of the fighting in France, in 1929. However, Neville had little chance to make his mark before dying suddenly in 1930. The matter of his replacement would bring to the forefront the previously fairly quiet division between the two subcultures.

Culture Clash and Consolidation in the Corps, 1930–35

The obvious candidate to replace Neville was Smedley Butler. In addition to his two Medals of Honor, he was now the senior general in the Marine Corps. Butler himself certainly expected the appointment, but he had been vocally obstreperous too many times to merit the Commandant's billet. He had also lost critical political patronage when his father, a congressman and member of the House Committee on Naval Affairs, died in 1928.[84]

Butler was therefore passed over in favor of Ben Hebard Fuller. Fuller had spent the bulk of the 1920s at Marine Headquarters, and so had observed both sides of the cultural ferment. He was not heavily invested in either; he had participated in imperial policing missions but worked extensively on War Plan Orange. He had, however, been a graduate of the first class at the School of Application, which he subsequently commanded. As such, he was committed to the unified managerial culture that had developed in the Corps.[85]

Almost immediately after becoming Commandant, Fuller was confronted with external threats to the Corps' well-being. The first was a general retrenchment and decline in U.S. military spending as the Hoover administration, penurious to begin with, struggled to cope with the Great Depression. The Marines' responsibilities were not curtailed, but their end strength and overall budget were. Further, Secretary of the Navy Charles Adams conspired with Army officers, including Army Chief of Staff Douglas MacArthur, to have the Corps absorbed into the Army. Congressional support for the Corps quashed this latter attempt, but Fuller nonetheless spent the first two years of his time as Commandant fighting to preserve the Corps.[86]

While the Commandant of the Corps sought to ensure its survival, the Marine Corps schools Commandant, Brigadier General Randolph Berkeley, initiated an effort to "develop and write the text for Landing Operations and Small Wars."[87] This decision would effectively validate both subcultures, yet the effort failed (for reasons that are opaque) in 1932. Nevertheless, these two missions were acknowledged as central to the Marine Corps. In this context, a history of the Basic School notes that "staff and students were intensely indoctrinated in the peculiar mission and functions of the Marine Corps."[88]

The same year an Army-Navy Board convened to determine responsibilities in landing operations for the two departments. The result was heavily focused on large-scale amphibious-style operations and was seen as a major victory for the amphibious subculture. However, this amphibious triumphalism provoked a strong response from the small wars subculture. Assistant School Commandant Colonel Ellis Miller delivered a pointed lecture calling for the embrace of both subcultures: "Some officers contend that we MUST . . . take our maximum war effort as our Corps mission, the seizure and defense of advanced bases for the fleet. Those who thus contend forget the long record of constructive achievements and success in minor wars which has conclusively proved that the Marines have operated, during the last century and a half, in the execution of many important missions in no way related to a war with a first class power."[89] Ellis elaborated further on the importance of the small wars mission, and was eloquent enough that Commandant Fuller had bound copies of the lecture distributed to Marine officers.

The teaching of the Basic School at this point was heavily focused on the small-unit aspects of managerial and strategic culture that both Marine subcultures had in common. In terms of the size of units, training and exercises included company and smaller operations (platoon, squad, and so on). Officers were trained in hand-to-hand combat through the use of small arms and crew-served weapons. Patrolling and scouting were heavily emphasized, as were the Spanish language, military government, and "bush warfare," the latter three more relevant to small wars than amphibious missions.[90]

However, the following year the advance base subculture received another boost with the formation of the Fleet Marine Force (FMF). This would serve as a standing and dedicated force for large amphibious operations. Those assigned to the FMF in this period could not be transferred without the Commandant's permission, so it was institutionally on firm footing.[91]

Further, Commandant Fuller retired and was replaced by Major General John Russell in 1934. Russell would be a major advocate for the FMF and the amphibious subculture, yet he had considerable small wars experience as well. From 1919 to 1922, he commanded the Marine Brigade in Haiti and then was appointed High Commissioner to Haiti. This position placed him in charge of all U.S. efforts in Haiti, military and civilian. Russell was clearly comfortable in this role, serving until 1930, though an uprising in 1929 may possibly have soured him somewhat on small wars. Regardless, he embodied the Marine Corps' cultural openness to working with other services and agencies as well as with local civilian and security forces (in this case the Marine-led Haitian gendarmerie).

As Commandant, Russell oversaw the final consolidation of the Marine Corps around both the small wars and advance base mission. In 1934 he directed the creation of the first Marine Corps manual for the advance base mission, entitled *Tentative Manual on Landing Operations*. The following year the new school commandant, Brigadier General James Breckenridge, oversaw the creation of the *Manual for Small Wars Operations*.[92]

From the mid-1930s onward, the Marine Corps would be defined by a unified managerial culture and two strategic subcultures. The managerial culture of small-unit operations with relatively little emphasis on staff functions was embraced by all, in keeping with the overall "every man a rifleman" ethos. The small wars and advance base subcultures would oscillate in terms of relative power within the Corps, depending on the external environment (both international and domestic).

Marine Culture, 1935–60

The Marines' experience in World War II, though dramatic, was in many ways similar to that of World War I. They were mostly restricted to the Pacific theater but accomplished their assigned tasks of taking and occupying enemy islands. The amphibious subculture was clearly validated by the experience, as many of the iconic and evocative images of the modern Marine Corps are from the Pacific campaign.[93] The most exemplary of these images, the flag raising at Mount Suribachi during the Battle of Iwo Jima, has been immortalized in the Marine Corps War Memorial in Arlington, Virginia.

Despite amphibious successes, World War II caused considerable disruption in the Marine Corps. First, the expansion in personnel was enormous and antithetical to the Marine Corps' small-unit professionalism. From a total of just under 20,000 personnel in 1939, the Corps expanded to about 475,000 by 1945. This overwhelmed the Basic School, as the number of junior officers needed for such large-scale war was enormous—officer totals leaped from 1,380 in 1939 to just over 37,000 in 1945.[94]

After demobilization, the Marine Corps returned to its historical mission focus. During the early Cold War, the Marines continued to be a relatively small force that operated in conjunction with the Navy to project U.S. influence. The Marine experience in Korea was similar to that of World War II but on a smaller scale, with notable success in some operations, including the landing at Inchon and the retreat from the Chosin reservoir.[95] This was despite expansion of the Corps mandated by congressional legislation following World War II. The Corps did retain a significant presence in East Asia as rapidly deployable reserves for contingencies such as renewed hostilities in Korea.[96]

The Marines continued to be used for small interventions abroad. The U.S. population and much of the rest of the world were relatively comfortable with this role, at least in comparison to sending the Army. The "ambassadors in green" had a deft touch with locals, were less heavily equipped, and had a history of often leaving soon after arriving (though they made frequent returns).[97]

In the period immediately prior to the commitment of ground combat forces to Vietnam, the Marines were used in two successful interventions, one in Lebanon (1958) and one in the Dominican Republic (1965). In Lebanon, the participants in the ongoing civil struggle welcomed the Marine presence, and order was quickly restored through negotiations without a Marine firing a shot. In the Dominican Republic, the effort to restore peace was more violent, but still successful.[98]

At the same time, the amphibious subculture had waned somewhat in influence within the Corps. The rapidly increasing range and firepower of carrier aviation made the seizing of advance bases nearly obsolete. The Army and Air Force dominated the European theater, leaving little role for the

Marines.[99] Finally, the potential for nuclear use raised the specter of a "nuclear Gallipoli," making large-scale landings ever more risky. This was the state of Marine culture as the Corps was committed to combat in Vietnam.

The Marine Corps' first war was typical of that of the "army" of a maritime power, with close involvement in imperial policing and naval matters. Beginning with the professionalization of the U.S. Navy, the Marine Corps was forced to develop its own professional culture. The Marine Corps quickly coalesced around a managerial culture emphasizing small-unit leadership with an infantry ethos.

Yet its strategic culture reflects two different but related first war experiences. The demand for rapid intervention in the burgeoning U.S. empire created one strategic subculture oriented around "small wars" that especially emphasized close relations with the U.S. State Department and indigenous forces. The Navy's demand for shock troops to seize advance bases led to another strategic subculture oriented around amphibious operations that especially emphasized close relations with the Navy.

The result is a Marine organizational culture that is homogenous in managerial culture, as exemplified by the small-unit emphasis of the Basic School. At the same time, the small wars and amphibious subcultures have waxed and waned in dominance over the Marine Corps, though neither has ever triumphed completely. In the early 1960s the small wars subculture was ascendant as the Marines were confronted with the challenge of counterinsurgency.

A Family of Regiments

British Army Professionalization, 1856–1948

The British Army is unique among military organizations. It has retained to a degree seen in only a few other organizations the character and tradition of its premodern origins. Central to this is the social class and especially the educational background of its officer corps, specifically the English "public school."[1] Even in the 1980s, just over half of all entrants into the Standard Military Course at Sandhurst (the gateway to officership in the Army) were from public schools.[2] Moreover, the combat arms, particularly the elite infantry regiments and armor units, were still dominated by graduates of the upper tier of public schools (Eton, Harrow, and so on) in the 1970s.[3]

Other military organizations strongly tied to class have followed similar patterns. As discussed earlier, the Prussian and later German officer corps is perhaps the most striking example of this phenomenon. Exclusively composed of poorly educated aristocrats in 1800, by 1870 its officers, now leavened with educated members of the middle class, were the model of technocratic excellence.[4]

However, compared to those in Britain, the German reforms and similar reforms elsewhere on the continent took place more rapidly and were more comprehensive. The geography of Britain has provided insulation from the pressure to modernize felt by continental powers. The Royal Navy was always the principal means of defending the homeland, so the Army was not responsible for the survival of the nation in the way the Prussian Army was. This muted the willingness of Britain's citizens to tolerate intrusive measures such as conscription that were the norm on the continent.

Further, the British Army was strongly associated with tyranny, particularly the tyranny of the monarchy, making it a potential instrument of repression. Parliament therefore had little interest in building a large and cohesive force that might threaten it. Civilians adopted a general attitude of benign neglect toward the Army, which in turn carried on as it had for centuries.

However, British interest in both the balance of power on the continent and controlling a vast empire eventually forced professionalization on the Army. The basic model for the professional British Army was in place within three decades of two crucial wars. The first, the Crimean War, showed the need to professionalize for coalition war on the continent. The second, the Sepoy Mutiny in India, made the British Army responsible for policing a vast colonial empire. This combination, interacting with the British public school system, produced the culture of the British Army, though full consolidation would not occur until the twentieth century.

Preprofessionalism: Three Hundred Years of Solitude, 1509–1809

The antecedent to the modern British Army begins with the reign of Henry VIII. Henry was confronted with both the need to defend the homeland from the Scots (not yet part of the United Kingdom) and his desire to press his claims in France with an expeditionary force. A levied militia force provided the means to achieve the former, while a mix of English volunteers and foreign mercenaries made the latter possible. Neither force would achieve anything like a permanent standing presence, in contrast to the emerging national armies of the continent.[5] The same pattern would hold under Elizabeth I, though impressment was used to raise some of the rank and file for expeditions (an early form of conscription, but only for the poor and on a limited scale). Many of Elizabeth's efforts to build the Army were dismantled by her successors.[6]

In 1642 the English Civil War pitted elements of society, none possessing much in the way of military expertise, against one another. After two years of war in which neither side made much progress, the forces loyal to the Parliament were reformed into "a New Model Army." This at last produced a standardized army on a nationwide basis, which won the Civil War and established a new regime under the Lord Protector, Oliver Cromwell.[7]

Unfortunately, the Army was the bedrock of the Commonwealth and Cromwell the bedrock of the Army. His death was followed by a brief split within the Army and then by the Restoration, which in turn led to a diminution of the Army as a standing entity and a return to a militia system. The standing army had become associated with the tyranny of the late Protectorate period, which would have important and lingering consequences for British Army professionalism. Indeed, from 1660 until the 1750s, England would not have a fully recognized "army"; instead, parliamentary estimates referred to "guards and garrisons."[8]

Beginning about 1740, the British at last began to generate a stable and enduring army establishment. The Royal Military Academy, Woolwich, was opened to train artillerymen and engineers (who had earlier been made a permanent corps) in 1741.[9] Finally accepting that both a militia and a standing army of some sort would be needed, Parliament enabled the Duke of Cumberland, "a soldier in the German School," to establish a standing central command centered in Whitehall at the new Horse Guards building in 1751.[10]

This army, still leavened with foreign troops, fought reasonably well against the rebellious American colonists but was unable to subdue them.[11] The years between the end of the American Revolution and the beginning of the Napoleonic Wars were a time of rapid demobilization and economy in military spending. It is therefore unsurprising that the British Army did less well in the initial battles against the French after the French Revolution. This would spark several reforms that would lead to proto-professionalization of the Army.

Proto-professionalism: Sandhurst, Wellington, and India, 1809–54

The 1795 expedition against the French in Holland of the Duke of York, commander in chief of the Army, ended in an ignominious withdrawal. The Duke as a result became interested in army reform and thus looked favorably on a 1799 proposal by one of his subordinates, John Le Marchant, for a national school for officers. However, the Duke felt that the incumbent officer corps would prevent the realization of the proposal.[12]

One of the central reasons for this resistance was that the British Army officer corps was essentially a rentier class that invested a sum in a position that guaranteed steady returns. Commissions in the British Army were at this point obtained principally by purchase (occasionally by royal favor), and as a result education and capability varied widely. Promotion was also by purchase when vacancies in a regiment came open, so, as one historian notes, this system "often produced twelve-year-old ensigns who, if their parents' pockets were deep enough, could become colonels at twenty."[13]

This was, as can be imagined, not a system likely to produce a highly effective officer corps. Yet the entire officer corps had already invested significant capital in it; an attempt to institute mandatory professional education seemed like an attack on their investment and future prospects. Only an act of Parliament or the monarch could overcome this resistance.

Fortunately, the Duke of York remained committed to the project and formed a special commission, with himself as head, to investigate the need for a national military college. Unsurprisingly, the committee recommended that one should be established. As a result, a royal warrant was issued blessing Marchant's private efforts to educate officers (conducted in an inn at High Wycombe) as "the Royal Military College." Subsequently, it was agreed that the college be established permanently on the Sandhurst estate.[14]

However, the Treasury was slow to authorize money for the college, and with the resumption of war with France in 1803 after the one-year Peace of

Amiens, the college languished. Finally, in 1808 the king issued a new royal warrant supporting and expanding on the previous warrants. The warrant specified that those meeting all requirements of the college for the position of lieutenant would be commissioned without purchase in an infantry or cavalry regiment. That same year, the Treasury was persuaded to provide the funds for building at Sandhurst.[15]

The British launched another continental campaign in that year as well, this time on the Iberian Peninsula. It was commanded by Arthur Wellesley, soon to be the Duke of Wellington. An able soldier and former politician, Wellington proved a worthy opponent for Napoleon's armies over the next five years. In particular, Wellington was able to create an effective military apparatus in the field, including adopting a divisional structure for the Army.[16]

The campaigns against France also expanded British Army involvement in India. Prior to the late eighteenth century, the East India Company, which maintained its own army and military establishment, had been principally responsible for the subcontinent. However, the alliance of various Indian potentates with the French increased Parliament's and the British Army's interest in securing the region. Wellington himself had participated in one of these wars, the Fourth Anglo-Mysore War.[17]

Wellington's subsequent triumph at Waterloo in 1815 cemented his place in British military legend. Yet his army at that point was still far from a national one; only slightly more than a third of its members were British, while the rest were a mix of Germans, Belgians, and other continentals. Following the end of the war, the British Army lapsed into quiescence and failed to institutionalize many lessons from the war.[18]

Sandhurst, completed in 1813, had an ample budget for the remaining two years of the Napoleonic Wars, but once peace returned, penury came back as well. The neglect of Sandhurst was not helped by Wellington himself, who loomed over military and political life until his death in 1852, as he was proud of "his success in the field with little formal military education."[19] Correlli Barnett more picturesquely describes the British Army under Wellington and his Napoleonic veterans: "Under their ancient and hallowed hands, the army remained preserved like a garment in a bottom drawer, sentimentally loved, but rotted and rendered quaint by the passage of time."[20]

Finally, in 1832, after more than a decade of decline, Sandhurst was cut loose from the public purse. It would survive only by the most stringent economies and the collection of fees from students. In addition to stunting professional education per se, this also had the effect of preventing any increase in homogeneity or "corporateness" in the officer corps of the British Army (apart from class). There was minimal incentive to pay a fee to attend Sandhurst when one could buy a commission, so there was no place of instruction to provide a common experience for officers.[21]

Indeed, it was something of misnomer to refer to a British officer corps or even a British Army. Rather, there was a collection of regiments and regimental officers. The regiments were scattered across the countryside and the world with no higher headquarters other than the overall command at the Horse Guards. No brigades or divisions, much less corps formations, existed, even on paper. The individual regiments seldom exercised units larger than a battalion.[22]

This lack of corporate identity at the level of the entire Army was of minimal concern as long as no fighting was required on the continent, and Europe was at peace for decades after the fall of Napoleon. Instead, the regiments were called on to fight in India both against and alongside native forces, who were no more professional and often less well armed. This experience began to generate regimental identity as well as emphasizing the importance of small-unit leadership, including personal bravery, for officers. Even in India, however, the political administration continued to be provided by the East India Company, which retained its own rival army (actually multiple armies).[23]

Domestic opinion in Britain during this period, though appreciative of heroes like Wellington, also remained concerned about the perils of a powerful and integrated army, particularly one strongly loyal to the monarch. Comments by senior officers, including Wellington, seemed to show that the monarchy retained the first loyalty of the Army, so civilians remained reluctant to see increasing military professionalism. Even the rather innocuous formation of the United Service Club (a gentlemen's club in London for senior officers of the Army and Navy) was a cause of concern.[24]

A Critical Five Years: The Crimean War and the Sepoy Mutiny, 1854–59

The long "Wellingtonian twilight" came to an end with the outbreak of the Crimean War in 1854.[25] This war, along with the subsequent Sepoy Mutiny in India, would be the foundational experience of the professional British Army officer corps. While perhaps not the most strategically sound war, the Crimean War nonetheless fit with the overall pattern of offshore balancing that the British government had pursued for decades. In this case, the perceived threat was potential Russian dismemberment of the Ottoman Empire, granting the Russians control of the Bosporus and thus menacing the route to India.

Alongside the French Army, the British Army, dispatched en masse for the first time in four decades, laid siege to the Russian Black Sea port of Sevastopol. The expedition was, if not a disaster, at a minimum poorly managed. Troops were dramatically short of supply in the initial months of the war, owing to the fragmented and outmoded system of supply and transport (to be fair to the Army, the supply system was entirely in civilian hands at this time).[26]

Most notably, the infamous Charge of the Light Brigade at the Battle of Balaclava in October 1854 highlighted the shortcomings of professionalism in the British Army. The Light Brigade was composed of five separate cavalry regiments, dispatched to the front and formed into a brigade under Major General James Brudenell, Lord Cardigan. The brigade itself was paired with a similarly cobbled together Heavy Brigade of cavalry into the Cavalry Division, the division commanded by Lieutenant General George Bingham, Earl of Lucan. The overall commander of British forces was General Fitzroy Somerset, Baron Raglan.[27]

On October 25, Raglan instructed Lucan to prevent the Russians from withdrawing with naval guns they had emplaced on the Causeway Heights (on the right of the cavalry at that time). When the order was transmitted to Lucan, by a young captain, it was misinterpreted; Lucan believed that Raglan wanted him to seize the guns emplaced at the far end of the valley formed by the Causeway Heights and the Fedyukhin Heights. Lucan in turn ordered Cardigan to charge with the Light Brigade. This initial charge would be followed up by the Heavy Brigade.[28]

The Russians, with artillery on both heights and at the end of the valley, inflicted devastating losses on the Light Brigade. Cardigan survived, though the young captain who relayed the order to Lucan did not.[29] The disaster was subsequently widely publicized in British newspapers, with Lucan and Raglan trading letters trying to scapegoat one another.[30]

This disaster could have been written off as an aberration, except that the three commanders, Raglan, Lucan, and Cardigan, were typical of British officers at the time. All three were upper class and had attended elite public schools (Westminster and Harrow). All had availed themselves of the purchase system; Lucan was thus a regimental commander at the age of twenty-six. Cardigan became a regimental commander at thirty-five despite a troubled and combative history; he would subsequently be removed from service, only to be reinstated by the king. Raglan had been a key aide to Wellington during the Napoleonic Wars. All had been members of Parliament and, demonstrating the tight-knit nature of the upper class at the time, Lucan and Cardigan were brothers-in-law (who detested one another). Of the three, only Lucan showed any dedication to military education through studying military history.[31]

Further, even in successful battles the British officers often succeeded due more to the professionalism of their enlisted soldiers than to any professional skill of their own. At the Battle of Alma in September, an advance of the First Division (consisting of the elite Guards and Highland Brigades) under Prince George, the Duke of Cambridge, broke apart due in large part to his lack of military training. However, the disciplined troops of the Grenadier and Coldstream Guards were able to reconstitute and demolish the charging Russians with steady fire.[32]

Cambridge, a member of the royal family, had been made a regimental commander at twenty-three and, unsurprisingly, was a believer in the importance of social breeding rather than professional education as the bedrock of officership. His performance, while not disastrous as with Cardigan and Lucan, was not very good. He too apparently misunderstood orders from Raglan and hesitated in deploying his troops at Alma, leading to the problems in the advance of the First Division.[33]

There were a few exceptions to the gentlemanly amateur stereotype. Perhaps the most outstanding was one of Cambridge's brigade commanders, Sir Colin Campbell. Campbell was born a commoner and enlisted in the service of the Duke of York just before the Peninsula Campaign. He was outstanding in that war as well as in the expedition against the Americans in 1814. A devoted student of military science, he would not become a regimental commander until he was in his forties; he would then go to the East, where he commanded units in the First Opium War and the final Anglo-Sikh War. It was for excellence in this latter war that he was knighted in 1849.[34]

He proved to be an able officer commanding the Highland Brigade in the Crimean War, first at Alma and then later at Balaclava. In the latter battle his resolute defense in the face of a major Russian assault inspired the phrase "the thin red line." Campbell was a careful, prepared commander, as disciplined as his elite troops.[35]

The shortcomings of the British Army in the Crimean prompted an array of committees and commissions to review the organization of the Army and the War Department. Sandhurst was reorganized following recommendations by three of these committees. Most notably, a staff college for more-senior officers was created and competitive examinations for entry were put in place for Sandhurst in 1858.[36] This examination requirement initiated the links between Sandhurst and British public schools that would soon come to define the officer corps.[37]

Even as these changes were under way, another dramatic conflict began for the British Army. In May 1857, Indian troops (known as sepoys) employed by the East India Company mutinied on a large scale over pay and perceived abuses, including to their religion. While small-scale mutinies had taken place before, those in 1857 were of an entirely different scale. They were a profound shock to the British national psyche, which one author compares to the effect of the attack on Pearl Harbor or the terrorist attacks of September 11, 2001.[38]

Sir Colin Campbell was dispatched in July to command the British effort to quell the mutiny. Arriving in August, Campbell assembled the British Army and the East India Company force, including those sepoys who had remained loyal. Campbell, with his usual care, then personally directed those forces against the captured city of Lucknow and, in November, successfully evacuated the city. Campbell then prepared to spend the rest of 1857 clearing and securing other regions, planning to return to recapture Lucknow the following year.[39]

However, the Governor-General of India, Charles (Viscount) Canning, believed that leaving Lucknow to the mutineers "would show there was a viable alternative to British rule and thus encourage all those still fighting against it . . . Campbell accepted that as head of government, Canning had the right to determine the direction of the campaign, and a new plan was devised to meet his wishes." Campbell spent the next few months gathering forces and prepared to move in February 1858. However, one of the key local allies of the British, the Gurkha ruler Jang Bahadur, was not yet ready. Campbell and Canning, fearing alienation of a vital ally, agreed to wait.[40]

In March, Campbell began moving his troops into position, linking up with Jang Bahadur's forces. Campbell began methodical clearing operations against Lucknow, by now heavily fortified by the mutineers. In just under three weeks, the city was back in British hands, though many mutineers managed to escape. In the entire operation pitting tens of thousands of men against entrenched defenders, Campbell lost only sixteen officers and 111 men killed. One historian declares this operation "one of the British Army's greatest feats of arms."[41]

Campbell wanted to finish securing the province around Lucknow, but was directed by Canning to seize Rohilkhand, the last area still fully under mutineer control. Campbell again changed his plans without complaint and began another methodical advance. His caution, born of experience and study, caused some officers to term him "Sir Crawling Camel," yet his approach time and again proved effective and efficient, as surprise attacks were repulsed and fortifications demolished without loss of British troops.[42]

In November 1858, the East India Company was dissolved by royal decree and all of its functions directly taken up by the British crown. The decree also guaranteed amnesty for all rebels seeking it, except for those who had promoted the mutiny or murdered British civilians. By December 1858, Campbell's campaigning had driven the last mutineers to flee to Nepal. In January 1859, a group of rebel leaders approached Campbell seeking amnesty; he made it a point to receive them with courtesy.[43]

Campbell would return home in triumph, soon promoted to the rank of field marshal and made a baron; he received thanks from both houses of Parliament and a generous pension for life. While he would retire the following year and then die in 1863, his India command set an example for a host of British officers who served under him, including thirteen of the twenty-seven nonroyal field marshals (not including Campbell himself) appointed from 1862 to 1908. One of these in particular, Garnet Wolseley, a valiant captain during the campaign against the mutineers, would be of major importance to the subsequent professionalization of the officer corps.[44]

As Campbell enjoyed his success, the dissolution of the East India Company was having a profound effect on the Army. All of the former Company units manned by Europeans were absorbed into the regular British Army. At the same time, the sepoy units were reduced in number, and a so-called Indian Staff Corps was created to provide British officers for the remaining native units. Even after the reduction in native units, there were still dozens of native regiments in need of officers. There was thus a dramatic expansion in the officer corps and the overall size of the Army.[45]

The impact of this expansion on Sandhurst, already seeking to modernize after the Crimean War, was dramatic. The college had only 178 cadets in 1853, but by 1859 plans were made to expand enrollment to 500; space constraints tempered this to 400. New construction began, and the entire enterprise was revitalized; one historian calls it "the beginning of a new era."[46]

These two experiences, the Crimean War and the Sepoy Mutiny, are the formative experience or "first war" for the professional British Army. One additional event, which would prove important in later decades, closed out these dramatic formative years. A war scare with France in 1859 sparked the birth of the "Volunteer" movement, which would produce a middle-class and later working-class vehicle for military aspirations. The Militia and Yeomanry, the other options for "citizen-soldiers," at this point were moribund and moreover dominated by the same upper-class elites that dominated the Regular Army. Volunteer units were initially derided as incapable, but they created a bridge between the long-service professional soldiers (who enlisted for life) and the untrained mass of British citizenry.[47]

Reform and the Regiments, 1860–95

While the expansion of Sandhurst proceeded, the core of the Army remained unchanged (other than its expansion) immediately after the Crimean War and the Sepoy Mutiny. Most of the decade following those two events was passed in deadlock between advocates of the status quo and advocates of reform. The former were represented by the queen's cousin and now commander in chief of the British Army, the Duke of Cambridge (whose poor performance in Crimea provided some of the impetus for reform). Reformers, to the extent that they had a champion, were represented by Major General Jonathan Peel, who served as Secretary of State for War in 1858–59 and 1866–67.[48]

Peel, younger brother of a former prime minister, also served on or appointed various royal commissions making recommendations for change after the Crimean War and the Sepoy Mutiny. While many of the recommendations of these committees were accepted (such as the abolition of the East India Company), one of the most far-reaching, the abolition of purchase of commissions in the Army, was rejected. Peel, an advocate for all officers attending a military college, was unable to push this reform through the opposition of the current officers, but he succeeded in laying some of the groundwork for his successor, Edward Cardwell, notably the establishment of a reserve for the Army.[49]

The initial deadlock between advocates of the status quo and those wanting professionalization highlights the importance of leadership in interpreting the lessons of the "first war." Peel and the Duke of Cambridge had drawn different conclusions about the lessons of Crimea and the Sepoy Mutiny, so the result was limited professionalization. This mirrors the initial deadlock in professionalization in the U.S. Army after Sherman and Grant began feuding.

However, just as Sherman was eventually able to incorporate the lessons he drew from the Civil War into the professionalization of the U.S. Army, eventually Peel's successor was also able to incorporate the lessons of Crimea and India into British Army professionalization. A brilliant and experienced politician, Cardwell became Secretary of State for War in 1868 and was able to force many of the reforms Peel and others had been unable to implement. Together these reforms sought to make the British Army capable of fulfilling the twin aims of being able to intervene on the continent and police the empire.

One of the lessons of the Crimean War was that continental intervention required more manpower than could effectively be maintained in the Regular Army. At the same time, the Regular Army needed to be able to function in far-flung locales, particularly the nearly one million square miles of British India. All of this had to be accomplished without resort to conscription.[50]

The Cardwell Reforms, as they are known, consisted of three central elements: the abolition of purchase for commissions; the localization and standardization of regiments; and the introduction of short service for enlisted men. The abolition of the sale of commissions was the most contentious of these reforms and at the same time the most vital. Apart from increasing professionalism, the sale of commissions impeded virtually all of Cardwell's other reforms. At stake was whether a regiment and its men were in effect the property of the regimental commander, who after all had paid for it, or were under the command of the state.[51]

Cardwell knew that abolition would be deeply unpopular, so he agreed to pay compensation to current officers. However, after a sharp clash in Parliament, the centerpiece of his reforms, the Regulation of the Forces Bill, failed to pass the House of Lords. Cardwell took the unusual step of asking the queen to abolish the purchase system by royal warrant. As the entire system rested on earlier warrants, this was a constitutional act, and the queen agreed to it.[52]

At a stroke, Cardwell had disarmed much of the opposition, and the Regulation of the Forces Bill was subsequently passed. The bill gave each regiment a territorial home county, where it would establish a training and recruiting depot. Regiments that did not previously have two regular battalions (many of the non-Guards regiments did not) would be amalgamated to produce regiments that did. This enabled one battalion to be serving abroad while another remained at home. These regular regiments were then linked to the Militia regiment of their home country, providing a reserve force. The Militia was also transferred fully from the control of the County Lord

Lieutenants to the crown (though the former continued to administer the Militia); for all practical purposes it had become an element of the Army rather than an alternative. Cardwell was not able to implement change for all regiments, but in 1881 the then Secretary of War Hugh Childers completed this reorganization.[53]

The introduction of short service made Regular Army duty more attractive and also enabled the Reserve established by Peel, somewhat moribund, to be made effective. Infantry enlisted men were now able to choose between terms of service. A "lifer" could enlist for twenty-one years. A short-service enlistment could be either a full six years or three years followed by enlistment in the Reserve.[54]

In addition, Cardwell expanded on the post–Crimean War reorganization of the War Department. Most notably, the Commander in Chief of the Army, still the Duke of Cambridge, was formally made subordinate to the Secretary of War. This helped allay concerns about professionalization of the Army, for it was now clearly subordinate to Parliament. In practice, the Commander in Chief, still the conservative Duke of Cambridge, had considerable autonomy. Most notably, Cambridge blocked the formation of a British general staff. Yet overall the concern that the Army would be used as a tool of the monarchy against Parliament or the people began to recede significantly.[55]

The Cardwell Reforms had a fundamental and indelible impact on the British Army and in particular on the officer corps. First, the elimination of purchase required a new system not only of entrance into the Army but also of promotion. The method of entrance would be competitive examination. The method of promotion would be seniority within the regiment, tempered by merit. This system therefore placed the careers of all officers in the hands of two institutions: Sandhurst (or Woolwich) and the regiment.

Sandhurst, a neglected orphan in 1853, would be central to the British officer corps a little more than two decades later. With the establishment of competitive examinations for commissions in 1871, Sandhurst shifted its instruction to preparing students for the examination. The initial system introduced in 1871 had all newly appointed officers become sublieutenants, who would take their examination after a probationary period; however, this proved suboptimal from a budgetary and effectiveness standpoint.[56]

Under Cardwell's successor, Gathorne Hardy, the War Office took control of Sandhurst. In order to rectify the initial problems of the new system for granting commissions, Sandhurst would in 1877 become the training ground for all Regular Army officers not entering the artillery or engineers. Prospective officers would enter Sandhurst as cadets and then leave for the regiments as lieutenants. The same system was in place at Woolwich for those seeking entrance to the artillery or engineers.[57]

The barriers to entry for Sandhurst and Woolwich were high. After passing an initial examination at age fifteen or sixteen while still at school, the prospective officer then had to pass the Army Entrance Examination. This examination was intense and geared toward testing that the officer candidate had a good general education, so that he could then be schooled in purely military affairs at Sandhurst or Woolwich. Subjects included mathematics, history, Latin, and the like, in essence, those things covered by a good public school education at the time.[58]

Competition was so fierce that so-called cram schools were often used to supplement public school education (though many public schools had "modern" or "Army" courses of study to prepare for the exam). Notes on Sandhurst cadets in 1885 showed that while 85 percent of cadets had been to public school, 79 percent had also gone to cram school. This was driven in large part by the fierce competition for cadet slots; from 1876 to 1882 less than one in four taking the examination was given a place at Sandhurst; Woolwich was scarcely less competitive. Achieving entry as an infantry or cavalry cadet was even more competitive, as only the very top received those positions. After attending a cram school, Winston Churchill passed on his third try as ninety-fifth out of 389 and still missed the cut for infantry (he made it only when a few candidates ahead of him did not take their places).[59]

Public school, cram school, and even Sandhurst all cost money (though Sandhurst had provisions for adjusting fees, particularly for orphans), so, although outright purchase had been eliminated, family money was still a clear requirement for those seeking to become officers. However, by harnessing the monetary requirement to an education requirement, the reforms of the 1870s ensured that officers would be capable as well as wealthy. This provided an opening to the sons of the wealthy middle class attracted to the lifestyle and social standing of officership; from 1870 to 1890 the proportion of Sandhurst candidates from the middle class rose from 10 percent to 37 percent.[60]

The Sandhurst course in this period varied in length from six months (during crises in Egypt) to eighteen months. Students studied tactics, fortification, map reading, military law and regimental administration, reconnaissance, drill, and riding. Each was thus well prepared to lead a small unit of men in battle.[61]

Sandhurst and its intensely competitive examinations were crucial to creating a common culture in the British officer corps, yet as soon as they left the college the new officers entered new and highly individual institutions: the regiments. The process of joining a British regiment is not like that in many other armies, where the top students are given a choice of branch and then assigned to a unit. Instead, regiments with vacancies look for candidates that they believe will fit the regimental culture. In many cases, they choose individuals who already have some tie to the regiment, such as being from its territory or having a family member who served in the regiment.[62]

After the Cardwell Reforms, promotion, as noted, was within the regiment by seniority, tempered by merit. In practice, this meant that once an officer entered the regiment, he would in most cases be part of it until he retired or was promoted above the rank of colonel. His promotion was thus in the hands of his fellow regimental officers, who could block his advancement regardless of his seniority if he was deemed unsuitable. The new lieutenant, already selected because he was believed to match the regiment's culture, had every incentive to further assimilate. Regular service in India, where regimental officers formed a small and tight-knit social cadre, further strengthened regimental culture. The result was that the British regiment is routinely compared to a family due to the strength of the ties.[63] Many of the various elements of regimental culture are, from the standpoint of doctrine and operations, irrelevant.[64]

However, the centrality of the regiment to the British officer corps, along with the importance of Sandhurst, provides an excellent indicator of the managerial culture of the British Army. Officers were trained at Sandhurst to lead small units and then spent their entire careers in regiments, which in turn often operated as battalions on the frontiers of empire. Larger units, such as brigades and divisions, were rarely used in the field.

The strategic culture of the officer corps was oriented toward cooperation with other organizations, principally the civilian colonial administrators, the natives of the colonies, and other military organizations. The importance of the civilian partners was always taken for granted; as noted, Sir Colin Campbell never questioned the importance of political issues in overall strategy. Civilian officials would sometimes even accompany the Army on expeditions as political officers.[65] Conversely, senior British officers would often be named as colonial administrators, so officers had to be comfortable in that role. Moreover, both the Army and the civil service recruited heavily from the same public schools, meaning officer and civilian often had similar early life experiences and outlook, making cooperation easier.

Similarly, cooperation with indigenous forces was of paramount importance. Sir Colin Campbell's experience in the Sepoy Mutiny, where managing relations with the Gurkha ruler Jang Bahadur was crucial, would provide a lasting example of how to get along with the sometimes fractious princes of India, who were signatories of treaties with the crown rather than mere subjects. Many British officers also served in the Indian Staff Corps, providing leadership to indigenous Indian units (generally these officers had served in a British regiment before being sent to a native unit).[66] After the creation of the Indian Police Service in 1860, the police were an important partner as well; until 1893 British Army officers would be seconded to the Indian Police Service to provide senior officers.[67]

Other military organizations included both the Royal Navy and the armies of the continent. The Navy was always going to be the means by which the Army arrived at the battlefield, as the Crimean War demonstrated, so even if the two services did not always agree, Army officers nonetheless were required to know how to work with the Navy. Equally important were relations with allied armies on the continent, also demonstrated in the Crimean War, where the French actually provided the bulk of troops.

The British Army was highly active in its imperial policing role throughout this period. From 1860 to 1895, the Army launched more than forty campaigns, from Canada to New Zealand.[68] Some of these were as brief and uneventful as the Red River Expedition led by Colonel Garnet Wolseley in 1870. This expedition put down rebellion in western Canada without firing a shot.[69] Others were larger and of longer duration; the conquest and pacification of Burma by General Frederick Roberts lasted from 1885 to 1892 (or 1896 depending on when one dates all resistance over).[70]

Wolseley and Roberts, veterans of Campbell's campaign in the Sepoy Mutiny, were national heroes in this age and had a profound effect on the Army. Wolseley, who earned the nickname "our only general," was Cardwell's principal military adviser and one of the most vocal advocates of Army reform. Roberts, soon known as "our only other general," was anti-Cardwell, believing that short service and the linked battalions were ineffective for empire.[71]

Despite their differences, both men nonetheless represented the emerging culture of the British Army. Both worked closely with various politicians and colonial officials in addition to serving stints as colonial administrators themselves. Both cooperated with indigenous rulers and commanded local troops, Wolseley raising them during his 1873 Ashanti campaign, while Roberts's entire career was spent commanding or working with indigenous troops in India.[72]

Finally, in 1895 the champion of the old order, the Duke of Cambridge, left the post of Commander in Chief of the Army after nearly forty years. He was replaced by Wolseley, who was reaching the end of his long career. However, the powers of the Commander in Chief, zealously guarded by Cambridge, were at last reduced. A War Office Council and an Army Board were established, and Wolseley began to act as a chief of staff; in effect, a proto–general staff had been created.[73] The last barriers to full professionalization were gone just in time for a major war.

Empire, Continent, and Reform, 1896–1914

In 1896 Wolseley made an attempt to estimate the needs of the Army for empire. It seemed clear to him that the Army was well short of the size needed to effectively maintain the empire and further that one of the major causes of this was the commitment to India. Despite the cost, Wolseley was able to obtain an increase in the size of the Army, but the problem of policing the empire with an all-volunteer force without bankrupting the country proved intractable. At the end of 1898, Wolseley noted that the expansion of the Regular Army meant scraping the bottom of the barrel for enlisted men. He wrote of the current recruits, "Over one third are below even the low physical standard laid down for recruits. In fact at this moment over one half of the Home army are unfit to carry a pack or do a week's—I might perhaps say a day's—hard work in the field."[74] It was this Army that would be called on to fight in 1899 in South Africa against an enemy that was well organized and equipped with modern weapons.

Disputes between the British around the Cape and the descendants of Dutch colonists, known as Boers, had originated in the early nineteenth century but until 1880 had been nonviolent. In that year, British attempts to exert control over the newly declared Boer republics led to war. The Boers were not the usual colonial enemy; hardy pioneers armed with rifles and suffused with nationalism, they proved superior to the British forces sent against them, defeating them in a series of battles culminating at Majuba Hill. Rather than commit more scarce resources, Parliament sued for peace, although the dispute was not truly resolved.[75]

In 1899 the British once again went to war with the Boers. An expeditionary force of Regular Army troops under General Redvers Buller was dispatched to join forces already in South Africa. Expectations were for a fairly short war, as the Boers lacked a regularly constituted professional army, instead relying on militia formations, known as commandos, which elected their own officers.[76]

This expectation proved wrong, and from the beginning of the war the Boers proved a tough opponent. At the Battle of Talana Hill / Glencoe in October 1899, the British forced a Boer retreat but took heavy casualties; the Boers were highly effective with their magazine-loading Mauser rifles. Tellingly, the British suffered significant casualties in the officer corps, including senior officers, as leading from the front was a major part of the managerial culture. A lieutenant general and three lieutenant colonels were among those killed at the battle.[77]

After a major British victory of Elandslaagte, the Boers regrouped and moved against the city of Ladysmith. British forces stationed there were defeated and the city besieged at the end of October. The hopes of a short war were fading but not gone, as the Regular Army expeditionary force had just arrived.[78]

Following the arrival of General Buller and his forces, the British prepared to go on the offensive. Unfortunately, the subsequent offensives were near-disasters. In the "Black Week" of December 10–15 the British suffered serious defeats at Stormberg, Magersfontein, and Colenso.[79]

Buller was blamed for these failures, and Field Marshal Frederick Roberts was dispatched to take overall command of British forces. The Army has now fully dominated by veterans of the Sepoy Mutiny, with Wolseley Commander in Chief and Roberts commanding the major field army. Buller would still command a significant portion of British forces (in Natal), and Roberts brought with him as chief of staff a new national hero, Herbert Kitchener, who had made his career around the Mediterranean and in Egypt.[80]

The disaster of Black Week also prompted the British government to mobilize the Reserves and auxiliary forces (the Militia, Yeomanry, and Volunteers). The latter was done on a strictly voluntary basis, as none of the auxiliaries could be compelled to serve overseas. Fortunately, Black Week had stoked British nationalism, so there was no shortage of volunteers. Over the course of the rest of the war, seventy-five thousand men from the Militia would transfer into the Regular Army, while another forty-five thousand would serve while still in the Militia. More than fifty thousand additional men would serve against the Boers in either the Yeomanry or the Volunteers. This was the first major mobilization of citizen-soldiers for an overseas conflict and would have important consequences after the war.[81]

The first of these reinforcements began arriving in early 1900, and, combined with adjustments in British tactics, the tide of the conventional war quickly began to turn. Advances by the British seized Bloemfontein, capital of the Boer Orange Free State, in March. The capital of the Transvaal, Pretoria, surrendered in June, and by November the British had defeated the Boer forces in a series of pitched battles. Victory seemed at hand, so Buller and Roberts both returned to England, leaving Kitchener in command.[82]

However, this predicted victory was ephemeral, as the Boers turned from conventional battle to guerrilla war. This was the first time the British Army had encountered such effective opposition; in most previous colonial campaigns a number of set-piece battles and the seizure of key cities would suffice to force a negotiated settlement. This had eventually been the resolution of the Sepoy Mutiny. Even in cases where lengthier pacification was required, as in Burma, the difference in discipline and armaments meant engagements were almost always won easily by the British, and major resistance was quickly broken.[83]

Moreover, the British punitive response, a common colonial technique, was counterproductive. Beginning in late 1900, the British under Roberts began burning farms to deprive the Boers of supplies and to punish the families of recalcitrant commandos. Looting was also allowed if not actively encouraged. This served to strengthen the Boers' resolve rather than forcing them to sue for peace. Buller, in contrast to Roberts, forbade his troops to conduct burning and looting.[84]

Kitchener continued Roberts's policy, but also sought a generous and early negotiated settlement including amnesty for the commandos. In contrast, Alfred Milner, the high commissioner of the Cape Colony and now responsible for the occupied Boer territory, wanted to avoid burning the Boer farms but also wanted a maximalist settlement to incorporate the Boer republics into the empire. This split, combined with continued intransigence from many Boer leaders, led to a collapse of peace negotiations in early 1901.[85]

Milner and Kitchener continued to disagree about an acceptable end to the war but otherwise worked together reasonably well throughout 1901. Milner was responsible for the administration of territory cleared and "protected" by Kitchener's forces (principally the cities). The solution to the problem of guerrilla war was consonant with the emerging British Army culture, particularly in reliance on local allies and civilian administrators. As the historian Thomas Pakenham notes of the winning methods, "The new policy was Milner's, the new weapons were Kitchener's."[86] However, the strength of Boer nationalism was such that this approach also required tens of thousands of British troops.

Kitchener's strategy first divided territory into sections by the use of fortified blockhouses, barbed wire, and railroads. He then used mobile columns to clear each of these sections, including destroying food supplies for the commandos. Initially, Kitchener began to relocate the civilian population of Boers in these areas to early concentration camps. However, this policy was later abandoned after an outcry from civilians, including the British public. The destruction of food supplies, however, meant that life was soon worse for Boers (mostly women and children) left on the veldt.[87]

Kitchener made extensive use of local allies, both white and black. The whites were Boers known as National Scouts. Blacks served extensively as labor but also provided a substantial portion of Kitchener's troops. Most importantly, as Pakenham notes, "it was these Africans who were the main source of each column's intelligence."[88]

It was ultimately this last aspect of Kitchener's strategy, the use of blacks, that proved decisive in bringing the Boers to the negotiating table again. Pakenham notes that Kitchener's arming of the blacks "struck terror into the Boers." As the war went on, blacks in the Transvaal, previously oppressed by the Boers, began to rise up. Most notably, in May 1902, Zulus seeking revenge for recent Boer attacks (motivated by Zulu cooperation with the British) launched a reprisal raid on Boers. Ominously for the Boers, "the women and children in this district had not been molested, but the Zulus had been restrained with difficulty."[89]

The Boers, though in dire straits, were not militarily broken at this point; indeed, in February and March 1902 the commandos scored their biggest successes. They dealt a smashing defeat to a column of over a thousand men and forced the surrender of a British general. Kitchener almost collapsed when he received this news. Further, there were over twenty thousand commandos left at large at this point. Kitchener was desperate to be done with the war. He felt that the continued conflict was wrecking the Army and the empire.[90]

Fortunately for the British Army, the Boer commandos had grim visions of the future that brought them back to peace talks. Kitchener's blockhouses and sweeps were having an effect. More importantly, the suffering of Boer women and children on the veldt, combined with their vulnerability to black

Africans and a worry that more and more fellow Boers were joining the British cause, made continued fighting seem hopeless. The British were now willing to accept less and offer more (including reconstruction money) for peace, so at the end of May 1902 the war was brought to a close.[91]

The war had been extraordinarily difficult for the British Army. In both men and money, it had been expensive. Moreover, its duration and scale showed the limitations of the Regular Army, particularly when it was confronted with well-armed nationalists. This gave a strong impetus to additional reforms that, when completed, would solidify British Army professionalism.

The assessments from the war were that there were still problems with both the enlisted and officer corps. With the enlisted, the problem remained that only those citizens with virtually no other option, meaning the least developed physically and mentally, signed up for the Regular Army. The various auxiliary units, such as the Militia and Yeomanry, were generally of better quality.[92] However, these units often lacked discipline that had been drilled into the regulars; indeed, the embarrassing defeat in March 1902 that almost broke Kitchener's nerve resulted from the scattering of newly recruited Yeomanry.[93]

With the officer corps, the critique leveled by an investigating committee was that, however competitive entry to Sandhurst was, once a cadet was there he had minimal incentive to work hard. The curriculum itself needed to focus even more on practical exercises. For example, only sixty hours in the course were devoted to tactics, half of which were indoors, and the subject represented only a little more than 10 percent of the final examination (the "passing out" exam). The exam itself, like promotion exams, was judged far too easy. Better-qualified instructors were needed as well.[94]

Finally, at an overall level, it was apparent that however much the reforms of 1860–96 had prepared the Army for policing the empire, they had failed in readying it for larger-scale war, as would be required in a continental intervention. Both the higher-level command and management functions and the size of the force were insufficient. War scares with Germany, with its massive army, underscored the inadequacy of current arrangements. This argued for further changes in the upper ranks of the Army.[95]

With remarkable speed, given its previous glacial pace, Parliament and the British Army effected changes to address (if not entirely solve) these shortcomings. For the enlisted man, Parliament acted to provide better education for the poor (the 1902 Education Act, known as the Balfour Act), better nutrition and medical care for these young students (1906 and 1907 acts), and better physical fitness training for these potential soldiers (the 1902 Model Course and subsequent revisions). While it would be an overstatement to argue that all of these progressive acts were purely military, they were at the time explicitly tied to national defense and the problems of the Regular Army enlisted man.[96]

For the higher-level military functions, the office of commander in chief was abolished in 1904 (to the chagrin of the current officeholder, the venerable Field Marshal Roberts, who replaced Wolseley in 1900). It was replaced by a general staff headed by a chief of staff. An Army Council was created to handle issues of higher policy, but final recommendations were to be made by the Secretary of State for War. The chief of staff would gain an expanded sphere of influence to offer guidance to the forces in the Dominions and India in 1909 when the position was renamed chief of the Imperial General Staff.[97]

These early actions post war were soon supplemented by a set of actions taken by the Liberal Secretary of War Richard Haldane, who took office at the end of 1905. He was most concerned with efficiency in the Army, but only scarcely less with efficacy. The Haldane Reforms explicitly set out to increase the Army's ability to act in coalition with allied powers on the continent.[98]

Haldane's first reform was to prepare an expeditionary force for the continent that would be organized in peacetime. This called for six ready divisions and corps headquarters. All of these were established with an Army order on January 1, 1907, with the first corps based at Aldershot. These divisions, however, would be built up from the existing regiments (though to save money Haldane disbanded some battalions), so the essence of the Cardwell system was preserved.[99]

This expeditionary force would need reinforcement and replacements, yet with conscription still out of the question Haldane had to rely on volunteers. He therefore sought to reform the existing auxiliary units. After political wrangling, the Militia was converted into the Special Reserve, explicitly under the War Department and part of the Army, ending the already tenuous distinctions among the Regular Army, the Reserve, and the Militia.[100]

The Yeomanry and Volunteers were amalgamated into a new Territorial Force. Ostensibly this was to defend the homeland while the Regular Army and Special Reserve went to the continent, but it is clear that Haldane believed that if war broke out, the Territorials would volunteer for overseas duty. The Territorials would therefore be constituted into fourteen divisions, which could be mobilized and sent fairly quickly to support the six Regular Army divisions on the continent.[101]

The Reserves and Territorials would need someone to train them, and they would need officers as well. The solution for the first group was to produce more Regular Army officers, and so the Army sought to increase output from Sandhurst while improving the curriculum. This was quickly done, with Sandhurst seeking to train 650 cadets every eighteen months, dispatching some to Woolwich for lodging. Though the goal of 650 was not reached for budgetary reasons, 420 cadets were at Sandhurst in 1912.[102]

By 1907 Sandhurst's curriculum was much more focused on practical exercises under modern conditions. The tactics course was extended, and signaling courses were made mandatory. By 1912 the end-of-term exams had become substantially more difficult, with some cadets held back for poor performance.[103]

In addition to requiring more Regular Army officers, the Reserve and Territorials needed their own officers. This led to the formation of the Officer Training Corps at public schools and universities. This Corps, a part of the War Department that incorporated previous voluntary organizations, would essentially provide initial military training while students were still in school. Those successfully completing the course and passing an exam would receive a certificate that would reduce the training time required to become an officer in the Reserve (which could be done without having to join the Regular Army) or exempt the holder from all or part of the examinations for becoming a Territorial officer.[104]

Additionally, the certificate would grant the holder bonus points should he choose to take the entrance exam to Sandhurst or Woolwich. This served to strengthen the link between the public schools and the Regular Army, as it gave a substantial boost to the chances of passing the rigorous exam. The public schools embraced the new Corps enthusiastically, and by April 1911 there were contingents at 153 schools as well as 20 universities.[105]

The combination of the major Cardwell and Haldane Reforms along with other more minor reforms over the fifty years from 1860 to 1910 had at last made an Army well positioned to carry out the twin maritime power imperatives of coalition warfare on the continent and imperial policing. Moreover, the Army was no longer viewed with suspicion by any but the most ardent pacifists. The British Army was in 1914 almost exactly what both the officer corps and its civilian masters wanted it to be: professional, efficient, and voluntary. The culture of the British Army was essentially set, built around regiments prepared for coalition warfare on a relatively small scale and for imperial policing. Unfortunately, this proved to be suboptimal for the coming conflict, which was of a scale that made the Boer War seem a mere skirmish.

War and the Decline of Empire, 1914–47

The outbreak of World War I should have been a high point for the British Army. The British Expeditionary Force (BEF) that went to the continent in August 1914 "was the best equipped, organized and prepared army that Britain had ever sent abroad at the beginning of a war."[106] The effectiveness of the Regular Army and its Reserves was proved at the Battle of Mons on August 23 when slightly more than nine British battalions held off four German divisions.[107]

However, this victory was followed by a retreat as the BEF commanders realized that their four divisions (two more were initially held in Britain against a possible invasion) were in the path of the strong right wing of the

Schlieffen Plan. They, and the French, were being overwhelmed by the sheer mass and firepower of the German First Army. After a long retreat the BEF would contribute to the "Miracle of the Marne," turning back the Germans.[108]

By the end of 1914, after a series of fierce battles, the stalemate on the western front was complete. Barbed wire and trenches ran from the Belgian coast to the Swiss frontier, and the combatants began to realize that this would be a long war fought by armies of a previously unimagined scale. The previously envisioned continental commitment of six Regular and fourteen Territorial divisions would be little more than a drop in the bucket.[109]

The remainder of the war saw the British improvise a mass army, finally resorting to conscription. The British also created a war economy to provide for this army, and industry began to produce the weapons to arm it. This took time, and fortunately the French were able to provide most of the manpower for holding the front while this new force was generated.[110] The Indian Army made a substantial contribution to the British effort, in both peripheral theaters such as the Middle East and, for the first year of the war, at the western front.[111]

The British Army, like all the combatants, was forced to formulate new tactics to cope with the challenge of mass armies and industrial war. It would do so over time as the information environment became increasingly unambiguous. Frontal assault and massive, lengthy artillery bombardment did little, as the Battle of the Somme illustrated in 1916. Yet the Army learned from these expensive failures. By 1918 the British had developed infiltration tactics, artillery orchestration, and a host of other techniques to deal with the challenges of the western front. These tactics were similar, though not totally identical, to those developed by the Germans in response to the same environment.[112]

Yet the experience of industrial warfare made little lasting impact on the British Army. After the war, the officer corps returned "to the life of the regiment, to small wars in hot places and police duties in India and Ireland, and even in the unhappy industrial areas of Britain."[113] Sandhurst and Woolwich "were busy 'getting back to normal.' Their role was unaltered; their establishments were much the same as at the outbreak of hostilities."[114] The Territorial Force was reconstituted as the Territorial Army after the war, but its function remained the same, though it was also given a role in keeping civil order.[115]

Twenty years after the end of World War I, the Army was again called on to provide a contingent to support continental allies. The experience was similar to that of the earlier war, with the conversion of much of the economy to the war effort and mobilization of the population on a massive scale. The armament, particularly aircraft and tanks, were new, and so again new tactics needed to be developed, but as in the previous war the unambiguous information environment of total war led to convergence in doctrine and operations across combatants during the war. However, the British Army was slower to adapt to the challenges of this environment than armies culturally better suited to this type of war.[116]

As with World War I, World War II had minimal lasting impact on the culture of the British Army. However, after the war three major events did lead to peripheral change. The first was the consolidation of Woolwich and Sandhurst, with Woolwich closing and Sandhurst being renamed the Royal Military Academy Sandhurst. The new academy opened in 1947 and, though its exact course would change several times over the next forty-five years, its focus would remain on preparing junior officers.[117] As of 1992, the Commissioning Course for almost all Regular Army officers (including women) was consolidated at Sandhurst.[118]

The Army did have a brief experience with peacetime conscription after World War II. From 1947 to 1960, Britain had a National Service system which made all eighteen-year-old men liable for military service in the Regular Army for up to two years, followed by four in the Reserves. Regular Army recruitment continued during this period, and the two types of enlisted men were often mixed together. However, this aberration had little effect on the Army.[119]

The Indian Army came to an end in 1947 as well, with the independence and partition of India. Four regiments of Nepalese Gurkhas were transferred from the Indian Army to the British Army, while all other units were transferred to either Pakistan or India. This removed the largest force where British Army officers led indigenous troops. However, the British Army continued to work with a variety of other local forces throughout the remainder of empire.[120]

The Special Air Service: An Elite Regiment (but Still a Regiment)

During World War II, the need for high-risk raids and other special missions led to the creation of commando units in 1940. These units transformed into several other special operations units, most notably the Special Air Service (SAS). The SAS, which eventually comprised several regiments, served in North Africa, Italy, and France, performing a variety of missions, including raids, partnering with local partisans, and reconnaissance.[121]

The unit was briefly disbanded after the war but was then reconstituted as a Territorial Regiment, the Twenty-First Special Air Service Regiment (Artists Rifles). This regiment combined the wartime SAS with a long-standing volunteer unit. In 1952, Twenty-One SAS was used as the genesis for a new Regular Army SAS regiment, the Twenty-Second, though Twenty-One SAS continued in existence as a Territorial unit.[122]

Unlike U.S. Army Special Forces, the SAS does not constitute a counter subculture in the British Army. Its officers are all Sandhurst graduates, often come from public schools, and have served in other regiments. Rotation between Twenty-Two SAS and other Regular Army regiments is encouraged (sometimes mandated), and former SAS officers frequently serve in senior general officer positions. For example, in 2002–3, after a career that included several SAS commands, Lieutenant General Cedric Delves served as senior British liaison to U.S. Central Command; commander, Field Army (the most senior operational Army command overseeing both Regular Army divisions); and commander in chief, NATO Headquarters Armed Forces North. Delves might have achieved further promotion were it not for a medical discharge.[123] General Mike Rose followed a similar trajectory, as did Lieutenant General Graeme Lamb, with both reported as commanding Twenty-Two SAS before eventually becoming commander, Field Army.

The SAS thus illustrates the importance of culture over function for at least certain types of intraservice relations. U.S. Army Special Forces and the SAS perform similar functions yet have very different relations to their respective armies. Special Forces relations with the U.S. Army are at best distant, while the SAS is an integral and accepted regiment within the British Army.

The British Army culture that emerged in the decades after the Crimean War and the Sepoy Mutiny was based on the lessons drawn from those experiences. It sought to prepare officers for the dual missions of imperial policing and coalition warfare. The professionalizing Army officer corps, built around education at Sandhurst, focused on small units, as they were unlikely to see a formation larger than a battalion with any frequency. The officer corps was also routinely expected to work intimately with other military services, indigenous forces, and civilians while serving abroad. The British Army viewed war as a common but not total experience—conscription and mass mobilization were aberrations.

The Special Air Service, unlike the U.S. Army's Special Forces, was well integrated into the broader British Army culture. Its officers routinely served in other units and were frequently promoted to senior ranks. SAS was a special regiment, but a regiment nonetheless.

In the 1950s, the British Army would face the challenge of modern counterinsurgency. Initially the British Army confronted it in Malaya and Borneo, but it would be in Kenya that this challenge would emerge most powerfully.

"A Nasty, Untidy Mess"

U.S. Counterinsurgency in Vietnam, 1960–71

This chapter details the response of three organizational cultures (the U.S. Army, the U.S. Marine Corps, and the U.S. Army's nascent Special Forces subculture) to the challenge of counterinsurgency in South Vietnam. It provides evidence on both written doctrine and actual operations conducted by those organizations during three periods of U.S. involvement across the years 1960–71, though U.S. involvement in South Vietnam actually began in 1954. At that time, following a war with the French, the country was divided into a Communist north and a non-Communist south.

For the remainder of the 1950s, the United States supported the government of Ngo Dinh Diem in the south. Diem, an authoritarian Catholic in a majority Buddhist country, provoked considerable resistance from both Communists and non-Communists alike. However, the North Vietnamese leadership, busy trying to establish a functioning state and hoping for peaceful reunification, counseled patience to those agitating against Diem in the south. There was thus no real insurgency against the South Vietnamese government for most of the 1950s.

By 1960, however, the southerners, undergoing extensive and brutal repression at the hands of Diem, felt they had no choice but to begin armed resistance. The government in the north had also lost hope of peaceful reunification and at the same time felt secure enough domestically to take action. Communist cadres who had relocated to the north in 1954 returned south to link up with those who had stayed behind, and an insurgency began.[1] The challenge of counterinsurgency in Vietnam therefore dates to about 1960. The involvement of U.S. ground troops and the insurgency itself both dwindled by the end of 1971 (the insurgent threat principally replaced by conventional North Vietnamese forces).

This eleven-year span can be broken into three periods. The first period is 1960–65, years in which officers from each of the three U.S. military organizations served as advisers to the South Vietnamese forces conducting counterinsurgency. The second period is 1965–68, from the introduction of U.S. combat forces to Vietnam to the massive insurgent Tet Offensive of 1968. The third period is 1968–71, as U.S. forces responded to Tet and then began to withdraw from Vietnam.

By comparing the organizational responses to insurgency in the same country over time, most variables other than organizational factors can be held relatively constant. This increases confidence that any variation in response is due to differences in the organizations. In addition to the broad comparison across three time periods presented in this chapter, chapter 7 details a natural experiment from the period 1966–68, where U.S. Army units replaced Marine units in the northern part of South Vietnam.

Counterinsurgency and the Gathering Storm over Vietnam, 1960–65

With the election of President John F. Kennedy in 1960, counterinsurgency (COIN) became one of the foremost concerns of the U.S. government. Kennedy believed that insurgencies intended to undermine governments friendly to the United States were a major threat to national security. Within a year of taking office, he formed an interagency Special Group (Counterinsurgency) to study the problem. This group, which included the Departments of Defense and State as well as the Central Intelligence Agency (CIA), produced an overall counterinsurgency doctrine (also called "overseas internal defense") that would be embodied in National Security Action Memorandum (NSAM) 182 in August 1962.[2]

The ideas embodied in NSAM 182 would provide the overarching framework within which early COIN doctrine would develop in the U.S. Army and Marine Corps.[3] In defining insurgency and the appropriate targets for countering it, NSAM 182 noted:

> Insurgency is grounded in the allegiances and attitudes of the people. Its origins are domestic, and its support must remain so. The causes of insurgency therefore stem from the inadequacies of the local government to requite or remove popular or group dissatisfactions . . . The U.S. must always keep in mind that *the ultimate and decisive target is the people.* Society itself is at war and the resources, motives and targets of the struggle are found almost wholly within the local population.[4]

NSAM 182 also described how counterinsurgency should be organized and practiced. It noted:

> In insurgency situations indigenous military action will be required. U.S. operational assistance may be a necessary adjunct to the local effort. In these

situations, U.S. programs should be designed to make the indigenous military response as rapid and incisive as possible while parallel reforms are directed at ameliorating the conditions contributing to the insurgent outbreak ... Anticipating, preventing, and defeating communist-directed insurgency requires a blend of civil and military capabilities and actions to which each U.S. agency at the Country Team level must contribute.[5]

NSAM 182 thus articulated a vision of what counterinsurgency should be. Backed by the Special Group for Counterinsurgency, which in turn had Kennedy's personal support, this represented a major effort to produce a coherent doctrine for counterinsurgency in the U.S. government.[6] Further, it did so at a time wherein there was concern at the highest levels of the U.S. government that the challenge of insurgency was real and important. This concern was buttressed by the intelligence community's alarming reports on the insurgency in South Vietnam and by the introduction of military advisers to the country. The latter would number more than sixteen thousand at the end of 1963.[7]

In response to both the direct pressure from the administration and the commitment of large numbers of advisers to a country facing an insurgency, the Army and the Marine Corps created doctrinal manuals for counterinsurgency. These manuals should ostensibly have provided guidance on how operations should be conducted. The next section examines what the Army and Marines claimed they would do to confront the challenge of counterinsurgency in this early period.

Early Army Written Doctrine, 1961–65

In defining the problem of counterinsurgency, Army written doctrine embraced the propositions of NSAM 182. FM 31-16, *Counterguerrilla Operations*, from February 1963, notes: "The fundamental cause of a resistance movement is the real, imagined, or incited dissatisfaction of a portion of the population with prevailing political, social, or economic conditions."[8] Another variation is used in the Army capstone manual FM 100-5, *Field Service Regulations—Operations*, from February 1962: "The fundamental cause of large-scale irregular activities stems from the dissatisfaction of some significant portion of the population, with the political, social, and economic conditions prevalent in the area."[9]

Army doctrine therefore emphasized the importance of reform while stressing that military force was only part of counterinsurgency, as noted in FM 100-5.[10] Similarly, FM 31-16 recommends the establishment of "pacification committees" at the brigade and battalion level. These committees would include representatives from the military, paramilitaries, and civilian agencies.[11] FM 31-16 also emphasizes small-unit patrolling and reconnaissance as well as ambush. It further notes that police/population control operations will often have to take place concurrently with combat operations.[12]

FM 31-16 also describes the importance of intelligence to counterinsurgency. It labels attempts to conduct operations against insurgents without sound intelligence as a waste of "time, material, and troop effort."[13] FM 31-16 also comments that "a basic essential in any type of counterguerrilla intelligence operation is a thorough understanding of the target area and society, in all its aspects."[14] The importance of social and cultural knowledge for COIN is echoed in FM 100-5.[15]

Early Marine Written Doctrine, 1961–65

The Marine Corps issued one of its first counterinsurgency manuals in August 1962 (roughly the same time NSAM 182 was published), Fleet Marine Force Manual (FMFM)-21, *Operations against Guerrilla Forces.* It was similar in many respects to the Army's FM 31-16, *Counterguerrilla Operations.* In defining the problem confronted in operating against guerrillas, it noted that "resistance stems from the dissatisfaction of some part of the population."[16]

Like the Army manuals, it devotes considerable attention to the population, noting: "Commanders must realize that operations against guerrillas will seldom solve the problems of the area in which they occur. The guerrilla force is only a symptom of the overall problem which caused the resistance movement to arise in the first place. Throughout military operations, a positive program of civil assistance must be conducted to eliminate the original cause of the resistance movement."[17] All of FMFM-21's chapter 10 and appendix B are devoted to population considerations and population control.

The Marine Corps' written doctrine also accepted the need for close coordination in counterinsurgency with both other U.S. agencies and the host nation. On U.S. agencies, FMFM-21, *Operations against Guerrilla Forces*, notes, "Close coordination is effected with the diplomatic mission and other U.S. agencies."[18] On the host government, it states, "One of the most important duties to be performed by the commander in an operation against guerrilla forces is to gain the cooperation and assistance of local police and judicial agencies."[19]

In terms of operations, the Marines focused on battalion and smaller units, with considerable autonomy given to these lower-echelon commanders. FMFM-21 describes battalion task forces (battalions with attachments such as psychological operations units) as conducting operations of an "independent or semi-independent nature."[20] The units actually doing the bulk of operations were smaller than battalions. The two main operations are described as patrolling and reaction force; the former is conducted by units from squad to reinforced company size, while the latter is conducted by units ranging from a reinforced platoon to a reinforced company. Patrols are specifically noted as potentially requiring independent action for a long period of time and also as potentially including civilians such as "local guides, trackers, and members of the civil police."[21]

FMFM-21 also places an extremely heavy emphasis on intelligence in counterinsurgency. It bluntly notes that "counterguerrilla operations without sound intelligence wastes [sic] time, material, and troop effort."[22] It goes on to list the need for more intelligence personnel and interpreters in counterinsurgency than in other operations.

Army Doctrinal Rhetoric and Reality, 1961–65

Doctrine as it appeared in print was thus in broad agreement in both the civilian and military realms from 1961 to 1965. Yet at the same time, public comments by some senior officers betrayed a hesitance to fully embrace the implications of the written doctrine. Appearing to dismiss the differences between conventional war and COIN, Army Chief of Staff George Decker notably stated, "Any good soldier can handle guerrillas." His successor, Earle Wheeler, argued, "It is fashionable in some quarters to say that the problems in Southeast Asia are primarily political and economic rather than military. I do not agree. The essence of the problem in Vietnam is military."[23]

The differences between written doctrine and actual practice would become glaringly apparent. First and foremost, the principle of unity of effort between civil and military elements of the U.S. COIN effort enshrined in written doctrine was not upheld. The 1962 terms of reference for the creation of the position of commander, United States Military Assistance Command Vietnam (COMUSMACV, or MACV) clearly indicate that, while COMUSMACV might nominally be subordinate to the ambassador, he was in fact autonomous.[24] Ambassador to Vietnam Frederick Nolting complained about this command relationship at some length, to no avail.[25]

Other deviations from written doctrine were observed in Vietnam. During this period, many observers also felt that the training of South Vietnamese forces was more appropriate to conventional conflict than COIN. President Kennedy's military adviser, General Maxwell Taylor, after visiting Vietnam in late 1961, reported, "It is our clear impression . . . that, by and large, training and equipment of the Vietnamese armed forces are still too heavily weighted toward conventional military operations."[26] Roger Hilsman, director of the State Department's Bureau of Intelligence and Research, came to similar conclusions after visiting in early 1963, and further pointed out that this was in part a result of American advice and support: "You have also the impression that the military is still too heavily oriented towards sweep-type operations. There is still the same emphasis on air power as there was before. Almost every operation so far as I can tell still begins with an air strike which inevitably kills innocent people and warns the Viet Cong that they should get moving for the troops will be coming soon. I think . . . that the Americans are as much to blame for this as the Vietnamese."[27] This emphasis on conventional over COIN operations by many (though not all) U.S. advisory personnel has been noted by many subsequent observers, as was the overall preoccupation with a conventional invasion from North Vietnam.[28]

U.S. Army Special Forces and COIN, 1961–65

Not all U.S. Army operations adhered to the approach just described. The U.S. Army Special Forces sought to put doctrine into practice by providing area security and development. They did so by participating in several CIA programs in South Vietnam that were initiated by Chief of Station in Saigon William Colby in 1961.

The most notable of the programs, the Civilian Irregular Defense Groups (CIDG), grew out of a contact between CIA and a young development volunteer who had been in South Vietnam's Central Highlands.[29] The CIA and Colby saw an opportunity to work with the tribes of the Central Highlands, who had been neglected by the South Vietnamese government. Colby and others believed CIA should establish a program to aid and support one of these tribes, the Rhade, with the goal of creating a local defense force.[30]

Colby negotiated an agreement with Ngo Dinh Nhu, the security chief for South Vietnam and brother of President Ngo Dinh Diem, to initiate the program by mandating the participation of Vietnamese Special Forces (VNSF) in the program.[31] The CIDG program brought in a U.S. Army Special Forces team (an Operational Detachment Alpha, or ODA) along with VNSF to train and advise the villagers. The program, which combined small development projects and medical treatment with the training of the local defense force, quickly took off, drawing in more U.S. and Vietnamese Special Forces over the course of 1962.[32]

The CIA / Special Forces program was emphatically defensive in nature. The Special Forces, along with VNSF, trained village defenders in basic small arms. Village defenders were expected to fight if attacked and remained at home. A small mobile strike force was trained and paid for full-time operations, but was intended to patrol the area between villages and provide a quick-reaction force for villages rather than to take the offensive.

Defensive did not mean inactive, as the program's essence was active defense and intelligence. As a U.S. Special Forces history describes, this active defense "consisted of small local security patrols, ambushes, village defender patrols, local intelligence nets, and an alert system in which local men, women, and children reported suspicious movement in the area . . . Strike force troops remained on the alert in the base center at Buon Enao to serve as a reaction force, and the villages maintained a mutually supporting defensive system wherein village defenders rushed to each other's assistance."[33]

The program grew quickly. In April 1962 there were forty villages with about 1,000 village defenders and a 300-man strike force. By July there were 3,600 village defenders along with 650 men in strike forces in the Central Highlands. By August more than 200 villages had joined, and by November, 23,000 men were under arms either as defenders or strike forces. In less than a year a small army had been successfully established with only twenty-four ODAs and a relative handful of CIA personnel.[34]

At this point MACV began to expand U.S. military activity in South Vietnam. MACV replaced the earlier Military Assistance Advisory Group, which was a much smaller organization. A special warfare branch was created in the operations section of MACV staff. MACV then arranged that CIA and this branch jointly operate the CIDG program, which was using Army troops (though funded and supported by the CIA). By June 1962, CIA and the Department of Defense concluded that the CIDG program had expanded so much that it was no longer covert and should be fully military (that is, no CIA involvement).[35]

The transfer of the program from CIA to MACV was known as Operation Switchback, incorrectly implying that the programs had previously belonged to MACV. However, MACV commander General Paul Harkins felt that CIA should continue its involvement with the program.[36] Harkins was also concerned about losing CIA's political skill and relationships with government of Vietnam (GVN) officials. This was echoed by the commander of Special Forces in Vietnam, Colonel George Morton. Morton was also worried about logistics, as he was losing CIA's flexibility.[37]

MACV proved unable to manage the political dynamics required to make CIDG viable. During Switchback, the number of villages in the program expanded rapidly even as the quality of the training and support fell. Switchback also revealed serious deficiencies in the GVN.[38] Most importantly, Switchback changed the fundamental nature of the program, as the emphasis on what operations were to be undertaken was reversed. At MACV direction, strike forces were reoriented to offensive operations and their camps shifted to new sites, while training of village defenders ended in April 1964.[39] The official history of the Special Forces in Vietnam bluntly states: "By the end of 1964 the Montagnard program was no longer an area development project in the original sense of the term. There was a shift in emphasis from expanding village defense systems to the primary use of area development camps or centers (CIDG camps) as bases for offensive strike force operations."[40]

This shift to offensive operations was accompanied by gradual conventionalization and standardization of strike force units. This in turn led to a "growing tendency to utilize CIDG units as conventional forces, a task they were neither trained nor equipped to carry out."[41] Combined with the shifting of camps far from their homes, this misuse contributed to "recruiting problems and high AWOL and desertion rates."[42]

The Special Forces subculture had created a program based on population security by allying with an outside entity, the CIA. When the Army reestablished control, it turned the defensive program into an offensive one and sought to make it larger as quickly as possible. Without the CIA to support and protect them, the dominant Army culture would dictate operations to the Special Forces subculture.

Following the co-optation of CIDG, Special Forces would receive new missions, including reconnaissance both inside South Vietnam and across the border in Laos, and covert operations into North Vietnam. These were conducted by MACV Studies and Observation Group (MACV-SOG), a bland cover organization created in 1964. MACV-SOG, though military, also worked closely with, and included officers from, CIA.[43]

The cross-border mission into Laos was conducted by OP 35, the Ground Studies Group component of MACV-SOG, initially under Operation Shining Brass. OP 35 utilized small reconnaissance patrols, generally composed of a few U.S. Army Special Forces and several locally recruited tribesmen (a total team size of about twelve) to locate infiltrators and then call in airstrikes on the targets. Additionally, the OP 35 patrols would emplace sensors, perform bomb damage assessment, and even conduct missions to capture prisoners or destroy facilities.[44]

In addition to the cross-border OP 35, Special Forces camps along the Vietnamese side of the border provided ability to gather intelligence aimed at interdicting infiltration. These camps grew out of the CIDG program and were known as Projects Delta, Sigma, and Omega, intended to locate insurgent bases inside Vietnam. These operations were also conducted by small teams of Special Forces working with locals.[45]

Finally, Special Forces continued to train other local irregular forces for CIA, usually at the base at Vung Tau near the coast. Most notable among these were the Counter-Terror Teams, a small unit of what the program's creator termed "deserters and small time crooks," which would enter Vietcong territory to target Communist leaders or installations. These teams were subsequently renamed Provincial Reconnaissance Units and would exist throughout the rest of the war.[46]

Marine Corps Counterinsurgency, 1961–65

In contrast to the Army, which had a major advisory presence in Vietnam, and Army Special Forces, which were committed to CIA operations in Vietnam, the Marine Corps' direct involvement in Vietnam before 1965 was small. Beginning in 1954, a Marine lieutenant colonel served as adviser to the South Vietnamese Marine Corps. This sole officer was supplemented by a couple of captains and a handful of noncommissioned officers later in the decade.[47]

With the formation of MACV in 1962, the Marine advisory presence grew to several dozen, including a two-star Marine general who served as MACV chief of staff.[48] Marine helicopter units were also dispatched to South Vietnam to provide mobility to South Vietnamese units.[49] However, the Marine presence in Vietnam was still relatively small compared to both the size of MACV (over sixteen thousand by the end of 1963) and the Marine Corps as a whole. For example, by 1964 the Marine helicopter support task unit, based at Da Nang, was only 450 total personnel.[50]

Yet despite this minimal direct involvement in Vietnam, the leadership of Marine units stationed in the Pacific was attuned to the likelihood of their involvement in counterinsurgency. In 1961 Lieutenant General Alan Shapley, the commanding general of Fleet Marine Force, Pacific (FMFP), created a program known as On-the-Job Training (OJT). OJT dispatched Marine officers to South Vietnam for a few weeks at a time to observe the developing situation and demands of counterinsurgency.[51]

The commanders of the Third Marine Division, based in Okinawa and the most likely candidate for involvement in Southeast Asia, took the issue of counterinsurgency even more seriously. Major General Donald Weller, commander in early 1961, had been instructed to lead a task force preparing for a possible intervention in Laos.[52] He subsequently gave orders to his staff to begin developing a counterinsurgency program for the entire division to supplement the OJT program.[53]

Weller's successor in late 1961, Major General Robert Cushman (a future commander in Vietnam as well as Commandant), accelerated the development of a counterinsurgency program. Early in 1962, he established a training program led by graduates of the British Jungle Warfare School in Malaya and the Army Special Warfare School. The Jungle Warfare School was set up by the British in response to the challenge of counterinsurgency in Malaya, and the Special Warfare School was the home of the Army Special Forces. The division's training was thus led by graduates of schools founded by services with maritime or unconventional war archetypes who had recent experience in counterinsurgency in Asia. The training was focused on intense company- and platoon-level infantry operations in northern Okinawa, with a less involved course for battalion staffs intended to prepare them "to support their companies in a counterinsurgency environment." Officers with OJT experience in South Vietnam helped prepare the division training.[54]

Assessing Theoretical Explanations for Written Doctrine and Operations, 1961–65

The evidence on Army doctrine and operations from 1961 to 1965 alone provides little that is dispositive in terms of the proposed alternative explanations for doctrine. What is most striking about this period in terms of the Army is the deviation from written doctrine made in the statements of senior Army officers and in the actions of advisers on the ground. Why would an organization write manuals it did not actually follow? One possible explanation is organizational inertia—large organizations take time to change, so even after NSAM 182 and FM 31-16, the Army would take time to adjust. Another possible explanation is that the written doctrine was instrumental speech, intended to demonstrate compliance with NSAM 182, which the Army had no intention of following. A third possibility is that the doctrine was written with the best of intentions, yet because it ran counter to Army culture it had minimal impact on operations. This first period does not provide sufficient evidence for a dispositive conclusion, but the point will be revisited in subsequent sections.

The evidence from the Special Forces experience in this period appears to lend somewhat more support to the organizational culture explanation, as Special Forces cooperated closely with the CIA and indigenous forces in very small units. This appears very different from the bigger Army's focus on preparing the Army of the Republic of Vietnam (ARVN) for conventional war.

As with the other organizations in this same period, no firm conclusions about hypotheses on doctrine can be drawn from the Marine experience between 1961 and 1965. The Marine Corps doctrine and practice seemed to be aligned, but the actual practice was on a very limited scale. As with U.S. Army Special Forces, the Marine experience in this period is suggestive without being definitive.

Overall, the period 1961–65 does little to demonstrate any enduring differences in Army, Army Special Forces, and Marine counterinsurgency operations. However, this period provides a necessary initial observation, setting the stage for the next two periods. Most importantly, it demonstrates that when U.S. combat units were introduced to South Vietnam in 1965, they were not confronted with a challenge or a country that their respective organizations had no experience with.

Across the Rubicon: Counterinsurgency Operations, 1965–68

The years from 1963 to 1965 saw the situation in South Vietnam go from bad to worse. Coup followed coup in Saigon, while the Vietcong grew stronger throughout the countryside. The complete collapse of South Vietnam seemed at hand despite increasing U.S. efforts. In March 1965, U.S. combat forces were introduced into Vietnam, initially to secure airfields. However, this mission would rapidly expand, and by the summer of that year U.S. forces were conducting offensive combat operations. This section details operations conducted during this period. It begins with a telling episode in which the Army not only rejected its own written doctrine for counterinsurgency—it also rejected a plan sponsored by the organization's highest-ranking officer.

General Harold Johnson, who had become Army Chief of Staff in 1964, was one of many deeply troubled by U.S. counterinsurgency efforts in Vietnam. Upon returning from Vietnam in March 1965, Johnson directed a select group of officers to undertake a reappraisal of efforts in Vietnam. This study was completed and issued in March 1966, with the title *A Program for the Pacification and Long Term Development of South Vietnam*, universally referred to by the acronym PROVN.

PROVN was a lengthy and thoughtful study but provided few if any truly new ideas. It principally sought to put into practice the tenets embodied in the Army's written doctrine for COIN. In essence, PROVN sought to provide a blueprint for the operationalization of COIN doctrine.

First and most importantly, PROVN reiterated the doctrinal point that development and good governance should be central to all U.S. efforts: "A viable, non-communist government in SVN is fundamental to the achievement of U.S. objectives. Failure to develop such a public supported political order not only will preclude winning a true military victory, it will ensure losing a negotiated peace . . . Long-standing and legitimate causes of insurgency are still present. Promises of reform melt into maintenance of the *status quo*."[55] PROVN readily acknowledged that development required security, but pointed out that security was to enable development rather than being an end in itself.

PROVN also called for a "single manager" for Vietnam, responsible for all aspects of U.S. activity there, and further argued that this should be (at least initially) the U.S. ambassador. In addition, PROVN stated:

> To succeed, we must actually decentralize and delegate to Americans and Vietnamese at district and province levels the requisite resources and authority to accomplish the tasks at hand. Their exercise of this authority must be buttressed and sustained up through the chain of command . . . Unity of command and effort is required now at province level, with the province chief directing all GVN [Government of Vietnam] activities (military and nonmilitary) in the province. His counterpart, the SUSREP (Senior U.S. Representative), must direct all U.S. activities.[56]

This was a directive for actually implementing FM 31-16's recommendation to establish "pacification committees," as well as NSAM 182's call for unity of civil and military effort.

PROVN additionally stressed the importance of language training and knowledge of political and social factors for COIN. It repeatedly noted that wide variations between the situations in different provinces and even between different districts in the same province are to be expected. This variation would require detailed awareness of the specific local environment where those conducting COIN would be assigned.[57]

Despite being an honest attempt to implement the doctrine that the U.S. government and the military services had promulgated, PROVN did not receive a warm welcome in the Army. The officer who was nominally in charge of the study, Deputy Chief of Staff for Operations Lieutenant General Vernon Mock, refused to sign off on it for distribution, saying to the authors, "Why don't you come in early some morning and have one of the cleaning ladies sign it?" PROVN did not receive much more of a welcome from CO-MUSMACV General William Westmoreland.[58]

In short, PROVN was an attempt to bring operations in Vietnam in line with written doctrine that failed because it ran counter to the essence of U.S. Army culture. This was despite PROVN's initiation and endorsement by the Army's most senior officer. Nor, as the third period of Vietnam will demonstrate, would this be the last time a senior Army leader's plans to alter operations would be frustrated.

Army Counterinsurgency Operations in Vietnam, 1965–68

The introduction of U.S. ground forces in a combat role in March 1965 began a rapid cascade of U.S. involvement in Vietnam. Most significantly for operations, it meant that at last COMUSMACV Westmoreland had combat troops to command rather than to merely advise. He quickly began employing them in operations, yet these operations were not grounded in COIN doctrine as promulgated.

The essence of Army operations from 1965 to 1968 was to apply maximum firepower to large enemy "main force" units (those most similar to conventional military units) in order to destroy them. By destroying enemy forces faster than they could be replaced, MACV sought to bring the war to a favorable conclusion via attrition. To this end, U.S. forces would seek contact with large units and then destroy them, an approach known as search and destroy.

This approach was premised on the idea of the massive application of firepower. COMUSMACV Westmoreland provided a one-word summary of his antiguerrilla strategy: "firepower."[59] In a less terse summary, Westmoreland stated that if the enemy did not quit, "we'll just go on bleeding them to the point of national disaster for generations."[60] General Westmoreland's operations officer, Brigadier (later Lieutenant) General William Depuy, summarized the MACV strategy in a statement to the press: "We are going to stomp them to death."[61] After being promoted to major general and receiving command of the First Infantry Division, Depuy described the approach in more detail to Daniel Ellsberg: "The solution in Vietnam is more bombs, more shells, more napalm . . . till the other side cracks and gives up."[62]

Army operations more than lived up to this rhetoric. Over four million tons of indirect (air and artillery) ordnance were expended over South Vietnam from 1965 to 1973.[63] Artillery alone expended more than twenty million rounds of all calibers.[64] Much of this firepower employed was not even in direct support of troops, instead being fired in so-called harassment and interdiction missions. This meant firing unobserved into areas thought likely to contain the enemy, despite posing severe risks to civilians in the vicinity.[65]

In addition to emphasizing firepower with minimal discrimination, combat forces in Vietnam were oriented toward centralized large-unit operations rather than decentralized small-unit operations. Beginning with the First Cavalry Division's battle in the Ia Drang valley in November 1965, Army units were consistently employed in multibattalion operations.[66] Operations increased in size, as Operation Attleboro in September 1966 illustrated. Beginning as a search and destroy operation by battalions of the 196th Light Infantry Brigade, Attleboro grew to include over twenty-two thousand U.S. and allied troops.[67] Attleboro would be followed in 1967 with the even larger Cedar Falls–Junction City operations. Both would be multidivisional operations with massive fire support, with Junction City utilizing over twenty-five thousand U.S. and allied forces.[68]

The Army's own measures of progress reinforced this focus on firepower and large operations.[69] Jeffrey Record, who was in Vietnam as a civilian, concluded that the body count became such an important metric for success that it corrupted much of the war effort: "amassing kills became the standard of career success for U.S. commanders, and therefore an often irresistible temptation to abuse in both the infliction and reporting of enemy casualties."[70] Another metric that encouraged search and destroy over pacification was "battalion days in the field." This counted the number of days each battalion spent conducting combat operations as a measure of performance. While time spent in search and destroy counted in this metric, pacification missions did not.[71] Other measures intended to ensure aggressive action against main force units included number of combat sorties flown, bomb tonnage dropped, ammunition expended, and ratio of U.S. deaths to enemy deaths.[72]

Finally, civil-military integration would was not well developed in this period. Not until 1967 was a real organization established to manage all civilian efforts and to attempt to integrate them with military efforts. This organization, known as Civil Operations and Revolutionary Development Support (CORDS), was headed by Robert Komer, who was made a deputy to COMUSMACV Westmoreland. While this was a step forward in integration, Komer still had limited ability to affect how U.S. forces would be employed. Rather than the civilians being supported by the military, or at a minimum the military and civilian aspects being coequal, the military (actually the Army) was now firmly in charge. This was clearly not the desired arrangement advocated in doctrine and articulated in PROVN.[73]

Army Special Forces Operations, 1965–68

Special Forces operations changed little in this period. Unlike the Regular Army, which had been unable to conduct combat operations until the introduction of combat troops in 1965, Special Forces had been conducting small-unit operations for years. Living with and running irregular units of locals (CIDG) and training locals for CIA's Provincial Reconnaissance Units, and other small-unit reconnaissance both in South Vietnam and in Laos, continued to be the bread and butter of Special Forces. The Laos mission was expanded in scope and renamed Operation Prairie Fire in March 1967 but remained a small-unit operation conducted in conjunction with locals (either Montagnards or ethnic Chinese known as Nungs). The same year similar cross-border reconnaissance into Cambodia, Operation Daniel Boone, was initiated.[74]

There was also a different sort of expansion of the small-unit reconnaissance mission. In September 1965, Fifth Special Forces Group began a program to train newly arriving Special Forces soldiers in long-range reconnaissance patrolling techniques in Southeast Asia. Upon learning of this course, COMUSMACV Westmoreland directed a study of the need for additional reconnaissance capabilities, which determined that this would be useful. Westmoreland tasked the Fifth Special Forces Group commander to establish a school to train volunteers from conventional units in these techniques.[75]

This school, known as Recondo School, was created in September 1966 at Nha Trang. The graduates of the school were returned to the divisions they originated from, where they were formed into Long Range Reconnaissance Patrol (LRRP) companies and detachments. They would then be used as division- or brigade-level assets or sometimes detailed back to Fifth Special Forces Group. LRRPs would operate in very small units during actual operations, generally less than a dozen men.[76]

LRRPs represented something of a half-step or perhaps bridge between Special Forces and regular Army cultures. Drawn from conventional units, LRRPs were expected to be highly motivated and exceptional soldiers; those who were not were washed out of Recondo School. Lieutenant General William Peers, commenting on the program at an LRRP conference in 1968, bluntly stated: "In my judgment, not every soldier, not every combat soldier is qualified for LRP duties for several reasons. The first reason is that an individual must be qualified both physically and psychologically."[77] His remarks were echoed by Colonel Harold Aaron, Fifth Special Forces Group commander and Recondo School commandant.[78]

Yet despite being volunteers with exceptional qualifications, LRRPs were not Special Forces either. They had not been through the Q Course, which was much more extensive than the three weeks of Recondo School. Though operating in small units, LRRPs were clearly adjuncts to the large Army units from which they were drawn.

The Special Forces interaction with the regular Army was contentious throughout this period. MACV, and particularly commander Westmoreland, considered SOG and Special Forces to generally be a sideshow at best.[79] Even in choosing commanders for SOG, the Army tried to pick officers who also had good credentials in the regular Army. For example, the third commander of MACV-SOG, Colonel Jack Singlaub, was an experienced special operator dating back to covert operations during World War II. However, he also had impeccable regular Army credentials including command of infantry units.[80]

In addition, Special Forces Group command and MACV-SOG were the highest-ranking billets the Army created for Special Forces officers in Vietnam. Yet these were billets for colonels, effectively shutting Special Forces out of the general officer ranks. Moreover, few colonels in these billets were promoted to general officer. Singlaub, with his Regular Army credentials, would make general, but many others would not. For example, Francis Kelly, commander of Fifth Special Forces Group in Vietnam in 1966–67, was shuffled off to a National Guard posting in 1970 before retiring as a colonel in 1972.[81]

Marine Counterinsurgency Operations in Vietnam, 1965–68

Two battalions from the Ninth Marine Expeditionary Brigade (MEB) landed at Da Nang in March 1965, initially to provide security for the large airbase there. These units were the first U.S. combat forces in South Vietnam. The Ninth MEB was commanded by Brigadier General Frederick Karch, the assistant division commander for the Third Marine Division.

The Marines immediately began attempting to form relations with South Vietnamese security forces. One of the battalions tried to set up a joint checkpoint with the local Popular Forces (PF) militia unit. However, this effort was unsuccessful, as the PF unit showed up at the checkpoint but then wandered off. Though frustrated by this lack of discipline, the Marines continued to try to build ties to the South Vietnamese militia.

In late April, the Marines began conducting joint patrols around Da Nang and Phu Bai (a nearby airfield and intelligence collection post) with ARVN units. At the same time additional reinforcements arrived at Chu Lai, a newly established Marine base. The ongoing expansion of Marine presence in South Vietnam led to the replacement of Ninth MEB with the III Marine Amphibious Force (III MAF), consisting of a Marine division and air wing, under Major General William Collins.

The expanding Marine presence and loosened operating guidelines enabled Marine battalion commanders to finally initiate counterinsurgency operations. The first major operation was initiated by Lieutenant Colonel David Clement, commanding Second Battalion, Third Marine Regiment (3/2); it held an area overlooking the village of Le My, a cluster of hamlets eight miles northwest of Da Nang. Conversations with the Vietnamese district chief revealed that this village had been swept by ARVN several times, but security was never maintained.

Clement resolved to provide security to the village. In early May 1965, he accompanied the district officer on a visit to the village. This exploratory trip led to a skirmish with the Vietcong, and Clement realized that the village would have to be cleared. A week later one of 3/2's companies returned and occupied the village. The company then enlisted the villagers in clearing traps and destroying insurgent bunkers. After three days, the PFs, supported by Regional Forces (RFs), occupied the village proper while the Marines moved to provide security around the village.

In addition, Clement's battalion began working to improve the village. His Marines trained the local PFs, built village defenses, and initiated civic action programs such as medical stations and school building. The goal of this activity, according to the battalion intelligence officer, Captain Lionel Silva, was "to create an administration, supported by the people, and capable of leading, treating, feeding, and protecting themselves by the time the battalion was moved to another area of operations."[82]

Senior Marine officers enthusiastically supported 3/2's approach to counterinsurgency. Major General Collins, III MAF commander, remarked that the "Le My operation may well be the pattern for the employment of Marine Corps forces in this area." On a visit to III MAF in mid-May, the commander of FMFP, Lieutenant General Victor Krulak, described the operation at Le My as "a beginning, but a good beginning. The people are beginning to get the idea that U.S. generated security is a long term affair."[83]

Major General Collins was replaced as III MAF commander by Major General Lewis Walt in June 1965. Walt also embraced the pacification mission, famously noting about Da Nang that "over 150,000 civilians were living within 81 mm mortar range of the airfield, and consequently, the Marines were into the pacification business."[84] Walt, though a veteran of high-intensity conflict in World War II and Korea, explicitly claimed affiliation with the small wars subculture, recalling that "as a young officer he learned the fundamentals of his profession from men who had fought Sandino in Nicaragua or Charlemagne in Haiti."[85] Walt was an equally strong proponent of Marine small-unit managerial culture, which he helped cultivate as the commandant of the Basic School from 1954 to 1956.[86]

Some of Walt's battalion commanders also embraced the small wars subculture. In addition to Clement, Lieutenant Colonel William "Woody" Taylor, commanding the Third Battalion, Fourth Marine Regiment (3/4) at Phu Bai, also emphasized the importance of the population. In June 1965, Taylor, acting on advice from his adjutant / civil affairs officer, negotiated with the local ARVN division commander for authority to work with the PFs to secure villages in Zone A, an area north and east of Phu Bai.

Taylor received permission and limited operational control of the PFs in July. His executive officer drew up plans to incorporate a Marine squad into four of the six PF platoons in Zone A. Taylor then briefed the plans to his superiors, including Major General Walt, who gave him permission to proceed and detailed a Vietnamese-speaking Marine first lieutenant named Paul Ek from headquarters to assist him in establishing a "joint action company."

The Marines who participated in the joint action company were all volunteers. Each was personally vetted by First Lieutenant Ek, who would command the joint company. He also spent several weeks instructing the Marines about Vietnamese life.

The company was joint but American-dominated. In practice, the Marine squad leader became the combined platoon commander, with the PF commander his deputy. Ek also had a South Vietnamese warrant officer as his deputy. However, the Vietnamese district chief retained administrative responsibility for the unit, while each platoon had to work with the chief of the village they were securing. Each Marine platoon commander was therefore called upon "to maintain harmonious relations among his subordinates, the village chief, and his PFs."[87] The unit, renamed the "combined action company" in October, engendered loyalty in both PFs and Marines, with several Marines volunteering to extend their tours to remain with their PF comrades.

Other Marine units also began to work with Vietnamese local forces, including the PFs and the RFs. General Walt was a supporter of all these efforts, considering the PFs in particular to be critical to security despite their poor training and equipment. He noted of the PF: "He had a signal advantage over all others; he was defending his own home, family, and neighbors. The Popular Force soldier knew every person in his community by face and name; he knew each paddy, field, trail, bush, or bamboo clump, each family shelter, tunnel, and buried rice urn. He knew in most cases the local Viet Cong guerrilla band, and it was not uncommon for him to be related to one or more of them by blood or other family ties." Walt also persuaded the ARVN corps commander to release more PFs to Marine operational control in November, and then persuaded the general to expand the combined action approach to all three Marine areas (Da Nang, Chu Lai, and Phu Bai) in January 1966.[88]

In addition to working closely with South Vietnamese government and security forces, the Marines also sought to integrate with U.S. civilian agencies in South Vietnam. In August 1965, Walt met with his civilian equivalent, Marcus Gordon, the regional director for the Marine area (known as I Corps) for the United States Operations Mission. They agreed to form a Joint Coordinating Council (JCC) that would include Gordon, the deputy U.S. adviser to the Vietnamese corps commander, and the III MAF civil affairs officer.

Walt then persuaded General Tri, the ARVN corps commander, to send a representative as well.[89]

The I Corps JCC soon became the central coordinating mechanism for counterinsurgency. Walt considered the JCC important enough to appoint his deputy as his personal representative in November 1965. Gordon would subsequently praise Walt and the JCC for ensuring that coordination of U.S. military, U.S. civilian, and South Vietnamese activity took place. Walt also restructured the staff of the MAF and its subordinate regiments and battalions by creating a G-5/S-5 section for "civic action" in order to ensure adequate support for these activities.[90]

The Marines also undertook larger-scale operations in this period, including a two-battalion operation that combined an amphibious landing with a helicopter blocking force. Known as Operation Starlite, this operation in August 1965 was initiated based on signals intelligence (SIGINT) that located a Vietcong regiment on a peninsula south of Chu Lai. The Marines encountered stiff resistance from insurgents operating from well-defended positions, and SIGINT subsequently determined that the operation succeeded only in disrupting the enemy regiment's communications for a few days despite the casualties the Marines inflicted.[91]

Walt continued to pursue the same basic course in 1966: cooperation with the Vietnamese and U.S. civilians to secure the population, with sporadic larger-unit operations. He pursued this course with the full support of Commandant Wallace Greene and FMFP commander Krulak and against the opposition of COMUSMACV Westmoreland. Westmoreland sought to get the Marines to undertake more large-scale search and destroy operations. Greene and Krulak did what they could to protect Walt, defending him and his approach against both Westmoreland and an impatient secretary of the Navy, Paul Nitze.[92]

The institutional Marine Corps also took the war in South Vietnam seriously. In August 1966, the Southeast Asia Village was opened at the Basic School. A replica of villages that many of the junior officers at the Basic School would soon be fighting in, the village was used for the conduct of small-unit exercises.[93] The staff of the Basic School also sent detachments to observe operations in South Vietnam in 1967 to ensure that the curriculum was successfully preparing officers for operations there.[94]

The Marines in I Corps made extensive use of intelligence collection from both patrolling and local sources. Though they also used SIGINT collection, this was generally a supplement to other sources in the early part of Marine involvement in Vietnam. One of the most notable of these sources took advantage of an existing program, the Chieu Hoi (Open Arms) amnesty program, which allowed guerrillas to defect from the insurgency and rally to the government without penalty.

In the spring of 1966, several insurgents turned themselves in to Marines west of Da Nang. Local insurgents claimed that these defectors were killed by the Marines, but the Marines countered by having the defectors go talk to locals. This convinced both Marines and U.S. civilians in the U.S. Agency for International Development (USAID) that these defectors could be useful for their detailed knowledge of the insurgency and local conditions. The Marines and civilians began working together to create a viable program. USAID produced some money to pay the defectors, who began working with Marine units as intelligence sources and scouts; the program was named the Kit Carson Scouts by Major General Herman Nickerson, commander of the First Marine Division.[95]

For the remainder of 1966, the program expanded across Marine units. In 1967 the funding was picked up by MACV and broadened to cover all units operating in South Vietnam. However, through the end of 1967, Marine units recruited the vast majority of scouts—171 of the 244 Kit Carson Scouts were in I Corps.[96]

The Marine Corps also developed very different metrics for evaluating units and the progress of the war. Unlike the Army, which focused on metrics to assess firepower employed and offensive operations, the Marines developed a matrix for evaluating the pacification of villages. Initiated in February and March 1966 and using metrics such as efforts to develop economic opportunities for villagers and level of village security, the Marine matrix was an attempt to systematically measure the inputs to pacification in the same way the Army sought to measure the inputs to attrition. This matrix would form the basis for the CIA-created Hamlet Evaluation System (HES).[97]

The Marine Corps continued to expand the combined action program in 1966, focusing on the platoon element of the program, known as the Combined Action Platoon (CAP).[98] Walt set a goal of seventy-four CAPs for the end of 1966. However, the Marines failed to reach this goal. The central limiting factor was not Marine willingness or personnel, although, as discussed later in the chapter, other demands on personnel emerged in 1966. Instead, it was PF recruitment and the unwillingness of many Vietnamese province and district chiefs to participate in the program that explained the limited expansion of CAP.[99]

However, the Marines faced a new challenge beginning in early 1966. Large units of North Vietnam's regular army, the People's Army of Vietnam (PAVN) began to launch attacks across the border between North and South Vietnam, known (without irony) as the Demilitarized Zone (DMZ). The first attack was by two PAVN regiments against a remote U.S. Army Special Forces camp in March 1966.[100] Three months later, intelligence indicated that roughly five thousand men of the PAVN 324B Division were south of the DMZ in Quang Tri Province. A three-division offensive across the DMZ was expected.[101]

General Walt had little choice but to shift forces north to handle this new conventional threat. He moved the Third Marine Division north to the border, leaving the First Marine Division to continue operations against insurgents further south in I Corps. The Third Marine Division and the First

ARVN Division launched Operation Hastings against these regular PAVN units in July 1966. The largest U.S. operation in the war up until that point, Hastings preempted the PAVN offensive. Yet the threat from guerrillas to southern I Corps had not vanished. The Marine historian Jack Shulimson summarizes the essence of the emerging Marine problem in I Corps: "By the end of 1966, the two Marine divisions of III MAF were fighting two separate wars. In the north, the 3d Marine Division fought a more or less conventional campaign while the 1st Marine Division took over the counterguerrilla operations in the populous south. Although by December 1966, III MAF numbered nearly 70,000 troops, one Marine general summed up the year's frustrations, '. . . too much real estate—do not have enough troops.'"[102]

The lament of not enough troops pointed to another major effect of the commitment of Marine combat forces to Vietnam, the rapid expansion of the Corps. The Marine Corps' end strength expanded from 190,000 in 1965 to 261,000 in 1966.[103] The Marine Corps had to rely on draftees for the first time since World War II and was further forced to accept some of the so-called New Standards men, who could not meet normal enlistment criteria. The ethos of the Corps, built around the volunteer professional nature of both enlisted and officer corps, began to erode in the face of these pressures.[104] The sergeant major of III MAF in 1967–68 and 1970–71, Edgar Huff, commented, "If I were asked to sum up the 'Marine Experience' in Vietnam, I would say that the Corps grew far too fast and that this growth had a devastating impact on our leadership training and combat effectiveness."[105]

As 1967 opened, the III MAF continued to confront the two-front war, with differentiation in approach. In opposing the large conventional PAVN units, the Marines were forced to shift to larger-scale operations, sometimes including multibattalion operations, as exemplified by the Prairie series of operations (I–IV). These operations in northern Quang Tri Province began in late 1966 and continued through 1967.[106]

Yet even against PAVN, the Marines would often rely on smaller units. Long-range patrols by well-trained small units (platoon or smaller and drawn from specialized Marine reconnaissance battalions) were used to make contact with larger PAVN units and then target them with artillery and air support. This tactic, known as Stingray, was widely used against both PAVN units and larger guerrilla formations.[107]

In the southern part of I Corps, the Marines continued to emphasize small-unit pacification operations, though with fewer personnel given the demands of the conventional war along the DMZ. Nonetheless, programs such as CAP expanded, numbering seventy-five CAP units in mid-1967, reaching Walt's earlier goal for the end of 1966 only six months late in spite of the difficulties the program encountered.[108] The Marines also continued to cooperate with civilians through the JCC, with Walt "exercising personal suasion" to ensure a coordinated civil-military pacification campaign.[109]

In June 1967, Lieutenant General Walt was replaced as III MAF commander by Lieutenant General Robert Cushman. Cushman, who, as noted earlier, had heavily promoted counterinsurgency as Third Marine Division commander, retained Walt's focus on pacification. He had a poor relationship with COMUSMACV Westmoreland, who felt that Cushman was complacent, while Cushman sought to mollify Westmoreland without actually conceding any autonomy.[110]

However, the war with PAVN attracted increasing attention from the Army-dominated MACV command staff. This had serious consequences for the Marines, as the injection of large numbers of Army forces into I Corps would constrain Marine autonomy (previously substantial). It would also shift the location of Marine forces within I Corps away from the southern pacification effort and toward the frontier battles with PAVN.

The initial Army entrance en masse (there had been a few scattered battalions previously) into I Corps was Task Force (TF) Oregon, a provisional division cobbled together in the spring of 1967 from units of the 101st Airborne Division, the 196th Light Infantry Brigade, and the Twenty-Fifth Infantry Division. TF Oregon was stationed at Chu Lai in southern I Corps and was given responsibility for that area. This freed Marine units to be shifted north toward the DMZ and the emerging frontier battles.[111] The move also gave the Army responsibility for pacification in part of I Corps, and the approach was notably different, as will be discussed in more detail in chapter 7.

The Marines, now concentrated in northern I Corps, confronted an increasingly well-armed conventional threat. Marine fire bases were established along the DMZ, the western anchor being the base at Khe Sanh near the Laotian border. PAVN artillery based in North Vietnam, including new 152 mm guns, pounded these bases as well as Marine efforts to secure the DMZ itself. Some PAVN troops were reported to be equipped with flak vests and even flamethrowers, hardly the hallmarks of a guerrilla force.[112]

In September 1967, the Marine fire base at Con Thien was besieged by units of the PAVN 324B and 324C Divisions. The PAVN units relied principally on artillery and rockets, and the United States responded with a massive air campaign against the artillery positions. Ultimately, the PAVN units made no attempt to overrun the fire base, and the siege lifted in October.[113]

Even as pressure on Con Thien eased, SIGINT (which had grown in importance as the Marines faced conventional units on the border) detected PAVN units massing near the Marine firebase at Khe Sanh. By January 1968, regiments from three PAVN divisions had been detected on all sides of the base. The stage was set for a major conventional PAVN offensive, which opened on January 21 with skirmishes in the hills around the base, followed by an artillery barrage against Khe Sanh.[114]

The battle around Khe Sanh was unambiguously conventional. PAVN units made lavish use of artillery, including the newly deployed 130 mm field gun, which had nearly double the range of the U.S. 155 mm howitzer.

The North Vietnamese also employed armor in Laos and South Vietnam for the first time. Infantry supported by PT-76 light tanks (which were more effective than heavier tanks in the mountainous jungle) overran the Special Forces camp at Lang Vei west of Khe Sanh on February 7.[115] The U.S. response was the most massive use of aerial bombardment for tactical purposes in history, hammering PAVN artillery positions with ninety-five thousand tons of ordnance over the next six weeks.[116]

Even in the middle of this unambiguously conventional fight, the Marines continued to pursue some of the programs for building local security forces they had initiated. Most notably, there were platoons from a Combined Action Company of Marines and Popular Forces militia guarding Khe Sanh village proper and some of the approach routes to the fire base. These units put up a tough resistance to the conventional PAVN assault for a few days before withdrawing from the village.[117]

Marine forces continued to move north as more Army units moved into southern and central I Corps. As this shuffle of forces took place, MACV commander Westmoreland, whose low opinion of Cushman had not changed, felt that another headquarters was needed in I Corps. On January 25, 1968, Westmoreland instructed his deputy, Lieutenant General Creighton Abrams, to establish MACV-Forward to oversee the clash with PAVN in northern I Corps. MACV-Forward would allow Westmoreland (via Abrams) "to observe, direct, and if necessary, control operations in the threatened northern provinces."[118] In short, Westmoreland did not trust Cushman to run a large-unit conventional war.

Only days after Abrams began working to create MACV-Forward, the Tet Offensive erupted across South Vietnam. In I Corps, all provincial capitals were attacked, but the major enemy efforts were assaults on Quang Tri City, the capital of Quang Tri Province, and Hue, the old imperial capital. Both assaults, though initiated by sappers who had infiltrated the two cities, were essentially conventional efforts.

In Quang Tri City, the attack was launched by the 812th Regiment of the 324C Division and the 808th and 814th Main Force Battalions. Nominally Vietcong units, the 808th and 814th had been heavily leavened with PAVN troops sent from the north. The assault was also supported by rocket artillery, likely from the Fifty-Fourth Artillery Regiment. The defenders, including city police, Regional Force paramilitaries, and units from the ARVN First Infantry Division, put up stiff resistance. A rapid counterattack by the First Cavalry Division (one of the Army units shifted into I Corps) ensured that within twenty-four hours the attack had been substantially repulsed with heavy PAVN losses.[119]

Hue proved to be a much more ferocious conventional fight, as PAVN had assembled the equivalent of at least fourteen battalions around the city. Armed with everything from rocket artillery to brand-new RPG7 antitank weapons, this strike force (which merited the formation of its own special command, the

Hue City Front) rapidly overwhelmed many of Hue's defenders. PAVN forces would be dislodged only after more than three weeks of intense conventional urban fighting by U.S. Army, Marine, and ARVN units.[120]

Assessing Theoretical Explanations for Counterinsurgency Operations, 1965–68

The evidence from this period, combined with evidence from the earlier period, indicates a powerful role for organizational culture in determining the actual conduct of counterinsurgency. There appear to have been significant and persistent differences in Army, Army Special Forces, and Marine operations in this period. Further, these differences were greatest in areas where information was ambiguous and least where information was most clear (for example, the border battles with PAVN), though the differences never disappear entirely.

Civilian intervention also appears to have had little effect. President Kennedy had died in 1963, but his successor, Lyndon Johnson, kept many key officials in place, such as Secretary of Defense McNamara, so there was strong policy continuity. The single major success in terms of civilian interventions was the creation of CORDS, yet, far from making the military and civilian efforts coequal, CORDS merely confirmed the supremacy of the military.

Further, throughout most of this period the bulk of Congress was highly supportive of the executive branch, indicating little reason to believe that civilian intervention had been stymied by legislators. The chairs of the critical Armed Services Committees, Senator Richard Russell and Representative Carl Vinson (and later Representative Mendel Rivers), were supporters of both the Kennedy and Johnson administrations. They were unlikely to strongly challenge the way the executive branch was handling the war even if they had misgivings.[121] The only substantial criticism on strategy from both the House and the Senate was the need to shorten the war as much as possible, and bomb more heavily in the north to do so.[122] As Deborah Avant notes, "both Kennedy and Johnson enjoyed general support in Congress for their activities on behalf of unconventional warfare. Congress seems to have had little active role in the story."[123]

The Army also did not gain resources, autonomy, or prestige for conducting operations as it did. All of Westmoreland's requests for forces were granted prior to Tet. Yet there is little reason to believe this had anything to do with the way the Army conducted operations.

Organizational culture explains both why the Army conducted the operations it did and why it wrote the doctrine it did not follow. The operations conducted are fully predicted by the Army culture derived from the Civil War and reified in the Command and General Staff College: firepower, indifference to or active targeting of civilians, large-unit operations, management of mass mobilization, and the like. The written doctrine, in contrast, was merely a smokescreen to limit civilian intervention in actual operations.

Evidence from this period on Army Special Forces operations tends to support organizational cultural explanations. It is clear that Special Forces did things very differently than the regular Army, as many of its operations were covert, it worked very closely with locals and with civilian organizations like the CIA, and its basic operating unit was the tiny ODA, barely the size of a regular Army squad. It is telling that Army Special Forces operations, with their small size and local orientation, tended to more closely resemble Marine operations rather than the rest of the Army.

Combined with the evidence from the period 1960–65, the evidence on Marine operations from the period 1965–68 also strongly supports organizational culture as an explanation for doctrine. However, the hypothesis that doctrine is a purely rational response to environment is almost as strongly supported. The Marine response to the bifurcated war in I Corps seems entirely rational, with small-unit support to local forces predominating in the south and larger units with artillery and air support predominating in the north.

This convergence in the two hypotheses is a result of the unambiguous signal sent by the large PAVN units in northern I Corps. The complex political-military-social phenomenon of insurgency was almost entirely absent in this part of the war, so the effects of culture tended to be least operational here. However, as approaches like STINGRAY patrols illustrate, even here managerial culture still had some effect, as Marines used small-unit approaches to the big-unit war.

The Marines also gained little in terms of resources, autonomy, and prestige. Marine autonomy was guaranteed early in the war by exclusive control of I Corps, which was independent of the Marine approach to COIN. Autonomy eroded later for reasons equally independent of the Marine approach to COIN. Resources were equally abundant regardless of approach. Moreover, the Marines actually grew in end strength more rapidly than the organization would have liked, further indicating the indeterminacy of generic propensities.

Evolution of Written Doctrine in the Army and Marine Corps, 1967

By March 1967, U.S. combat forces had been engaged in Vietnam for two years. New doctrine manuals began to appear in this period and, as one might expect, there had been some evolution. For one, the new manuals were longer. The March 1967 version of FM 31-16 was about 25 percent longer than the February 1963 version. Some shifts in terminology are also visible; FM 31-16 uses the term "internal defense and development" rather than counterinsurgency; this shift is also seen in the September 1968 version of FM 100-5: "The term 'counterinsurgency' is used by the joint services, other governmental agencies, and many foreign countries. Within the U.S. Army, depending on the context, use of 'stability operations' or 'internal defense and internal development' is preferred to 'counterinsurgency.'"[124]

Yet despite these cosmetic differences, the doctrine produced in this period is fundamentally similar to earlier doctrine. For example, the 1967 version of FM 31-16 notes the primary importance of the population and the need for civil-military integration.[125] Similarly, the 1968 version of FM 100-5 describes the roots of insurgency much as earlier versions did: "Government ultimately depends on the acquiescence if not the active support of its citizens . . . Thus, the basic causes of insurgency are the existence of one or more grievances and lack of faith in the government's ability or desire to correct them."[126]

In terms of organization for COIN, the 1967 FM 31-16 reiterates the call for the establishment of pacification committees, though they are renamed "area coordination centers" or ACCs. It goes into somewhat more detail on this organization than the earlier version; it specifically calls for the establishment of ACCs at all levels of political organization, especially the province, district, and village levels. The membership of the ACC is also enumerated, with the military, intelligence agencies, paramilitary, and police being the foremost members. FM 31-16 also calls for Civil-Military Advisory Committees to be established to advise the ACCs, with members including judges, religious leaders, labor unions, and other respected members of the community.[127]

In terms of operations, the revised doctrines of the late 1960s are still similar to their predecessors, though again often with more elaboration. FM 31-16 reasserts the importance of the population and provides a caution on the use of firepower.[128]

Doctrine in this later period continued to emphasize the critical importance of intelligence for COIN. Cultural, political, and economic intelligence was still seen as important alongside traditional order of battle. In addition, FM 100-5 states that the need for and staffing requirements of intelligence in COIN are higher than in normal operations.[129]

Besides the formal and general doctrine produced by the Army, MACV also began to produce its own COIN doctrine specific to the conflict. One example is the *Handbook for Military Support of Pacification*, published in February 1968. This guide provides descriptions of pacification and the military role in supporting pacification, as well as numerous specific tactics, techniques, and procedures (TTPs) for COIN. The beginning of its introduction provides perhaps as clear and succinct a definition of COIN as can be found:

Pacification, as it applies in the Republic of Vietnam[,] is the military, political, economic, and social process of establishing or re-establishing local government responsive to and involving the participation of the people. It includes the provision of sustained, credible territorial security, the destruction of the enemy's underground government, the assertion or reassertion of political control and involvement of the people in the government, and the initiation of economic and social activity capable of self-sustenance and expansion . . . The key to pacification is the provision of sustained territorial security. Territorial security is security from VC local forces and guerrilla units and VC/NVA main force units, if any are in or threatening the area. It also includes the protection of the people within a hamlet from the VC infrastructure and bullies.[130]

The handbook also provides guidance on how many of the other elements of COIN doctrine relate to the specific environment of Vietnam. Yet practice continued to diverge from doctrinal rhetoric.

Marine written doctrine likewise evolved in response to the Vietnam experience but did not fundamentally change. In December 1967, the basic guidance for COIN, FMFM-21, was reissued with a new title, FMFM 8-2, *Counterinsurgency Operations*. The new manual was approximately 50 percent longer than the previous one, yet this was principally elaboration on the same themes presented in FMFM-21.

In terms of the basic concept of insurgency and counterinsurgency, FMFM 8-2 used the same definition as FMFM-21 essentially verbatim.[131] It also reiterated the importance of intelligence collection, noting that requirements were higher in COIN than in conventional war.[132]

The new manual did expand significantly on the importance of small-unit operations. It devoted an entire chapter to the subject, summarized as follows: "Operations against guerrillas are characterized by small unit actions."[133] The managerial locus of Marine COIN clearly remained at the battalion level and below.

A Better War? Counterinsurgency Operations in Vietnam, 1968–71

The Tet Offensive of 1968 finally provided Westmoreland with a chance to effectively apply the firepower he had amassed in Vietnam. The results were devastating to the Vietcong, but the mere fact that the Vietcong could launch such a major effort after almost three years of search and destroy was equally devastating to Westmoreland. He was "kicked upstairs" to become Army chief of staff, while his deputy, General Creighton Abrams, replaced him in July 1968.[134]

ARMY COUNTERINSURGENCY, 1968–71

Abrams's understanding of the war was clearly different from Westmoreland's, though probably less so than his most ardent supporters might claim.

After observing the war for several years, he had come to accept, as written COIN doctrine elaborated, that pacification was a more appropriate strategy than search and destroy. He therefore began acting to shift operations toward small-unit action, pacification, and more restraint in firepower. Some credit him, along with Ambassador Ellsworth Bunker and the CIA's William Colby, with shifting the Army to effective pacification, which was undone by the 1972 and 1975 conventional offensives of the North Vietnamese Army.[135]

Closer inspection of what actually took place after Tet reveals that change was more apparent than real. Even a commander as senior and well respected as Abrams was unable to alter Army operations substantially. Abrams bemoaned the inability of various subordinates, including battalion and division commanders, to change their conception of the war and thus the actual conduct of operations.[136] This was in part because battles like Khe Sanh and Hue, in which the enemy stood and fought, often with heavy artillery, appeared to validate the large-unit/firepower-intensive operations the Army had been pursuing.

Those of Abrams's senior subordinates who accepted his shift in approach experienced similar frustrations in attempting to change the conduct of their own subordinate units. Lieutenant General Melvin Zais, commander of the Twenty-Fourth Corps in 1969–70, described many of his subordinate units as "thrashing around spending untold thousands of man-hours looking for an elusive enemy." He similarly noted a failure by his division commanders to make their own brigade and battalion commanders "understand our pacification goals and developed proper attitudes with Vietnamese officials and other personnel in populated areas."[137]

Yet less than eight months prior to voicing these complaints about his division commanders, Zais himself had commanded the 101st Airborne Division when it launched a bloody attack on the strategically unimportant Hill 937. This attack, in May 1969, was conducted during Operation Apache Snow, an attempt to clear the A Shau valley using three battalions of the 101st. The attack on the heavily fortified Hill 937, dubbed "Hamburger Hill" by those who fought for it, was consonant with earlier firepower-intensive search and destroy operations. Zais himself was forced to admit this; an official Army history notes: "Defending the operation, the commander of the 101st, Maj. Gen. Melvin Zais, acknowledged that the hill's only significance was that the enemy occupied it. 'My mission,' he said, 'was to destroy enemy forces and installations. We found the enemy on Hill 937, and that is where we fought them.'"[138]

Other accounts reinforce the view that despite Abrams's efforts to force change from the top, Army operations remained constant. Robert Graham, an infantry sergeant in the Fourth Infantry Division during 1969–70, candidly noted that "unofficially, attrition remained in force."[139] Graham further noted, "We relied heavily on firepower . . . It was standard practice for American units upon contacting the enemy to sit tight and summon fire support."[140]

Another assessment argues that the attitude of Abrams toward harassment and interdiction (H&I) fire was fundamentally no different than Westmoreland's. While Abrams did change rules of engagement for artillery to some degree, H&I fire was still allowable in designated areas despite the risk to civilians it created. While there was a decline in H&I under Abrams, it actually began under Westmoreland and in both cases seems to have been driven by the cost of ammunition rather than concern for collateral damage.[141]

The career under Abrams of Lieutenant General Julian Ewell provides concrete evidence of the limits of change. Ewell commanded the Ninth Infantry Division in the densely populated Mekong Delta in 1968–69, where his obsession with body counts and kill ratios earned him the nickname "Delta Butcher." Informed of Abrams's desired shift in approach, Ewell is alleged to have protested, "I have made my entire career and reputation by going 180 degrees counter to orders such as this."[142]

Ewell, aided by his division chief of staff, Ira Hunt, would subsequently make plain the Ninth Infantry Division approach. Writing in 1973 in an Army official publication, Ewell and Hunt defended search and destroy:

> When one first observes the fighting in Vietnam, there is a tendency to assume that the current tactics are about right and that previous tactics were rather uninspired if not wrong. The first conclusion is probably correct, the second is probably wrong. For example, one hears much criticism of the Search and Destroy Operations which were extensively used in 1967 and before. However, if one looks at the situation then existing and what was actually done, the tactics were pretty well chosen and did the job. Any reasonably effective commander, after observing the enemy operate a while, can cope with him reasonably well.[143]

Elsewhere in the same publication, he derides pacification via development: "More often than not, units in Vietnam emphasized pacification by stressing civic action efforts. In our opinion, this was a mistake as long as the enemy retained even a modest military capability. In the 9th Division, we always stressed the military effort."[144]

As for the negative effects of firepower, Ewell states that he was careful to avoid civilian casualties. Yet it is telling that in a volume devoted to statistical assessment of performance that includes a quarterly breakdown of kilometers of road constructed by the Ninth Infantry Division, Ewell is unable or unwilling to provide a numerical estimate of civilian casualties, merely claiming, "We had only moderate civilian casualties and damage."[145] That an officer so enamored of operations research would not bother to track this number (or having tracked it would not want to include it) says much about Ewell's priorities.

Moreover, Ewell conducted Operation Speedy Express, a massive six-month operation using three brigades of the Ninth Infantry Division. From December 1968 to May 1969, the operation used massive amounts of fire-power, including over three thousand airstrikes. The official body count claimed by Ewell was a staggering 10,899 enemy dead. Yet only 748 weapons were captured; subsequent reporting indicates that Speedy Express was perhaps the most brutal and indiscriminate U.S. operation of the entire war, with some suggesting that the toll of civilian deaths may have been half of the reported body count. Moreover, this took place in the Mekong Delta, an area where large insurgent units were rare and PAVN conventional units essentially absent.[146]

Ewell was even blunter in a debriefing report on his time commanding the Ninth Infantry Division. He noted that "these days (1969) one seldom plans or carries out attacks or operations, one conducts reconnaissance. Once a contact is gained an attack is organized rapidly to exploit the situation. The attack is normally by firepower—artillery, tac air, gunships or, sometimes, B-52 strikes."[147]

Ewell also described his views on pacification and firepower:

I guess I basically feel that the "hearts and minds" approach can be overdone. In the Delta the only way to overcome VC control and terror is by brute force applied against the VC . . . By stressing discriminate and selective use of firepower, one can minimize beating up the countryside. The 9th fought constantly through areas which looked quite peaceful and unharmed from the air. In other areas, where this emphasis wasn't applied or wasn't feasible, the countryside looked like the Verdun battlefields. On the other hand, one has to lower the boom occasionally and battalion commanders have author-ity to use heavy firepower in populated areas.[148]

It is telling that even in the areas where Ewell believes firepower was lim-ited, his only standard is that they appear unharmed from the air.

One would not expect an officer advocating such an approach to prosper if operations actually changed significantly under Abrams. Yet Abrams praised Ewell and promoted him to command II Field Force, an Army corps command, where he continued to serve under Abrams in 1969–70.[149] The Army historian Andrew Birtle refers to Ewell as "one of the more successful commanders during the Abrams years," while affirming that Ewell always stressed military operations against enemy formations.[150]

An exchange between Abrams and Ewell during a weekly intelligence meeting in June 1969 underscores that Ewell's attitude fundamentally had not changed:

EWELL: Anybody stealing gas is a VC sympathizer. You knock off about five and the rate of stealing in that general area will go down precipi-tously.

MILDREN: Yeah, but you can't shoot people for petty larceny.

EWELL: B-u-l-l-shit.

ABRAMS: Now wait a minute, wait a minute, wait a minute.

EWELL: If you have a pipeline, you put out rules that people aren't supposed to steal gas . . . and that we're going to get these VC that are doing it and just go *shoot* them.

ABRAMS: You've got to think about these people here. *Shooting* them— "Well, that'll stop it." Christ, these people have been shot at for the last twenty years! I don't—going out there and *killing* a few of them is not, in my opinion, going to have the *effect*. I think they're *all* sort of fatalists.

EWELL: Well, I don't agree with you, General. You can get a sapper unit mining the road, and you kill two or three and they'll knock it off. It may be that a month later they'll come back. These people can *count*. And boy when you line them up [bodies] and they count one, two, three, four, their enthusiasm is highly reduced. That's the way we opened up Highway 4—just killing them. It doesn't take many.

ABRAMS: All right, we'll study it. [Laughter][151]

Despite the concluding laughter, this exchange illustrates that whatever Abrams himself may have believed about COIN, much of the rest of the Army continued to do more or less the same type of operations it had undertaken under Westmoreland. Moreover, it continued to reward those who did it well, as Ewell would subsequently serve as a military adviser at the peace talks in Paris before concluding his career as chief of staff of NATO Southern Command.

Other operations followed the same pattern as Speedy Express, if somewhat less egregiously, through the end of the war. For example, as late as February 1970, the Americal Division launched a multibattalion sweep of the Batangan Peninsula known as Operation Nantucket Beach. The Army historian Richard Hunt concludes that operations such as this and the offensive at Hamburger Hill "challenged the notion that U.S. forces were operating differently under Abrams."[152] He further notes that there is little evidence that "subordinate commanders heeded Abrams's new operational precepts."[153] Despite a concerted effort by a widely respected four-star operational commander, Army operations did not change substantially over the course of the war.

MARINE COUNTERINSURGENCY OPERATIONS, 1968–71

In the wake of the Tet Offensive and Khe Sanh, the Marines began working to restore order to the countryside. However, the two subsequent Communist offensives (the so-called Mini-Tets of May and September 1968) and the enduring PAVN threat on the border limited progress. The latter in particular limited Marine ability to do more in terms of counterinsurgency, as General Cushman later lamented.[154]

Among other effects, the demands of the border war had limited expansion of the CAP program. The target for the end of 1967 had been 114 platoons, but only 79 were functional.[155] However, post-Tet the Marines resumed expansion (albeit slow) of the program. By July 1968, there were 93 platoons in the program.[156] By the end of the year there were 102 platoons.[157]

In addition to the border war with PAVN and continuing problems recruiting Popular Forces for the program, the expanding Army presence in I Corps limited the growth of CAP. MACV-Forward was converted to a Provisional Army Corps in March 1968, which then became the XXIV Corps in August 1968. This corps was given responsibility for the border war, effectively controlling tactical units in northern I Corps. While it was nominally subordinate to III MAF, like the American Division earlier, XXIV Corps had substantial autonomy. Note that this created the curious phenomenon of an Army three-star general being responsible for many Marine units in northern I Corps, while Army units in the south reported to a Marine three-star general.[158]

Neither the Army corps nor its subordinate divisions had much use for CAP. The Army's First Cavalry Division sought to keep CAP Marines out of its area of operations in early 1968.[159] Later in the year, Lieutenant General Richard Stilwell, the XXIV Corps Commander, was reported to be "very vociferous to his staff with respect to the CAP Program . . . [and later] voiced strong objections to having them [Combined Action Platoons] placed along the LOCs [lines of communication]."[160] As CAP units had to rely on local U.S. units for support if attacked, this Army disdain led Cushman to cancel plans to expand CAP in the Army area of responsibility between Hue and Quang Tri.[161]

Marine operations for the remainder of the war continued to combine larger-unit actions against PAVN forces near the border with small-unit actions against local guerrilla forces around population centers. The larger-unit operations decreased in 1969, as PAVN units became less active while recovering from the intense fighting of 1968. A Marine operational summary for September 1969 notes that the Marines conducted fifteen battalion or larger operations that month without making significant contact.[162]

One of these large-unit operations, Defiant Stand, was an exception in that it was not on the border. Instead, it was a major amphibious combined operation with the Korean Marine brigade against an island south of Da Nang, proving that the advance base subculture was still alive and well. The nearly superfluous nature of this amphibious operation is clear even in the official account, which notes that the landing was unopposed and encountered no large enemy units.[163] Operation Bold Mariner in January 1969 was similar: an amphibious operation conducted jointly with the American Division's Russell Beach on the Batangan Peninsula. Bold Mariner, like most Marine amphibious operations during Vietnam, was not particularly successful, yet the Marines kept at them.[164]

Despite the pressure on the border, which was reduced but not absent, the Marines continued to conduct small-unit operations. The Marines conducted over 4,000 small-unit patrols and 249 company-size operations in September 1969, despite Marine troop withdrawals begun earlier in the year. In addition to these small-unit operations near population centers, the Marines continued to maintain frequent Stingray reconnaissance patrolling in outlying areas.[165]

The Marines also continued to maintain the combined action program, though the program's expansion remained slow due to continuing shortages of both U.S. and South Vietnamese personnel. The program reached 114 platoons in August 1969, remaining at that level through March 1970. The number of platoons in the program peaked at about 120 before beginning to decline in July 1970.[166]

This is particularly noteworthy because Marine troop withdrawals from Vietnam had begun in 1969, indicating that the Marines remained committed to the program even as available manpower fell.[167] In March 1970, the command arrangement for III MAF and XXIV Corps was reversed to reflect the plummeting number of Marines in Vietnam.[168] With the Marines now under the direction of an Army higher headquarters, Marine autonomy, which had previously been high, was constrained. It is therefore not surprising that by the end of 1970, the combined action program had contracted to only thirty-eight platoons before being formally ended in May 1971 as the final Marine units left Vietnam.[169]

Marine total end strength peaked in 1969–70 at almost 310,000.[170] This was the largest the Marine Corps had been since World War II, and the strains on the force were high. Commandant Leonard Chapman, who had replaced Greene in 1968, oversaw a rapid decrease in Marine Corps end strength, explicitly embracing the return to small-unit professionalism that was central to Marine Corps culture.[171] By 1972–73, Marine end strength was down to 198,000. It would fluctuate only modestly around this number for the remainder of the Cold War (the low being just over 185,000 and the high just under 200,000) even though defense budgets varied widely.

ASSESSING THEORETICAL EXPLANATIONS
FOR DOCTRINE AND OPERATIONS, 1968–71

The evidence from this period further underscores the power of organizational culture in explaining U.S. Army counterinsurgency, as the senior operational commander, Abrams, was unable to change operations. Many in the Army continued to conduct operations as they had in the prior period, buoyed by the border battles like that at Khe Sanh, where the enemy, sometimes even wearing uniforms, chose to stand and fight conventionally. At the same time, written doctrine continued to proclaim an entirely different approach than that actually used.

Similarly, in this period, the Marine Corps continued to emphasize and conduct small-unit operations. It further continued to focus extensively on cooperating with local forces and other organizations, most notably though the combined action program. The U.S. Army Special Forces continued to do likewise.

The U.S. Army, U.S. Army Special Forces, and U.S. Marine Corps, confronted with the murky military-political challenge of counterinsurgency in South Vietnam, pursued very different operations. In contrast, when confronted with the unambiguously conventional PAVN divisions on the border, Army and Marine operations converged, though they did not become identical. This indicates that the structure of the information environment seems to have some effect on operations, yet some other factor is required to explain variation.

The Army's response to counterinsurgency is the most puzzling of the organizational responses. It promulgated a doctrine for counterinsurgency in the early 1960s, which it subsequently revised, yet ignored it throughout the war, this in spite of having sent thousands of officers to advise the South Vietnamese before 1965 and then participating with combat forces from 1965 to 1971. Further, both the senior Army officer (Chief of Staff Johnson) and the senior operational commander (COMUSMACV Abrams) tried to force compliance with this doctrine, yet both failed.

The failure of both Army Chief of Staff Johnson and Abrams to change operations significantly underscores the limited power of principals to control agents even in very hierarchical organizations. Due to limits on the time and attention of principals, as well as the need for some level of autonomy for agents, change relies heavily on organizational culture to ensure that agents understand and comply with directives from principals. Where culture and attempts at doctrinal/operational change are compatible, change is relatively easy. The U.S. Army's adoption of helicopters for mobility and firepower during the Vietnam era supports this contention, as helicopters, though a radical new technology, were easily compatible with Army culture's emphasis on mass maneuver and firepower.

Yet attempts to shift to smaller-unit operations that were more integrated with civilian and indigenous forces were not compatible with Army culture. Therefore even when senior officers in the Army sought to impose change, the effects were limited. As the case of Lieutenant General Ewell demonstrates, the broader Army, and even Abrams himself, continued to support those who conducted operations more consonant with Army culture.[172]

In contrast, the Marines and Special Forces, while confronting various obstacles in their counterinsurgency operations, seemed to have little internal dissent about those operations. Senior leaders supported subordinates' close cooperation with locals (CIDG, Kit Carson Scouts, and CAP) as well as the extensive use of small-unit operations. Both cooperated closely with civilian agencies (CIA and USAID). They appear to have accomplished all this with little or no organizational friction, except for the Marines' rapid expansion in personnel.

None of the existing hypotheses on military doctrine and operations can fully account for this pattern of behavior. Hypotheses on the role of the external environment, both international and domestic, cannot account for this pattern. If doctrine and operations are a rational response to the international environment, the operations of the Army and Marines should have converged across South Vietnam, not just on the border. If doctrine and operations respond to the intervention of domestic civilians, then there should have been convergence across the organizations at least during 1961–69. Virtually the same senior national security civilians were in place, with the exception of the president, for almost this entire period. Further, these civilians were not indifferent on counterinsurgency; rather, they had views expressed in NSAM 182.

Similarly, explanations that focus on universal or generic aspects of organizations cannot account for this persistent variation. If doctrine and operations are chosen to maximize resources, there should have been convergence on a common set of resource-maximizing operations. An organizational drive for autonomy might explain variation, yet in Vietnam autonomy for the Army and Marines preceded choices about operations.

Finally, organizational inertia or simple lag is not a convincing alternative explanation given the duration and scale of U.S. military involvement in Vietnam. By 1971 the U.S. military had been in South Vietnam for a decade either advising South Vietnamese forces conducting counterinsurgency operations or conducting those operations with U.S. forces. Both the Army and the Marines had similar written counterinsurgency doctrines for seven years at that point, which each had updated, and MACV had produced its own written guide to counterinsurgency specific to Vietnam. Moreover, organizational inertia should predict no convergence in any operations, when in fact the border operations against PAVN look quite similar for the Army and the Marines.

The only hypothesis than can explain the variation observed in operations is that of organizational culture. Culture had the greatest effect in the ambiguous information environment of counterinsurgency and the least impact in the unambiguous conventional border battles. Chapter 7 reinforces this conclusion through a more detailed comparison of Marine and Army operations in a single province.

A Natural Experiment in I Corps, 1966–68

As briefly noted earlier, in 1967 large Army formations were introduced into I Corps for the first time, beginning in southern I Corps. This provides an excellent natural experiment for comparing Marine and Army counter-insurgency operations, as the Army units replaced Marine units shifted northward to the DMZ and the Laotian border. Army units would therefore begin operating in the exact same terrain and presumably against the exact same enemy the Marines had. Any differences in operations are therefore likely due primarily, perhaps even exclusively, to differences in the two organizations rather than to environmental effects.

This chapter focuses on operations in a single province of I Corps, Quang Ngai, in 1966–68. Quang Ngai is a good environment for a comparison of the two services, as it was the southernmost province in I Corps, yet the Vietcong political-military infrastructure was very strong in it. Therefore, unlike northern I Corps, it was not attacked by large PAVN divisions presenting an unambiguously conventional threat, nor was it an area with little insurgent presence. Instead, the robust insurgent presence produced an ambiguous information environment where culture would, if the proposed theory is correct, strongly influence doctrine and operations. This chapter begins with a brief description of the geography and history of Quang Ngai before turning to Marine operations in the province in 1966–67. It then contrasts this with Army operations there in 1967–68.

Quang Ngai is located along the South China Sea coast of Vietnam. Now roughly at the midpoint of unified Vietnam, it was one of the northern provinces of South Vietnam. In the 1960s, much of the population was close to the coast, which has many rivers and good land for rice cultivation. West of the coast, the land becomes higher and hillier as it climbs into the Annamite Mountains; population density is much lower in this region. The province was buffered from infiltration (particularly of large PAVN units) from the west via Laos or Cambodia by neighboring provinces Kontum and Quang Tin. The large Marine base and airfield of Chu Lai was just across the northern border of Quang Ngai in Quang Tin Province.[1]

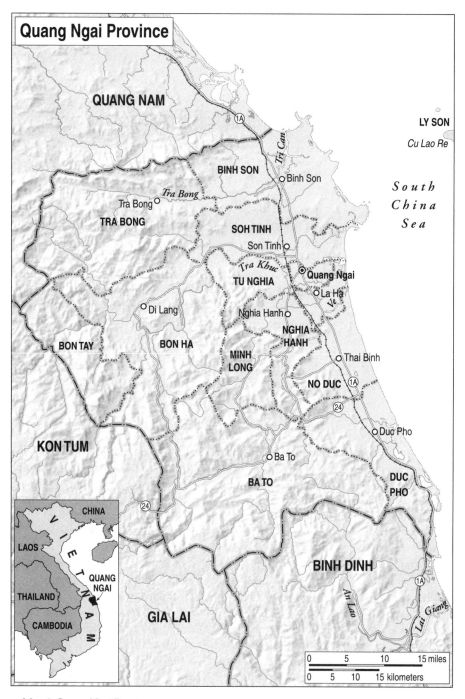

Map 1. Quang Ngai Province

Quang Ngai had allegedly been known for strong sympathy with North Vietnam and the insurgency since 1954. While there is some debate about exactly how strong insurgent presence was before 1964, it was clear to all observers that by 1964–65 the insurgency was extremely well established in the province. According to several sources, it had replaced the government in most if not all villages, leaving the provincial capital, Quang Ngai City, and the smaller district capitals islands in a hostile sea.[2]

As noted earlier, this part of I Corps was the last to see the introduction of Marine forces, which took place with the establishment of the Chu Lai base in May 1965. Operation Starlite, the first amphibious assault of the war, took place in Quang Ngai three months later. However, Marine operations in this area for most of 1965 were limited principally to establishing a perimeter around Chu Lai, though some training of local Popular Forces (PF) troops took place.[3]

This would change in 1966 as the Marines expanded personnel and operations in the area. The First Marine Division was deployed to Chu Lai early in the year, and the division commander, Major General Lewis Fields, was given responsibility for all forces in the Chu Lai AO, which included Quang Ngai. At the same time, III MAF commander Walt received permission from the Vietnamese to introduce the Combined Action Platoon (CAP) program into the Chu Lai AO (see map 1).[4]

Marine Operations in Quang Ngai, 1966

One of the first Marine operations of 1966 was ordered by MACV as part of a larger offensive (according to one source, this was an intentional move on the part of COMUSMACV Westmoreland to force the reluctant Marines to participate in a large-unit offensive).[5] This offensive, Operation Masher/White Wing, would be the first to cross corps area boundaries and would involve Marines, soldiers, Korean Marines, and ARVN soldiers.[6] The U.S. Marine component of this offensive was Operation Double Eagle, which would be the largest amphibious assault since Korea, ultimately using four battalions.

Double Eagle would be conducted in the southernmost district of Quang Ngai, known as Duc Pho, beginning on January 28. The Army's First Cavalry Division would launch its portion of the operation across Quang Ngai's southern border in the province of Binh Dinh on January 24. The ARVN and Korean Marines would provide additional support.[7]

Realizing that the enemy would likely avoid contact, the Marine commander for the operation, Brigadier General Jonas Platt, deployed small reconnaissance teams to a Special Forces camp in the inland hills of Quang Ngai on January 12. These units immediately began patrolling, sighting several insurgent units and, in Stingray patrol fashion, would often call air or artillery strikes on them.[8]

The amphibious assault, though plagued by bad weather, was unopposed. The Marines sweeping inland encountered no significant enemy resistance. B-52 Arclight strikes scheduled by MACV for January 30 took place despite Platt's request to delay them until he could make better use of them. The Marines turned south in February, sweeping to the province border in several teams composed of two rifle companies with an 81 mm mortar platoon. General Platt apparently found this operation not particularly effective, choosing to close it on February 17 even as the First Cavalry to the south continued attempting to find and fix the enemy.[9]

The after-action report for Double Eagle, while attempting to draw lessons for future operations, has a pessimistic tone about such large-unit sweeps, as the enemy can too easily avoid contact.[10] Perhaps the most telling sign of Marine dissatisfaction with Double Eagle is the fact that no similar large-unit operations would be launched by Marines in this area of Quang Ngai.[11] All would be smaller and much shorter.

At the same time, Marines undertook many small-unit operations in Quang Ngai. In the month of February 1966, the three battalions of the Seventh Marine Regiment conducted a total of 1,306 small-unit patrols and ambushes. This represented 10 percent of all small-unit actions conducted by all U.S. ground forces in Vietnam during that month.[12] Seventh Marines would be responsible for Quang Ngai for the rest of the Marines' time in the province, though the battalions in the province would change, as discussed later.

The following month, the Marines conducted three large-unit operations in Quang Ngai: Operations Utah, Texas, and Indiana. These operations were in northern Quang Ngai. Each was small and brief relative to Double Eagle, involving only two Marine battalions each and lasting from three to six days. Tellingly, Texas and Indiana were launched in response to an attack by a large enemy unit on a South Vietnamese unit (a fairly unambiguous signal). Only Utah was launched offensively, based on intelligence on the location of a main force unit (likely through signals intelligence.[13] The Marines, while generally seeing little profit after Double Eagle in simply beating the bush for large enemy units, were willing to respond to large enemy attacks with equal or greater numbers.

At the same time, small-unit actions continued. There was a slight drop, as each of the three battalions of Seventh Marines was involved in the three large-unit operations. Nonetheless, 1,178 small-unit operations were conducted in Quang Ngai.[14] Note that the small-unit totals include only actions by Marine line infantry battalions. They do not include Stingray-type patrols, which were conducted by separate Marine reconnaissance units.

In April 1966, two large-unit operations were launched in Quang Ngai. The first was Operation Nevada, which sent two Marine battalions to the

Table 6 Number of small- and large-unit operations, May–December 1966

Month/Year	Large-unit operations (number)	Large-unit operations (duration per operation)	Small-unit operations
May 1966	4	2–6 days	2,073
June 1966	1	3 days	1,346
July 1966	1	4 days	1,167
August 1966	1	3 days	437 (some data may be missing)
September 1966	0	0	583
October 1966	0	0	1,187
November 1966	0	0	892
December 1966	0	0	987

Batangan Peninsula, where Operation Starlite had been conducted. It lasted only six days and, by Marine assessment, produced few results. The second, Operation Hot Springs, was launched when a defector gave the location for an insurgent regimental headquarters in the area where the three operations from the previous month were conducted. Two reinforced Marine battalions were dispatched and overran the headquarters in the course of a single day, though the operation officially lasted four days.[15] Small-unit operations in the province for the month increased to 1,219.[16]

This pattern of few or no large-unit operations per month and a major emphasis on small-unit operations would continue for the remainder of 1966. Table 6 details the number of large-unit operations and their duration as well as the number of small-unit operations.[17]

In parallel to the efforts of the line Marine units, the Combined Action Platoon (CAP) concept was also employed in Quang Ngai. CAPs were introduced to Quang Ngai Province in the summer of 1966. One of the first was at the village of Binh Nghia, with Marines entering the village on June 10.[18] Other CAP units were created in the province throughout the remainder of 1966.

Marine Operations in Quang Ngai, 1967

In late January 1967, Marines in Quang Ngai initiated a new operation that differed from both the lengthy large-unit sweeps that the Marines used sparingly and the small-unit patrols and ambushes that formed the bulk of operations. This operation, De Soto, was a relief of an ARVN battalion in the Duc Pho district of Quang Ngai. This ARVN unit would be transferred elsewhere, leaving the Marines responsible for its former area of operations.[19]

The Third Battalion, Seventh Marines was chosen to replace the ARVN battalion. This battalion had been one of those responsible for Quang Ngai until its focus was shifted north to Quang Tin and participation in the battles near the DMZ. De Soto would represent a new type of operation for the Marines, because the entire battalion would remain in the former ARVN position rather than conducting operations from Chu Lai or outposts near the large base. This posed significant logistical challenges and would expose the battalion command post to attack. However, Marine leadership deemed a longer-term presence in this area sufficiently important to make the operation worthwhile.[20]

De Soto began on January 26 and would continue through early April. During that time, additional companies or even battalions would enter the area of operations, making it a large-unit operation. However, with two major exceptions, the activity undertaken as part of De Soto took the form of small-unit patrols and ambushes. Operating from Nui Dang, small units of the Third Battalion patrolled and "set up numerous ambushes every night."[21]

The first exception to this pattern of small-unit activity came in the initial phase of the operation. The ARVN battalion had rarely ventured forth from its base, so insurgents had been able to establish fortified positions in nearby villages. Marine companies attempting to search these villages encountered heavy enemy fire from concrete bunkers. Despite extensive use of indirect fire assets, including air strikes and naval gunfire, Third Battalion's rifle companies took substantial casualties.[22]

As a result of this fierce resistance, two companies from Third Battalion, Fifth Marine Regiment were brought in as reinforcements. After nearly two weeks of intense fighting, during which the battalion command post was attacked by an insurgent unit, all of these heavily fortified villages were cleared. The Marines were then able to shift to small-unit operations, gradually expanding the area patrolled.[23]

The second exception to small-unit activity came about ten days after the last fortified village was cleared. This was a separate operation conducted by Marine amphibious forces in the same region as De Soto. Known as Deckhouse VI, this amphibious operation was conducted in the southern tip of Quang Ngai where a spur of the Annamite Mountains runs to the coast. Deckhouse VI met little resistance but likewise achieved little other than to indicate that the amphibious subculture in the Marine Corps still had adherents.[24]

De Soto ended a little more than a month later when Task Force Oregon assumed control of southern Quang Ngai. For this remaining period of De Soto no other large-unit operations took place in the province. At this point, Revolutionary Development teams were able to operate in this region of Quang Ngai, which had been far too dangerous for them before.[25]

While De Soto was under way in southern Quang Ngai, Second Battalion, Seventh Marine Regiment continued to conduct small-unit operations elsewhere in the province. In January it conducted 1,223 small-unit operations.[26] In February it reached 1,472, and in March, 1,706.[27]

Assessing Marine Operations in Quang Ngai, 1966–67

Marine operations in Quang Ngai after Double Eagle (which was at least partly imposed on the Corps by MACV) heavily emphasized small-unit actions and minimized large-unit operations. From February 1966 to March 1967, Marine battalions conducted nearly seventeen thousand small-unit operations in the province (not counting those conducted as part of De Soto). In contrast, during the same period it conducted only seventeen large-unit operations in the province, none larger than two battalions. These operations lasted on average between three and four days each, with only one, Deckhouse VI, lasting longer than a week. There was also a five-month period (September 1966–January 1967) in which no large-unit operation was conducted.

Moreover, it is telling that the Marines kept sufficiently detailed records of small-unit operations that such precise figures can be produced for the province. This is also something of an undercount, as it does not include patrols and ambushes conducted by reconnaissance Marines, such as Stingray patrols. These operations were clearly important to the organization.

The use of firepower was more varied. At one end of the spectrum, the early battles of De Soto were marked by extraordinary levels of firepower against heavily fortified positions. Similarly, the Stingray patrol concept was predicated on firepower. At the other end of the spectrum, CAP units rarely if ever relied on firepower other than that of their organic small arms unless they were in danger of being overrun by a massed enemy.[28] Indeed, in 1970 an after-action report from the American Division, the provisional Army division that emerged from TF Oregon in southern I Corps, noted, "Few artillery fire missions were requested by CAPs because team members were inexperienced and lacked confidence in the capabilities of artillery to support them."[29]

This variation in firepower was principally a result of target sets. The Marines were willing to use firepower extensively in environments that unambiguously required it, such as the De Soto fights against an enemy in concrete bunkers. In other contexts, the key distinction was the civilian population. Stingray operations took place "in the hinterland . . . on Viet Cong and North Vietnamese troops far inland, in areas where the enemy least expects contact with our forces."[30] The combination of remote location and observed artillery fire meant that there was little risk to the civilian population from Stingray. Likewise, CAP Marines eschewed firepower, as it was far too likely to harm the population they were protecting.

This is not to argue that the Marines never caused civilian casualties or created refugees by destroying homes. Over the course of 1966, the Marines reported that 117,000 new refugees were displaced in I Corps.[31] A substantial portion of these refugees were doubtless due to Marine operations, particularly in the northern provinces where the heaviest fighting took place.

Overall, however, the Marines worked to secure the population rather than target it.

The Army Takes Over, 1967–68

TF Oregon units began arriving at Chu Lai on April 12, 1967, quickly settling in to the base. On April 26 the Marines turned the southern part of I Corps, including Quang Ngai, over to the Army. TF Oregon, under the command of Major General William Rosson, wasted little time in getting to work.

The first operation, Malheur (supposedly named for a town in Oregon rather than for the French word for bad luck), was initiated on May 11 in Duc Pho district, near where De Soto and, earlier, Double Eagle had been conducted. The operation was large, using all three battalions of the First Brigade, 101st Airborne Division plus an additional battalion each from the 196th Infantry Brigade and the Second Brigade, Twenty-Fifth Infantry Division as a ready reserve at Chu Lai and Duc Pho. The units would air assault into target areas and conduct search and destroy operations.[32]

Malheur was the largest operation in Quang Ngai since Double Eagle. It was also the longest, lasting until June 8 (a total of twenty-nine days—a week longer than Double Eagle).[33] This was despite (or perhaps because of) the recent De Soto operation in the area.

Malheur was also marked by massive use of firepower, particularly artillery. Records listing number of artillery rounds used in the operation are available for nineteen days of the operation. The total for those days was 23,368 rounds, with a low on the first day of 360 rounds and a high of 3,506 rounds on May 31. The average was 1,230 rounds per day.[34]

These numbers tell little absent context. If the fighting resembled the tough fights of the early part of De Soto or was conducted against large enemy units in the hinterland, as with Stingray patrols, this would clearly resemble Marine operations. However, this does not appear to be the case. For example, on May 31, the day of peak artillery expenditure in available records, contact with enemy was reported as light. This contact apparently consisted of a single U.S. company, and no mention is made of fortified positions or large enemy units.

Even more tellingly, on June 5, 954 rounds were fired. This was a day of "negative contact" with the enemy. Nor were any casualties reported for either side. TF Oregon had expended more than 75 percent of the daily average number of rounds for the operation on a day in which no enemy were observed.[35]

This hardly seems discriminate, and in all likelihood it was not. In August 1967, a reporter visited the Fire Direction Center of the Army unit that occupied Duc Pho district after Malheur was completed. He noted that of the

7,116 fire missions (each mission averaging about eight rounds) the unit had fired, 6,266 (88 percent) were harassment and interdiction (H&I) fires. These missions were fired almost randomly into large areas to keep the enemy off balance, but with little regard to civilians outside of major cities.[36] This is a probable explanation for the 954 rounds fired on a day of negative contact during Malheur.

Two days after Malheur ended, on June 10, TF Oregon began Operation Malheur II. This operation used the same units as Malheur (plus one additional cavalry troop, the equivalent of an additional company) but shifted those forces northwest from Duc Pho into the Song Ve valley. This operation would last until August 1, a total of fifty-three days.[37] The Army was thus clearly committed not only to Malheur II specifically but also to the type of large-unit operation it represented.

In terms of firepower, Malheur II was comparable to Malheur, perhaps even slightly higher. In terms of artillery fires, the daily average was lower. For the forty-eight days for which data are available, the average was about 818 rounds per day.[38] However, the use of airpower appears to have been more extensive, with 671 sorties flown by fixed-wing tactical aircraft in support of the operation by July 31. Moreover, thirty naval gunfire missions and nine B-52 Arclight strikes were used to support Malheur II.[39]

Like Malheur, the fighting in Malheur II also does not appear in most cases to have been against a heavily entrenched and/or massed enemy. For example, on July 17, a day of light contact, three insurgents were killed by small-arms fire in three unrelated incidents, and no U.S. casualties were reported. Yet despite this minimal resistance, the Army expended 1,240 rounds of artillery.[40]

After Malheur II, TF Oregon immediately launched Operation Hood River. The brigade of the 101st moved north again, this time operating in the Song Tra Khuc valley. The operation would last until August 13 and was similar in size and execution to Malheur I and II.

According to the brigade's after-action report for the operation, "the same techniques of artillery employment that have proven successful in the past were employed." This report lists 3,838 artillery rounds expended for the entire operation, yet this appears to be an underestimate of the firepower employed.[41] Based on counts from nine days of available operational records, over 7,500 rounds were fired, averaging 835 rounds per day.[42] In addition, by August 11 the operation had used 126 fixed-wing air strikes.[43] Further, a reporter observing the last two days of the operation noted that "troops, and the artillery and aircraft that supported them, did, however, destroy most of the villages in the river valley and on the coastal plain at its mouth."[44]

Additional evidence suggests that this expenditure of firepower was not only lavish but that it was at a minimum indiscriminate and may have been intentionally targeted on the general population. The surge in the number of refugees generated in Malheur I and II and Hood River was described as "meteoric" by the U.S. civilian official responsible for refugees in Quang Ngai. He reported the creation of 31,888 refugees in Quang Ngai between mid-June and the end of August, completely outstripping U.S and South Vietnamese capacity to provide even minimally for those displaced.[45] Three U.S. Army operations in a single province had in roughly two and a half months created more than a quarter as many refugees as the Marines had reported in all of I Corps for an entire year. Put another way, the Army appears to have been creating refugees at least five times faster than the Marines did the year before.[46]

This refugee explosion was not accidental. In Malheur II, the U.S. Army evacuated more than five thousand Vietnamese from the Song Ve valley. It then destroyed their homes and sprayed the area with chemical defoliant before declaring the entire area open to H&I fire.[47] According to one U.S. civilian official in Quang Ngai, the H&I fire served the dual purpose of hampering insurgent movement and discouraging civilians from returning to the area. The same official noted that when a mortar attack was determined to be coming from inside one of the haphazard camps, TF Oregon, despite being informed that the area was full of refugees, blasted the area with counterbattery artillery fire, with devastating results.[48]

After Hood River, the units of TF Oregon shifted operations north again, this time into Quang Tin Province. In September 1967, TF Oregon was reorganized as the Twenty-Third Infantry Division (Provisional), also called the American Division. No large-unit operations were conducted in Quang Ngai from September to November 1967.

The Army did not totally eschew small-unit operations in I Corps. According to III MAF records, of the slightly less than thirty-six thousand small-unit operations in I Corps during October 1967, Army units conducted fewer than four thousand (about 11 percent of the total).[49] This is quite small considering that in that month the American Division represented between a third and a quarter of the combat power in I Corps.

Moreover, Marine units were increasingly concentrated along the DMZ and the Laotian border in Quang Tri Province, where they faced conventional PAVN divisions. Those units conducted relatively few small-unit operations. The vast bulk of Marine small-unit operations (twenty-nine thousand in October 1967) were conducted around Da Nang, where the enemy was still principally an insurgent force.[50] The American Division was facing a similar enemy in southern I Corps yet conducted far fewer small-unit operations despite having more combat power available than was available at Da Nang (which was less than a full Marine division).

On December 24, units from the American Division launched Operation Muscatine in northern Quang Ngai. Initially the operation was conducted by the 198th Infantry Brigade (using all three of its battalions), but in early January 1968 the operation was taken over by the Third Brigade, Fourth Infantry Division. Near the end of January, the 198th again took over the operation before relinquishing it to the Eleventh Infantry Brigade in early February. The operation would continue until June, a total of nearly six months.[51]

Throughout this period, contact with the enemy was light, with most U.S. casualties coming from mines and booby traps.[52] Nevertheless, U.S. Army operations appear to have relied heavily on massive firepower, even in populated areas. An after-action report of the operation from one of the Eleventh Brigade's battalions notes, "Artillery support for the operation was timely, massive, and very effective." It also commends support from both helicopter and fixed-wing units.[53] The American Division artillery standard operating procedure from this period also makes clear that the civilian population was at best a secondary consideration: "Hamlets and villages may be attacked without warning if the attack is in conjunction with a ground operation involving the movement of ground forces, and if in the opinion of the ground commander, his mission would be jeopardized by such warning . . . None of the above controls abridge the right of self-defense, and artillery may be fired without clearance at the request of any unit in contact. The decision to do so will be made by the senior officer present."[54]

Despite the shift of Marine infantry battalions to the north, the CAP program remained in place in Quang Ngai. The CAP Marines' relations with the Army units tended to vary from cordial if formal to simply poor. In general, the CAP Marines simply preferred that the Army, like artillery, stay away from their villages unless a massive attack was under way.[55] The Army units also made no attempt to emulate CAP.

Assessing Army Operations in Quang Ngai, 1967–68

Army operations in Quang Ngai Province were substantially different from Marine operations in 1966–67. The principal differences were size of operations, level of firepower, and targeting of firepower. Moreover, there was no convergence toward the Marine operational model over the course of the fourteen months from April 1967 to June 1968.

In terms of size of operations, the Army concentrated overwhelmingly on multibattalion operations of long duration. Malheur I and II, Hood River, and Muscatine were all brigade-size operations using at least three battalions. The operations varied in duration from two weeks to over six months. The only period in which the Army did not conduct large-unit operations in Quang Ngai, September to November 1967, occurred because those large units were committed in Quang Tin Province to the north. Small-unit operations were neglected, with the Army conducting a small fraction of those conducted by the Marines.

In terms of firepower, the Army consistently used high levels of firepower in all operations, almost regardless of level of enemy resistance. As noted, even on some days with no contact, Army units made extensive use of artillery during Malheur. In other cases, minimal contact was met with the full array of firepower, including massive B-52 Arclight strikes.

This firepower was also targeted with either minimal concern for the civilian population or with the intent of forcing the population to relocate. Whether targeting insurgent mortar units in the middle of a refugee camp or using H&I fire to prevent refugees from returning home, the Army viewed civilians as at a minimum an almost irrelevant nuisance to operations. In other cases, civilians were ruled a legitimate target, as they provided active or passive support to insurgents. No attempt was made to actually protect or isolate the population from the insurgents by living among them as in the CAP program.

This natural experiment in Quang Ngai provides the strongest evidence for the importance of military organizational culture to doctrine and operations. The Army was placed in exactly the same insurgency environment as the Marines who had just been shifted north. Yet its approach to COIN was, according to independent observers, radically different. The Army provisional division relied extensively on often indiscriminate firepower and depopulated the area through the creation of massive flows of refugees. Further, the division developed little connection to the ARVN units in its area, much less the local security forces such as the PFs the Marines had embraced with the CAP program.[56]

This shift in COIN approach seems inexplicable by the other three hypotheses. A rational response would predict continuity in at least overall approach between the Marines and the Army in southern I Corps, as both organizations would be expected to respond similarly to the same environment. The hypotheses on civilian intervention would make a similar prediction, as civilian intervention applied equally to both services. The quest for resources, autonomy, and prestige would predict that the Army might use a different approach if it would be rewarded for doing so, yet there is little evidence that the Americal Division was rewarded (or expected to be rewarded) for its alternative approach.

Indeed, the autonomy of the Americal Division was guaranteed regardless of its approach to COIN. The division commander, Major General Samuel Koster,

> maintained a rather informal command relationship with General Cushman [the III MAF commander]. Several years later, Koster remembered that he would visit the III MAF commander at Da Nang once a week "to tell him what we were doing." Although nominally under the operational control of the Marine command, the Army division commander stated, "I got the distinct feeling that [I was] to work my TAOR as I saw fit." General Cushman later asserted that he treated the Army division the same as he did Marine units, but admitted that General Westmoreland would not "let me move his Army divisions without there being a plan that he'd okayed."[57]

In other words, Army autonomy in I Corps preceded operational methods, rather than the reverse.

The natural experiment in Quang Ngai provides a fine-grained test of theories of military doctrine and operations. Fighting the same enemy, in the same terrain, at almost the same time, the U.S. Marine Corps and the U.S. Army undertook radically different operations despite written doctrine that was functionally identical. This provides high confidence that the difference in operations can be attributed to factors intrinsic to the two organizations.

Moreover, both organizations generally had substantial autonomy. The Marines, with only a few modest exceptions such as the cross-boundary White Wing / Masher / Double Eagle, were similarly free to conduct operations in I Corps as they saw fit. Similarly, once the Army units that comprised TF Oregon / American Division entered I Corps, they had autonomy to choose how to conduct operations, reporting in only occasionally to higher headquarters. Thus in most instances operations were not imposed over organizational objections.

Only the cultural hypothesis can explain this wide divergence. In the ambiguous information environment of Quang Ngai, where a powerful insurgent organization was capable of building heavily fortified bunkers in civilian villages, the Marines and the Army drew heavily on their respective organizational cultures to craft operations. The Marines gravitated to small-unit operations, cooperation with indigenous local forces, and limited firepower. The Army, in contrast, immediately engaged in extensive use of firepower and large-unit operations, creating refugees in lieu of cooperating with local forces. Yet Vietnam could be an outlier or an artifact of the Cold War, so chapters 9 and 10 explore change and continuity in counterinsurgency after the Cold War in Iraq and Afghanistan.

Out of Africa

British Army Counterinsurgency in Kenya, 1952–56

The end of World War II began the unraveling of the British Empire. As noted earlier, India was given independence in 1947, and soon anticolonial movements were multiplying across the globe. One of the first was in Malaya, where a Communist movement among the Chinese minority began fighting the colonial government in 1948.

Most of the scholarship on British counterinsurgency during the Cold War has focused on Malaya. It is perennially cast as an example of the "right" way to conduct counterinsurgency and contrasted with efforts by the French and Americans in Indochina. For example, John Nagl's *Learning to Eat Soup with a Knife* is built around contrasting the British in Malaya and the Americans in Vietnam.[1] Robert Cassidy refers to actions of the British in Malaya as "in many ways the archetypal counterinsurgency campaign."[2]

However, Malaya was in many ways an "easy case" for a counterinsurgent. Many ethnic Chinese, often squatters, were easily won over to resettlement programs. The conflict was isolated by virtue of Malaya's island/peninsular nature, limiting outside support or sanctuary. Economic growth in the country, based largely on tin and rubber exports, boomed with the beginning of the Korean War and a spike in American demand.[3]

This relative easiness of the campaign, combined with the extensive coverage of the conflict, make counterinsurgency in Malaya a less fruitful case for exploration. In contrast, the British experience in Kenya is both understudied and, in some ways at least, was more challenging than counterinsurgency in Malaya. The presence of British settlers in large and influential numbers, for example, greatly complicated the political aspect of the conflict, and the sprawling slums of Nairobi forced the British to confront urban insurgency, which was almost entirely absent in Malaya. Moreover, lessons from Malaya led to creation of written doctrine for counterinsurgency. Kenya thus provides a way to observe the convergence or divergence between counterinsurgency operations and written doctrine. This chapter describes British Army counterinsurgency doctrine and operations in Kenya from 1952 to 1956 and uses that evidence to evaluate the four hypotheses on military doctrine.

British Rule in East Africa, 1888–1952

The British Empire came relatively late to the part of Africa that would eventually be called Kenya. In 1888 the British East Africa Company began to develop the territory between Mombasa on the coast and Lake Victoria (which included both modern Kenya and Uganda), principally by building a railroad to connect the two. The territory lacked some of the mineral resources of South Africa but proved to be good cropland, especially for coffee.[4]

However, the British East Africa Company was not as adroit as some of its predecessor companies and had a much shorter life span. The British crown declared a protectorate over the territory in 1894–95, and a commissioner was appointed to govern the new protectorate. In 1907 the capital was moved inland, from Mombasa to Nairobi. White settlers (almost all British) also began to move into the interior, setting up lucrative plantations and ranches on land grants.

Following World War I, the protectorate was reorganized, with Kenya and Uganda becoming separate colonies. The years between World War I and World War II were tumultuous, with the worldwide boom of the 1920s followed by the Great Depression mirrored in Kenya. Labor shortages and rapid expansion in the economy gave way to unemployment and contraction as agricultural prices collapsed; only government intervention in the 1930s prevented greater economic dislocation.

The coming of World War II once again drove demand up, but the Depression had revealed how dependent on cheap labor the agricultural economy was. This labor was provided by Africans, who were the overwhelming majority of the population yet had little political representation. While this imbalance in power had earlier been acceptable to many Africans, particularly the class of chiefs who had been empowered by the British colonial government, a group of educated nationalist Africans began to emerge in this period. This emerging nationalist movement, embodied initially in groups such as the Kenya African Union (KAU), was opposed by the white settler community, which rightly saw it as a challenge to their privileged position.[5]

After World War II, the British colonial administration, led from 1944 to 1952 by Sir Philip Mitchell, was essentially tasked with managing the inevitable conflict between the nationalists (who were not entirely unified) and the coalition of white settlers and African beneficiaries of the colonial order. Mitchell advocated a "multiracial" Kenya that gave Africans greater status, yet his policies, based on the need for cheap African labor and a paternalist view of the Africans, increased rather than decreased tension between nationalists and the old guard. Mitchell's policy ran against the emerging policy in the cabinet office of the colonial secretary, which sought to give more political representation to Africans, yet absent a crisis London was reluctant to force the issue. Crisis would come just as Mitchell was leaving Kenya in 1952, with the bloody eruption of the Mau Mau rebellion.[6]

African versus Kikuyu, Moderate versus Militant: Resistance in Kenya, 1947–52

The Mau Mau movement had its roots in the nationalist KAU, which began to mobilize more and more Africans in the period 1947–52. The KAU's strongest constituency was the Kikuyu tribe, and from the beginning it was often difficult to categorize Mau Mau aims. There was no doubt a strong African nationalist element of the movement, yet it was equally true that the vast majority of support for the movement came from a single tribe.[7]

Further, there was a division between those who advocated nonviolent political mobilization and more militant nationalists. The former were represented by leaders such as Jomo Kenyatta, a missionary-educated Kikuyu. The latter were exemplified by the "Forty Group," an urban criminal gang with ties to nationalist politics.[8]

Mau Mau (the name the British gave to the movement) was born out of this combustible mix of motives and factions. It began with the administering of oaths of loyalty to the Kikuyu tribe among various communities in the late 1940s. These oaths were said to have mystical power, so a quasi-religious aspect was also injected into the movement.[9]

By 1950 the colonial government was concerned enough about the spread of oathing among the Kikuyu to outlaw the movement. From 1950 to 1952, the suppressed movement continued to spread, though the British initiated "counter-oathing" ceremonies as well.[10] This struggle remained relatively nonviolent until May 1952, when militants killed a village elder and a police informer. More deaths followed as militants killed those who refused to take oaths or worked to support the colonial regime.[11]

The new governor, Sir Evelyn Baring, arrived at the end of September 1952, and within days "the most senior African official under Kenya's colonial administration," Chief Waruhiu wa Kungu, was found murdered. Baring determined that violence in Kenya was in danger of getting out of control but that the situation was not irreparable with swift, decisive action. He asked London for permission to declare a state of emergency, which was approved.[12]

Early Emergency, October 1952–May 1953

The state of emergency was declared on October 20, 1952. Simultaneously, Operation Jock Scott was launched by the Kenya Police, including the intelligence-gathering Special Branch, supported by the British Army. This operation sought to arrest all suspected Mau Mau leaders. This list included both true militants and moderates like Kenyatta; unfortunately, leaks within the government meant that many on the list were prepared. Groups of militants fled to the dense forest regions, while the moderates were arrested. Rather than decapitating Mau Mau, Jock Scott empowered the militants by removing the moderates and also aided Kikuyu mobilization by the insurgents, as it provided a major symbol of colonial oppression.[13]

British Army involvement in this early period of the Emergency was limited. The Army command in Kenya was a relative backwater in 1952, with no European units. Instead, the Army was represented by the Kenya Regiment, a Territorial Army unit that recruited white settlers, and the King's African Rifles, which recruited Africans from across British colonies in Africa. At the beginning of the Emergency, a battalion of the Lancashire Fusiliers was flown to Kenya from the Suez Canal zone, principally to reassure the white settlers.[14]

It was the Kenya Police and the Kenya Police Reserve (KPR) that were initially responsible for operations against the Mau Mau. Both were white settler–dominated organizations, though the police would be supplemented by contract officers from Britain. The KPR were police auxiliaries drawn from the white settlers, most of whom worked only part time for the KPR.[15] These forces were supplemented beginning in November 1952 by African loyalist militia units known as Home Guard (also called Kikuyu Guard).[16] Recruitment for these units, bolstered by incentives such as the issuance of weapons and an exemption from the poll tax, expanded rapidly. Writing about this period, the historian David Anderson notes, "For the first eight months the British military stood back and let the white highlanders, the police and—increasingly—the Home Guard get on with it."[17]

This proved deeply problematic, as the KPR in particular consisted of armed white settlers with little discipline. This indiscipline, combined with settler hostility to any manifestation of African nationalism, which threatened their privileged position, led to rampant abuse. Further, the settlers were no more willing to compromise on any political issues than they had been earlier. This combination only strengthened Mau Mau, as the security forces were seen by many Kikuyu not as protectors but as oppressors.[18]

During this period Mau Mau developed two principal strongholds. The first was in the highland forests around Mount Kenya and the Aberdare Mountains. It was to here that many of the Mau Mau leaders fleeing Jock Scott had traveled, and initially it proved to be an extraordinarily good insurgent base. Heavily forested and with an elevation of over eight thousand feet, these highland forests were difficult terrain. At the same time, the forests were close enough to Kikuyu population concentrations that the guerrillas were able to obtain food and supplies.[19]

The second base was urban, principally in the African neighborhoods around Nairobi. Known as Eastlands, these neighborhoods varied from public housing estates to shantytowns. Many parts of Eastlands had, in the years before the Emergency, become almost lawless. Many of the gangs associated with Mau Mau, such as the Forty Group, were based here, so it was natural that this area became home to the urban resistance.[20]

Mau Mau quickly demonstrated its power and resilience through operations in and around both base areas. In November 1952, barely a month into the Emergency, one of the major leaders of moderate middle-class Africans in Nairobi, Tom Mbotela, was murdered in Eastlands.[21] In March 1953, guerrillas operating from the Aberdare Forest massacred loyalist African families in the village of Lari in Kiambu District; the Home Guard and KPR immediately launched a retaliatory massacre.[22]

Both Governor Baring and the government in London were shocked into further action by the rising tide of violence. In January 1953, Major General W. R. Hinde was dispatched to act as staff officer to Baring to provide more high-level professional leadership. Hinde, unfortunately, had relations among the white settlers, with whom he sympathized. Combined with his very general brief from London, which was simply to "jolly things along," his settler sympathies meant that Hinde proved ineffective as a leader (though he was generally regarded as a good officer who laid the groundwork for later success). His position was clarified early in April 1953 when he was made Director of Operations.[23]

Even in this very early period, elements of the British Army's organizational culture were apparent. The policy directives for the first half of 1953 note the critical importance of intelligence and the threefold task of the Army: help secure police posts until the police and Home Guard could operate alone; act as a reserve for emergencies; and conduct mobile operations against large gangs. Likewise, airpower and other firepower were to be used if required, though "experience shows that suitable targets are rare in present conditions."[24] In addition, the role of the Home Guard is emphasized as being of "*paramount importance.*"[25] Thus, from the beginning the Army defined its role as requiring close cooperation with both other government organizations (for example, police) and indigenous forces (for example, the Home Guard).

In addition to the dispatch of Hinde, additional Regular Army units were sent to support the security forces. In April 1953, Thirty-Nine Brigade, consisting of a battalion from two regiments (the Devons and the Buffs) arrived in Kenya to provide additional military capability. In addition, two additional battalions of the King's African Rifles under Seventy Brigade had been moved into the country, bringing the total to six battalions. Yet despite this buildup, the Army continued to remain on the sidelines, principally acting in a defensive role, though it did make sweeps in and around the Aberdares.[26]

British Written Doctrine for Counterinsurgency, 1952

By 1952 the British experience in Malaya had produced a written doctrine of sorts for counterinsurgency. It was entitled *The Conduct of Anti-terrorist Operations, Malaya* (generally referred to as ATOM) and sought to encapsulate lessons from the ongoing conflict in Malaya. This manual was written for distribution outside Malaya to spread operational insights from the conflict.[27]

ATOM differed from previous colonial policing and colonial internal security but in ways that were consonant with those previous experiences. For example, ATOM emphasized the importance of integration with civilian agencies (the colonial administration and police) through a system of war executive committees from the most senior levels down to the district level.[28] It devotes one chapter to the organization and operations of platoons and two to small-unit patrolling.[29] It also noted the importance of controlling food supplies to deny support to insurgents.[30] "Home Guards," locals who were recruited to protect villages part time, were to be used to protect the population from the insurgents (as noted, this was done in Kenya even before the Army arrived in force).[31] Finally, it emphasized the importance of collecting intelligence from a wide variety of sources.[32]

The Army Acts: Erskine and Counterinsurgency, June 1953–May 1955

In May 1953, the commander in chief for the Middle East visited Kenya and, after conferring with the War Office in London, decided to establish a separate military headquarters for East Africa (previously subordinate to Middle East Land Forces command) to allow more attention to Kenya. The officer chosen for the new position was General George "Bobbie" Erskine. Erskine was a veteran of both World War II and interwar India. A product of public school, Sandhurst, and a Rifle regiment, he was highly representative of the British Army officer corps.[33]

When offered the job, Erskine initially wanted powers similar to those held by Sir Gerald Templer in Malaya. This would have made him the "Supremo" over both the security forces and civilian administration. While this was turned down, he was given operational control over the nonmilitary security forces.[34]

Erskine's arrival meant that the Army was now firmly in command of security force operations, and changes began to take place almost immediately. Erskine emphasized the political nature of the conflict and that its solution would be political as well as military. This would require careful organization and administration of the political-military campaign. He sought to combine improved intelligence collection with offensive operations in order to break up the guerrilla bands in the forest. Unsurprisingly, he requested copies of ATOM almost as soon as he arrived (and would request more copies later in the year).[35]

Erskine's assessment placed much of the blame for the insurgency on the colonial administration, initially attributing all the problems of Kenya to "rotten administration . . . [I]n my opinion they want a new set of civil servants and decent police."[36] He also took a very dim view of the white settlers. In his letters home to his wife, he called Kenya "a sunny land for shady people."[37] He later wrote, "I hate the guts of them all . . . they are middle class sluts."[38] Yet he was equally aware that he would have to work with the settlers as well as the colonial administration. Improving the civilian side of administration and integrating military efforts were thus Erskine's top priorities.

The system of counterinsurgency administration that was initially put in place in 1953 was similar to that in Malaya. At the top was the Colony Emergency Committee, whose membership included the governor, the deputy governor, a representative of Erskine, several other colonial administrators, and a representative of the settlers, Michael Blundell. This body made policy decisions, which were then implemented by the Deputy Director of Operations' Committee.[39]

This arrangement at the top would be streamlined further in March 1954, after the promulgation of a new constitution that enabled a multiracial government for Kenya. The new organization was termed the War Council and consisted of only Governor Baring, the deputy governor, Erskine, and Blundell, with support from a dedicated staff. This arrangement further increased high-level policy coordination among the security forces, colonial administration, and the white settlers. In terms of the latter, the clear intent was "to co-opt and to use the advice of the more moderate Europeans—and to bring home to them the realities of both the military and the wider political situation—and to isolate the more militant."[40]

Below this level were provincial-, district-, and divisional-level Emergency Committees.[41] The district-level committees were actually created first; the membership of these committees included the district commissioner, senior police and military officers in the area, and relevant colonial officers. The settlers wanted to control these committees by appointing both a chairman and an executive officer to them. A compromise was reached whereby a settler would frequently be appointed executive officer, but the chairmanship remained firmly under the civilian colonial administration.[42]

There was, perhaps unsurprisingly, frequent friction between the military and those committees most dominated by white settler influence. The settlers were interested in preserving their economic livelihood, whereas the military was focused on eliminating the insurgents. Differences emerged over such issues as static protection of farms (the settler preference) versus patrolling (the military preference). However, despite this friction, the system of extensive political-military integration was never abandoned.[43]

In addition to political coordination, Erskine also believed that discipline and professionalism were critical elements of the campaign. Within a month of taking command, he issued orders banning the practice of paying bounties to soldiers for killing Africans and declaring that he would personally be involved in the investigation of any outside complaints of abuse by the security forces. He dismissed the brigade commander of the King's African Rifles for allowing indiscipline and abuse in his troops and court-martialed a captain in the unit for gross abuse of prisoners.[44]

Erskine also launched military offensives against the insurgents. His initial military efforts to engage Mau Mau units in the forest, undertaken with the police and Home Guard, proved deeply frustrating. Operations Primrose, Buttercup, and Carnation swept into the forests in July and August 1953 with minimal success. After these initial offensives, Erskine requested and received additional British battalions in September 1953. The Lancashire Fusiliers were replaced by the elite Black Watch (a regiment of the Highlanders). Forty-Nine Brigade, consisting of the Royal Northumberland Fusiliers and the Inniskillings, was dispatched as well, bringing the total number of British battalions to five; in November the King's Own Yorkshire Light Infantry would arrive, for a total of six British battalions (the maximum level attained), not including the battalions of the King's African Rifles. Erskine then launched more offensives, seeking to pursue the insurgents by constant patrolling.[45]

The Army's review of Operation Buttercup is telling, as it specifically notes that the operation produced no major contacts with gangs of insurgents, in part because the units used were too big. It described the operation as covering too much area too fast, while at the same time calling for more training of the Home Guard. More deliberately paced operations, with smaller units covering smaller areas, was the preferred solution.[46] Erskine thought Operation Carnation had been more effective than Buttercup but noted that getting past the insurgent sentries remained difficult in these operations, presumably in part due to their scale and the size of the units involved.[47]

The emphasis on small-unit operations would appear repeatedly in operational assessments and planning. One such assessment noted that "past experience has proved that large scale (company or more) operations . . . do not produce results comparable with the effort involved.[48]

Firepower was limited in these operations. Most firepower was provided by mortars integral to infantry units. Erskine's main source of heavy firepower was provided by outmoded aircraft, principally Harvard light bombers and Lincoln heavy bombers. However, these were used only deep in the forest areas, which were all but uninhabited (apart from the insurgents) and had been declared off limits to the population. Erskine noted that he "refused flat to use them [the Air Force] . . . anywhere, in an offensive role, except in the prohibited areas."[49]

There were procedures in place to allow troops in close contact with large gangs of insurgents to call in air support. This mechanism, referred to as the Mushroom procedure, still restricted the use of aerial firepower to twenty-pound bombs, which could be delivered accurately with little risk of collateral damage.[50] According to one source, this procedure was used only nine times between June 1954 and July 1955.[51]

Additionally, Erskine had one artillery battery and an armored car squadron which were used as a mobile column in open terrain. Neither the aircraft nor the mobile column was thought to have much military utility.[52] Erskine commented that the mobile column was useful for morale but did not produce spectacular results.[53] Over the course of the entire Emergency only about twenty-four thousand rounds of artillery were fired by the battery.[54]

In addition to political-military integration and offensive operations, Erskine greatly expanded intelligence collection. However, Erskine realized that the Army could not and should not be the only source of intelligence. Instead, the intelligence demands of the war required extensive integration of Army officers with police, local informers, and turncoat insurgents.

The initial improvements in intelligence began with the reorganization of intelligence in Kenya in 1953. Acting on the advice of the Director of the Security Service (a.k.a. MI5, Britain's domestic intelligence agency), Sir Percy Sillitoe, and senior Security Service officer A. M. MacDonald, a series of intelligence committees were created at the national, provincial, and district levels to integrate intelligence. MacDonald remained in Kenya as the intelligence adviser to the governor, chairing the national intelligence committee and working to improve the capabilities of the Police Special Branch.[55]

In order to further improve intelligence, Erskine and his intelligence staff began sending sergeants from the Kenya Regiment to supplement Police Special Branch activity. These sergeants were termed field intelligence assistants (FIAs); as natives they were believed to have good local knowledge that would make them excellent collectors. However, some level of oversight was needed, so Regular Army officers were soon dispatched as district military intelligence officers (DMIOs) to provide that oversight and ensure that intelligence was properly integrated.[56]

One of those British Army officers selected to be a DMIO was Captain Frank Kitson. Kitson had the same background as Erskine: public school, Sandhurst, and a commission in the Rifle Brigade. He was thus an equally typical example of the British Army officer corps; however, unlike Erskine, Kitson had no colonial experience. Before Kenya, his entire Army career (1945–53) had been as an infantry officer in Germany. In addition, he had no background in police or intelligence operations.[57]

Kitson arrived in Kenya in late August 1953 and was assigned as the DMIO of Kiambu District in the Central Province. This district was strongly contested by the insurgents, as it was located between the southern end of the Aberdare Forest and Nairobi. It was thus a key link between the insurgent rural sanctuary and the urban resistance in Nairobi. Kitson was subsequently made responsible for the neighboring district of Thika as well as Nairobi itself.[58]

Kitson was given high levels of autonomy in his role as DMIO; he essentially defined his own job and could carry it out as he saw fit. Kitson, despite his lack of training in intelligence, quickly realized that he would have to build an intelligence collection network relying heavily on other organizations.[59] In his memoir of this period he writes:

> I had no idea of how to get information because I had no training on the subject and knew no language other than English. This was a sobering fact which led me to decide that my only logical course was to organize other people to collect information for me . . . I only had one part-time K.P.R. officer, one full-time K.P.R. officer, and a recently married sergeant of the Kenya Regiment to do the collecting for me. They could only pick up a small proportion of the information I wanted. As a result I decided that I should have to collect information from every single person who came on it. Soldiers, policemen, district officers, Kikuyu Guard officers and the C.I.D. [Criminal Investigation Department] all had some. Until I had a larger organization of my own I would have to get it from them. The only way to do this was by visiting them often and making friends with them.[60]

Even after he received additional personnel, Kitson continued to work closely with all other elements of the security forces as part of the intelligence committees.

Operations in late 1953 continued to consist principally of small-unit activity. Kitson describes one on Christmas Eve 1953. A patrol from a company of the Black Watch received intelligence about the location of a group of insurgents and set out in pursuit, accompanied by a squad of police. After they caught up with the insurgents, a brief engagement took place, and the British took casualties, including the Black Watch company commander. Trapping the insurgents in a small valley, the Black Watch unit called for reinforcements, which were principally from the KPR, though supplemented by "most of the Black Watch company" and police. The KPR district commander arrived and took charge of the situation, yet he too was killed. Control passed back to the military when a replacement company commander arrived from the Black Watch. No indirect fire was used against the trapped insurgents, and the Black Watch assaulted the insurgent position the following morning.[61]

In addition to small-unit activity, the British Army believed that the Home Guard remained critical to success. The operating instructions for Thirty Nine Brigade for 1954 placed emphasis on both conducting small patrols and training the Home Guard.[62] Erskine repeatedly noted the importance of the loyal Kikuyu as the solution to the problem, even though (or perhaps because) the loyalists would likely be brutal in their actions. In June 1953 he wrote to the Chief of the Imperial General Staff that "there may be a tendency to cry 'Don't be too beastly to the Mau Mau' which we must resist. The loyal Kikuyu must be given an opportunity in every area to tidy up their own affairs—they will do this much better than the Government, and my operations are designed to give them the opportunity."[63] Writing a month later, he approvingly related an incident when "a certain dead Mau Mau was brought into a post held by a Lancashire Fusilier company and the Home Guard. One of the Home Guard identified the dead Mau Mau as his son and was delighted that his son had been killed."[64]

The Home Guard expanded rapidly in this period, numbering over twenty-five in Central Province by 1954.[65] Over this period the Home Guard acted much as Erskine seemed to desire, "tidying up their affairs" in an often "beastly" fashion, frequently as retaliation for Mau Mau violence. Abuses were common on both sides of what was essentially a civil war in the Kikuyu community.[66]

Yet at the same time the British Army also made extensive use of amnesty and former insurgents who changed sides. Erskine launched a surrender offer known as Green Branch in August 1953, over settler objections. It met with limited success but would be followed by other efforts.[67] Eventually both rank and file and insurgent leaders would be incorporated in the British effort.

One of the most notable leaders the British sought to use was Waruhiu Itote, known by the nom de guerre General China. One of the most prominent insurgent commanders, China was captured in January 1954 and interrogated extensively before being sentenced to death. However, he was offered a chance to help negotiate the surrender of Mau Mau forces in exchange for a pardon. China accepted, and several months of negotiations with other insurgent leaders, called Operation Wedgwood commenced. Though the surrender negotiations eventually collapsed, in part due to suspicion from within both the government security forces and the insurgents, China nonetheless proved an excellent source of intelligence.[68] When the surrender negotiations collapsed, the British Army executed preparations it had made for such an eventuality and launched Operation Overdraft, a highly successful targeted operation based on China's intelligence.[69]

In April 1954, Kitson interrogated a captured insurgent who proved willing to defect and begin working with the government. This provided not only intelligence but also the idea that Kitson could form his own groups of faux insurgents (termed "pseudo-gangs"). These pseudo-gangs, led by whites but principally composed of both former insurgents and loyal Africans, would be sent out to interact with real insurgent groups to gather intelligence. Pseudo-gangs were very small unit operations, consisting of only a handful of men. Kitson felt that this was the most effective intelligence-gathering technique, and it was soon expanded to other areas of Kenya on Erskine's instruction.[70]

The use of pseudo-gangs was amplified by the creation of other small special units. So-called Trojan teams were created to support and rapidly act on intelligence gathered by the DMIOs. Tracker teams were also formed to pursue small insurgent gangs in the forest.[71]

April 1954 would prove to be a turning point against the urban resistance in Nairobi. Following months of planning, the British Army, in conjunction with the police, the KPR, and the Home Guard, launched Operation Anvil. This operation sealed off three of Eastlands' housing estates and slums with five battalions of British troops and a battalion of the King's African Rifles along with hundreds of police, KPR, and Home Guard. The total force numbered about twenty thousand, making this the largest operation of the conflict.[72]

Once the areas were sealed, search teams led by a combination of colonial administration district officers, colonial labor officers, and the KPR began to sort through the inhabitants. Those who were lacking documentation, lacked a place of residence in the city, or were identified by informers as Mau Mau were detained. According to a campaign history written by Erskine for the military, 30,000 men were screened, with 16,538 detained.[73] They were then sorted and classified in detention camps.[74]

Lasting from April to July 1954, Operation Anvil broke up much of the Mau Mau apparatus in Nairobi, though it did not entirely eliminate it. The struggle between insurgents and the government would continue until late 1955. However, it had principally become a contest between the police, particularly Special Branch, and very small numbers of insurgents. Some of these insurgents would be those released from the detention camps after being incorrectly classified as uninvolved with the insurgency, indicating that the intelligence apparatus was far from infallible.[75] Indeed, the entire process of screening was difficult, relying heavily on Africans identifying and classifying fellow Africans.

In addition to Operation Anvil, the British also sought to concentrate the population in secured areas controlled by the Home Guard. Fortified camps were constructed, and much of the rural population in Kikuyu areas was resettled in them. By early 1955, hundreds of thousands of Kikuyu were resettled as part of the "villagization" strategy. By October 1955, villagization was essentially complete, with roughly 1.75 million Kikuyu concentrated in 845 villages.[76] This strategy hinged on the existence of loyal Home Guard and chiefs willing to work for the colonial administration, as the British Army provided only minimal oversight through the Emergency Committee system.[77]

Following Anvil, Erskine turned operations toward securing the areas around Nairobi and isolating the insurgents in the forest sanctuaries. Ditches were dug with forced labor along the forest edges; the ditches were kept under observation by the Home Guard. Offensive operations were launched along the forest borders as well.[78]

An example of the type of operations conducted during this period is an engagement to the northwest of Nairobi in October 1954. The security forces in the area were informed by a young African worker that a large group of insurgents was camped in a swampy area on a nearby plantation. A platoon of police surrounded the insurgent base and attacked but was repulsed. The police commander then called for reinforcements, which took the form of Kenya Regiment officers leading Kikuyu Guards, more police, and a platoon of the Royal Northumberland Fusiliers. After a surrender offer was made to the insurgents and rejected, the Fusiliers shelled the enemy position with mortars before assaulting in the morning, while the other security forces maintained the cordon.[79]

Erskine at this point felt confident enough in how operations were progressing to create his own equivalent to ATOM. Thus in 1954, his command issued *A Handbook on Anti–Mau Mau Operations*. Based on ATOM, it also incorporated the specific context and lessons of Kenya.[80] Like ATOM, it had a chapter dedicated to the system of war executive committees.[81] It also had a chapter on intelligence and two on patrolling.[82] It also detailed the limits of airpower as well as the Mushroom procedure for calling for limited fire support outside the prohibited areas.[83]

By late 1954, the forest sanctuaries were deemed sufficiently isolated to launch a major offensive against them. Operation Hammer was launched against the Aberdare Forest sanctuary in December 1954. It was intended to take an "inside-out" approach against the insurgents; British forces would begin in the very high moorlands of the mountain range and seek to force the insurgents down toward the barriers set up along the forest edge. Operation First Flute, using a similar approach, began around Mount Kenya in February 1955.[84]

Even as British offensive operations took place in the forests, Erskine prepared another amnesty offer. This offer was made in conjunction with a major effort to reform and reorganize the Home Guard, which had been a source of abuse of the population and in some cases now seemed to be prolonging rather than ending the conflict. In January 1955, "insurgents were told that they would not be prosecuted for any terrorist offenses (even those liable for the death penalty) though they would be detained, and the Home Guard were told of the forthcoming reorganization and assured that no action would be taken in respect of the past but strict discipline would be required for the future." The offer was to be open through July 1955; roughly 1,000 insurgents surrendered, leaving an estimated 4,500 to 5,000 in the forests.[85]

Erskine's tour as commander ended in May 1955. At that point, the insurgency had been broken. The insurgents in the forests were forced to break up into small bands constantly on the move. The areas outside the forest and in Nairobi were much more secure, if not entirely safe. This increased security accelerated the process of drawing down the British Army units in Kenya, which began in 1954, in the last few months of Erskine's tour.[86]

Assessing Theoretical Explanations for Counterinsurgency Operations, 1953–55

British Army operations in Kenya under Erskine were characterized by small-unit operations, close cooperation with locals and civilian organizations, and limited and discriminate use of firepower. In terms of operations, Erskine had at most only six British and six African battalions for the entire country. Operations using more than one battalion were extremely rare, the main exception being Operation Anvil. Instead the focus was on operations of battalion size and smaller, including the very small pseudo-gang operations begun by Kitson.

From the beginning, the British Army worked closely with locals (in the form of the Kenya Police, KPR, and Home Guard) as well as civilian organizations. This was most clearly exemplified by the system of committees instituted at the national, provincial, district, and division levels of government. Firepower was very limited outside of the forest areas, and even in the forests was considered an auxiliary to sweeps and patrolling.

There was also little difference between written doctrine and operations. Initially taking ATOM as written doctrine, Erskine and his subordinates implemented most if not all of the guidance in that document. After gaining additional experience with the unique circumstances of Kenya, Erskine's command created a handbook based on ATOM to give specific doctrinal guidance for operations against the Mau Mau.

The hypothesis that military organizations respond rationally to their environment is supported by the evidence from this period of British Army counterinsurgency in Kenya. Erskine's operations proved extraordinarily effective against the insurgency, reducing it from a rising threat across the country to scattered bands in the forests in barely two years. Hypotheses relating to civilian intervention are not supported, as apart from approving Erskine's appointment as the commander of forces in Kenya, the civilian government of Britain did nothing to direct operations. Similarly the hypothesis that doctrine is shaped by the search for resources, autonomy, and prestige also receives little support; Erskine was given significant autonomy and resources as soon as he was appointed. His choice of operations had little effect on either. Finally, the cultural hypothesis is also supported by evidence from this period, as operations conformed to the maritime army cultural archetype.

Mopping Up: Lathbury and Counterinsurgency, May 1955–November 1956

Erskine's replacement was Lieutenant General Gerald "Legs" Lathbury. Lathbury was, like Erskine, a public school and Sandhurst product. He was commissioned into the Oxford and Buckinghamshire Light Infantry

Regiment before being intimately involved in the creation of British Parachute units in 1941.[87]

The environment he inherited was one that was simultaneously much more secure and more difficult than the one Erskine had found in 1953. Both Nairobi and the rural areas outside the forests had been all but totally pacified thanks to Anvil and villagization. The rebel bands in the forests were increasingly fragmented, poorly supplied, and all but incapable of mounting major offensives. Yet the very fragmentation of the insurgent groups, combined with the skill they had developed in evading security forces, made finding and eliminating them much more difficult.

Lathbury's response to this environment was to initially continue with Erskine's policies. He left the amnesty offer made early in 1955 open for another month while continuing to reorganize and demobilize the Home Guard, with those not demobilized absorbed into a tribal police and police reserve system totaling about nine thousand personnel. He also continued the offensive operations in the forest regions, beginning with Operation Gimlet at the end of May 1955.[88]

The operations for the most part remained small-unit patrolling in the forest regions, with each battalion given a section of forest to patrol and set up ambushes.[89] For example, the Gloucestershire Regiment rotated into Kenya in April 1955, and, after establishing a base at Gilgil, its "various companies were allocated areas of responsibility in which they set up temporary camps. These were frequently on European owned farms, where they were made very welcome. Companies actively patrolled their areas with the help of local guides, looking for Mau Mau gangs." The companies in turn dispatched platoon-size patrols in the forest and its boundaries.[90]

In June 1955, the British also took steps to enable the creation of an alternative to Mau Mau by legalizing African political organizations at the district level. Both the governor and Lathbury felt that as the Emergency was ending as a military crisis, a political solution was more vital. Lathbury noted that "gaining the fullest possible information on African political activity, particularly among the Kikuyu, is now and will be an intelligence task of equal if not greater importance than keeping track of the terrorist."[91]

With the expiration of the amnesty offer in July, Lathbury decided to increase pressure against the forest strongholds. In July and August, Operations Dante and Beatrice would be launched against the Aberdare and Mount Kenya regions, respectively. Dante was one of the largest operations since Anvil, using four battalions of troops (three British and one King's African Rifles), who would surround an area known to contain insurgent groups. This area would be bombed and shelled, with the intent to drive insurgents toward ambushes set up by the battalions. This part of the operation would last seven to ten days, after which the troops would move in toward the center of the area.[92]

Dante was marked by only modest success. The plan worked to some degree, with over thirty engagements by the ambushing units in the first four days. However, the number of insurgents killed was very small, as they apparently broke contact quickly in the dense forest. Kitson, who was present during the operation, also noted that the troops, many of whom were National Service draftees, were not very good marksmen.[93]

Dante would be the last large-unit operation for the British Army in Kenya. Lathbury would subsequently reorient the Army in Kenya toward training for "silent movement, the use of trackers [typically surrendered Mau Mau] and tracker dogs, and quick and accurate shooting," the latter apparently confirming Kitson's critique of the soldiers' marksmanship. Lathbury also felt that the need for battalion-size formations was decreasing, echoing earlier critiques of large-unit operations: "mounting of large scale operations involving a heavy concentration of forces was unlikely to be profitable except [when] it became clear that considerable numbers of terrorists were located in a given area."[94] Accordingly, he announced at the beginning of September 1955 that a brigade headquarters and roughly thirty-five hundred British Army and King's African Rifles soldiers would be withdrawn over four months.[95]

Central to this new approach was small-unit action by the pseudo-gangs pioneered by Kitson. These units were renamed Special Forces Teams and centralized as an element of Special Branch under Assistant Police Superintendent Ian Henderson. Crucially, Lathbury and Henderson decided to allow the Special Forces Teams, unlike the pseudo-gangs, to operate without any white oversight despite being composed mostly of former insurgents. They would be armed and sent autonomously out into the forest to hunt their former comrades; clearly, the level of trust in these locals was extraordinarily high.[96]

Lathbury also implemented further restrictions to limit the insurgents' access to food and supplies. This included prohibition of food cultivation within three miles of the forest sanctuary. By December 1955, the insurgents were desperately short of food and ammunition, even as the small units harried them. Only 2,000 to 2,500 insurgents were estimated to be left.[97]

These remaining insurgents, however, showed no signs of surrendering as of January 1956. This was likely due to a combination of fear of being subjected to the death penalty and the continuing presence of powerful leaders among the insurgents. Most notable among the leaders was Dedan Kimathi, who had been one of the main commanders in the forest throughout the insurgency. Kimathi was the most nationalist of the Mau Mau leaders, an inspiring symbol and an effective insurgent. As long as he remained at large, it seemed that the insurgency would sputter on.[98]

Even as Kimathi continued to elude capture, the Special Forces Teams and small-unit operations by the British Army eliminated other leaders. From

January to July 1956, roughly fourteen hundred of the remaining insurgents were accounted for, leaving an estimated five hundred in the forests. Over this period, Lathbury reduced the British Army presence by two more battalions and "planned to transfer responsibility for the conduct of day-to-day operations from the army to the police between October and the end of the year."[99]

Finally, on October 21, 1956, a concerted manhunt by Ian Henderson and his Special Forces Teams cornered Kimathi in the forest. He was wounded and captured while trying to flee; at this point estimates were that there were only four hundred fifty insurgents remaining. Both the governor and Lathbury took this as a sign that the Army was no longer required, so on November 17, 1956, the Army was withdrawn from operations in Kenya.[100]

Assessing Theoretical Explanations for Counterinsurgency Operations, 1955–56

British counterinsurgency operations in Kenya in 1955–56 were essentially the same as those from 1953 to 1955. With the exception of Operations Beatrice and Dante, they were focused on small-unit operations. Indeed, after those two large operations, the British under Lathbury redoubled efforts to conduct effective small-unit operations. Firepower would also remain limited. Dante was the last use of heavy firepower such as artillery and airpower in Kenya, with the bomber aircraft withdrawn by September 1955.[101]

Cooperation with both local natives (African and whites) and civilian authorities continued to be a vital part of British Army counterinsurgency. By 1956 Lathbury was relying heavily on Special Forces Teams composed of former insurgents under Henderson's civilian police Special Branch. He would certainly give credit to Henderson, noting, "Ian Henderson has probably done more than any single individual to bring the emergency to an end."[102]

As with the first period of operations, this period gives support to both the hypothesis that military organizations respond rationally to their environment and to the cultural hypothesis. The British Army's operations were very effective and adjusted to the environment as it changed, as the abandonment of anything other than small-unit operations in mid-1955 demonstrates. However, the rapidity and smoothness of these adjustments (taking place in less than four years) suggests that culture helped the British Army adjust to the challenge of counterinsurgency in Kenya.

Kenya presented a difficult and ambiguous challenge to the British Army. It was forced to function in both urban slums and forested highlands, working among a population with both hostile and loyal elements. The white settlers provided valuable allies but also were the primary source of the political and economic grievances fueling the insurgency.

The British Army responded to this ambiguous challenge in ways that were often highly coercive, yet always consonant with the elements of British Army culture. Operations in Kenya were based principally around small-unit operations, close cooperation with locals and civilians, and limited firepower. Ultimately this combination proved highly successful, though Kenya would subsequently be given independence.

Counterinsurgency in the Land of Two Rivers

The Americans and British in Iraq, 2003–8

The U.S.-led invasion of Iraq in March 2003, which included a substantial British element, reintroduced the U.S. Army and Marines and the British Army to the challenge of counterinsurgency in a foreign land. This provides an opportunity to further test the hypotheses on doctrine for each organization. The conduct of counterinsurgency by each of the three in the same country at the same time also allows for the control of many variables, including the terrain, weather, language, and, to a somewhat lesser degree, population and enemy.

This chapter presents evidence on two issues. The first is cultural change and continuity for each of the three organizations in the period between the end of its experience in counterinsurgency in Vietnam or Kenya and the beginning of the Iraq War. The second is counterinsurgency doctrine and operations conducted in Iraq during the period 2003–8.

There are limits to what can be conclusively demonstrated about the organizations' activities in Iraq at present. Most publicly available information is derived from news reporting, which is by its nature somewhat fragmentary. Some additional accounts based on interviews are beginning to appear. Yet much history remains to be written, particularly as presently classified documents become available. The following discussion of Iraq is therefore much more tentative than the previous discussions of Vietnam and Kenya.

Fortunately, I am able to draw on two sets of information that amplify news reporting and current histories. The first is conversations and briefings with U.S. military and intelligence personnel on Iraq throughout the period 2003–9.[1] The second is my own experience as a civilian analyst and adviser to U.S. forces in Iraq, which totaled roughly nine months from August 2007 to August 2008. I then briefly returned to Iraq in 2009 as a consultant.[2] This additional information adds some level of granularity to this account that would otherwise be lacking, particularly for U.S. forces.

The U.S. Army, 1973–2003

The year 1973 was the low-water mark of the U.S. Army in the twentieth century. The Army had not brought the Vietnam War to a successful conclusion yet had reduced readiness in Europe to fight the war. Discipline was shaky, morale was low, and combat effectiveness poor at best.[3]

In terms of Army culture, there were three major developments in its environment in this period. The first and most important development was the end of the draft. It was to be replaced by an all-volunteer force (AVF), as the Vietnam experience had made the draft, never well liked by the American public, untenable.

The end of the draft struck at one of the bedrocks of Army managerial culture. No longer could it count on simply requisitioning huge masses of manpower that would be turned into corps, divisions, and brigades. Instead, it would have to persuade and cajole young Americans to join of their own free will.

The second development was the evolving U.S.-Soviet nuclear balance. Until the 1960s, U.S. superiority in strategic nuclear systems was the centerpiece of deterrence in Europe. By 1973 the era of nuclear parity had arrived, as the Soviets had a large and relatively survivable strategic force along with their own tactical and theater systems.[4] This cast doubt on the credibility of nuclear deterrence, yet at the same time made conventional forces more important to the United States and NATO.

The third development was the evolving nature of the technology of conventional war. From communications to lasers and precision-guided weapons, technology was increasing the mobility and firepower of conventional units at a rapid pace. Of course, this new technology was often complicated and so required well-trained personnel to utilize optimally.[5]

At precisely this moment, the U.S. Army witnessed another army, surprised and outnumbered, fight off two determined Soviet-trained and -supplied armies. This was the 1973 Yom Kippur War, in which the Israeli Army faced the Egyptian and Syrian armies. The central lessons of the Yom Kippur War appeared to be that modern combat was incredibly lethal, but that a smaller, well-equipped, and well-trained force could defeat larger armies even when beginning from a disadvantageous position. The U.S. Army, traditionally centered on deliberate mobilization, would have to be able to mobilize and win quickly.[6]

These three factors, particularly the end of the draft, combined with the Israeli example to shift Army culture over the course of the next fifteen years. The Army began to change in terms of managerial culture, as labor was no longer a free good. In particular, much more emphasis was given to producing units high in quality rather than just in quantity.

The changes to meet this requirement were extensive. Briefly summarizing, the Army sought to buy higher-quality equipment in somewhat lower quantity, while vastly improving training for units. On the acquisition side, this meant the so-called Big Five systems, including what would become the M1 Abrams tank and the M2 Bradley infantry fighting vehicle, as well as additional systems such as the multiple-launch rocket system (MLRS). On the training side, the Army constructed the high-technology National Training Center (NTC) at Fort Irwin and emphasized improving the quality of individual recruits.

However, even this cultural shift was limited. The Army continued to emphasize planning in terms of units of battalion size and larger, particularly divisions. NTC was tailored to prepare battalion- and brigade-size units for high-tempo mechanized warfare. The end of the draft may have forced some adjustment in Army managerial culture, but it remained limited.[7]

Although the Cold War ended in 1989 with no shots fired along the European central front, within a year the Army would be called upon to fight a mostly Soviet-equipped army after the Iraqi invasion of Kuwait in August 1990. The result was spectacular, with U.S. casualties minimal and the devastation of the Iraqi Army nearly total. This success validated the post-Vietnam Army's evolution, which despite the changes noted earlier still viewed the world in much the same way as the pre-Vietnam Army.[8]

U.S. Army culture in 2003 was therefore, despite significant changes in both its domestic and international environment, remarkably similar to what it had been at the end of the Vietnam era. The end of the draft had the most effect, as it removed a central element that Army culture had rested upon. This caused a modest change in managerial culture, focusing on improving the quality of both labor and capital to be managed. The overall strategic culture remained focused on employing large units and extensive firepower in high-intensity conflict while minimizing involvement with other services and agencies.[9]

The U.S. Marine Corps, 1973–2003

The Marines, who had been the first combat units into Vietnam, were the first service to be fully withdrawn from the conflict, with the last Marine units leaving in 1970. The Corps thus had something of a head start in planning for the future. Further, as noted, the Marine Corps had only briefly had to rely on the draft during World War II and Vietnam, so the subsequent shift to the AVF impacted it the least.

Despite these advantages, the post-Vietnam period was still challenging for the Corps and its two strategic subcultures. Defense budgets were tight, and the U.S. appetite for small wars had reached its nadir, while there was little resurgence in the need for or viability of amphibious operations. The country was refocusing on the threat posed by the Soviets, particularly to Western Europe. All three of the other services were focusing heavily on what their contributions to NATO would be in a future war. The Marine Corps thus began seeking a piece of the NATO mission.

Marine interest in NATO missions was not entirely new, as large exercises in the Mediterranean dated to the 1960s. However, a 1970 joint Norwegian-U.S. defense study provided a new opportunity. This study concluded that NATO's "northern flank" needed additional protection, particularly Norway's far north. The Marine Corps leapt at the opportunity. In 1975 a Marine Amphibious Unit conducted maneuvers in Norway and Germany, the Marines' first NATO operation away from the Mediterranean. By the end of the 1970s, brigade-size maneuvers were being conducted by the Marines in Norway.[10]

Even as it found a quasi-amphibious mission in NATO, the Marine Corps was seeking other missions. One of the most notable national security debates in the late 1970s was on the need for a Rapid Deployment Force (RDF) to quickly move to reinforce states threatened by Soviet expansion. By the late 1970s, the principal area of concern was the Middle East, as Soviet naval power in the Mediterranean appeared to be increasing even as the Soviets moved into Afghanistan to prop up their client state. Previously the United States had relied on a friendly Iran as its bulwark in the Persian Gulf, but the ouster of the shah changed the strategic environment dramatically.

Some in the Marine Corps, such as General P. X. Kelley, embraced the RDF concept as another mission for which the Corps was well suited.[11] However, confronting heavy Soviet forces would be challenging for a force that was traditionally organized for either a relatively brief amphibious assault or for low-intensity conflict. The Marines would be forced to increasingly resemble the Army (though still conducting a form of amphibious operation) if they seriously embraced this mission, so Marine participation in the RDF was contentious. Even as these debates took place, the Marine Corps continued to be the force of choice for small-scale U.S. interventions in places like Lebanon.

The end of the Cold War came as many of the debates from the post-Vietnam era became increasingly heated. On one side were the heirs to the amphibious school, which advocated the heavier, RDF-oriented force structure.[12] One the other side of the debate were the small wars Marines. They argued that low-intensity conflict was the most likely form of warfare the Marines would be called on to wage in the future and should therefore be the focus of preparation and doctrine.[13] Rather than getting heavier, the Marines should stay relatively light and avoid heavy reliance on prepositioning and the massive logistical requirements that were the hallmark of the Army.

This debate was embodied in the two Commandants of the late Cold War and early interwar period. P. X. Kelley, commandant from 1983 to 1987, was a major proponent of the RDF, which was developed during his tenure. His successor, Alfred Gray, Commandant from 1987 to 1991, was much more focused on low-intensity conflict and took steps to rein in Kelley's embrace of heavy units. Gray, for example, decided to cut back heavily on Marine acquisition of the M1 tank.[14]

However, just as Gray seemed in position to shift the Marine Corps away from maneuver warfare, Saddam Hussein's Iraq invaded neighboring Kuwait. In the space of only a few months, the advance base subculture advocates of the RDF saw their concepts validated as the First and Second Marine Divisions surged to Saudi Arabia. Further, the argument that low-intensity conflict was to dominate Marine deployments in the future, though not disproved, did not appear supported by the short, intense, and successful Gulf War. Among other things, this led to expanded Marine acquisition of the M1 in the early 1990s.

However, the small wars Marines did not lose all influence in the 1990s. Charles Krulak, Commandant from 1995 to 1999, continually stressed that the Marine Corps was about producing skilled Marines rather than relying heavily on technology. A common refrain among Marines was that the other services "man their equipment," while the Marine Corps "equips its men."[15] Krulak also promulgated such concepts as the "strategic corporal" and the "three block war," which focused on low-intensity conflict and the importance of skilled personnel.[16]

In 2003 Marine culture was therefore unchanged. The amphibious subculture and small wars subculture continued to oscillate slightly in terms of who dominated the Corps at any given time, yet neither was any closer to establishing a durable hegemony. At the same time, the Corps continued to embrace the importance of small-unit leadership, with the Basic School essentially unchanged in role and focus.

Revitalization of the Quiet Professionals:
U.S. Army Special Forces, 1973–2003

After Vietnam, the decline in interest in small wars led to a fallow period for the Special Forces. However, three events at the very of end of the 1970s would reinvigorate the Special Forces' vitality. By 2003 Special Forces would be more capable and autonomous than ever before and would play a major role in Iraq.

The first event was the beginning of a Communist insurgency against the government of El Salvador. U.S. policy was to support the government, but to do so with as few U.S. forces as possible. The Special Forces would provide many of the advisers to the Salvadoran military, ensuring the vitality of the Special Forces' unconventional warfare mission. This would last throughout the 1980s.[17]

The second event was the failed attempt to rescue U.S. hostages held in Iran. This prompted efforts to ensure that the U.S. would have capabilities to conduct special operations more effectively in the future. Among other things, a Joint Special Operations Command (JSOC) was created in the early 1980s.[18]

Finally, the Soviet invasion of Afghanistan prompted a general resurgence in U.S. interest in unconventional warfare. U.S. aid to Afghan rebels was principally handled by the CIA, but CIA links to Special Forces remained strong. Special Forces personnel apparently provided training to rebels in some instances.[19]

The increasing importance of special operations eventually resulted in major bureaucratic change. The Defense Authorization Act of 1987 established the Special Operations Command (SOCOM): a four-star unified command with responsibility for all special operations activities. Though this reorganization stopped short of making special operations forces a true fifth service, it did result in the unification of all special operations under a major command. In 1989 SOCOM was given limited budget autonomy through a funding mechanism separate from the military service budgets. The combination of a separate command and limited funding autonomy gave SOCOM greater latitude and clout than it had ever enjoyed previously.[20]

Special Forces were only one small component of SOCOM, but nonetheless they benefited from the increase in budget and autonomy. The end of the Cold War thus had less impact on Special Forces than on the broader Army. Throughout the 1990s, Special Forces conducted unconventional warfare operations in both the Balkans and Somalia.[21]

One emerging problem, however, was the division between Special Forces and other special operations forces, including the so-called Special Mission Units (SMUs) in SOCOM. SMUs were created to conduct missions similar to the Iranian hostage rescue and operated under JSOC. In addition, Navy SEALs and Army Rangers, elite commando-oriented forces, also existed under SOCOM.

These other forces, with only a few exceptions, had a different strategic culture than Special Forces. While Special Forces sought to integrate closely with locals, these other forces focused on conducting so-called direct-action missions, essentially commando raids. While these orientations were not necessarily mutually exclusive, as Special Forces were also effective commandos, these differences meant that even within SOCOM the Special Forces often felt marginalized.[22]

In 2001 Special Forces working with CIA were the spearhead of the U.S. campaign in Afghanistan. CIA and Special Forces partnered with local forces (the so-called Northern Alliance) and were able to combine these forces with U.S. airpower to rapidly defeat the Taliban.[23] At the same time, Special Forces began training and supporting the Philippine military in counter-insurgency operations against Muslim rebels.[24] By 2003 Special Forces were in a position to become a major part of the Iraq War.

The British Army, 1960–2003

Following the end of the Mau Mau uprising in Kenya, the British government began to liquidate even more of its imperial possessions and overseas bases. This was accelerated by the Harold Wilson Labour government in 1967, which formally announced a withdrawal from commitments "east of Suez" beginning with Aden (in what is now Yemen). Formal requirement for the British Army to defend the empire vanished along with the empire (or so it seemed, as the Falkland Islands campaign of 1982 proved otherwise).

Even with the end of empire, the British Army retained two missions. The first was the British continental commitment in support of NATO, embodied in the British Army of the Rhine (BAOR). The second, from 1969 on, was in Northern Ireland, where the conflict between Catholic Republicans and Protestant Unionists resulted in a nasty civil war.

BAOR, along with the Berlin Brigade in West Berlin, represented a substantial commitment to the continent (averaging nearly sixty thousand men for most of the 1960s and 1970s). Moreover, with the end of National Service in 1960, the British Army was once again a volunteer force. Apart from manpower, BAOR required heavy equipment to face the mechanized forces of the Warsaw Pact; three of the four divisions committed to BAOR were armored divisions.[25]

Even as the British Army ended the imperial commitment and became accustomed to the challenge of forward deployment in Germany, it was called on to mediate in Northern Ireland. First deployed in 1969 to keep the peace between Catholic and Protestant, the Army was soon fighting extremists from both factions. The Army would remain in Northern Ireland until 2007, though after the Belfast Agreement (also known as the Good Friday Agreement) in 1998 this presence was mostly symbolic.

Counterinsurgency in Northern Ireland was extraordinarily difficult for the Army. One of the central reasons for this was that the civilian and local partners the Army was so accustomed to supporting were either absent or compromised by partisanship. The Parliament of Northern Ireland, the Royal Ulster Constabulary, the Ulster Special Constabulary (the so-called B Specials), and essentially all aspects of the government were dominated by the Protestants.[26]

The Army was thus massively handicapped in the initial years but eventually began to make progress as civilian partners were reformed or eliminated. The B Specials were disbanded in 1970, but real progress was not made until 1972, when the Parliament of Northern Ireland was eliminated and replaced by direct rule by the British Parliament. From 1972 the Army began to make progress against the insurgency through the use of amnesty (including the so-called supergrass informers), coordination with the police (which were at least partially reformed), census taking, and generally discriminate use of force.[27]

Operations were generally conducted by small units, initially company and platoon size but shifting to four-man patrols known as "bricks" after 1972. There were a few exceptions to eliminate no-go areas fortified by the Republicans, such as Operation Motorman. Motorman used more than twenty thousand troops backed by armored vehicles; as a result it cleared the no-go areas almost without resistance.[28]

The Army was also confronted by the problem of conducting counterinsurgency at home rather than abroad. Methods that had proved acceptable in previous counterinsurgency campaigns did not survive the scrutiny of democratic society. Interrogation techniques such as forcing individuals to stand for prolonged periods, sleep deprivation, exposure to white noise, and the like were explicitly permitted as recently as 1967. However, these techniques, termed "interrogation in depth," produced immense controversy in Northern Ireland before Prime Minister Edward Heath finally disallowed them in 1972.[29]

Detention without trial proved similarly untenable. Initial internments were launched in 1971 under the name Operation Demetrius. Over a thousand individuals were interned over the next few years. However, like interrogation in depth, the practice provoked an outcry and was suspended in 1975.[30]

Even as the British Army was pulled deeper into Northern Ireland, it was also conducting a counterinsurgency campaign in Oman. In this case, however, it had almost ideal civilian partners. The old sultan, whose archaic attitudes had provided fuel to an insurgency that had begun about 1965, was overthrown in a bloodless coup by his energetic son, Qaboos, in 1970. Qaboos, who was a graduate of Sandhurst and had served in the British Army, made the ending of the insurgency his first priority and had the authority of an absolute monarch to accomplish that goal.[31]

Qaboos called upon the British for aid and received more than four hundred officers, either seconded or on contract to the sultan, to act as advisers. He also received Special Air Service (SAS) teams, who created and led local paramilitaries. Qaboos also proved willing and able to carry out the reforms the British advised. Together with his British advisers, Qaboos oversaw an integrated military and development campaign that ended the insurgency by 1975. The campaign, like the American campaign in El Salvador, was almost entirely fought by locals; however, Qaboos, probably the closest to an enlightened despot the twentieth century produced, proved a much more capable and adaptable local partner than the government of El Salvador.

By the 1980s, the situation in Northern Ireland had stabilized or perhaps stalemated. The Republicans had been reduced to terrorism rather than full-scale insurgency in the cities, where a tense and hostile peace punctuated by low-level shootings and occasional bombings reigned. In the south along the border with the Republic of Ireland, particularly in South Armagh, cross-border operations by snipers, bombers, and hit-and-run squads produced a higher level of violence, though one still relatively limited. Finally, the Republicans also launched a terror campaign in Britain proper as well as attacking servicemen in the BAOR in Germany.[32]

In the 1990s, the BAOR came to an end, replaced by the much smaller British Force Germany. At the same time, fitful negotiations between the factions began in Northern Ireland, culminating in the Belfast Agreement. The pace of violence dropped significantly during this period, with less than a dozen fatal casualties for the British Army after 1993 (out of a total for the entire war of just over seven hundred).

The effort against the Irish Republican Army, though deeply challenging to the British Army, did not fundamentally change its culture. If anything, it reinforced many of its cultural characteristics, such as affinity for working with other government organizations (particularly British intelligence agencies). It was this force that would be committed to Iraq in 2003.

COBRA II and After: The U.S. Army in Iraq, 2003–5

The results of the initial invasion of Iraq looked strikingly similar to that of the 1991 Gulf War. While this campaign, code-named Cobra II (a reference to Cobra, the breakout from the Normandy beachhead in 1944), was more ambitious in scope and did not go quite as flawlessly as 1991, it was nonetheless a massive triumph. In scarcely a month, Army units moved from southern Iraq to Baghdad, collapsing the regime.[33]

However, the collapse of the regime created a dangerous void, which was only partially filled by the Coalition Provisional Authority, the hastily constituted occupation government. Vast quantities of weapons scattered around the country were in many cases totally unsecured. Large numbers of aggrieved former regime officials with military experience were still free. Foreign Sunni Islamic extremists began entering the country and linking up with domestic Sunni extremists. Fighting erupted inside the southern Shia Islamic community, while in the north the Kurds sought to secure a quasi-independent Kurdistan.[34]

A Sunni insurgency against the U.S.-led coalition quickly emerged in this void. It consisted of former regime officers, nationalists (who often combined moderate Islamism with nationalism), domestic and foreign Sunni extremists, and pure criminals. By 2004 part of the Shia community began fighting the coalition as well.

The next section describes U.S. Army responses to this insurgency in terms of doctrine and operations. It begins with a description of Army written doctrine for COIN in 2003.[35] It is then followed by a discussion of some Army operations through 2005.

In February 2003, just before the invasion of Iraq, the Army issued a new version of FM 3-07, *Stability and Support Operations*, which included counterinsurgency. This edition (over two hundred pages long) is not specifically and exclusively about COIN, but it contains many familiar elements from previous COIN doctrine. It uses the term "foreign internal defense" (FID) rather than COIN in many instances, but nonetheless devotes an entire chapter to COIN.

In discussing stability operations generally, the manual emphasizes the importance of knowledge of local culture and social conditions.[36] It also stresses the importance of the population and of coordination between civilian and military efforts. The chapter devoted to FID claims that "success in counterinsurgency goes to the party that achieves the greater popular support."[37]

The chapter then discusses the need for amnesty programs, the importance of police and paramilitaries, the need to avoid using excessive force, and the need to remain on the strategic defensive (but tactical offensive) in COIN.[38] Though comparatively brief, the same basic discussions found in earlier Army COIN doctrine are present. The manual also contains appendixes on making interagency coordination work (appendix A) and the nature of insurgency (appendix D).

Thus, the U.S. military that entered Iraq in 2003 did not lack at least general doctrinal guidelines for COIN. However, the 2003 version of FM 3-07 was not ideal. It covered such a broad range of operations that it did not provide sufficient detail on COIN. It was further limited by its assumption that U.S. forces would typically provide advice and support rather than conduct combat operations themselves.

By the end of 2003, the U.S. Army realized that it needed a manual specific to COIN. The result, released in October 2004, was the Army's Field Manual–Interim (FMI) 3-07.22, *Counterinsurgency Operations*. FMI 3-07.22 elaborated on previous concepts (such as the importance of insurgencies that attempted to form a "counterstate" to replace the existing authority) but basically retained the same definitions and prescriptions for COIN. In discussing why insurgency happens and why the population is important, the manual notes:

The desire to form a counterstate grows from the same causes that galvanize any political campaign. These causes can range from the desire for greater equity in the distribution of resources (poverty alone is rarely, if ever, sufficient to sustain an insurgency) to a demand that foreign occupation end. Increasingly, religious ideology has become a catalyst for insurgent movements.

The support of the people, then, is the center of gravity. It must be gained in whatever proportion is necessary to sustain the insurgent movement (or, contrariwise, to defeat it).[39]

FMI 3-07.22 repeatedly asserts that the population is the center of gravity in COIN. Additionally, it argues that intelligence must cover cultural, social, political, and economic issues.[40] The importance of civil-military coordination is similarly emphasized.[41]

In discussing COIN combat operations, the FMI reprises familiar points from earlier doctrine. One example is the possible negative consequences of firepower: "The American way of war has been to substitute firepower for manpower. As a result, US forces have frequently resorted to firepower in the form of artillery or air any time they make contact. This creates two negatives in a counterinsurgency. First, massive firepower causes collateral damage, thereby frequently driving the locals into the arms of the insurgents. Second, it allows insurgents to break contact after having inflicted casualties on friendly forces."[42]

Other examples include the need for small-unit decentralized operations and the importance of patrolling out among the populace. The FMI also has a section that discusses the importance of "clear and hold" operations (during which insurgents are driven from an area that is subsequently secured and developed); these are essentially pacification operations.[43]

The U.S. Army's actual conduct of COIN in Iraq from 2003 to 2006 seldom matched the written doctrine in either FM 3-07 or FMI 3-07.22. One of the most often noted examples of deviation from written doctrine was the Fourth Infantry Division commanded by Major General Raymond Odierno in 2003–4. The division was operating north of Baghdad along the Tigris River valley, an area that included Saddam Hussein's hometown of Tikrit.[44]

This area would rapidly become a major center of the Sunni insurgency. Odierno's response, as related by one of his former subordinates, was to "increase lethality."[45] While perhaps understandable in the face of mounting attacks, such a response was not what any of the Army's COIN doctrine from Vietnam onward called for.[46]

Odierno revealed a considerable amount about his operational approach in an interview soon after returning from his tour in Iraq with the Fourth Infantry Division. First, he made extensive use of multibattalion operations:

We ended up conducting 11 major offensives during the next 10 months we were in Iraq. The first was "Peninsula Strike" on a peninsula formed by the Tigris River near Balad, just north of Baghdad. The mission was to defeat noncompliant forces still conducting operations against Coalition Forces. We conducted a combined air-ground assault with a 4,000-man heavy-light force. It included our 3d Brigade out of Fort Carson [Colorado] and the 173d Airborne Brigade out of Vicenza [Italy], which was OPCON to [under the operational control of] Task Force Ironhorse, as well as support from Special Operations Forces [SOF] and the Air Force.[47]

Odierno also discussed his attitude toward firepower:

> During Ramadan, I made a conscious decision to conduct some lethal operations. For about a three-week period, we used artillery and mortar H & I [harassing and interdiction] fires, CAS [close air support], and tank and Bradley direct fire on specific targets we knew were conducting these operations. Because of the amount of firepower we employed, the operations got a lot of play from the media. Using lethal operations was very important for a couple of reasons. One, we went after very specific targets and were able to take down a large number of insurgents by doing this. Secondly, it sent the right message: "We are here to help the Iraqi people, and anytime we need to, we can raise the level of conflict to lethal."[48]

H&I fire, the firing of artillery in areas where the enemy is suspected to be, was directly from the Vietnam era Army's mode of operation. Odierno further noted:

> We used our Paladins [155 mm artillery] the entire time we were there. Most nights, we fired H & I fires, what I call "proactive" counterfire. One of the enemy's techniques was to try to shoot mortars or rockets at large forward operating bases [FOBs] that had a lot of our Soldiers on them. We identified areas from which we knew the insurgents were shooting mortars and shot H & I fires into those areas . . . We also shot a lot of counterfire. We had free fire areas and became very good at clearing fires—good enough to respond with counterfire in less than a minute. We were careful about collateral damage.[49]

According to one officer serving in Iraq, Odierno's claim of concern about collateral damage is overstated. This officer noted that insurgents "would come up from Fallujah, set up next to a farmhouse, set off a mortar, and leave. And the 4th ID would respond with counterbattery fire."[50]

Even in discussing information and psychological operations, it is clear that Odierno's use of firepower was extensive:

> Because we were so careful about collateral damage and maximized IO, over time, we found the Iraqis, for the most part, understood what we were doing and why, even when we conducted lethal operations. Let me give you an example. We tried firing H & I less and less frequently, as long as we were not receiving mortar attacks. At one point, we went three weeks without firing H & I, the longest we had gone. But then we received some rocket attacks. So we went to the Iraqi leaders and said we were going to start firing H & I fires again—that we didn't want to have to do that, but we couldn't allow rockets to be fired at our forward operating bases.[51]

Despite Odierno's protestations to the contrary, it seems unlikely that Iraqis were particularly sympathetic to H&I fire of such volume that three weeks represented the longest time it was not used.

Nor were these beliefs limited to Odierno alone in the Fourth Infantry Division (ID). Many Fourth ID commanders, including battalion commander Lieutenant Colonel Steve Russell and brigade commander Colonel David Hogg, were reported to have embraced the same methods of operation. Only a few Fourth ID officers, such as brigade commander Colonel Frederick Rudesheim, were reported to have not fully embraced this operational approach.[52]

However, the influence of commanders like Rudesheim was apparently minimal. One of his subordinates, battalion commander Lieutenant Colonel Nathan Sassaman, embraced the Odierno approach, essentially ignoring Rudesheim's guidance to the contrary. "We are going to inflict extreme violence," he is reported to have told subordinates. Sassaman's unit lived up to this statement in a variety of ways, including destroying the family homes of individuals suspected of being insurgents, in effect making refugees of their families, and using white phosphorous mortar rounds to burn down wheat fields used by insurgent snipers. Sassaman would subsequently be discharged from the Army for helping cover up the drowning of an Iraqi one of his subordinate units had detained.[53]

Odierno, who would go on to command all forces in Iraq before becoming chief of staff of the Army, may have been an outlier, but other divisions in 2003–4 conducted operations that did not conform to written doctrine. The Eighty-Second Airborne Division, operating in Anbar Province west of Baghdad in 2003–4, was also quite reliant on firepower and violent raids rather than population security. This was most notable around the city of Fallujah.

Almost from the beginning, the Eighty-Second Airborne was quick to use significant firepower in dealing with Iraqis. On April 28, 2003, a demonstration in Fallujah confronted soldiers from the unit, who were provoked into firing on the crowd, killing between six and seventeen Iraqis (accounts vary) and wounding many more. The exact nature of the provocation is unclear, but all of those killed appear to have been unarmed.[54]

A similar incident took place two days later, when a convoy of the Eighty-Second encountered another group of demonstrators. The convoy was provoked into firing on the crowd with crew-served weapons (reportedly including a .50 caliber machine gun). Accounts of the casualties and provocation in this instance also vary.[55]

In September 2003, after some unit shuffling, the city was passed to the Third Brigade of the Eighty-Second. This brigade pursued a very raid-intensive strategy in the early months of its deployment, allegedly relying heavily on firepower, as had the previous units of the Eighty-Second.[56] However, the unit is reported to have subsequently decreased patrolling the city proper, increasingly giving responsibility to the hastily created Iraqi Civil Defense Corps (ICDC).[57] This shift, while reducing the use of firepower, essentially abdicated securing the population.

This pattern of raids and firepower rather than the population security and development called for in written doctrine continued. Two operations from November 2005 demonstrate the Army's disregard of its own COIN doctrine. Operation Kennesaw Dragon, launched on November 14, 2005, involved Iraqi Army units, which cordoned the town of Ad Dawr, and the U.S. Army Third Infantry Division's First Brigade Combat Team, which air assaulted to the outskirts of the town. After a one-day sweep that encountered little resistance, the units returned to Forward Operating Base Wilson.

Operation Clean Sweep which occurred nearly simultaneously in southern Baghdad, was similar to Kennesaw Dragon, lacking only the air-assault element. Neither operation provided any enduring security to the population or did much to garner its support. Indeed, the area covered by Clean Sweep had been swept only a month before yet continued to be problematic.[58]

In addition to heavy use of firepower and brief raids and sweeps, the Army relied extensively on detention of military-aged males (MAMs). MAMs were all males from roughly the age of sixteen to sixty. Though sometimes driven by intelligence on specific individuals, detention was often less discriminate, as a Department of Defense review in August 2004 noted that "units conducting raids found themselves seizing specifically targeted persons, so designated by military intelligence; but . . . they reverted to rounding up any and all suspicious looking persons—all too often including women and children."[59]

Detainees were introduced into a system that was capricious at best. Army battalions and brigades could hold detainees for only two weeks without additional authorization from higher headquarters. In that time, detainees were interrogated, and a decision would be made on whether to release them or send them along to the theater detention system, which included large facilities such as the Abu Ghraib prison west of Baghdad, Camp Cropper near Baghdad International Airport, and Fort Suse in northern Iraq. At the theater level detainees were sometimes interrogated further but for the most part were simply "out of circulation."[60]

Mass detention enabled the Army to conduct an easy sorting of an ambiguous environment. In effect, a detained Iraqi was no longer the unit's problem. The detainee population swelled rapidly as a result of the embrace of detention. By October 2003 there were seven thousand detainees at Abu Ghraib alone.[61]

The scandal associated with abuse of detainees at Abu Ghraib acted to curb the use of mass detention to some degree but did not end the practice. By August 2005, despite large releases from the theater-level facilities, the number of detainees had reached almost eleven thousand.[62]

Finally, the body count once again became a significant metric for the Army in Iraq, despite senior leadership specifically arguing early in the war that the body count would not be used. In an interview in November 2003, Secretary of Defense Donald Rumsfeld said bluntly, "We don't do body counts on other people."[63] Before the Iraq War began, General Tommy Franks, head of U.S. Central Command, had made a similar statement.[64]

Yet the metric inevitably returned, as operations were focused on killing and capturing insurgents. Despite senior leadership efforts to the contrary, Army culture drifted back to this metric. The body count (and the related statistic of number of detainees taken) was in use internally to the Army by June 2003.[65] By 2005 it had become common practice to publicly report a number of enemy killed or detained with every operation.[66]

The foregoing is not to argue that no Army officers understood and attempted to implement COIN doctrine as written. One example of a senior officer attempting to do so was Major General David Petraeus, commanding the 101st Airborne Division in 2003–4, in northern Iraq around Mosul. Enabled by a relatively benign security environment, Petraeus emphasized the security and development approach called for by doctrine.[67]

However, assessments of the 101st experience suggest that the environment was extremely calm, making the operation more akin to humanitarian relief than counterinsurgency. One history notes that the 101st encountered "a spate of small firefights" in its first week in Mosul but little real resistance.[68] In some areas around Mosul, such as the Sinjar region, soldiers of the 101st encountered essentially no resistance.[69]

At the next lower echelon of command, the Third Armored Cavalry Regiment's (Third ACR) Colonel H. R. McMaster embraced COIN with zeal, conducting extensive predeployment training that, as doctrine would support, focused nearly as much on language and culture as on fire and maneuver.[70] This would enable Third ACR, which benefited from a small surge of other U.S. and Iraqi forces, to conduct operations in Tal Afar in western Iraq during 2005–6 that would be held up as a model of COIN.[71] However, some who served in Tal Afar believed that McMaster's operations were successful only due to ethnic cleansing of Sunni Arabs from the city by the Shia Arab community.[72]

Yet for every McMaster or Petraeus, there seemed to be several commanders who did not embrace written COIN doctrine. At least a partial explanation for McMaster's and Petraeus's deviation from Army culture is that both had spent considerable time away from Army education in civilian graduate schools. Petraeus had earned a PhD in international relations from Princeton, and McMaster held a PhD in history from the University of North Carolina. Moreover, both had written dissertations on the U.S. Army and Vietnam, indicating that they had spent far more time reflecting on the problem of counterinsurgency than the vast majority of their peers.

Assessing Explanations for Army Doctrine and Operations, 2003–5

The evidence for the period 2003–5 is somewhat inconclusive from the per-spective of hypotheses on doctrine but is nonetheless instructive. The hypothesis that militaries respond rationally receives little support. As with Vietnam, the Army's written doctrine and actual operations bore little resem-blance to one another.

The hypotheses on civilian intervention are indeterminate in this period, as there was very little intervention. Senior civilians such as Secretary of Defense Rumsfeld initially refused to use the term "insurgency" to describe the problems in Iraq. Even after accepting that an insurgency was under way, the leadership did little to pressure the Army to adopt new doctrine.

Likewise, there is little support for the hypothesis that doctrine is driven by the search for resources, autonomy, or prestige. There is little evidence that the Army's doctrine or operations generated autonomy, resources, or prestige. Indeed, the lack of civilian intervention indicated that the Army had a high degree of autonomy to decide its actions. Similarly, the main constraint on resources was available manpower, and this was a constant in this pe-riod regardless of what doctrine the Army chose to follow. The Army was able to requisition billions of dollars a month for the war, and no evidence indicates that this was dependent on choice of doctrine. Finally, Army op-erations contributed to events like the Abu Ghraib scandal that actually *reduced* Army prestige.

The cultural hypothesis receives some support. The Army continued to focus on large-unit operations, such as Fourth ID's Peninsula Strike, and relied heavily on the use of firepower. Granted, the scale of both units and firepower was smaller in Iraq than in Vietnam, but the pattern remained the same. More importantly, this pattern was again almost exactly the opposite of the Army's own written doctrine, a paradox difficult to explain unless some set of causal beliefs and norms about war supersedes the written doctrine.

War along the Western Euphrates: Marines in Al Anbar, 2003–5

The Marine Corps would have a major part in Operation Iraqi Freedom, as the eastern part of the push to Baghdad would be undertaken by the First Marine Expeditionary Force (I MEF). The Marine drive to Baghdad was the longest Marine armored movement in history.[73]

Marine forces in Iraq were rapidly reduced in the summer of 2003. As the insurgency worsened in the fall, the Marines began preparing to return. I MEF arrived in Anbar in March 2004, taking responsibility from the Eighty-Second Airborne and other detached Army units. The killing and mutilation of four security contractors in Fallujah on March 31, 2004, highlighted the growing lawlessness and violence in Anbar. At this point Fallujah had become a bastion for the insurgency and was essentially not under control by either the provincial government or the coalition.

I MEF attempted to restore order in Fallujah in April with Operation Vigilant Resolve. However, tough insurgent resistance in the urban environment meant that the city was being destroyed and civilians killed. After a few days the operation was halted, and by the end of the month the Marines withdrew entirely from Fallujah proper. An attempt was made to use an Iraqi unit cobbled together from various tribes to secure Fallujah. This attempt was doomed from the start, and Fallujah remained an insurgent stronghold through the summer of 2004.[74]

In November 2004, the Marines, along with U.S. and Iraqi Army units, launched a second offensive, Operation Phantom Fury (also referred to by the Arabic name *Al Fajr* [The Dawn]), to retake Fallujah. This massive force was opposed by heavily entrenched insurgents.[75] After more than a month of intense urban combat that devastated the city, the insurgents were forced out after taking massive casualties. Insurgent operations shifted west, with the group Al Qaeda in Iraq (AQI) increasingly dominating the insurgency.[76]

The nationalist insurgents and tribesmen who had previously supported the religious fundamentalist group AQI began to have second thoughts beginning in early 2005. Many of the nationalists in this period were beginning to consider participation in the political process, as the alternative seemed to be more battles like Fallujah to no gain. Tribesmen were increasingly angry as AQI took over their lucrative gray and black market activities, such as smuggling.[77]

The first open break between AQI and Anbaris came around Al Qaim in early 2005. Tribes from the area formed a paramilitary unit known as the Hamza Brigade (later known as the Desert Protectors). Initial attempts to establish a partnership between the Hamza Brigade and the Marines were unsuccessful, apparently due to miscommunication. A May 2005 Marine offensive, Operation Matador damaged the city and killed members of Hamza Brigade, ending attempts at cooperation for several months.[78] In November 2005, a major partnership between the Hamza Brigade and the Marines began. This partnership led to the launch of a major offensive around Al Qaim called Operation Steel Curtain which eventually drove AQI out and secured the town.[79]

Around Ramadi, other Anbaris began attempting to fight AQI. Sheikh Abdul Sattar Bezia al-Rishawi, a tribal smuggler, gathered some fighters, but they were crushed by the superior organization of AQI. Nationalist insurgents in Ramadi also decided to turn against AQI at some point during mid- to late 2005. These nationalists, operating under a new umbrella organization called the Anbar People's Council (APC), fought against AQI and also sought to help the Marines protect the elections for the new national government in December 2005.[80] The Marines by 2005 were thus both able and willing to cooperate with local security forces, even those that were former insurgents.

ASSESSING EXPLANATIONS FOR MARINE DOCTRINE AND OPERATIONS, 2003–5

As with the Army, there is little that is dispositive about this early period of Marine involvement in Iraq. The rational response hypothesis receives some support given that Marine operations varied from the massive conventional Phantom Fury in Fallujah to cooperating with tribal fighters in Al Qaim—this could be a rational response. As with the Army, civilian intervention cannot be tested, as civilians were not interested in forcing operational change.

The hypothesis that doctrine is driven by the pursuit of resources, autonomy, and prestige receives little support, as Marine operations, like those in the Army, were not tied to the level of resources or autonomy. Like the Marines in I Corps during Vietnam, the Marines in Anbar had very high levels of autonomy from Multinational Force I (MNF-I). I MEF (and subsequently II MEF) constituted Multinational Force–West (MNF-W), a major subordinate command of MNF-I analogous to the role played by III Marine Amphibious Force in Vietnam.

The cultural hypothesis receives support, as Marine operations varied with the information environment. In Fallujah in 2004, the Marines confronted an enemy and an environment that most resembled Hue in 1968. Insurgents in Fallujah, as at Hue, occupied fortified urban positions in large numbers. The response, unsurprisingly, was similar. However, elsewhere the Marines cooperated with locals and conducted small-unit patrols.

"Masters of Chaos": Army Special Forces Operations in Iraq, 2003–5

Army Special Forces were a major component of the initial invasion of Iraq. Operating independently in western Iraq, and with Kurdish peshmerga militia, the CIA, and a few conventional units in the north, and supporting conventional units in the south, Special Forces were ubiquitous across the battlefield. After the invasion, Special Forces supported efforts to provide security in the chaotic environment.[81]

Special Forces organization in Iraq had some similarities to organization in Vietnam, but there were a few key differences. As in Vietnam, the senior Special Forces officer was only a colonel, the commander of the Fifth or Tenth Special Forces Group (Airborne). However, this commander was placed in charge of Combined Joint Task Force–Arabian Peninsula (CJSOTF-AP), which commanded all special operations forces in Iraq that were not detailed to

JSOC.[82] JSOC maintained a separate task force, focused on targeting "high-value individuals."[83] CJSOTF-AP thus oversaw Army Special Forces, Navy SEALs, and other elements of Army special operations. The CJSOTF arrangement gave Special Forces considerable autonomy. The commander of CJSOTF-AP reported directly to the commander of Multinational Corps and Multinational Force and was responsible for special operations forces across all of Iraq.

CJSOTF subordinate commands were based on regions within Iraq and reported directly to the CJSOTF commander. This gave them near-total autonomy to conduct operations as they saw fit. Sometimes these operations were closely coordinated with local commanders, sometimes less so.[84]

One example of Special Forces operations in this early period was securing Ar Rutbah in western Anbar Province. A Special Forces company secured the town, worked with local leaders, and began building local security. Unfortunately, the unit rotated out and was not replaced.[85]

In late 2003, Special Forces began to train Iraqi special operations forces (ISOF). This mission would expand to include training Iraqi police Special Weapons and Tactics (ISWAT) teams. This training took place across all parts of Iraq.[86] These training missions, when done by Special Forces, were conducted by a twelve-man Operational Detachment Alpha, which remained the central unit of Special Forces.[87]

Special Forces units also built local intelligence networks throughout Iraq, using sources to locate insurgents and understand local dynamics.[88] The CJSOTF-AP commander was one of only two officers (the other being the MNF-I C2, the senior intelligence officer in Iraq) who could authorize the wearing of civilian clothes by military personnel during operations.[89] This was presumably to enable better blending in with the local population for intelligence collection.

ASSESSING EXPLANATIONS FOR SPECIAL FORCES
DOCTRINE AND OPERATIONS, 2003–5

As with the Marines, Special Forces operations in 2003–5 appear to support both rational response and cultural hypotheses. Special Forces operations could have been a rational response to the environment but were also consonant with the Special Forces subculture. There is no support for the other hypotheses, though the civilian intervention hypothesis, as with the other cases, is indeterminate.

All Quiet on the Shatt al-Arab? The British Army, 2003–5

The British Army was, like the U.S. Marine Corps, a major component of the invasion of Iraq in 2003. It contributed over forty thousand personnel to its component of Cobra II, known as Operation Telic. This operation was no less successful than any of the other components, and the British rapidly occupied the far south of Iraq, including the populous city of Basra and the vital Shatt al-Arab waterway to the Persian Gulf. In total, the British would be responsible for four provinces: Maysan, Dhi Qar, Muthanna, and Basra (a province as well as a city).

The British Army, like the U.S. Army, had a written counterinsurgency doctrine when the invasion began. Encapsulated in publications such as the 2001 *Counterinsurgency Operations*, the doctrine was not dissimilar to that of the U.S. Army and Marine Corps.[90] It was somewhat more up to date and lengthy (nearly three hundred pages), unsurprising given the ongoing British experience with counterinsurgency in Northern Ireland.

The manual defined insurgency as "the actions of a minority group within a state who are intent on forcing political change by means of a mixture of subversion, propaganda and military pressure, aiming to persuade or intimidate the broad mass of people to accept such a change. It is an organized armed political struggle, the goals of which may be diverse."[91]

Intelligence is also given an entire chapter in the manual. It opens with discussion of "the preeminence of intelligence" in counterinsurgency:

> Good intelligence is vital in any phase of war. In counterinsurgency operations it will be in constant and continuous demand. Operations require steady success, built up over time, which will wear down the insurgent movement, restricting its capability and reducing its morale. Accurate intelligence will permit commanders to conduct operations with precision, reducing the detrimental effect on the local population and minimising casualties among friendly forces. The combined effect will be to secure and maintain the morale among the security forces and raise their standing with the civilian population. Effective and precise use of force will earn respect; vital in the campaign for hearts and minds. Ill-directed and indiscriminate use of force will serve merely to alienate any local population.[92]

This prescription thus notes both the importance of intelligence and the need for discriminate use of force, with minimal collateral damage.

The manual also gives six principles for counterinsurgency: political primacy and political aim; coordinated government machinery; intelligence and information; separating insurgents from their support; neutralizing the insurgents; and longer-term postinsurgency planning. The section on coordinated government machinery makes clear the importance of civilian agencies and the need for close coordination with them, potentially in a committee system. It notes that the best approach "is for the government to give one person overall responsibility for the direction of the government campaign allowing differences of opinion between agencies to be resolved by an impartial Director." The manual also discusses the importance of police and police auxiliary units.[93]

The British would clearly seek to implement their doctrine in southern Iraq. Within weeks of the invasion, the British Army was seeking to partner with locals and work with civil authority. By mid-April the British were recruiting police and conducting joint patrols south of Basra.[94] Violence against the British was initially quite limited, though mass looting took place (as it did across Iraq). By the summer, civil disturbances and lethal attacks against British troops began to occur. However, they remained mild compared to the burgeoning insurgency to the north.[95]

Violence erupted in Basra in early 2004, as the British were confronted by militiamen loyal to Shiite cleric Moqtada al-Sadr.[96] The British battled sporadically with militias, principally Sadr's, throughout the south for the remainder of the year. British operations were marked by restraint and concern for collateral damage, as well as continued efforts to work with both local police and politicians.[97] Unfortunately, the attempt to support locals was doomed, because the locals with power were all affiliated with militias and/or criminals.

British efforts to build police were frustrated, as militias simply infiltrated the new force en masse. Police jobs in fact became a form of patronage for militia leaders and politicians. Attempts to cooperate with tribes turned into "barely concealed protection rackets," where payments were all but explicitly made to prevent attacks on the British and the nascent Iraqi government.[98]

In mid-2004 Iraqi sovereignty was returned, and the British Army found itself lacking civilian partners. A 2007 analysis of British operations notes that prior to the return of sovereignty, coalition civilians and military officers had worked together "to intervene in local politics." However, after the departure of many British civilians, "the rotating Basra and Maysan battle groups stepped back from involvement in Iraqi factional politics in the autumn of 2004 and instead focused on a range of necessary missions concerned with their own force rotation, logistical sustainment, force protection, and reconstruction support."[99] The British Army culture, so dedicated to supporting civilians and working with local forces, found itself adrift without them.

The British Army presumably still had support from the British intelligence community. Reports indicate that the Secret Intelligence Service (SIS), the British CIA equivalent, and other British intelligence organizations maintained a presence in southern Iraq. However, these organizations were limited in size, particularly compared with their American brethren, and were also committed to Afghanistan. It is likely that they were unable to fully provide the support the British Army needed. The SAS and related special operations units were also present.[100]

By early 2005, Basra was all but lawless, a haven for criminals and militias, while Maysan Province to the north was dominated by Sadr's militia. Both levels of violence generally and attacks against the British specifically continued to increase. These attacks increasingly took the form of lethal armor-defeating roadside bombs known as explosively formed penetrators. The British were forced to devote more and more effort to force protection, for example, by shifting from single-vehicle patrols to multivehicle convoys, and to rely less on Land Rovers and more on heavy vehicles such as the Warrior infantry fighting vehicle. The British also began to spend more time on their bases, where they were nonetheless subjected to mortar and rocket bombardment.[101]

An event in September encapsulates the situation the British were in by late 2005. On September 19, two British special operations soldiers acting as human intelligence collectors (and out of uniform) were arrested by Basra police affiliated with one of the militias.[102] They were taken to a Basra jail, where the British began to negotiate for their release. This proved fruitless, and the British launched an assault on the jail using Warriors. Though successful, the raid provoked a violent riot and a major outcry from the provincial government.[103]

Little information about SAS operations in southern Iraq is publicly available. However, it has been reported that the SAS was a major component of the JSOC-led special operations task force focused on high-value individual targeting. The SAS apparently commanded the subordinate task force responsible for southern Iraq, and later around Baghdad, known as Task Force Black.[104]

Even as the British Army in southern Iraq shifted to an increasingly defensive posture (beginning to resemble the U.S. Army's elsewhere in Iraq), others in the British Army chided the U.S. Army for its heavy-handed tactics. Most notable was an essay by a British general officer, Brigadier Nigel Aylwin-Foster, who had served with MNF-I in Baghdad in 2004. Published in the U.S. Army's journal *Military Review*, the essay argued that the American approach made more enemies than it eliminated.[105]

While Aylwin-Foster's essay did not explicitly point out the British approach as a superior alternative, its tone made this argument implicit. Yet the dissonance between Aylwin-Foster's view of British counterinsurgency and the actual posture of the battle groups in southern Iraq in 2005 was striking. This was immediately pounced on by those seeking to defend the U.S. Army, including Colonel Kevin Benson, one of the planners of the initial invasion.[106]

Assessing British Counterinsurgency Doctrine and Operations, 2003–5

The evidence on British Army counterinsurgency doctrine and operations, like that regarding the Marines, supports both the rational response and cultural hypotheses to some degree. While initially pursuing their written doctrine, the British adjusted operations in accord with the environment. There is little evidence supporting the pursuit of resources, autonomy, and prestige, as the British Army, also like the Marines, had a very high degree of autonomy in its area of operations. There is no evidence of civilian interest in the specifics of doctrine, so civilian intervention cannot be evaluated.

The dissonance between Aylwin-Foster's implicit view of British Army operations (or at least what those operations should have been) and the change in the actual conduct of operations in Basra from 2003 to 2005 is important evidence for the cultural hypothesis. Aylwin-Foster clearly had a set of beliefs about how counterinsurgency should be conducted. His beliefs appear to have matched both British written doctrine and the early operations of the British Army in the south.

However, those early operations, so predicated on local police and civilian agencies that were absent, anemic, or infiltrated, resulted in an environment that was increasingly chaotic and hostile. By late 2005, the British were forced by increasingly lethal attacks to adopt many of the same measures Aylwin-Foster decried in his essay and even to attack the very police force they had been working to construct. Rod Thornton of the Joint Services Command College aptly summed up this central dissonance in a memorandum to the House of Commons Defence Committee, noting that in most of the British Army's previous counterinsurgency campaigns "there would be an extant police force and public administration run by fellow-countrymen. There would be people who knew how to run the countries and how best to deal with the indigenous populations. Intelligence would be available, there would be a high degree of cultural awareness, and there would be many people who spoke the local languages. In essence, all the Army had to do was to use its military muscle in aid of a civil power who would know how to target such muscle." Thornton noted that the British lacked all of these assets in Iraq.[107] Yet operations were conducted as though they were present, despite increasing evidence throughout 2004 and early 2005 that they were ineffective. The result was an environment becoming so unambiguously violent that the British Army had little choice but to adopt extensive force protection measures.

SAS operations, to the extent anything can be said about them, appear to conform to the cultural hypothesis as well. The SAS worked effectively with both the British Army and American special operations forces. SAS operations were very small unit (in the September 2005 incident, only two men) and heavily oriented toward intelligence collection and targeted direct action.

On the Tigris: Army Doctrine and Operations, 2006–8

General George Casey, the commander of the overall coalition command known as MNF-I, noted the failure of commanders to adhere to written doctrine. Frustrated, in 2006 he opened a so-called COIN Academy (officially called the MNF-I Counterinsurgency Center for Excellence) at Camp Taji north of Baghdad in order to ensure that all commanders fully absorbed COIN doctrine. As MNF-I commander, Casey exercised his authority to make attendance compulsory for all officers going to command in Iraq.[108]

In addition to training and education, this academy produced a guide similar to MACV's *Handbook for Military Support of Pacification*, entitled simply MNF-I *Counterinsurgency Handbook*. It provides a significant amount cultural and historical context for Iraq and gives reasons why this knowledge is important for COIN operations.[109] It also provides a brief discussion of both COIN and FID, particularly noting the importance of avoiding "kinetic-only" operations focused just on killing insurgents.[110] It also devotes an entire chapter to intelligence in COIN, reiterating the importance of concepts such as "every soldier an intelligence collector."[111] Finally, it notes the vital importance of the population and civil-military operations and coordination.[112]

Despite the opening of the COIN Academy, operations in Iraq still showed limited acceptance of written doctrine. For example, in March 2006, the 101st Division, under the command of Major General Thomas Turner, launched Operation Swarmer near Samarra. This operation, conducted jointly with substantial numbers of Iraqi troops, was described as the largest air assault operation since the initial invasion. Though touted by many as a success, Operation Swarmer appears to have been a brief sweep through an area, encountering little resistance. U.S. and Iraqi forces departed after rounding up suspected insurgents and some weapons caches.[113]

Even a cursory look would suggest that Operation Swarmer was not doctrinal COIN and that it did little to improve the security situation around Samarra.[114] Further, Operation SWARMER, far from being unique, was only the largest and most notable of this type of operation. As MNF-I spokesman Major General Rick Lynch noted at a subsequent press briefing: "Operations like this continue all across Iraq. This happened to be a brigade-level operation in the Salahuddin Province."[115]

Army metrics also continued to focus on the number of alleged insurgents killed or detained. One variation from the body count in Vietnam was a greater focus on insurgent networks and leadership. For example, a briefing given in December 2006 focused on about thirty senior and midlevel leaders of Al Qaeda in Iraq (AQI), a Sunni insurgent group, detained or killed in 2006. In the briefing, MNF-I spokesman Major General William Caldwell made the link between killing/capturing and success clear: "The more we can bring down al-Qaida and other terrorist organizations, the greater probability of reducing violence."[116]

Even as COIN operations continued in Iraq, new doctrine was produced. In June 2006, the Army and Marine Corps issued the final draft of a new joint manual, FM 3-24/FMFM 3-24, *Counterinsurgency*. This draft shows more nuance in definitions and descriptions than previous manuals, in part because it incorporates significant input from academics.[117] Yet the basic substance remains similar. In defining the objective of COIN, the joint manual states that "the primary objective of any counterinsurgent is to foster the development of effective governance by a legitimate government. All governments rule through a combination of consent and coercion. Governments described as 'legitimate' rule primarily with the consent of the governed, while those described as 'illegitimate' tend to rely mainly or entirely on coercion."[118]

The manual also devotes a chapter to the importance of civil-military integration, highlighting in particular the need for unity of command and unity of effort:

> For all elements of the U.S. government engaged in a particular COIN mission, formal command and control using established command relationships within a clear hierarchy should be axiomatic. Unity of command should also extend to all military forces supporting a host nation. The ultimate objective of these arrangements is for local military forces, police, and other security forces to establish effective command and control while attaining a monopoly on the legitimate use of violence within the society . . . All elements supporting the COIN should strive for maximum unity of effort. Given the primacy of political considerations, military forces often support civilian efforts.[119]

The draft provides several examples of mechanisms for civil-military coordination, including Joint Interagency Coordination Groups, host-nation Country Teams, and Civil-Military Operations Centers. It also notes two models employed in the field, the Provincial Reconstruction Team pioneered in Afghanistan and CORDS in Vietnam.[120]

The importance of intelligence is also highlighted in the draft in both a chapter and a more-detailed appendix. The manual notes that COIN "is an intelligence war. The function of intelligence in COIN is to facilitate understanding of the operational environment, with emphasis on the populace, host nation, and insurgents, so commanders can best address the issues driving the insurgency. Both insurgents and counterinsurgents require an effective intelligence capability to be successful. They attempt to create and maintain intelligence networks while trying to neutralize their opponent's intelligence capabilities."[121]

The official version of FM 3-24 was released in December 2006; the Marine Corps official designation was changed to Marine Corps Warfighting Publication (MCWP) 3-33.5. It is substantially similar to the June 2006 draft; indeed, the only major change appears to be the incorporation of an appendix on intelligence into the main body of the text.[122] Like the draft manual, it emphasizes the importance of intelligence, civil-military operations, population security, and legitimate government.

In January 2007, General Casey was replaced by General Petraeus, the former 101st commander. Petraeus had in the interim between 2004 and 2007 overseen much of the writing of FM 3-24. He intended to change how the Army was conducting operations in Iraq, seeking compliance with written doctrine. He would also benefit from a decision made in late 2006 to send additional troops to Iraq (the so-called surge).

Petraeus had some success in adjusting Army operations, principally in Baghdad. It was to Baghdad that the bulk of surge troops would go, with four out of the five additional brigades being deployed either in the city or to its immediate south. Petraeus used these troops, in conjunction with Iraqi security forces, to launch an ambitious campaign to secure Baghdad.

This campaign, initiated in February 2007, was called Operation Fard Al Qanoon (Enforcing the Law). A principal part of the plan was to open joint security stations and combat outposts throughout the city to secure the population. By May sixty-five of these small bases were operating in the city.[123] This new approach was hailed by some as the Army finally "getting" counterinsurgency.

Closer examination suggests that results in Baghdad were more mixed. Soldiers at the new outposts did not necessarily act any differently than they had before. Several complained that they still felt they were just a "show of force" with no purpose, as they had not been given guidance on the purpose of being at the new bases.[124] Another noted, "They say we are spending more time 'in sector,' which we are doing—we live here . . . But we aren't spending the time patrolling."[125] Another junior officer commented, "I just know it's not much different than it was seven months ago . . . We are retaking the same ground every day."[126]

Moreover, whatever success Petraeus achieved in ensuring Army compliance with written doctrine in Baghdad was limited outside the capital. This is perhaps unsurprising given that Petraeus's headquarters was at Camp Victory, just outside the city. As with Abrams in Vietnam, he could at least observe and cajole commanders near him. Operations "far from the flagpole" of the commander would remain unchanged. One alleged exception was the First Brigade, First Armored Division around Ramadi in Anbar.[127]

Yet whatever the situation in Baghdad and Anbar, the Army behaved differently elsewhere. In Diyala Province, which received the fifth of the surge brigades, the Army continued to perform operations having little accord with written doctrine. In June 2007, the Army launched a massive offensive around the city of Baqubah, using roughly ten thousand troops from four brigades, known as Operation Arrowhead Ripper. The operation began with a night air assault and relied heavily on firepower from attack helicopters and fixed-wing aircraft.[128] The operation concluded in July and was followed in August by the equally large-scale (sixteen thousand U.S. and Iraqi troops) Operation Lightning Hammer in the Diyala River valley.[129] Lightning Hammer II was launched in September with twelve thousand U.S. and fourteen thousand Iraqi troops.[130]

These operations were reported to be highly successful in driving insurgents out and disrupting networks. However, the continued violence in Diyala and particularly in Baqubah in 2008 tends to cast doubt on the success of these operations.[131] Moreover, by focusing on attacking insurgents rather than securing the population, the Army continued to ignore its own written doctrine.

Anecdotal evidence suggests that any protection of the population was transient and ineffective. I visited Diyala Province in November 2007, shortly after the conclusion of Lightning Hammer II. While there I interviewed five members of an Iraqi family from a village about ten kilometers from Baqubah about their recent experiences. They said that around August 2007 (the time frame of Arrowhead Ripper and Lightning Hammer) U.S. troops had occupied an abandoned house in their village.[132]

While the villagers had no problem with this and got along with the soldiers, the U.S. unit left sometime in September or October. Almost immediately after, masked gunmen from AQI came to the village and ordered the villagers not to cooperate with the coalition forces. The villagers felt extraordinarily insecure, trapped between AQI, Shiite militias, and U.S. forces. This was due to the possibility of being killed by U.S. firepower, as one of their cousins had been, or being detained by U.S. forces.

This second concern, detention, is supported by the booming number of detainees in U.S. custody in 2007. By April 2007, the total number of detainees in U.S. theater facilities at Camp Cropper and Camp Bucca (south of Basra) had reached eighteen thousand. A thousand of those detainees were reported to have reached the facilities in March alone.[133] By August that number had reached nearly twenty-five thousand.[134]

The Army continued to track the body count and number of detainees throughout 2007. While it is impossible at this point to tell if the inflation of the body count that took place in Vietnam was taking place in Iraq, a suggestive trend can be observed. From January to September 2007, the monthly number of reported enemy killed was two to five times the number of enemy reported injured, which is almost the inverse of the normal pattern of wounded to killed in combat. Between two and three thousand detainees were taken each month as well, though not all ended up being sent to the theater facilities at Camp Cropper and Camp Bucca.[135]

South of Baghdad the Army's Third Infantry Division (Task Force Marne) followed a similar pattern of operations to those north of Baghdad in 2007. It launched numerous multibattalion operations with names like Marne Avalanche, which used one battalion as a blocking force while inserting another via air assault.[136] Other operations were even larger. Marne Torch used most of the division to clear the area around Arab Jabour.[137]

The division's attitude toward firepower was strikingly similar to that of Major General Odierno and the Fourth Infantry Division in 2004. In describing Marne Torch, division historian Dale Andrade underscored division commander Major General Rick Lynch's approach: "From the start, General Lynch placed a premium on firepower as the price of clearing territory. A total of 786 fire missions were called during the one-month operation, more than half of which were area denial strikes . . . An additional forty-one artillery strikes were counterfire missions in response to enemy rocket or mortar attacks. General Lynch wanted the insurgents to know that every assault they made on a U.S. base or patrol would have a cost. 'Whenever there is incoming, I want immediate outgoing,' he often said."[138]

Army operations in 2008 continued to follow the same pattern. Multi-National Division–North launched Operation Iron Harvest, spearheaded by a U.S. brigade, in late December 2007. The operation, part of a larger set of division and brigade operations directed by Multinational Corps–Iraq (MNC-I) known as Operation Phantom Phoenix, was reported to have detained or killed "hundreds" of insurgents by February 2008, indicating that the body count was alive and well in 2008.[139] In July 2008, four squadrons of U.S cavalry were committed in support of more than thirty thousand Iraqi Army and police in the Iraqi-led Operation Bashaer al-Kheir (Augurs of Prosperity).[140]

The Third Infantry Division launched its part of Phantom Phoenix, known as Marne Thunderbolt, in January 2008. It was a multibattalion sweep in the Tigris valley. During the operation General Lynch emphasized that his attitude toward firepower remained "blow it up before it kills our soldiers."[141] In ten days of the operation, U.S. aircraft dropped 114,500 pounds of bombs, alongside additional tube and rocket artillery. While a significant portion of this firepower was in sparsely inhabited areas and was more precise than Vietnam-era firepower, it is a striking contrast to written doctrine, particularly since only a handful of the targets were fortified.[142]

Army culture also had a significant effect on other areas of counterinsurgency. Two in particular, development of local security forces and intelligence, are discussed in more detail in the next section, on the Marines in Iraq. It is in these two areas that the Army and Marine cultural differences stand out most starkly in Iraq, making presentation of the two side by side important.

ASSESSING EXPLANATIONS FOR ARMY DOCTRINE AND OPERATIONS, 2006–8

The evidence from the second period of U.S. Army operations in Iraq provides much stronger support for the cultural hypothesis. Despite the publication of new doctrine and a new senior commander, change in operations was modest and occurred mostly in Baghdad. In Diyala and south of Baghdad, the Army continued to conduct large operations that interacted only briefly with the local population. Even in Baghdad, where Petraeus was headquartered, the shuffling of soldiers out to smaller outposts appears to have produced only limited operational change. This argues strongly that doctrine, as in Vietnam, was used more for instrumental purposes than for actual operations.

The Tide Turns in Anbar: Marine Doctrine and Operations, 2006–8

AQI's response to Anbaris turning against the organization was ruthless and devastating. AQI assassinated key leaders, including the well-respected Sheikh Nassir al-Fahadawi in February 2006. Others were intimidated and cowed by these actions. Many sheikhs also fled to Jordan or Syria. The combination of assassinations (often carried out by members of the same tribe), intimidation, and sheikh flight began to undermine the power of the tribe.[143]

Attacks against Marines were astronomical in this period, outside of a few areas like Al Qaim where local cooperation was effective. In Ramadi, according to Marines stationed there in this period, attacks ranging from mortars to ambushes to suicide truck bombs were almost continuous. Despite this, Marine firepower was, if not insignificant, at least discriminate. Two of the weapons of choice for fire support were the Guided Multiple Launch Rocket, a GPS-guided 227 mm rocket, and the laser-guided Maverick missile. Both enabled very effective attacks on insurgent defensive positions with minimal collateral damage.[144]

In the summer of 2006, tribal leaders around Ramadi, including Sheikh Sattar, formed an anti-AQI movement that would eventually be called the Anbar Awakening.[145] Under Sattar, tribesmen began cooperating with Marine forces against AQI, which at this time dominated much of Ramadi. In cementing this alliance, the Marines worked closely with special operations forces and, it seems likely, CIA.[146]

The situation was so dire in all of Anbar that an August 2006 Marine Corps intelligence assessment deemed that social order had all but collapsed and that AQI held sway over most of what was left.[147] However, as with the Desert Protectors in Al Qaim, the combination of Marine capability with the tribal leaders' local knowledge rapidly began to reverse the situation. With Marine support the Awakening spread quickly across Anbar.[148]

Note that this interpretation of the origin of the Awakening is at odds with the current public narrative, which gives credit for the Awakening to the Army brigade commander in Ramadi in 2006, then-colonel Sean Mac-Farland.[149] Based on conversations with U.S. personnel familiar with the origin of the Awakening and with the Marines' embrace of tribal fighters around Al Qaim nearly a year earlier, I believe the initial driving force was not Colonel MacFarland. Crucially, my initial conversations on this subject took place immediately after these personnel rotated back from Iraq in the fall of 2006, before there was any publicity for the Awakening (indeed, the term was not even in common use). I believe my interpretation is further supported by the rapidity and manner with which Marines elsewhere in Anbar began working with local tribesmen, in contrast to the Army response noted subsequently. However, it will be some time before declassification makes a definitive history possible.

The year 2007 saw almost all of AQI's gains in Anbar reversed. Though AQI was successful in assassinating some key leaders, including Sheikh Sattar, its intimidation failed this time, as the Marines continued to support resistance and Sattar's brother, Ahmad, replaced him.[150] In Fallujah there was no equivalent to the Awakening, but an insurgent turned police chief, Colonel Faisal Ismail al-Zobai, also worked with the Marines to secure the city.[151] By the end of 2007, Anbar was, if not secure, nonetheless radically safer.

During this period, the Marines also focused on collection and analysis of economic and political intelligence. Realizing the importance of the local relationships and dynamics that made the Awakening possible, Marine intelligence officers wrote intelligence collection plans to gather this information. Not one but two elements were created to assess this intelligence under the MEF G2. The first was the Economic and Political Intelligence Cell (EPIC) formed in the MEF Intelligence Battalion. The second was the Security, Governance, and Economics (SG&E) section formed in the MEF Radio Battalion.

In the author's experience, U.S. Army units in Iraq had no comparable organizations, much less two. Army units may have collected and analyzed similar information, but it was not readily apparent that they did so in a systematic fashion. If this information was collected and assessed, based on author and colleagues' attempts to access the information from the Army, it was not readily available and therefore likely not to have been of high importance.[152]

A partial exception to the Army's relative indifference was the MNC-I Coalition Analysis and Control Element (CACE). CACE analysts did produce some political and economic analysis. However, CACE was not an Army-only organization; it was, as the name suggests, a coalition organization and thus both multinational and multiservice. Further, CACE analysts were based in Baghdad and thus were dependent on analysis and collection from units in the field. Given the limited interest in collection on political and economic topics of Army intelligence units, there was not much for these analysts to go on.

Marine intelligence collection and analysis in turn supported engagement with local civilians conducted by Marines. The MEF created a section to handle economic and political engagement and reconstruction, known initially as G3 CMO (for Civil Military Operations) and later reconstituted as G9. G9 personnel, in addition to conducting engagements, also supported very senior level engagements by one of the two deputy commanding generals of the MEF (the other focused on combat operations, producing a division of labor).[153]

The intelligence support to political engagement was mirrored at lower echelons of the Marines as well. At the regimental level, the S-2 (intelligence officer) or one of his subordinates conducted engagements with locals and also supported engagements by the regimental commander.[154] This was the practice with at least some Marine battalions as well.[155]

In 2007, after the Marine success with the Awakening had become widely appreciated, the Army began to adopt similar strategies. This, unsurprisingly, began around Baghdad, where Petraeus began to push Army units to emulate the Marine approach. However, there were critical differences in the two approaches.

In the Marine case, the local forces were incorporated into the formal Iraqi state as quickly as possible. Tribal fighters were encouraged to join the police or police auxiliary units known as Emergency Response Units (ERUs) or Provincial Security Forces (PSFs), which they did. The Marines were able to accomplish this due to their high levels of effective engagement with locals, supplemented by intelligence collection about local dynamics and Marine relations with special operations and other government agencies.[156]

In contrast, the Army essentially paid insurgents to shift from attacking U.S. forces to acting as militias. These groups, which were referred to as Concerned Local Citizens (CLCs) and then Sons of Iraq (SOI), were not in any way tied to the formal Iraqi state and were paid directly by the Army. Further, the Army often lacked the detailed knowledge of local dynamics the Marines had gathered. In November 2007, when the program had more than seventy thousand fighters on the payroll, Army spokesmen were admitting that they had problems with vetting.[157]

Indeed, according to some reports, the Army simply paid elites and asked few questions. One brigade commander south of Baghdad in late 2007 commenting on the program noted, "A lump sum is provided by U.S. military to local Iraqi leaders that is then divided among all the CLCs. The intent is to encourage Iraqis to keep the number of CLCs down, so that each man's salary does not suffer."[158] The Army approach was clearly very hands off, as it apparently left all hiring decisions to the locals. Given apparent Army indifference to collecting intelligence on local political dynamics, a hands-off approach is unsurprising.

ASSESSING MARINE OPERATIONS AND DOCTRINE, 2006–8

As with the Army, Marine operations in this second period of the Iraq War support the cultural hypothesis. Marine operations were much more focused on working with the local population than Army operations. This was particularly true in terms of intelligence collection and analysis. The Marines also worked more closely with civilian agencies and other services, particularly special operations forces. This was despite the two services having coauthored a joint counterinsurgency doctrine. Even when the Army deliberately sought to mimic Marine operations, as with the CLC/SOI program, the result was substantially different.

"By, With, and Through": Army Special Forces Operations 2006–8

There was relatively little change in Special Forces operations in this second period in Iraq. CJSOTF-AP continued to train ISOF and ISWAT units, collect intelligence, and conduct small-unit raids. The latter raids were often conducted with the ISOF and ISWAT units, in keeping with the Special Forces approach calling for working "by, with, and through" partners.[159] If there was a change in Special Forces operations in this period, it was an increase in the discretion of targeting and detention, such as a focus on being able to obtain sufficient evidence to legally prosecute those captured in raids rather than merely detain them.[160]

However, issues began to emerge during this period internal to the Special Forces community. Some in that community believed that Special Forces were becoming increasingly "kinetic," focusing too much on direct-action missions rather than working with locals. This was attributed to a combination of the exalted status within SOCOM of JSOC, the rapid expansion in the number of Special Forces soldiers after 2001, and, most crucially, a reported change in attitude of instructors at the Q Course.

JSOC maintains a virtual lock on command of SOCOM. SOCOM Commander in 2015 General Joseph Votel was formerly JSOC commander. Almost all previous SOCOM commanders have been either commander or deputy commander of JSOC or one of JSOC's component commands.

This dominance only expanded after 2001. Secretary of Defense Donald Rumsfeld became a major proponent of JSOC during his tenure. The commanding general of JSOC was promoted to three stars (the billet had previously been a two star) during this period. Budget priority and prestige within SOCOM followed accordingly.

Second, Special Forces began a rapid expansion after 2001. This brought in large numbers of new personnel, some with no previous Army experience through the "18X" military operational specialty. In 2008, Fifth Special Forces Group added a new battalion, created from scratch, and the other groups planned to do likewise over the next few years.[161] Some Special Forces personnel believed that these "X-Rays" had less appreciation for the traditional Special Forces mission and were more interested in direct-action raids.[162]

Finally, some individuals familiar with the Q Course have noted a change in the attitude of instructors. They claim that the focus has shifted from working with locals to conducting direct-action missions. While this cannot be confirmed directly, it fits with the observations and concerns former Special Forces officers expressed during this period.[163]

ASSESSING SPECIAL FORCES OPERATIONS, 2006–8

Special Forces operations, like Marine operations, tend to support the cultural hypothesis. There appears to have been significant divergence between Special Forces operations and those of the Army, while there was some degree of convergence between Marine and Special Forces operations. Indeed, the Anbar Awakening appears to have been a result of extensive cooperation among Special Forces, Marines, and, likely, CIA.

The signs of a cultural shift in Special Forces are not definitive. However, if true, the fact that much of it seems to stem from change in the core professional education school, the Q Course, underscores the importance of professional education to culture. By changing what the surge of new Special Forces soldiers are taught, the culture of the organization could possibly be changed, perhaps even dramatically, over the course of the next decade.

Trouble on the Persian Gulf: British Army Operations, 2006–8

The environment the British Army faced in southern Iraq grew yet more hostile in early 2006. Iraqi officials in Basra formally suspended cooperation with the British in February, allegedly in response to evidence and allegations of British abuse of Iraqis. This cooperation was not resumed until May; in the meantime a British Lynx helicopter was apparently shot down by surface-to-air missiles. The downing of the helicopter was followed by violent riots against the British forces seeking to reach the crash site.[164]

By the end of May 2006, Basra was in virtual anarchy, forcing Prime Minister Nouri al-Maliki to declare a state of emergency there.[165] The environment only worsened in June, with the British Armed Forces minister noting, "I am conscious of the fact that the first time I visited Iraq I was on the streets with our soldiers who were in soft hats, no body armour. I don't think that could happen now."[166] British casualties continued to mount over the summer, even as the Army turned over control of Muthanna Province to the Iraqis in July.[167]

The transfer of Muthanna Province was quickly followed by the transfer of Dhi Qar Province to the Iraqis in September.[168] Muthanna and Dhi Qar had been relatively quiescent, in large part because they were dominated by relatively pro-coalition affiliates of the Islamic Supreme Council of Iraq. In contrast, Maysan, dominated by affiliates of Sadr, and especially Basra, remained violent and anti-British.

The British therefore used many of the troops freed up from Dhi Qar and Muthanna to launch Operation Sinbad in Basra in late September. Sinbad was intended to break the militias' hold on the city and was conducted jointly with Iraqi forces. The operation concentrated on attempting to clean up the police force, yet also sought to demonstrate the British commitment to reconstruction.[169]

Sinbad's ambitious goals were scaled back within two weeks of its launch, as Basra politicians complained and militias counterattacked. Some questioned whether there was ever any intention to actually achieve the original ambitious goals. A British defense analyst and Territorial Army officer who had served in Iraq earlier in 2006 believed Sinbad was "almost a last attempt to be seen to be doing something."[170]

As the scope of the operation was reduced, the tactics became larger and more dramatic. In December the British launched a major multibattalion attack led by Warrior infantry fighting vehicles on the same police station they had raided in September 2005. The station, home to a police unit alleged to be little more than a militia front, was demolished after more than one hundred Iraqi prisoners were freed.[171]

These occasional dramatic efforts, like similar large-scale U.S. Army efforts, produced only ephemeral gains. By February 2007, the British were under near-total siege. A reporter in Basra summed up:

> Today, life has become so precarious for the British that all movement of personnel is conducted by helicopter and at night. The main palace complex, which houses soldiers and government officials, is permanently under siege from rockets and mortars. Every building is protected by sandbags or blast-proof concrete walls. Helmets and body armour are compulsory. Diplomats are not allowed to leave the compound. Soldiers rarely venture beyond the perimeter in anything less conspicuous than a large armoured force, usually only deployed in battle . . . Even mundane missions are difficult, dangerous and costly. The patrol we joined, which led to the soldier being shot by a sniper, was providing protection for a small police training unit checking on an Iraqi police station. At the cost of one near fatality and the resources of dozens of troops and two helicopters, a local police commander received money to buy mattresses for his officers.[172]

SINBAD ended in March 2007; in April Maysan Province was transferred to Iraqi control despite the continued dominance of Sadr affiliates.[173]

Over the summer of 2007, the environment in Basra remained unrelentingly hostile. By August the majority of British troops had pulled out of bases in the city proper to the air station outside of town.[174] At the beginning of September, the British left Basra Palace, their last base in the city. While the Army sought to portray this move in the most positive light, several independent commentators noted that it could hardly be called anything other than "a defeat" or "a strategic retreat."[175]

This withdrawal also marked a de facto end to significant British operations inside Basra. Prime Minister Gordon Brown announced that British troops would begin substantial withdrawals in the spring. In December the British passed control of Basra to the Iraqis despite the province's manifest instability.[176]

From January until March 2008, Basra remained anarchic. In late March, the Iraqi government launched a massive assault on the city to restore order. Known as Operation Charge of the Knights (Saulat-Fursan in Arabic), the operation was led by Iraqi Army, ISOF, and ISWAT units (the latter two working with U.S. Special Forces) with no British participation. The battle proved difficult, and after four days the British began to provide artillery support for the Iraqis.[177] By April the British, alongside Americans, were providing both advice to Iraqi troops and air support in addition to artillery.[178] However, British combat forces were not directly committed to the operation inside the city.

While regular British Army forces may have been increasingly defensive during this period, the SAS, working with U.S. special operations forces, remained active. Few details of these operations are publicly available. However, incidents reported in the media provide some insight into these operations.

The first of these incidents for this period was the capture in early 2007 of a senior Lebanese Hezbollah officer in Basra. This officer, Ali Musa Daqduq, was in Basra to provide advice and training to militias supported by Iran (Hezbollah's patron). He was captured in a targeted raid that also detained two of his associates along with substantial physical evidence.[179] While the SAS were not specifically noted as being part of the operation, it is likely that British special operations forces at a minimum helped provide intelligence supporting it.

The second was an SAS operation in Baghdad in 2008 against an AQI cell. This operation was publicly praised by MNF-I commander Petraeus.[180] Additionally, SAS soldiers were killed in raids in or near Baghdad in November 2007 and March 2008.[181]

The rest of the British Army in Iraq (with the exception of a small contingent also in Baghdad) remained confined to Basra airfield and its environs for the remainder of 2008. British defense secretary Desmond Browne's visit to Basra in May 2008 was a major exception, as he was escorted by British troops; but this was clearly not a combat mission.[182] The visit by his successor, John Hutton, in October was a similar exception (though one report indicates that Hutton's security in the city was provided by Iraqis).[183]

ASSESSING BRITISH OPERATIONS, 2006–8

The British Army in this period made one last attempt to execute the kind of operations it had been trying since 2004. With extra forces available after turning over other provinces, Sinbad was a last-ditch effort to clean up the police, and it failed. Thereafter, the British essentially ceded the bulk of Basra to the militias.

This period provides some additional support for the cultural hypothesis, as the British persisted in conducting the same type of operations from 2004 to 2007 despite mounting evidence that those operations were ineffectual. Yet once the information environment indicated that Basra was unambiguously hostile and that these operations were not working, the British changed their approach and launched a few large operations (such the assault on the police station in December 2006) before giving up.

Ironically, the Iraqis proved willing to launch exactly the sort of assault on Basra the British had been unwilling to conduct. It ultimately proved effective, even though the British refused to commit combat troops. The British Army was then able to salvage some of its reputation, as security had improved markedly by the end of 2008.

The preliminary evidence from Iraq generally supports the cultural hypothesis. The U.S. Army's experience was markedly similar to that in Vietnam, including large operations and heavy firepower followed by a new senior commander who wanted to change the conduct of operations. Improvements in security in Iraq, as in Vietnam circa 1970, have been attributed to that commander and his changes in operations.

However, closer inspection reveals that changes in operations in Iraq, as in Vietnam, appear to have been more apparent than real. The improvement in security stemmed largely from other factors, one of the major ones being a decision by many Sunni insurgents to ally with U.S. forces against AQI. This decision was aided and the alliance initially consummated by Army Special Forces and the Marines working closely with other government agencies while looking for local allies. This pattern is also as the cultural hypothesis predicts.

The British attempt to do likewise in southern Iraq met with some initial success in 2003 but after the removal of much of the civilian apparatus began to fail. Local allies in Basra proved unreliable and the enemy highly effective, in part due to Iranian support. Operations in Basra thus resembled the early days of Northern Ireland, only more violent.

The British Army continued its effort to build civilian and police capabilities in Basra even as the lethality of the environment forced ever greater levels of force protection. However, even redoubled effort (embodied in Sinbad) to produce effective local allies in late 2006 failed, principally because there was no threat to the militias comparable to AQI for the Sunnis. Absent this threat, the militias saw little need to seek external allies like the British.

Culture thus led the U.S. and British armies down two very different operational paths in Iraq, yet neither ultimately proved particularly successful. The Marines were more successful than either in the long run, but from

2004 to 2006 the Marines appeared to be the least successful, even according to their own intelligence assessments. Only a fortunate alignment of Marine culture and a shift in calculations by Anbaris resulted in success, and even then it was a success that was subject to reversal. Culture, although it determines in large part how an organization operates, does not guarantee triumph.

Counterinsurgency in Afghanistan, 2003–11

Even as the Iraq invasion began in 2003, the Americans and British were drawn into counterinsurgency in Afghanistan. Initially relatively peaceful after the collapse of the Taliban regime following the U.S.-led invasion after the attacks of September 11, 2001, Afghanistan was becoming increasingly violent in 2003. This chapter summarizes the events in Afghanistan from 2001 to 2003 and then presents a very brief overview of counterinsurgency operations in Afghanistan conducted by the U.S. Army, U.S. Marine Corps, British Army, and U.S. Army Special Forces from 2003 to 2011.

Initial Operations in Afghanistan, 2001–3

The attacks of September 11, 2001, on the World Trade Center and the Pentagon prompted a rapid U.S. response. Once it became clear that the Taliban regime, dominated by ethnic Pashtuns, would not hand over Al Qaeda leader Osama bin Laden, the United States initiated plans to topple the regime. Central to these plans was the use of local allies supported by the CIA and Special Forces along with massive use of airpower. The local allies, referred to as the Northern Alliance, were a collection of mostly non-Pashtun warlords, such as the Uzbek Rashid Dostum and the Tajik Mohammed Qasim Fahim, who were locked in a losing war with the Taliban.[1]

This combination of locals, the CIA, Special Forces, and airpower proved devastating to the Taliban. Organized for conventional operations but not of any particular impressive skill, Taliban forces were routed in a few months and suffered devastating losses to precision airpower. Bin Laden himself managed to escape to Pakistan, as did Taliban leader Mullah Omar, but their respective organizations were in utter disarray.[2]

However, neither gave up the fight. Operating from sanctuary in Pakistan's periphery in Baluchistan and the North-West Frontier Province as well as the semigoverned Federally Administered Tribal Area, the two men began to rebuild. By 2003 the Taliban, along with allied groups such as the organization of former anti-Soviet guerrilla leader Jalaluddin Haqqani and the Party of Islam led by Gulbuddin Hekmatyar were ready to begin a serious insurgency in Afghanistan.[3]

While the Taliban were rebuilding, the U.S.-led coalition had overseen the creation of an interim government led by Hamid Karzai, a Pashtun, though with strong representation for the Tajik and Uzbeks who had made up the Northern Alliance. Under a United Nations Security Council resolution, a separate International Security Assistance Force (ISAF) was established to help rebuild Afghan institutions. Subsequently led by NATO, from 2001 to 2003 it did not operate outside Kabul.

This left the bulk of security and combat operations outside Kabul to the Americans. However, American military planners were occupied with plans for Iraq, and few forces were committed to Afghanistan in this period. This left most of the Pashtun regions of Afghanistan, which bordered Pakistan, up for grabs at the beginning of 2003 as distracted American and international forces were suddenly confronted by a Taliban-led insurgency in those areas.

Eastern Promises: The U.S. Army and Counterinsurgency in Afghanistan, 2003–9

In 2003 the new commander of U.S. forces in Afghanistan, Lieutenant General David Barno, recognized that the reconstituted Taliban and other groups were an insurgency (as opposed to terrorists or criminals). He reorganized his forces into two brigade formations, known as Regional Commands (RCs), one operating in the east (RC East) and one in the south (RC South). The two commands had various battalions committed to them to conduct counterinsurgency operations as well as supporting organizations known as Provincial Reconstruction Teams, which combined military and civilian personnel.[4] RC East was the main focus for the Army, where it was the dominant force.

The operations conducted in 2003 were principally large-unit sweeps, though some level of small-unit patrolling did take place. Examples of the former are Operations Warrior Sweep and Mountain Viper in July–September 2003. Warrior Sweep used a total of more than one thousand Afghan National Army (ANA) and U.S.-led coalition personnel, including soldiers from the Eighty-Second Airborne, to clear the Zermat valley in Paktia Province. Mountain Viper was a similar operation conducted in Zabul Province using ANA and soldiers from the Tenth Mountain Division. In neither operation did forces appear to stay in place for long, instead engaging enemy forces, destroying insurgent caches when found, and moving on.[5]

In 2005 and 2006, this pattern of large-unit sweeps continued. For example, in northern Kandahar, soldiers from the Eighty-Second and 173rd Airborne, along with ANA and other coalition forces, conducted Operations

Diablo Reach and Diablo Reach Back in May and June. These operations, in the Shah Wali Kot district, involved more than a battalion of U.S. troops alongside several companies of ANA, yet did not establish an enduring presence in the district.[6] In April 2006, more than twenty-five hundred coalition and ANA personnel launched Operation Mountain Lion in Kunar Province.[7]

In June a force of roughly eleven thousand U.S., British, Canadian, and Afghan troops launched the largest operation of the war, Mountain Thrust (an infelicitous name choice). This operation lasted through July and spanned four provinces (Zabul, Helmand, Kandahar, and Uruzgan). As with the other large-unit operations, it did not leave any substantial forces in place at the conclusion of the operation. The Second Battalion, Eighty-Seventh Infantry Regiment, for example, deployed to a newly built forward operating base (FOB), Little Round Top in Helmand Province, for the duration of operations before returning to their normal location at FOB Salerno in Khost Province.[8]

The large-unit operations continued in 2007–9. In October 2007, a reinforced battalion of U.S. and ANA forces launched Operation Rock Avalanche, a six-day sweep of several valleys in Kunar Province.[9] In July 2009, Operation Mountain Fire, a battalion-size operation, was launched in Nuristan Province.[10]

The operations just mentioned are particularly noteworthy because U.S. force levels were much lower than in Iraq, much less Vietnam. In Iraq, force levels were about 120,000–160,000 for most of the period 2003–8, while in Vietnam they were in excess of 200,000 (up to about 500,000) for most of the period 1966–70. In contrast, Afghanistan ranged from less than 10,000 in 2002 to 32,000 in 2008.[11] It is therefore all the more telling that despite very low force levels, operations of battalion size or larger still took place with some frequency, though clearly less often than in Iraq or Vietnam.

As in Iraq, dissatisfaction with the state of counterinsurgency operations in Afghanistan led to the creation of a Counterinsurgency (COIN) Academy. Established in 2007 at Camp Julien on the outskirts of Kabul, the COIN Academy was intended to provide training to U.S. and other forces in counterinsurgency theory and practice. As in Iraq, it appears to have had minimal effect on actual operations and was not well resourced.[12] While not definitive, this pattern suggests a broad similarity in Army counterinsurgency in Iraq and Afghanistan. A final aspect of U.S. counterinsurgency in Afghanistan, the Provincial Reconstruction Team, is discussed in more detail in the section on the British Army.

The U.S. Marine Corps and Counterinsurgency in Afghanistan, 2003–11

The Marine role in counterinsurgency in Afghanistan was fairly limited from 2003 to 2008. The Corps did dispatch a few units, but they were sent piecemeal for short periods. For example, in 2004 the Twenty-Second Marine Expeditionary Unit (MEU) deployed to Afghanistan for four months. In 2005–6 the Second Battalion, Third Marine Regiment spent roughly six months there. It was relieved by the First Battalion, Third Marine Regiment, which was deployed for a similar period. Some Marine special operations units were also deployed to Afghanistan in this period.[13]

However, a major influx of Marines into Helmand Province began in the summer of 2009. An MEU had been deployed to southwest Afghanistan in the summer of 2008, a foot in the door but still only a reinforced battalion in terms of combat troops. This limited force was unable to cover many areas, and when they did they often ran into large insurgent formations. In the remote Gulistan valley of Farah Province, for example, a Marine platoon was nearly overrun by a force of over a hundred heavily armed fighters.[14]

This presence expanded to a Marine Expeditionary Brigade (MEB) in 2009, with the MEB moving into Helmand in early summer. Under the command of a one-star general and with a defined area of operations, the Marines in Helmand appear to have had more autonomy than their battalion-size predecessors. The Marines then launched Operation Khanjar (Sword Stroke in Pashto) in conjunction with the ANA and Afghan police in July.

Khanjar involved most of a Marine Regimental Combat Team, so it was clearly a large-unit operation. However, at least initial reporting made the operation sound more like the Vietnam-era De Soto, which used a large unit to occupy an area and then conduct small patrols, rather than a transient sweep. One July report noted that the Marine units "are under orders to set up outposts in the villages and stay there to convince local people that the Taliban will not be allowed to return and that it will be safe to take part in next month's presidential elections."[15] The MEB commander, Brigadier General Larry Nicholson, declared, "Where we go we will stay, and where we stay, we will hold, build and work toward transition of all security responsibilities to Afghan forces."[16]

Subsequent reporting seemed to support Nicholson's assertion. A report from September 2009 described a Marine company that had been in place in the village of Mianposhteh since early July. The company commander, faced with nearly continuous daily combat (six engagements in one day in late August), still made time to attempt to build rapport with locals. Moreover, the commander partnered with a Pashtun-speaking British Army captain serving as an adviser to the ANA, making him the Marines' "ambassador" to the locals.[17] In the Garmser district of Helmand, the Marines relied heavily on a civilian adviser detailed from the State Department.[18]

In the Nawa district of Helmand, a reinforced company from the First Battalion, Fifth Marines moved into the district center, where a team of British advisers and ANA troops had been stationed since 2006. The insurgent presence was so heavy in Nawa that this British-Afghan force had been unable to patrol at any distance from the district center. The Marine presence greatly expanded the combat power available, and the new British-Afghan-Marine team launched into two weeks of daily fighting with significant Taliban formations. After this initial period of fighting, the combined team began conducting frequent platoon-size patrols in conjunction with the Afghan National Police.[19]

The Marines also limited their use of firepower. As a 2012 assessment of the Nawa operations noted, the Marines limited use of mortars and airpower. This included refraining from using any bombs for fear of collateral damage.[20]

Army Special Forces and Counterinsurgency in Afghanistan, 2003–11

Early in the Afghan campaign, U.S. Special Forces continued to conduct operations similar to those that began the war in 2001. The focus was on U.S. forces in conjunction with Afghan militia forces searching for Taliban, Al Qaeda, and other extremist remnants. These operations were led by U.S. units, but the fighting was mostly done by Afghans.[21]

In describing the 2004 campaign plan for Combined Joint Task Force–Afghanistan (CJSOTF-A), a monograph written by a Special Forces officer makes clear the small-unit focus of Special Forces. "Five named operations were conducted with most of the effort oriented all the way down to the SF Operational Detachment-A. These were a series of major operations conducted across Afghanistan employing small units in large areas of operation."[22] It further details that one of these named operations, Independence, involved just two Operational Detachment Alphas (ODAs) (twenty-four men total), one on each side of the Baghran valley, in July 2004. The monograph also indicates that Special Forces continued to work with local forces, including tribal militias.[23]

Even in launching unsuccessful operations, the emphasis remained on using Afghan forces for the bulk of operations. In one operation in the Deh Chopan valley in Zabul Province, a Special Forces unit acted on intelligence provided by its Afghan partners, who were not from the valley and so knew little about it. Unsurprisingly, the operation found few Taliban but provided an opportunity for the militia forces to loot the valley's inhabitants, requiring Special Forces soldiers to then pay reparations.[24]

Special Forces units remained closely tied to indigenous forces throughout the period 2001–11, some tied to the formal state and others not. Formal state partners were mostly elite Afghan units. These included the Afghan National Army Commandos, the Afghan National Army Special Forces (ANASF, an explicit copy of U.S. Special Forces), Afghan National Police Provincial Response Companies, and the Afghan National Civil Order Police (ANCOP).[25] These units conducted a variety of missions, ranging from local security to targeted raids against the Taliban.

Other indigenous allies had few or no ties to the formal state. As militia units were formally disbanded, these local allies came to be called the Afghan Security Guards (ASG). This is a generic term that encompasses a variety of local allies, ranging from literal security guards who do nothing but protect bases to forces that provide security over larger areas in partnership with Special Forces.[26]

An example of the role of ASG units (sometimes known as "campaign forces" to Afghans) is the force led by Commander Azizullah in eastern Paktika Province. Azizullah commands an ASG force in the region around Orgun and Bermal, and has been working with U.S. Special Forces almost since the beginning of the war. His unit and others like it have been referred to as some of the most effective units in Afghanistan, in part because of their strong connections to Special Forces.[27]

In June 2009, U.S. Special Forces sought to further expand their links to village-level indigenous forces through a program called the Community Defense Initiative. This program did not initially involve the Ministry of Interior, instead working directly with village leaders who had decided to resist the Taliban and supporting those leaders with a special operations team living in or near the village. In December 2009, the program was renamed the Local Defense Initiative.[28]

Over the next year, the Local Defense Initiative expanded despite resistance from the U.S. embassy and the Afghan government. Both were concerned that the program might allow the return of predatory militias. In mid-2010 an agreement between the U.S. and Afghan governments made the local defense force part of the Ministry of Interior, and in August President Karzai signed a decree creating the Afghan Local Police (ALP).

Numbering more than seven thousand in forty-three districts in August 2011 and reportedly over thirteen thousand by May 2012, with an eventual goal of thirty thousand (or possibly more), ALP have defensive responsibilities and operate mainly near their villages.[29] Members of the unit are volunteers from the community between the ages of eighteen and forty-five who sign a one-year contract. They are nominated by a village *shura* (meeting) and then vetted by the Ministry of Interior with support from the National Directorate of Security (the Afghan internal security intelligence organization). Members work part time and are paid approximately 60 percent of the basic police salary.

The ALP are thus a clear analog to the Special Forces experience in Vietnam with Civilian Irregular Defense Groups (CIDG). Based around a very small unit embedded with an indigenous local security force, the ALP concept has been heralded as a breakthrough in counterinsurgency in Afghanistan. Yet, like CIDG, the expansion of the program carries risks akin to those in Operation Switchback, with the larger U.S. Army culture altering the ends and means of the program.

The records to fully document the operations of U.S. Army Special Forces in the ALP program will not be available for some time, but as a participant-observer I have had several opportunities to observe operations firsthand. In particular I observed multiple Special Forces units in Khakrez district of Kandahar Province over the course of a year. While this time series of one district is hardly definitive, it is probably a unique set of observations for examining Special Forces operations in Afghanistan.[30]

In June 2010 I arrived in Khakrez, where two Special Forces ODAs represented the only U.S. forces in the district. One ODA was based in the district center, the small village of Darvishan. It was colocated with ANA and Afghan police units in a series of small compounds. A Special Forces team had been in this position on a rotational basis since 2009.

The second ODA had arrived only a few months earlier and occupied a very small compound that had been built with Japanese foreign aid. It had promptly been taken over by the Taliban, who fled when the ODA began preparing to seize the building but left behind a variety of explosive traps. This second team was assigned the mission of building a local defense force as part of what was then called the Local Defense Initiative. Its location was referred to as the Green Zone, as it was situated in an agricultural area of several very small villages. For clarity I will refer to the two different ODAs by their base locations—Darvishan and Green Zone, respectively.

At the time the principal challenge the Green Zone ODA had identified was that political power in the district was overwhelmingly concentrated in the hands of the Popalzai tribe (the tribe of Afghan president Hamid Karzai). Both the appointed district governor and the district chief of police were from that tribe. The district chief of police had been wounded in an attack and had appointed his son as acting chief of police despite his son's youth (roughly twenty years old), inexperience, and laziness. Economic benefits from government spending and government jobs went along with this concentration of political power.

The result was that the Popalzai tribe's rival, the Alikozai tribe, was disenfranchised politically and economically. Perhaps unsurprisingly, the Alikozai of Khakrez supported the Taliban. This was in contrast to their Alikozai tribal cousins in the neighboring Arghandab district, who were strongly anti-Taliban. The Green Zone area was predominantly though not exclusively Alikozai, many of whom grew opium poppy.

This was the environment the Green Zone team confronted in trying to build a local defense force. They acknowledged that it was not particularly propitious. This was confirmed the first night I stayed with team, as the team's compound was attacked by recoilless rifle fire from an Alikozai village a few hundred yards south. The team returned fire with small arms and medium machine guns. Fortunately, no one was injured on the team or in the village (the latter confirmed by a patrol to the village the next morning).

The Green Zone team did have one small advantage in that it had just received an Afghan unit to partner with—the first ANASF ODA. The ANASF ODA was explicitly copied from the U.S. model and so had a dozen reasonably well trained and motivated Afghan soldiers with specialized skills. The U.S. team thus had one set of indigenous partners to help them build the local defense force as well as conduct other operations.

The Green Zone team's operational plan was based on getting the Alikozai to participate in the local defense force. This required persuading the tribe that it was in their interest to do so, which in turn required determining who had authority in the tribe as well as redistributing some of the political power in the district to the tribe. The team concentrated on building intelligence networks as well as holding shuras and extensive foot patrolling of Alikozai villages. At the same time, the team mentored their ANASF partners as well as providing medical and development assistance to the local villages.

However, the team was unable to make progress in building a local defense unit, as it was not able to change the distribution of political power. Despite the team's efforts to engineer change, both the district governor and chief of police remained in place, funneling resources to the Popalzai tribe. In this situation, despite efforts to use minimal firepower and cooperate with a variety of indigenous forces, the team had little success.

In January 2011, I returned to Khakrez. Both the Darvishan and Green Zone teams I met previously had rotated out and been replaced by two new teams. The district governor remained the same, so the new Darvishan team, rather than seeking to replace the district governor, sought to mentor him. Their goal was to persuade him that sharing power with the Alikozai would ultimately be good for the district as well as both tribes. The Darvishan team also sought to expand the market in Darvishan through development efforts in order to foster economic growth.

This approach, again in keeping with Special Forces subculture, focused on close cooperation with indigenous forces, very small unit operations, and limited firepower. Yet in January this team had no greater success than the previous teams. The team also lost several members to an improvised explosive device placed by the Taliban.

I returned again to Khakrez in July 2011 to find some significant changes. First, both the Darvishan and Green Zone teams had rotated out, and two more new teams were in. Second, the district chief of police had been replaced with a well-respected Alikozai leader, Mullah Gul. Mullah Gul was, according to both the Darvishan and Green Zone teams, a very aggressive leader, though he was also believed to have family ties to the insurgency. He used his new position and tribal influence to get Alikozai tribesmen to join the local defense unit (which had by this point been christened the ALP). At the same time, the district governor used his influence to get members of his own tribe to join the ALP.

On the surface this at last represented progress for the Special Forces operations. Close cooperation with indigenous forces had at last yielded the desired result. Unfortunately, closer examination revealed this progress to be more apparent than real. As one Special Forces soldier noted, Mullah Gul had more or less browbeaten his tribesmen into joining the ALP, so their motivation to actually confront their insurgent kinsmen was low.

I observed a security shura with the leaders of the two Special Forces ODAs, the district governor, the Afghan National Army commander, Mullah Gul's deputy, and the ALP leaders. At this meeting one of the Special Forces teams asked the Alikozai leader of the ALP to set up night patrols around their villages. The leader demurred, citing a need for flashlights to do night patrolling. This was interpreted by the Special Forces personnel as a means of avoiding conducting night patrols that might actually encounter insurgents, but the Special Forces team promised to acquire flashlights for ALP. A subsequent communication from the Special Forces personnel after I left Khakrez indicated that after receiving flashlights, the Alikozai ALP then began complaining that the Taliban had night vision devices and that they could not be expected to patrol at night without having them as well. This was taken as further evidence that the ALP simply wanted to shirk.

In contrast to the Alikozai ALP, the Popalzai ALP did not appear to be coerced into serving. However, they all clustered around the district governor's home village. They were also led by the injured former chief of police. Special Forces personnel assessed that these ALP were more of an additional form of patronage than a serious defense force (though they would certainly fight if their home village was attacked).

On paper, then, the ALP program in Khakrez looked good. It had gone from nascent to having roughly a hundred ALP in only a year. Yet fundamentally, little had changed in terms of the insurgency. While I was there, an Afghan soldier was killed in an explosive attack near Darvishan amid suspicions many in the Alikozai were still supporting (or at least not opposing) the Taliban.

This vignette shows that at least in one district there was general continuity of operations that were in accord with the Special Forces subculture across multiple teams. At the same time, it demonstrates that even when effectively and appropriately applied, the tenets of this subculture—small units, discrete firepower (such as the return fire in the attack in June 2010), and intense cooperation with indigenous actors—do not always yield successful results. Like the British experience in Basra, this highlights the limits of foreign agency in counterinsurgency.

The Not So Great Game: The British Army and Counterinsurgency in Afghanistan, 2002–9

After dispatching nearly three thousand troops to Afghanistan in the spring of 2002, British Army force levels dropped precipitously later in the year as preparations for Iraq began in earnest. By late 2002, only three hundred British soldiers remained, mostly in Kabul.[31] However, the emergence of insurgency in 2003 forced the British government to recommit more forces to Afghanistan despite the ongoing war in Iraq.

The initial commitment to the counterinsurgency campaign was a reinforced battalion-size force known as the Afghanistan Roulement Infantry Battalion (ARIB). This force, based in Kabul, rotated roughly every six months and was responsible for three main tasks. First, it committed a company to patrolling Kabul. Second, it formed the Afghan National Army Training Team.[32] Third, it provided the military element to a Provincial Reconstruction Team (PRT) that the British established in the northern Afghan province of Balkh at Mazar-i-Sharif in 2003, with responsibility for five northern provinces. The PRT concept was intended to unify civil and military capabilities for counterinsurgency, particularly focusing on developing Afghan capabilities for security and governance. The British PRT in Mazar included representatives of the Department for International Development and the Foreign Office in addition to elements of the ARIB. In 2004 another PRT was opened in Maimana, the capital of the northern province of Faryab, with a similar composition.[33]

The PRT was not a uniquely British invention, though it clearly harkened back to the civil-military committees of Malaya and Kenya. Other ISAF nations, including the United States, also created PRTs during this period. However, not all PRTs were created equal, and there was substantial difference in the British and U.S. implementation of the concept.

The U.S. model was, like CORDS in Vietnam, dominated by the military. Moreover, it was often the combat units operating in an area that dictated to the PRT rather than the reverse. An interagency assessment of U.S.-led PRTs in 2006 noted:

> While interagency guidance gave civilians from USAID and DOS the lead on governance and reconstruction, PRT culture, people, and resources were predominantly military. Military dominance was reinforced by force protection and security concerns, and by the collocation of several Coalition PRTs with maneuver units. Moreover, subordination of PRTs to maneuver units threatened to dilute a core focus of the PRT, which was to strengthen the Afghan government's capacity to address issues underlying instability and support for insurgency.[34]

In contrast to the military-dominated U.S.-led PRTs, the British PRT in Mazar was a more truly integrated civil-military team. It also included an expert on the security sector detailed from the Afghan government. More-over, there was no British combat unit operating in Mazar, further ensuring that the military did not dominate. External observers gave the British model high marks, with a vice president of the nongovernmental organiza-tion International Crisis Group stating:

> Our assessment is that the British have done an excellent job in the north. Their model of running a PRT is the one that we endorse with the focus on security, stabilisation, for the most part keeping out of the development sphere and the humanitarian sphere. We particularly support the fact that they have operated mobile observation teams and have spread the security blanket throughout the area because this is a very important way of show-ing support for the Afghan government institutions . . . In terms of the de-velopment focus, we support the British view, which is that ideally you establish security which allows room for others or a better place to do development. The problem you see with the approach of some of the U.S. PRTs, for instance, is that you build a school but there are no teachers there because you have not integrated your development efforts with the rest of the development work that is going on, or you build a well, but who is there to maintain a well if it is not part of a cohesive approach? So the approach adopted in Mazar, which is the security blanket but enabling NGOs and/or the Afghan government to carry out development, is a better approach.[35]

The period 2003–5 was therefore one of British success in northern Afghan-istan. However, the environment was relatively nonviolent to begin with, far from the burgeoning insurgency in the south and east. The next year would be different as British forces were dispatched to the thick of the fight. Yet the British Army would continue to emphasize cooperation with the PRT.

By late 2005, it had become clear to senior ISAF leaders that Helmand Province in southern Afghanistan was in dire need of additional effective troops, as the mix of narcotics, tribal militias, and the insurgency was spi-raling out of control. The British government decided (or was persuaded) to dispatch a brigade-size task force to Helmand in the spring of 2006. At the same time, the PRTs in Mazar and Maimana were handed off to the Swedes and the Norwegians, while the British assumed control of the PRT in Helmand, based at the capital, Lashkar Gah.[36]

The British effort in Helmand was intended to be much like the effort in northern Afghanistan, with an emphasis on developing Afghan governance and security. The British Task Force Helmand and the PRT rapidly discov-ered that they had been handed a hornets' nest, a real insurgency to combat rather than the more peacekeeping-oriented environment in the north. Com-bat throughout the summer was ferocious as the British sought to establish a presence in district centers in northern Helmand.[37]

This so-called platoon house strategy, apparently requested by the pro-vincial governor but supported by the British Army commander, sent a company to occupy and defend government buildings in district centers such as Musa Qaleh and Sangin. However, the insurgents massed forces and began launching frequent attacks on these outposts, harassing them almost continuously and attempting to overrun them in several instances. The British had suffered only two fatal casualties in Afghanistan in 2003–5, but by the end of 2006 they had taken more than thirty additional fatalities, with a substantial number of injuries.[38]

In October 2006, the provincial governor and the British Army accepted an offer from tribal leaders around Musah Qaleh to form a tribal militia to keep the insurgents out. In exchange, the British troops left the district center. This local agreement was treated with disdain by U.S. military and civilian officials but apparently kept the town free of insurgent influence until January 2007, when a massed insurgent force retook the town.[39]

The British nonetheless did not abandon the hope of negotiations with local tribes and insurgent commanders. The British Secret Intelligence Service (SIS), also referred to as MI6, is reported to have negotiated with local commanders throughout the summer of 2007, supported by the British Army. In October successful negotiations, led by the Afghan government but supported by the British Army (and probably SIS as well), resulted in the defection of Mullah Abdul Salaam, a tribal leader supporting the insurgents in Musa Qaleh.[40]

Even as it continued to support negotiations, the British Army shifted to participating in larger-scale operations in parts of Helmand, this in part due to the realization that the Taliban were much stronger and better able to mass and maneuver than initial British estimates of the situation had assessed. The logic of these larger-unit operations was to disrupt Taliban large-scale forces in order to take pressure off smaller-unit security operations like the platoon houses (though with mixed success).[41]

The first large-unit operation was Operation Achilles, which brought together more than a thousand British, Canadian, American, Afghan, Dutch, Estonian, and Danish forces. Begun in March 2007, Achilles sought to secure Sangin, one of the areas where the platoon house strategy had foundered the year before. A major British component was Operation Silicon, which would eventually involve more than a thousand British troops in addition to Afghan security forces.[42]

The British continued with a series of operations in and around Sangin in 2007.[43] In the summer the British led Operation Chakush (Hammer). With more than two thousand ISAF and Afghan troops (fifteen hundred of which were British), this July 2007 offensive took place in the Upper Gereshk valley. It apparently did little to bring permanent security, as it was followed in September 2007 by the slightly larger Operation Palk Wahel (Sledgehammer Blow in Pashto) in the same area.[44]

In late November, following the defection of Mullah Abdul Salaam, ISAF command decided the time was right to retake Musa Qaleh. This led to

Operation Mar Kardad (Snake Pit), which used more than four thousand ISAF and Afghan troops, including more than twelve hundred British soldiers. This was a clearly conventional battle, as estimates indicated that roughly two thousand insurgents held the town. After weeks of intense fighting, the town was finally cleared in mid-December.[45]

The battles of Mar Kardad were followed by an apparent lull in major operations until the following summer. In June 2008, Operation Oqab Sturga (Eagle's Eye) was launched south of Musa Qaleh using hundreds of British, Afghan, and Dutch troops. This was followed in September by Operation Oqab Tsuka (Eagle's Summit), wherein roughly four thousand ISAF (about two thousand of which were British) and Afghan troops guarded the transport of massive hydroelectric generators to the Kajaki Dam.[46]

The large-unit operations did not indicate a complete abandonment of the earlier platoon house strategy. Throughout 2007 and 2008 companies were forward-deployed at small compounds in northern Helmand. These bases remained in constant danger of being overrun as well as taking frequent indirect fire. For example, FOB Inkerman at the upper end of the Sangin valley was renamed FOB Incomin' by its occupants. First occupied in 2007, beginning in 2008 it was manned by an ANA company in addition to the British company. Inkerman was one in a series of such bases across northern Helmand.[47]

This pattern of operations in central Helmand continued with over seven hundred British, Danish, and Afghan troops in Operation Aabi Toorah (Blue Sword) in March. In May focus shifted to neighboring Kandahar Province with Operation Sarak (Road). This operation dispatched over five hundred British soldiers along with an ANA company across the provincial border to help secure the road connecting the two provinces. Later in the month Operation Mar Lewe (Snake Wolf) sent a similar mixed British and Afghan force to clear an area just south of Musa Qaleh.[48]

British troops expanded the platoon house strategy into several of the areas cleared by operations in early 2009. For example, an outpost known as Patrol Base Argyll, containing a British company alongside an ANA company, was established in the area cleared by Operation SOND CHARA. The unit stationed there also worked closely with the district governor, among other things holding a weekly "security shura."[49]

In June the British launched Operation Panchai Palang (Panther's Claw) in the area north of Helmand's capital, Lashkar Gah. The operation began with an air assault by over three hundred soldiers supported by additional ground troops. Over the next five weeks the operation grew as it continued through several phases, eventually employing over three thousand British, Afghan, Danish, and Estonian troops.[50]

In addition to the search for indigenous allies, the British Army sought to deepen and expand its integration with civilian agencies, most notably the PRT. By 2009 the British operational military and PRT had become deeply intertwined, with the Army aiding in expanding the PRT. As Theo Farrell notes, the Army "developed greater integration with the expanding British-led PRT in the provincial capital, Lashkar Gah. The brigade planning section, J-5, were physically moved to the PRT HQ. Moreover, the deputy brigade commander, Colonel Neil Hutton, became one of the three PRT deputies . . . [T]he PRT more than doubled in size: the civilian staff grew from 45 to 94, and military personnel from 19 to 48."[51]

British operations in Afghanistan appear to support the cultural hypothesis and provide additional fidelity on how culture interacts with the information environment. In northern Afghanistan from 2003 to 2005, British operations conformed to cultural expectations, with an integrated civil-military team working closely with local allies to expand government capability. When operations shifted to Helmand, the British Army immediately attempted something similar with the platoon house strategy.

However, as with Basra in Iraq, the British in Helmand found themselves without effective local allies. Moreover, the Taliban massed and attempted to overrun the platoon houses. After about six months, it became clear that the number of enemy and their method of operation were much closer in many cases to those of a conventional army. This was particularly true around Musa Qaleh, where a British-backed tribal deal collapsed in the face of a reported two thousand insurgents, who seized the town and constructed extensive defenses.

The British, while not abandoning the platoon house approach, responded to this fairly unambiguous signal by shifting to more large-scale operations. The main operations of each year from 2007 to 2009 (Mar Kardar, Sond Chara, and Panchai Palang) sought to clear an area so that platoon houses could be established there while negotiations with tribal leaders and even some insurgents continued. The results of this shift were mixed, and the British essentially were confronted with the same problem encountered with Operation Sinbad in Basra: without local allies, aggressive operations were unable to hold areas that were cleared. In Musa Qaleh, reliable (or at least semi-reliable) local allies appear to have been more attainable (in the form of Mullah Abdul Salaam) than in other areas, such as Sangin.

Afghanistan provides additional support for the cultural hypothesis. In the case of the three organizations previously studied, there does seem to be similarity between operations in Iraq and Afghanistan. The British Army sought to do the same kind of operations in both northern and southern Afghanistan that it sought to do in Kenya and Iraq. In northern Afghanistan, the approach was successful, as local partners were readily available. In southern Afghanistan, as in Basra, the approach was less successful, as local partners were unavailable and the enemy was much more robustly organized into large quasi-conventional units.

With the U.S. Army, the same pattern as in Vietnam and Iraq appears to obtain. The focus of operations has consistently been on large units and fire-power. This is particularly telling given the troop limitations the Army faced, which meant that multibattalion operations would be difficult to assemble. Yet the Army nonetheless conducted at least a dozen such operations from 2002 to 2009.

Army Special Forces, in contrast, operated in small units in close cooper-ation with Afghan local forces. This pattern remained constant from 2001 to 2009, expanding in 2009–10 with the Local Defense Initiative and the Afghan Local Police. The emphasis on small units would sometimes conflict with limiting firepower, as the enemy in many cases would mass and oppose the Special Forces units in inhabited areas. U.S. Marine operations, which began on a large scale only in 2009, offer the least evidence but generally seem to support the plausibility of the cultural hypothesis.

Conclusions

The previous chapters have addressed two related puzzles of counterinsurgency doctrine. First, why do military organizations, despite agreement on the theoretical outlines of counterinsurgency doctrine, continue to diverge in terms of operations? Second, why does this variation in the conduct of operations not yield any reliably positive results? In other words, why does there not seem to be an equivalent to the "modern system" for counterinsurgency—a way of fighting that if effectively applied produces victory?

The first puzzle is best explained by the proposed hypothesis of organizational culture. All three of the organizations (and their subcultures) continued to conduct operations in accordance with their culture regardless of what written doctrine prescribed. The other competing hypotheses on doctrine are either indeterminate or do not explain the variation in operations. The geopolitical environment, level of civilian intervention, and structure of democratic institutions all vary across the cases yet seem to have little effect.

For example, civilian intervention in the United States to promote a certain type of counterinsurgency doctrine has had minimal effect on the Army at the operational level. Nor do the Army and Marine Corps ever experience substantial convergence in operations when information is ambiguous, despite conducting counterinsurgency in two countries for many years. Despite having different domestic political institutions, the British Army and the U.S. Marine Corps conduct similar counterinsurgency operations. The end of the Cold War seems to have had little effect on how any of the three confronted the challenge of counterinsurgency.

The desire to maximize resources and autonomy and minimize uncertainty also seems to have had little effect. In Vietnam the U.S. Army and Marine Corps had substantial autonomy that preceded conduct of operations. The British Army's access to resources in Kenya similarly seems to have been unaffected by choice of doctrine. All three organizations faced the same imperative to minimize uncertainty, yet the U.S. Marine Corps and the British Army accomplished this in a way significantly different from the U.S. Army.

Only in certain cases involving U.S. Army Special Forces was the effect of culture attenuated due to its subordinate status in the broader Army. In Vietnam, Special Forces initially had significant autonomy as part of a CIA program to work with mountain tribes. However, once the program was given to the Army-dominated Military Assistance Command Vietnam, it changed in ways that many in Special Forces were not comfortable with. Yet even in this case Special Forces continued to conduct operations as their culture would dictate, focusing on small-unit operations in conjunction with indigenous forces.

However, these varying operational responses have not led to systematically correlated outcomes. British success in Kenya was not duplicated in either Iraq or Afghanistan. Marine Corps engagement with indigenous forces in Vietnam produced no strategically significant effects, while similar efforts (in conjunction with civilians and U.S. Army Special Forces) in Iraq had a massive if fleeting strategic effect. Army Special Forces efforts with indigenous forces in Vietnam and Afghanistan likewise had limited effect.

This underscores the second puzzle of counterinsurgency doctrine: Why do none of the variations in operations seem to reliably lead to success? This puzzle is one that I did not initially anticipate. In beginning the research that resulted in this book, I believed that some organizational cultures were better than others for counterinsurgency. The U.S. Army, I thought, was culturally ill suited to counterinsurgency, whereas the British Army and the U.S. Marine Corps and Special Forces were well suited. Thus I expected to find the U.S. Army failing while the others succeeded.

The reality, as I witnessed firsthand in Iraq and Afghanistan, is different. The just-so narrative of the Iraq War—that the right general with the right doctrine leads to victory—does not withstand scrutiny. Even if it did, the same general with the same doctrine did not produce the same results in Afghanistan.

This has two major implications, one for theory and one for national security policy. Theoretically, culture provides a fruitful way of understanding variation in military doctrine and operations, most prominently in ambiguous information environments. It does so in ways that are more predictive than generic organizational theories, which can at best tell post hoc stories of organizational decision making. By referring to the organizational culture, the general outlines of a military's response to an environment can be predicted *ex ante*.

Because organizational culture will matter significantly when information is ambiguous or absent, it will be very important during extended periods of peace or during limited war. The observed decline in major interstate war since the nuclear revolution implies that culture will continue to be very important in the future. At the same time, this decline makes the continental armies increasingly out of step with the environment they exist in.

A related implication is that if change is to take place in military culture, it must affect military professional education. Without changes in not only the content but the context of professional education, it is unlikely that culture will change substantially. Related changes in promotion policy and force structure (such as shifting the focus of command training to platoons or companies rather than brigades or divisions) will also be required.

The policy implication is perhaps even more important, as it provides insight into the limits of the military tools available to policymakers. Continental armies, powerful as they may be against other armies, have distinct limitations in contexts and environments that do not match their cultural elements. Most notably, the ambiguous environment of counterinsurgency is a persistent mismatch to continental armies. They will therefore interpret that environment in ways that are often problematic, focusing on large units and purely military action to the exclusion of other aspects, including cooperation with locals and civilian agencies. Maritime armies, in contrast, have cultures much better suited in general to counterinsurgency. They will tend to interpret the ambiguous environment in ways that highlight the importance of small-unit operations, relatively limited firepower, and cooperation with locals and civilians.

However, maritime armies, despite a better generic fit, are not guaranteed success. The British Army in Kenya did extraordinarily well, as it had numerous effective local and civilian partners. However, the Marine experience in Vietnam was less successful, as was its effort in Anbar until 2005–6. Only the emergence of local partners in that period enabled Marine success in Iraq. Finally, the British Army in Iraq, despite nearly five years of persistent effort, was never able to find effective local partners and thus did quite poorly despite following the same set of practices that had proved successful before. Similar patterns appear to hold in Afghanistan as well.

This last point indicates the limits of counterinsurgency more generally. In the cases studied, it is the presence of effective local allies along with civilians with extensive local knowledge, as in Kenya, that appears to be the major determinant of success. The British Army in that case was vital for providing "muscle" and discipline, but absent the Home Guard, the Kenya Police Reserve, colonial administration, and the like, would have had a much more difficult if not impossible time quelling Mau Mau.

This is perhaps the key lesson of Iraq and Afghanistan: counterinsurgency is about much more than finding the right army, the right general, or the right doctrine. I began this research believing that there were organizations that were culturally "right" for COIN and that these organizations would succeed where others failed. The reality, as I saw firsthand, was different. Culture, doctrine, and operations mattered but were not dispositive.

Nothing drove this home to me more than the experience with Afghan Local Police. U.S. Army Special Forces, who are culturally well suited for

COIN, worked very hard under good generals to conduct COIN with local allies. Yet time and again the program ran up against the local reality that the government was unpopular and intransigent. Local allies were thus in short supply.

This indicates a line of future research on the causes and consequences of local allies. Why were the Marines able to find effective partners in Iraq, while the British were not? How was the Army able to copy to some degree the Marine success?

Another line of future inquiry would be to examine additional cases. Three cases that would provide substantial additional leverage are the Japanese Army, the French Army, and the Soviet/Russian Army. A study of the Japanese Army would be useful for two reasons. First, despite being the army of an island nation, it developed into a continental army focused on total war and conducted it during World War II in China, Southeast Asia, and the Pacific islands. It is therefore, like the U.S. Army, an example of the nonendogenous nature of culture. Second, it underwent a dramatic restructuring after World War II that might illuminate the steps needed to radically change culture.

Studying the French Army would be useful because its domestic environment, while democratic during the professionalization process, was substantially different from the British and American systems. Most notably, it was associated with conservative elements and was involved in several coups or near-coups. Further, France was a continental power, yet it had a substantial overseas empire as the French Army professionalized. It therefore had to perform a complex balancing act in terms of what lessons of warfare it sought to incorporate into its professionalization process; it had to be ready for war both with potential continental foes like Austria and Germany and with various tribes and ethnic groups overseas.

A study of the Soviet/Russian Army would be useful, as it began to professionalize in a domestic environment of hereditary autocracy. However, this domestic environment changed radically in 1917 and then again in 1991, becoming a one-party totalitarian system before transforming into a democracy (of sorts). These transformations and the wars associated with them, from the Russian Revolution to the counterinsurgency campaigns in Afghanistan and Chechnya, would provide a useful way to explore the effect of radical domestic change on organizational culture and military doctrine.

A final line of additional inquiry would be to examine other archetypes, such as the German/Israeli archetype noted in Chapter 2. The German Army, like the Japanese Army, underwent a radical restructuring that might show the limits of cultural continuity. Other archetypes might include those, such as Indonesia, that focus principally on internal security rather than interstate war, or the Swiss Army, which is essentially a guerrilla force in waiting.

Professional military organizations in the twenty-first century seem likely to spend much of their time in ambiguous environments. Major conventional wars are increasingly rare, meaning that these organizations will either have little information during times of peace or will be confronted with murky environments such as counterinsurgency. This means that for the foreseeable future culture will have a profound effect on military doctrine and operations. It therefore behooves military analysts and political leaders to understand the culture of these organizations as they plan strategy.

Notes

1. Military Doctrine and the Challenge of Counterinsurgency

1. For examples, see Kimberly Kagan, *The Surge: A Military History* (New York: Encounter Books, 2008); Linda Robinson, *Tell Me How This Ends: General David Petraeus and the Search for a Way Out of Iraq* (New York: PublicAffairs, 2009); and Thomas Ricks, *The Gamble: General Petraeus and the American Military Adventure in Iraq* (New York: Penguin, 2009). A more scholarly and nuanced treatment of the same basic narrative is Stephen Biddle, Jeffrey Friedman, and Jacob Shapiro, "Testing the Surge: Why Did Violence Decline in Iraq in 2007?," *International Security*, v. 37, n. 1 (Summer 2012).

2. U.S. Department of the Army and U.S. Marine Corps, Field Manual 3-24 / Fleet Marine Force Manual 3-24, *Counterinsurgency*, final draft, June 2006.

3. U.S. Department of the Army, Field Manual 31-16, March 1967, 7–8.

4. Lewis Sorley, *A Better War: The Unexamined Victories and Final Tragedy of America's Last Years in Vietnam* (New York: Harcourt, 1999).

5. For a broader critique of this "great man" theory of counterinsurgency, see Joshua Rovner, "The Heroes of COIN," *Orbis*, v. 56, n. 2 (Spring 2012).

6. For a similar critique, see Gian Gentile, *Wrong Turn: America's Deadly Embrace of Counterinsurgency* (New York: New Press, 2013); and Douglas Ollivant, *Countering the New Orthodoxy: Reinterpreting Counterinsurgency in Iraq* (Washington, DC: New America Foundation, 2011).

7. See, for example, Matt Bradley and Julian Barnes, "Iraq Army's Ability to Fight Raises Worries," *Wall Street Journal*, June 22, 2014.

8. See also the critique by Lieutenant General (ret.) Daniel Bolger, *Why We Lost: A General's Inside Account of the Iraq and Afghanistan Wars* (New York: Houghton Mifflin Harcourt, 2014).

9. U.S. Department of the Army and U.S. Marine Corps, Field Manual 3-24 / Marine Corps Warfighting Publicatoin 3-33.5, *Insurgencies and Countering Insurgencies* (May 2014).

10. Stephen Biddle, *Military Power: Explaining Victory and Defeat in Modern Battle* (Princeton, NJ: Princeton University Press, 2004).

11. For discussion of the challenges of counterinsurgency abroad, see Erin Simpson, "The Perils of Third Party Counterinsurgency" (Doctoral dissertation, Harvard University Department of Government, 2010).

12. See Robert Mackey, *The Uncivil War: Irregular Warfare in the Upper South, 1861–1865* (Norman: University of Oklahoma Press, 2004), esp. 113–22; and Lance Janda, "Shutting the Gates

of Mercy: The American Origins of Total War, 1860–1880," *Journal of Military History*, v. 59, n. 1 (January 1995): 14–17.

13. Michael Howard, *The Franco-Prussian War: The German Invasion of France, 1870–1871* (London: Rupert Hart-Davis, 1961).

14. See Robert T. Foley, *German Strategy and the Path to Verdun: Erich von Falkenhayn and the Development of Attrition, 1870–1916* (New York: Cambridge University Press, 2005), 14–37. One notable Prussian/German work on the subject is Fritz August Hoenig, *Der Volkskrieg an der Loire im Herbst 1870* [The People's War to the Loire in Fall 1870] (Berlin: Ernst Siegfried Mittler and Son, 1897).

15. See Robert B. Edgerton, *Warrior Women: The Amazons of Dahomey and the Nature of War* (Boulder, CO: Westview Press, 2000).

16. See Harold E. Raugh, *The Victorians at War, 1815–1914* (Santa Barbara, CA: ABC-Clio, 2004), 49–53; and Thomas Pakenham, *The Boer War* (New York: Random House, 1979).

17. Stanley Karnow, *Vietnam: A History* (New York: Viking Press, 1983), 135–40.

18. For more detailed discussion of the history of counterinsurgency theory, see Nils Gilman, *Mandarins of the Future: Modernization Theory in Cold War America* (Baltimore, MD: Johns Hopkins University Press, 2003); Austin Long, *On "Other War": Lessons from Five Decades of RAND Counterinsurgency Research* (Santa Monica, CA: RAND, 2006); D. Michael Shafer, *Deadly Paradigms: The Failure of U.S. Counterinsurgency Policy* (Princeton, NJ: Princeton University Press, 1988); and Jefferson Marquis, "The Other Warriors: American Social Science and Nation Building in Vietnam," *Diplomatic History*, v. 24, n. 1 (Winter 2000).

19. See Walt Rostow, *Economic Growth: A Non-Communist Manifesto* (Cambridge, MA: Center for International Studies, 1959), and Lucian Pye, *Lessons from the Malayan Struggle against Communism* (Cambridge, MA: Center for International Studies, 1957), for early thoughts on these issues. Samuel Huntington, *Political Order in Changing Societies* (New Haven, CT: Yale University Press, 1968), remains the definitive work on the tension between political development and order.

20. See, for example, Mao Tse-tung, *On Guerrilla War* (New York: Praeger, 1961); and Vo Nguyen Giap, *People's War, People's Army: The Vietcong Insurrection Manual for Underdeveloped Countries* (New York: Praeger, 1963).

21. See Roger D. Petersen, *Resistance and Rebellion: Lessons from Eastern Europe* (New York: Cambridge University Press, 2001); and Stathis N. Kalyvas, *The Logic of Violence in Civil War* (New York: Cambridge University Press, 2006).

22. For a review of the literature presented here, see Adam Grissom, "The Future of Military Innovation Studies," *Journal of Strategic Studies*, v. 29, n. 5 (October 2006).

23. For some of the roots of this basic set of beliefs, see Aaron Wildavsky, "The Self-Evaluating Organization," *Public Administration Review*, v. 32, n. 5 (September–October 1972); Morton Halperin, *Bureaucratic Politics and Foreign Policy* (Washington, DC: Brookings Institution, 1974), 51–58; and John Steinbrunner, *The Cybernetic Theory of Decision* (Princeton, NJ: Princeton University Press, 1974), 71–80.

24. Barry R. Posen, *The Sources of Military Doctrine: France, Britain, and Germany between the World Wars* (Ithaca, NY: Cornell University Press, 1984), conclusions on 239–41.

25. Jack L. Snyder, *The Ideology of the Offensive: Military Decision-making and the Disasters of 1914* (Ithaca, NY: Cornell University Press, 1984), conclusions on 205–11.

26. Deborah D. Avant, *Political Institutions and Military Change: Lessons from Peripheral Wars* (Ithaca, NY: Cornell University Press, 1994), conclusions on 130–33.

27. On value infusion and organizational goals, see Philip Selznick, *Leadership in Administration: A Sociological Interpretation* (New York: Row Peterson, 1957), 38–42; Herbert Simon, "On the Concept of Organizational Goal," *Administrative Science Quarterly*, v. 9, n. 1 (June 1964); Lawrence Mohr, "The Concept of Organizational Goal," *American Political Science Review*, v. 67, n. 2 (June 1973); and Halperin, *Bureaucratic Politics*, 28–29.

28. Stephen Rosen, *Winning the Next War: Innovation and the Modern Military* (Ithaca, NY: Cornell University Press, 1991), conclusions on 253–54.

29. Kimberly Marten Zisk, *Engaging the Enemy: Organization Theory and Soviet Military Innovation, 1955–1991* (Princeton, NJ: Princeton University Press, 1993), conclusions on 178–80.

30. Elizabeth Kier, *Imagining War: French and British Military Doctrine between the Wars* (Princeton, NJ: Princeton University Press, 1997), conclusions on 164–65.
31. Derived from Rosen, *Winning the Next War*, and Zisk, *Engaging the Enemy.*
32. Derived from Posen, *Sources of Military Doctrine.*
33. Derived from Avant, *Political Institutions and Military Change.*
34. Derived from Snyder, *Ideology of the Offensive*, and Halperin, *Bureaucratic Politics.*

2. Culture, Doctrine, and Military Professionalization

1. For a favorable review of the literature, see Alistair Iain Johnston, "Thinking about Strategic Culture," *International Security*, v. 19, n. 4 (Spring 1995). For a critical review of the literature, see Michael C. Desch, "Culture Clash: Assessing the Importance of Ideas in Security Studies," *International Security*, v. 23, n. 1 (Summer 1998). The business literature also has a long history of organizational culture argument at both the organizational and the national level. For discussion of culture at the organizational level, see, inter alia, Daniel R. Denison and Aneil K. Mishra, "Towards a Theory of Organizational Culture and Effectiveness," *Organization Science*, v. 6, n. 2 (March–April 1995); and Mary Jo Hatch, "The Dynamics of Organizational Culture," *Academy of Management Review*, v. 18, n. 4 (October 1993). At the national culture level, see Jeffrey A. Hart, *Rival Capitalists: International Competitiveness in the United States, Japan, and Western Europe* (Ithaca, NY: Cornell University Press, 1992).
2. Johnston, "Thinking about Strategic Culture."
3. Nathan Leites and Alexander George's concept of the operational code is certainly part of the lineage of organizational and strategic culture. See Nathan Leites, *The Operational Code of the Politburo* (New York: McGraw-Hill, 1951), and Alexander L. George, "The Operational Code: A Neglected Approach to the Study of Political Leaders and Decision-Making," *International Studies Quarterly*, v. 13, n. 2 (June 1969). Andrew M. Scott, "The Department of State: Formal Structure and Informal Culture," *International Studies Quarterly*, v. 13, n. 1 (March 1969), is also an excellent early work on organizational culture. See also Andrew M. Scott, "Environmental Change and Organizational Adaptation: The Problem of the State Department," and John E. Harr, "The Issue of Competence in the State Department," both in *International Studies Quarterly*, v. 14, n. 1 (March 1970).
4. Russell F. Weigley, *The American Way of War: A History of United States Military Strategy and Policy* (New York: Macmillan, 1973).
5. Jack L. Snyder, *The Soviet Strategic Culture: Implications for Limited Nuclear Operations* (Santa Monica, CA: RAND, 1977). Other RAND works examining the role of culture that followed include Arnold L. Horelick, *The Strategic Mind-Set of the Soviet Military: An Essay-Review* (1977), and Anthony H. Pascal et al., *Men and Arms in the Middle East: The Human Factor in Military Modernization* (1979).
6. Colin S. Gray, "National Style in Strategy: The American Example," *International Security*, v. 6, n. 2 (Fall 1981), as well as Colin S. Gray, *Nuclear Strategy and National Style* (Lanham, MD: Hamilton Press, 1986).
7. For example, Bradley S. Klein, "The Textual Strategies of the Military: or, Have You Read Any Good Defense Manuals Lately?," in James Der Derian and Michael J. Shapiro, eds., *International/Intertextual Relations: Postmodern Readings of World Politics* (Lexington, MA: Lexington Books, 1989); and Carol Cohn, "Sex and Death in the Rational World of Defense Intellectuals," *Signs: The Journal of Women in Culture and Society*, v. 12, n. 4 (Summer 1987).
8. Carl H. Builder, *The Masks of War: American Military Styles in Strategy and Analysis* (Baltimore, MD: Johns Hopkins University Press, 1989), and Andrew Krepinevich, *The Army and Vietnam* (Baltimore, MD: Johns Hopkins University Press, 1986).
9. Jeffrey W. Legro, *Cooperation under Fire: Anglo-German Restraint during World War II* (Ithaca, NY: Cornell University Press, 1995), and Elizabeth Kier, *Imagining War: French and British Military Doctrine between the Wars* (Princeton, NJ: Princeton University Press, 1997) are two of the best and most well-known examples. See also Kimberly Marten Zisk, *Weapons, Culture,*

and Self-Interest: Soviet Defense Managers in the New Russia (New York: Columbia University Press, 1997). Peter J. Katzenstein, ed., *The Culture of National Security: Norms and Identity in World Politics* (New York: Columbia University Press, 1996), contains essays from many of the new generation of writers on strategic culture.

10. H. H. Gerth and C. W. Mills, eds., *From Max Weber: Essays in Sociology* (New York: Oxford University Press, 1958), 280.

11. John Nagl, *Learning to Eat Soup with a Knife: Counterinsurgency Lessons from Malaya and Vietnam* (Chicago: University of Chicago Press, 2005).

12. Richard Downie, *Learning from Conflict: The U.S. Military in Vietnam, El Salvador, and the Drug War* (Westport, CT: Praeger, 1998).

13. Robert Cassidy, "Russia in Afghanistan and Chechnya: Military Strategic Culture and the Paradoxes of Asymmetric Conflict" (Carlisle, PA: U.S. Army War College Strategic Studies Institute, February 2003); Cassidy, *Peacekeeping in the Abyss: British and American Peacekeeping Doctrine and Practice after the Cold War* (Westport, CT: Praeger, 2004); and Cassidy, *Counterinsurgency and the Global War on Terror: Military Culture and Irregular War* (Westport, CT: Praeger Security International Press, 2006).

14. Nagl, *Learning to Eat Soup*, 35–55.

15. The anthropologist Clifford Geertz, for example, popularized the term "thick description" of culture but was skeptical of a "science" of culture. See Clifford Geertz, *The Interpretation of Cultures* (New York: Basic Books, 1973).

16. This definition is very similar to Edgar Schein's. Like Schein's, it does not include overt behavior and argues that these beliefs are so ingrained as to be taken for granted by an organization's members. See Edgar H. Schein, *Organizational Culture and Leadership* (San Francisco: Jossey-Bass, 1985), 8–9.

17. Jack L. Snyder, *The Ideology of the Offensive: Military Decisionmaking and the Disasters of 1914* (Ithaca, NY: Cornell University Press, 1984), 15–30.

18. Ibid., 30.

19. Ibid., 210–11.

20. This is similar to the process of value infusion described in see Philip Selznick, *Leadership in Administration: A Sociological Interpretation* (New York: Row Peterson, 1957), 38–65.

21. Thanks to Paul Staniland for suggesting this point, which is alluded to in different ways in Snyder, *Ideology of the Offensive*, and Stephen Rosen, *Winning the Next War: Innovation and the Modern Military* (Ithaca, NY: Cornell University Press, 1991).

22. Thomas Mahnken, *Uncovering Ways of War: U.S. Intelligence and Foreign Military Innovation, 1918–1941* (Ithaca, NY: Cornell University Press, 2002).

23. See Caitlin Talmadge, *The Dictator's Army: Battlefield Effectiveness in Authoritarian Regimes* (Ithaca, NY: Cornell University Press, forthcoming 2015).

24. Scott D. Sagan, "1914 Revisited: Allies, Offense, and Instability," *International Security*, v. 11, n. 2 (Fall 1986), presents the essence of this argument, summing up, "The key point for this critique of 'cult of the offensive' theory is not how this counterfactual debate is resolved but rather that it exists at all." See 159–61. See also John Mearsheimer, *The Tragedy of Great Power Politics* (New York: W. W. Norton, 2001), 58, 215–16, and Niall Ferguson, *The Pity of War: Explaining World War I* (New York: Basic Books, 1999), 315–16, for more recent comments on the potential viability and effectiveness of the Schlieffen Plan and German strategy.

25. James G. March with Chip Heath, *A Primer on Decision Making: How Decisions Happen* (New York: Free Press, 1994).

26. George F. Hofmann, "The Tactical and Strategic Use of Attaché Intelligence: The Spanish Civil War and the U.S. Army's Misguided Quest for a Modern Tank Doctrine," *Journal of Military History*, v. 62, n. 1 (January 1998).

27. James S. Corum, "A Clash of Military Cultures: German and French Approaches to Technology between the World Wars," paper presented at the U.S. Air Force Academy Symposium, Colorado Springs, Colorado, September 1994.

28. Morton Halperin, *Bureaucratic Politics and Foreign Policy* (Washington, DC: Brookings Institution, 1974), 28–29.

29. Ibid., 35.

30. James Q. Wilson, *Bureaucracy: What Government Agencies Do and Why They Do It* (New York: Basic Books, 1989), 101; see also 90–113 on organizational culture.

31. Barry R. Posen, *The Sources of Military Doctrine: France, Britain, and Germany between the World Wars* (Ithaca, NY: Cornell University Press, 1984), 13–14.

32. Barry Posen, "Still Strange Defeat? France 1940," unpublished paper, 1999.

33. Dan Carter provides a lucid discussion of why the poor specification of doctrine undermines its utility as a dependent variable. See Daniel Carter, "Innovation, Wargaming, and Armored Warfare" (master's thesis, Massachusetts Institute of Technology, 2005), 10–12. Carter's definition of doctrine is essentially identical to the one presented here.

34. See Robert Doughty, *The Evolution of U.S. Army Tactical Doctrine, 1946–1976* (Leavenworth, KS: Combat Studies Institute, 1979), and Ingo Trauschweizer, *The Cold War U.S. Army: Building Deterrence for Limited War* (Lawrence: University Press of Kansas, 2008).

35. Doctrine will vary along different lines for air and naval forces, which exist in a very different milieu than ground forces. The central differences are that neither sea nor air is home to human habitation on a significant scale, and both lack "terrain" in a meaningful sense. Combined with the capital-intensive nature of air and naval combat, these differences mean that air and naval doctrine are substantially different from ground force doctrine.

36. Some scholars refer to these shared beliefs as "mental models." See Douglass C. North, and Syed Shariq "Learning, Institutions, and Economic Performance," *Perspectives on Politics*, v. 2, n. 1 (March 2004); and Douglass C. North and Arthur T. Denzau, "Shared Mental Models: Ideologies and Institutions," *Kyklos*, v. 47, n. 1 (Winter 1994). Schein also argues that organizational founders play a major role in the formation of culture. See Schein, *Organizational Culture*, chaps. 7 and 9.

37. Barbara Farnham, ed., *Avoiding Loss/Taking Risk: Prospect Theory and International Conflict* (Ann Arbor: University of Michigan Press, 1994), and Yuen Foong Khong, *Analogies at War: Korea, Munich, Dien Bien Phu, and the Vietnam Decisions of 1965* (Princeton, NJ: Princeton University Press, 1992), present applications of analogical decision making to international relations.

38. Carl Builder even uses the term "institutional personality" rather than organizational culture. The two terms are used here synonymously. See Builder, *Masks of War*, 7–8.

39. For example, the preprofessional Prussian Army officer corps was drawn almost exclusively from the Junker upper class. See Karl Demeter, *The German Officer Corps in Society and State, 1650–1945*, trans. Angus Malcolm (New York: Praeger, 1965).

40. See Howard M. Vollmer and Donald Mills, eds., *Professionalization* (Englewood Cliffs, NJ: Prentice-Hall, 1966), especially Ernest Greenwood, "The Elements of Professionalization"; and Harold L. Wilensky, "The Professionalization of Everyone?," *American Journal of Sociology*, v. 70, n. 2 (September 1964). For discussion of the tension between bureaucracy and professionalism and attempts to balance the two, see Richard H. Hall, "Professionalization and Bureaucratization," *American Sociological Review*, v. 33, n. 1 (February 1968).

41. Professions are more than just abstract theory along with values and codes of conduct; they include the other aspects of culture noted earlier, such as shared language, rituals, dress, and the like. The most important elements for doctrine, however, are the theory and the values.

42. Morris Janowitz, *The Professional Soldier: A Social and Political Portrait*, 2nd ed. (New York: Free Press, 1971), 5–6.

43. For a recent work that proposes a "military operational code" that covers all professional militaries, see Colin Jackson, *Defeat in Victory: The Military, Politics, and Counterinsurgency* (forthcoming).

44. Corelli Barnett, "The Education of Military Elites," *Journal of Contemporary History*, v. 2, n. 3 (July 1967): 16–19, explicitly draws this link between educational reform and unsuccessful war. Barry Posen, "Nationalism, Military Power, and the Mass Army," *International Security*, v. 18, n. 2 (Fall 1993), discusses the improvement in the officer corps in the context of fully utilizing the capabilities of the mass army.

45. Barnett, "Education of Military Elites." See also Demeter, *German Officer Corps*; and Gordon Craig, *The Politics of the Prussian Army, 1640–1945* (London: Oxford University Press, 1955), 38–46.

46. On the importance of the mass army, see Posen, "Nationalism, Military Power, and the Mass Army." On the importance of directive-oriented command, see Demeter, *German Officer Corps*, and Martin van Creveld, *Fighting Power: German and U.S. Army Performance, 1939–1945* (Westport, CT: Greenwood Press, 1982). On the battle of annihilation, see Dennis Showalter, *Railroads and Rifles: Soldiers, Technology, and the Unification of Germany* (Hamden, CT: Archon Books, 1975), and Larry Addington, *The Blitzkrieg Era and the German General Staff, 1865–1941* (New Brunswick, NJ: Rutgers University Press, 1971).

47. An entire literature has emerged on geography's influence on the military and state formation. See Otto Hintze, "Military Organization and the Organization of the State," in *The Historical Essays of Otto Hintze*, ed. Felix Gilbert (New York: Oxford University Press, 1975); Charles Tilly, "Reflection on the History of European State-Making," in *The Formation of National States in Europe*, ed. Charles Tilly (Princeton, NJ: Princeton University Press, 1975); and Peter Gourevitch, "The Second Image Reversed: The International Sources of Domestic Politics," *International Organization*, v. 32, n. 4 (Autumn 1978).

48. Samuel Finer, "State and Nation Building in Europe: The Role of the Military," in Tilly, *Formation of National States*. Alan Milward's concept of "strategic synthesis" is somewhat similar. See Alan Milward, *War, Economy, and Society, 1939–1945* (Berkeley: University of California Press, 1977).

49. See Donald Abenheim, *Reforging the Iron Cross: The Search for Tradition in the West German Armed Forces* (Princeton, NJ: Princeton University Press, 1988), and Thomas U. Berger, *Cultures of Antimilitarism: National Security in Germany and Japan* (Baltimore, MD: Johns Hopkins University Press, 1998).

50. Posen, *Sources of Military Doctrine*, 183.

51. In an unpublished manuscript titled "The Evolution of Land Warfare," Barry Posen uses the similar concept of "mass mobilization–heavy." Posen, "Nationalism, Military Power, and the Mass Army" provides a good overview of this type of warfare.

52. I am grateful to Owen Coté and Brendan Green for many long discussions about the issues of maritime states' military policy, internal order, and the relationships between the two. See also Aaron Friedberg, *In the Shadow of the Garrison State* (Princeton, NJ: Princeton University Press, 2000).

53. See Michael Barnhart, *Japan Prepares for Total War: The Search for Economic Security, 1919–1941* (Ithaca, NY: Cornell University Press, 1987), and Edward Drea, *Japan's Imperial Army: Its Rise and Fall, 1853–1945* (Lawrence: University Press of Kansas, 2009).

54. For the role of language in organizations, see Martin Meissner, "The Language of Work," in Robert Durbin, ed., *Handbook of Work, Organization, and Society* (Chicago: Rand-McNally, 1976). Militaries in general and the U.S. military in particular are prone to extensive use of jargon. See Frederick Elkin, "The Soldier's Language," and Howard Brotz and Everett Wilson, "Characteristics of Military Society," both in *American Journal of Sociology*, v. 51, n. 5 (March 1946).

55. Eliot A. Cohen, "Making Do with Less, or Coping with Upton's Ghost," paper presented at U.S. Army War College Strategy Conference, Carlisle, Pennsylvania, May 1995, makes similar points.

56. See http://usacac.army.mil/cac2/CSI/docs/SRT_CSIRideMap.pdf (accessed October 1, 2014).

57. For example, on the more general and often remedial nature of education at West Point in the 1800s, see Russell Weigley, *History of the United States Army* (New York: Macmillan, 1967), 104–6; and Edward M. Coffman, *The Old Army: A Portrait of the American Army in Peacetime, 1784–1898* (New York: Oxford University Press, 1986), 269–71.

58. Gary Wade, "World War II Division Commanders" (Leavenworth, KS: Combat Studies Institute, 1983), 5–6.

59. See Max Weber, *The Theory of Social and Economic Organization*, trans. A. M. Henderson and Talcott Parsons (New York: Free Press, 1947), and James Q. Wilson, *Bureaucracy: What Government Agencies Do and Why They Do It* (New York: Basic Books, 1989), for discussion of the standard characteristics of bureaucracy and organization.

60. See Samuel Huntington, *The Soldier and the State: The Theory and Politics of Civil-Military Relations* (Cambridge, MA: Belknap Press of Harvard University Press, 1957), 16–18; and Jacques

Van Doorn, "The Officer Corps: A Fusion of Profession and Organization," *European Archives of Sociology*, v. 6 (1965).

61. See Erving Goffman, *Asylums: Essays on the Social Situation of Mental Patients and Other Inmates* (Garden City, NY: Doubleday Press, 1961), and C. A. McEwen, "Continuities in the Study of Total and Nontotal Institutions," *Annual Review of Sociology*, v. 6 (1980).

62. See Morris Janowitz and Edward A. Shils, "Cohesion and Disintegration in the Wehrmacht in World War II," *Public Opinion Quarterly*, v. 12, n. 2 (Summer 1948); Omer Bartov, *Hitler's Army: Soldiers, Nazis, and War in the Third Reich* (New York: Oxford University Press, 1991); and Jasen Castillo, *Endurance and War: The National Sources of Military Cohesion* (Stanford, CA: Stanford University Press, 2014).

63. Rosen, *Winning the Next War*, discusses the nonmonolithic nature of most military organizations, though he refers to them as branches or communities rather than subcultures.

64. Caren Siehl and Joanne Martin, "Organizational Culture and Counterculture: An Uneasy Symbiosis," *Organizational Dynamics*, v. 12, n. 2 (Autumn 1983). In the military context, Builder briefly mentions subcultures or "intraservice" distinctions (*Masks of War*, 25–26).

65. See Builder, *Masks of War*, chaps. 3, 6, and 12, for discussion of the general Air Force culture, and Mike Worden, *Rise of the Fighter Generals: The Problem of Air Force Leadership, 1945–1982* (Maxwell, AL: Air University Press, 1998), for discussion of the fighter vs. bomber pilot subcultures. Tom Wolfe, *The Right Stuff* (New York: Farrar, Straus and Giroux, 1979), also gives a good overview of Air Force culture and the hierarchy of various types of pilot subcultures.

66. For discussion of the Navy subcultures and how they interact, see, inter alia, Elmo Zumwalt, *On Watch* (New York: Quadrangle Books, 1976), and Malcolm Muir Jr., *Black Shoes and Brown Water: Surface Warfare in the United States Navy, 1945–1975* (Washington, DC: Naval Historical Center, 1996).

67. For more detail on Goldwater-Nichols, see James R. Locher, *Victory on the Potomac: The Goldwater-Nichols Act Unifies the Pentagon* (College Station: Texas A&M Press, 2002). For more detail on special operations culture and efforts to promote it, see Susan L. Marquis, *Unconventional Warfare: Rebuilding U.S. Special Operations Forces* (Washington, DC: Brookings Institution, 1997).

68. For example, Army officers who are members of the armor, artillery, or infantry branches will often (though certainly not always) express disdain for Army Special Forces as "cowboys" who "don't play well with others." See Marquis, *Unconventional Warfare*, chaps. 2 and 3.

3. "The Habits and Usages of War"

1. See William Skelton, "Samuel P. Huntington and the Roots of the American Military Tradition," *Journal of Military History*, v. 60, n. 2 (April 1996); and William Skelton, *An American Profession of Arms: The Army Officer Corps, 1784–1861* (Lawrence: University of Kansas Press, 1992).

2. Skelton, *An American Profession of Arms*; Russell Weigley, *History of the United States Army* (New York: Macmillan, 1967), 144–73.

3. Skelton, "Samuel P. Huntington," 329–30.

4. Weigley, *History of the United States Army*, 163–64.

5. John B. Wilson, *Maneuver and Firepower: The Evolution of Divisions and Separate Brigades* (Washington, DC: U.S. Army Center for Military History, 1998), 9.

6. Weigley, *History of the United States Army*, 160–63.

7. Wilson, *Maneuver and Firepower*, 11–12; Weigley, *History of the United States Army*, 182.

8. This characterization of two distinct and different professionalization experiences of the U.S. Army is drawn from Mark R. Grandstaff, "Preserving the 'Habits and Usages of War': William Tecumseh Sherman, Professional Reform, and the U.S. Army Officer Corps, 1865–1881, Revisited," *Journal of Military History*, v. 62, n. 3 (July 1998).

9. See Mark Grimsley, *The Hard Hand of War: Union Military Policy toward Southern Civilians, 1861–1865* (Cambridge: Cambridge University Press, 1995), 21–22.

10. Ibid., 31–33; Joseph Harsh, "Lincoln's Tarnished Brass: Conservative Strategies and the American Attempt to Fight the Early Civil War as a Limited War," in *The Confederate High*

Command and Other Topics: Themes in Honor of T. Harry Williams, ed. Roman Heleniak and Lawrence Hewitt (Shippensburg, PA: White Mane, 1990).

11. Grimsley, *Hard Hand of War*, 33–35; Richard Curry, "A Reappraisal of Statehood Politics in West Virginia," *Journal of Southern History*, v. 28, n. 4 (November 1962).

12. Grimsley, *Hard Hand of War*, 35–39.

13. Ibid., 67–92; Daniel Sutherland, "Abraham Lincoln, John Pope, and the Origins of Total War," *Journal of Military History*, v. 56, n. 4 (October 1992).

14. Grimsley, *Hard Hand of War*, 48–58.

15. Ibid., 154–62.

16. John F. Marszalek, *Sherman: A Soldier's Passion for Order* (New York: Free Press, 1993), 253–54. See also Grimsley, *Hard Hand of War*, 162–65.

17. Grimsley, *Hard Hand of War*, 166–67.

18. Both quotations from ibid., 168.

19. See Robert Mackey, *The Uncivil War: Irregular Warfare in the Upper South, 1861–1865* (Norman: University of Oklahoma Press, 2004), esp. 113–22; and Lance Janda, "Shutting the Gates of Mercy: The American Origins of Total War, 1860–1880," *Journal of Military History*, v. 59, n. 1 (January 1995): 14–17.

20. Grimsley, *Hard Hand of War*, 186–204.

21. See ibid., 171–73, and Marsalek, *Sherman*, 232–33, for examples of Sherman's justifications.

22. See Russell F. Weigley, *The American Way of War: A History of United States Military Strategy and Policy* (New York: Macmillan, 1973), 102–27, for discussion of Lee and the Confederates' search for decisive battle, and 133–39 for McClellan and the Union.

23. See ibid., 129–31, 139–46; and Brent Noseworthy, *The Bloody Crucible of Courage: Fighting Methods and Combat Experience of the Civil War* (New York: Carroll and Graf, 2003), 645–48.

24. Weigley, *American Way of War*, 108–9.

25. Ibid., 135.

26. In addition to previous cites, see Edward Hagerman, *The American Civil War and the Origins of Modern Warfare: Ideas, Organization, and Field Command* (Bloomington: Indiana University Press, 1988), 275–98.

27. See Noseworthy, *Bloody Crucible of Courage*, 496–518, 533–67.

28. Weigley, *History of the United States Army*, 250–52; Weigley, *American Way of War*, 139–45.

29. Noseworthy, *Bloody Crucible of Courage*, 564–67; Alfred James, "The Battle of the Crater," *Journal of the American Military History Foundation*, v. 2, n. 3 (Spring 1938).

30. See Marszalek, *Sherman*, 264–84, for examples of both Sherman's general preference to avoid battle and his willingness to undertake it when necessary.

31. See Hagerman, *American Civil War*, 293–97. Hagerman notes that Sherman made less use of artillery than Grant did in the same period, as he needed to move across greater distances and also faced less entrenched resistance.

32. See David Skaggs, "River Navies in the Civil War," *Military Affairs*, v. 18, n. 1 (Spring 1954), for a brief summary.

33. Weigley, *History of the United States Army*, 241.

34. See Grady McWhiney, "General Beauregard's 'Complete Victory' at Shiloh: An Interpretation," *Journal of Southern History*, v. 49, n. 3 (August 1983).

35. See Edward Hagerman, "Union Generalship, Political Leadership, and Total War Strategy," in *On the Road to Total War: The American Civil War and the German Wars of Unification, 1861–1871*, ed. Stig Forster and Jorg Nagler (Cambridge: Cambridge University Press, 1997), 150–54.

36. Ibid., 157–60.

37. Marszalek, *Sherman*, 259–64.

38. This summary is drawn from James E. Sefton, *The United States Army and Reconstruction, 1865–1877* (Baton Rouge: Louisiana State University Press, 1967).

39. See War Department General Order 56, 1866, quoted in Wilson, *Maneuver and Firepower*, 16.

40. Ibid., 14.

41. Robert Epstein, "The Creation and Evolution of the Army Corps in the American Civil War," *Journal of Military History*, v. 55, n. 1 (January 1999).

42. See Richard DiNardo, "Southern by the Grace of God but Prussian by Common Sense: James Longstreet and the Exercise of Command in the U.S. Civil War," *Journal of Military History,* v. 66, n. 4 (October 2002).

43. See Sherrod East, "Montgomery C. Meigs and the Quartermaster Department," *Military Affairs,* v. 25, n. 4 (Winter 1961); Erna Risch, *Quartermaster Support of the Army: A History of the Corps, 1775–1939* (Washington, DC: Center for Military History, 1989); and David Miller, *Second Only to Grant: Quartermaster General Montgomery C. Meigs: A Biography* (Shippensburg, PA: White Mane, 2000).

44. East, "Montgomery C. Meigs," 194.

45. E. G. Campbell, "The United States Military Railroads, 1862–1865: War Time Operation and Maintenance," *Journal of the American Military History Foundation,* v. 2, n. 2 (Summer 1938): 89.

46. Sherman, 385.

47. Ibid.

48. Ibid., 386.

49. This discussion of Sherman and Army professionalism draws heavily on Grandstaff, "Preserving the 'Habits and Usages of War.' "

50. *Report of the General of the Army, 1881,* 36–37, as quoted in Grandstaff, "Preserving the 'Habits and Usages of War.' "

51. Timothy K. Nenninger, *The Leavenworth Schools and the Old Army: Education, Professionalism, and the Officer Corps of the United States Army, 1881–1918* (Westport, CT: Greenwood Press, 1978), 28.

52. See Robert Utley, *The Indian Frontier, 1846–1890,* rev. ed. (Albuquerque: University of New Mexico Press, 2003), 104–6, quotation from 106.

53. Ibid.

54. Ibid., 109–21.

55. Ibid., 123–24.

56. See Lance Janda, "Shutting the Gates of Mercy: The American Origins of Total War, 1860–1880," *Journal of Military History,* v. 59, n. 1 (January 1995).

57. For an account of the campaign against Black Kettle, see Charles Brill, *Custer, Black Kettle, and the Fight on the Washita* (Norman: University of Oklahoma Press, 2002). Sheridan's own description of the engagement can be found in Philip Sheridan, *Memoirs of Philip Sheridan,* vol. 2 (New York: Charles Webster, 1888), 313–20.

58. Quotation from David Smits, "The Frontier Army and the Destruction of the Buffalo, 1865–1883," *Western Historical Quarterly,* v. 25, n. 3 (Autumn 1994): 314.

59. Ibid., 316–17.

60. Utley, *Indian Frontier,* 188–200.

61. Ibid., 170–75.

62. Smits, "Frontier Army," 326–28.

63. For discussion of the Guard and the Army in the Spanish-American War, see Jerry Cooper, *The Rise of the National Guard: The Evolution of the American Militia, 1865–1920* (Lincoln, NE: University of Nebrasak Press, 1997) 97–107; and Graham A. Cosmas, "From Order to Chaos: The War Department, the National Guard, and Military Policy, 1898," *Military Affairs,* v. 29, n. 3 (Autumn 1965).

64. Weigley, *History of the United States Army,* 299–302.

65. Ibid., 306, notes that V Corps, about 14,400 Regulars and 2,400 volunteers in the Rough Riders, and two National Guard regiments conducted most of the fighting.

66. Arthur A. Ekhirch Jr., "The Idea of a Citizen Army," *Military Affairs,* v. 17, n. 1 (Spring 1953); Phillip L. Semsch, "Elihu Root and the General Staff," *Military Affairs,* v. 21, n. 1 (Spring 1963). Note that neither act was uncontroversial. Some of the senior officers in the Army (who had not attended the Leavenworth school) were particularly opposed to the general staff.

67. Nenninger, *The Leavenworth Schools,* 53–60.

68. Quoted in Brian Linn, *The U.S. Army and Counterinsurgency in the Philippine War, 1899–1902* (Chapel Hill, NC: University of North Carolina Press, 1989), 153.

69. Nenninger, *The Leavenworth Schools,* 68–79.

70. Ibid., 82–130.

71. War Department, *Field Service Regulations, United States Army, 1905 (Amended, 1908)* (Washington, DC: Government Printing Office, 1908).

72. Linn, *U.S. Army and Counterinsurgency*, 70–86.

73. Ibid., 154–56.

74. Ibid., 157.

75. John Gates, *Schoolbooks and Krags: The United States Army in the Philippines, 1898–1902* (Westport, CT: Greenwood Press, 1973), 254–58.

76. Weigley, *History of the United States Army*, 347.

77. Nenninger, *The Leavenworth Schools*, 134–44.

78. Weigley, *American Way of War*, 201–7.

79. The National Defense Act of 1920 created an assistant secretary for mobilization in the War Department. The mass army would be a key element of the Army's primary mission, so selective service provisions were also included in the 1920 act. See Weigley, *American Way of War*, 207–10, 220–22; Ekhirch, "Idea of a Citizen Army," 5–7; Albert A. Blum and J. Douglas Smythe, "Who Should Serve: Pre–World War II Planning for Selective Service," *Journal of Economic History*, v. 30, n. 2 (June 1970).

80. Weigley, *American Way of War*, 313; Louis Morton, "War Plan ORANGE: Evolution of a Strategy," *World Politics*, v. 11, n. 2 (January 1959). Some in the Army War Plans Division wanted to abandon the Philippines and scrap the ORANGE plan entirely; see Ronald Schaffer, "General Stanley D. Embick: Military Dissenter," *Military Affairs*, v. 37, n. 3 (October 1973).

81. There is considerable debate on the quality of education received at the CGSS, yet most sources agree that what was taught was still focused on the traditional elements of Army strategic culture. The curriculum and composition of the classes at the CGSS had changed over time while still transmitting the tenets of Army culture. For a review of some of the debate and discussion of what was taught, see Timothy K. Nenninger, "Leavenworth and Its Critics: The U.S. Army Command and General Staff School, 1920–1940," *Journal of Military History*, v. 58, n. 2 (April 1994). Martin Blumenson is somewhat harsher than Nenninger in discussing Leavenworth but makes the same key points, that Leavenworth was the most important educational assignment for rising officers and exerted a homogenizing influence. See Martin Blumenson, "America's World War II Leaders in Europe: Some Thoughts," *Parameters*, v. 19 (December 1989).

82. Nenninger, "Leavenworth and Its Critics," 203.

83. Fred Greene, "The Military View of American National Policy, 1904–1940," *American Historical Review*, v. 66, n. 2 (January 1961): 358–59. This article relates Army and Navy views during the period to national policy or lack thereof. Greene argues that in the 1920s the Army was not planning for a return to Europe. However, the CGSS was educating officers for mass warfare somewhere, probably South America.

84. The Reichswehr would provide a good cadre of long-service professionals for the later expansion of the Wehrmacht. The U.S. Regular Army would serve much the same role, though there is debate about the relative quality of the two. Martin van Creveld, *Fighting Power: German and U.S. Army Performance, 1939–1945* (Westport, CT: Greenwood Press, 1982) argues that the Wehrmacht was more effective due in large part to its culture of decentralized command, while Michael D. Doubler, *Closing with the Enemy: How GIs Fought the War in Europe, 1944–1945* (Lawrence: University Press of Kansas, 1994), casts doubt on Van Creveld's conclusions. See also Russell F. Weigley, *Eisenhower's Lieutenants: The Campaign of France and Germany, 1944–1945* (Bloomington: Indiana University Press, 1981), and Geoffrey Perret, *There's a War to Be Won: The U.S. Army in World War II* (New York: Ballantine Books, 1997). Weigley is generally supportive of Van Creveld, while Perret is generally supportive of Doubler.

85. Weigley, *American Way of War*, 314–16; for discussion of Army interest in the Spanish Civil War, see George F. Hofmann "The Tactical and Strategic Use of Attaché Intelligence: The Spanish Civil War and the U.S. Army's Misguided Quest for a Modern Tank Doctrine," *Journal of Military History*, v. 62, n. 1 (January 1998).

86. The anti–armored warfare bias of the branches is discussed in Hoffman, "Tactical and Strategic Use," 120–25. Charles M. Bailey, *Faint Praise: American Tanks and Tank Destroyers in World War II* (Hamden, CT: Archon Books, 1983), and David E. Johnson, *Fast Tanks and Heavy Bombers:*

Innovation in the U.S. Army 1917–1945 (Ithaca, NY: Cornell University Press, 1998), provide a good summary of the development of Army thought on tanks in the interwar period.

87. Weigley, *American Way of War*, 317–59, provides a summary of the American war in both theaters; for a later analysis of the mobilization that argues that organizational and moral factors contributed heavily to victory, see Richard J. Overy, *Why the Allies Won* (New York: W. W. Norton, 1996).

88. Gary Wade, *World War II Division Commanders* (Fort Leavenworth, KS: Combat Studies Institute, 1983), 5–6, quotation on 6.

89. See Conrad C. Crane, *Bombs, Cities, and Civilians: American Airpower Strategy in World War II* (Lawrence: University Press of Kansas, 1993), for discussion of American strategic airpower, and W. A. Jacobs, "The Battle for France, 1944," in *Case Studies in the Development of Close Air Support*, ed. Benjamin Franklin Cooling (Washington, DC: Office of Air Force History, 1990), for discussion of the tactical use of airpower.

90. Quoted in Weigley, *Eisenhower's Lieutenants*, 28.

91. See David T. Fautua, "The 'Long Pull' Army: NSC 68, the Korean War and the Creation of the Cold War U.S. Army," *Journal of Military History*, v. 61, n. 1 (January 1997), for discussion of Army attitudes in the late 1940s and early 1950s, including the service's plans for a larger standing army. This standing army would still be supplemented by a massive influx of new soldiers in an actual war in Europe. He also points out that even as the Eighth Army fought a limited war in Korea, the Army was focused on building the Seventh Army for total war in Europe.

92. For a discussion of the 1950s and the Army's reaction to massive retaliation, see Andrew J. Bacevich, *The Pentomic Era: The U.S. Army between Korea and Vietnam* (Washington, DC: National Defense University Press, 1986).

93. For an overview of early Army advocacy of tactical use nuclear weapons, see Barton J. Bernstein, "Eclipsed by Hiroshima and Nagasaki: Early Thinking about Tactical Nuclear Weapons," *International Security*, v. 15, n. 4 (Spring 1991). For a discussion of the Army focus on airmobility as primarily an element of the nuclear battlefield, see John J. Tolson, *Airmobility, 1961–1971* (Washington, DC: Army Center for Military History, 1973), 10–12.

94. See Wilson, *Maneuver and Firepower*, chap. 10, for discussion of the concept and evolution of the Pentomic Division.

95. See Maxwell D. Taylor, *The Uncertain Trumpet* (New York: Harper, 1960).

96. The conflicting views of Kennedy and the Army on limited war are presented in Andrew Krepinevich, *The Army and Vietnam* (Baltimore, MD: Johns Hopkins University Press, 1986) 28–40. See also Robert E. Osgood, *Limited War: The Challenge to American Strategy* (Chicago: University of Chicago Press, 1957), chap. 10. Osgood's view of limited war as a conventional/theater nuclear contest below the strategic nuclear threshold is consonant with the Army's views.

97. Army Special Forces existed prior to Kennedy, but he was a major champion of the Special Forces and a proponent of a distinct subculture for them. For example, he authorized them to wear the green beret in 1961, distinguishing them from the elite of the regular infantry subculture, who wore maroon (Airborne) and black (Ranger) berets. See Francis John Kelly, *U.S. Army Special Forces, 1961–1971* (Washington, DC: Army Center for Military History, 1973), 2–6, 160–68. As noted earlier, Special Forces would be classified by Siehl and Martin as a "counter" subculture. Note that another counterculture of the Army, aviation, succeeded in breaking away from the Army into its own service. The increasing autonomy of U.S. Special Operations Command (USSOCOM), which now has its own budget apart from the services, may be an indication that Special Forces will eventually do the same.

98. See Alfred Paddock, *U.S. Army Special Warfare: Its Origins; Psychological and Unconventional Warfare, 1941–1952* (Washington, DC: National Defense University Press, 1982), 23–38.

99. Ibid., 69–110.

100. Ibid., 111–40.

101. Ibid., 150.

102. Charles M. Simpson, *Inside the Green Berets: The First Thirty Years; A History of the U.S. Army Special Forces* (Novato, CA: Presidio Press, 1983), 21.

103. Ibid., 22.

104. Kelly, *U.S. Army Special Forces*, 3–4.

105. Simpson, *Inside the Green Berets*, 22.

106. Paddock, *U.S. Army Special Warfare*, 230, 236–37.

107. William Meara, *Contra Cross: Insurgency and Tyranny in Central America, 1979–1989* (Annapolis, MD: Naval Institute Press, 2006), 14.

108. Ibid., 17.

109. See ibid., 18–21; Linda Robinson, *Masters of Chaos: The Secret History of the Special Forces* (New York: PublicAffairs, 2004), 26–29; and Janice Burton, "Robin Sage: World's Foremost Unconventional Warfare Exercise Turns 35," *Special Warfare*, v. 22, n. 2 (March–April 2009).

110. At various times, the Army has authorized a direct enlistment to Special Forces. These individuals, known as "SF babies," must still pass jump school and the Q Course.

4. From the Halls of Montezuma

1. See James A. Donovan, *The United States Marine Corps* (New York: Praeger, 1967), for a short discussion of the history of the Corps prior to Vietnam.

2. Allan R. Millett, *Semper Fidelis: The History of the United States Marine Corps*, rev. ed. (New York: Free Press, 1991), 90–92.

3. The most detailed treatment of the early period of Marine professionalization is Jack Shulimson, *The Marine Corps' Search for a Mission, 1880–1898* (Lawrence: University Press of Kansas, 1993), 10–29.

4. Ibid., 40.

5. Ibid., 40–45.

6. Ibid., 45–54.

7. Ivan Musicant, *The Banana Wars: A History of U.S. Intervention in Latin America from the Spanish-American War to the Invasion of Panama* (New York: Macmillan, 1990), 88.

8. Ibid., 84–85, 88, 95; Shulimson, *Marine Corps' Search*, 58–62.

9. Quoted in Musicant, *Banana Wars*, 95.

10. Shulimson, *Marine Corps' Search*, 61–62.

11. Ibid., 89–90.

12. Ibid., 90. See also John G. Miller, "William Freeland Fullam's War with the Corps," *U.S. Naval Institute Proceedings*, n. 101 (November 1975).

13. Ibid., 82.

14. See Jack Shulimson, "Daniel Pratt Mannix and the Establishment of the Marine Corps School of Application, 1889–1894," *Journal of Military History*, v. 55, n. 4 (October 1991).

15. Shulimson, *Marine Corps' Search*, 100–102.

16. Ibid., 101.

17. Ibid., 106–10, 143.

18. Ibid., 122–26, 136.

19. For detailed essays on the Marine Corps' role in the Spanish-American War, see Jack Shulimson et al., eds., *Marines in the Spanish American War, 1895–1899* (Washington, DC: History and Museums Division, Headquarters Marine Corps, 1998).

20. Shulimson, *Marine Corps' Search*, 172.

21. Ibid., 173–77.

22. Ibid., 184–88.

23. Ibid., 190.

24. Ibid., 196–97.

25. Ibid., 197–200.

26. Ibid., 200–202.

27. See Keith B. Bickel, *Mars Learning: The Marine Corps' Development of Small Wars Doctrine, 1915–1940* (Boulder, CO: Westview Press, 2001), 53–57.

28. See George McMillan, *Old Breed: A History of the First Marine Division in World War II* (Washington, DC: Zenger, 1983).

29. The argument here is not that the Marines do not or cannot do staff work at all, merely that it is not a primary part of Marine professionalism. See the discussion of Marine disregard for staff functions in Allan Millett, "Why the Army and Marine Corps Should Be Friends," *Parameters*, v. 24, n. 4 (Winter 1994–95).

30. Even in the present, for example, Marine medical services are provided by Navy corpsmen and religious/counseling services by Navy chaplains. This dependence on the Navy is one reason Carl Builder does not include an analysis of the Marine Corps in *Masks of War*. See Carl H. Builder, *The Masks of War: American Military Styles in Strategy and Analysis* (Baltimore, MD: Johns Hopkins University Press, 1989), 9.

31. See William W. Stickney, "The Marine Reserves in Action," and Arthur Roth, "Development of the Army Reserve Forces," both in *Military Affairs*, v. 17, n. 1 (Spring 1953).

32. See Harry Levins, "Forget the Unit Rivalries, Being a Marine Says It All," *St. Louis Post-Dispatch*, August 28, 2004. Levins does mention a "friendly rivalry" between East Coast and West Coast Marines, home of the First and Second Marine Divisions. Yet officers move back and forth between the two coasts and to Okinawa, home to the Third Marine Division, with enough regularity to prevent this from developing into a true subcultural distinction.

33. See Stephen K. Scroggs, *Army Relations with Congress: Thick Armor, Dull Sword, Slow Horse* (New York: Praeger, 2000), 128–32, for comparison of Marine and Army attitudes toward congressional and public relations.

34. See C. H. Metcalf, "A History of the Education of Marine Officers," *Marine Corps Gazette*, v. 20, n. 2 (May 1936): 18.

35. Ibid.

36. John Gates, *Schoolbooks and Krags: The United States Army in the Philippines, 1898–1902* (Westport, CT: Greenwood Press, 1973), 254–58; Bickel, *Mars Learning*, 38–39.

37. George Clark, *Treading Softly: U.S. Marines in China, 1819–1949* (Westport, CT: Praeger, 2001).

38. See John Major, *Prize Possession: The United States and the Panama Canal, 1903–1979* (Cambridge: Cambridge University Press, 1993), and Walter LaFeber, *The Panama Canal: The Crisis in Historical Perspective*, updated ed. (New York: Oxford University Press, 1989).

39. Millett, *Semper Fidelis*, 166.

40. Major, *Prize Possession*, 118–21.

41. Ibid., 122–32.

42. Millett, *Semper Fidelis*, 166–67; Bickel, *Mars Learning*, 32–33, 41–42; Richard McMonagle, "The Small Wars Manual and Military Operations Other Than War" (U.S. Army Command and General Staff College paper, 1996), 24–26.

43. Millett, *Semper Fidelis*, 167.

44. Metcalf, "Education of Marine Officers," 18.

45. Ibid.

46. Millett, *Semper Fidelis*; Musicant, *Banana Wars*, 137–38.

47. Merrill Bartlett, "Ben Hebard Fuller and the Genesis of a Modern United States Marine Corps, 1891–1934," *Journal of Military History*, v. 69, n. 1 (January 2005): 77–78.

48. Millett, *Semper Fidelis*, 272–73; Leo J. Daugherty III, "Brigadier General Dion Williams, USMC (1869–1952)," *Marine Corps Gazette*, v. 82, n. 2 (February 1998): 88.

49. Millett, *Semper Fidelis*, 273–74.

50. Ibid.

51. M. Bartlett, "Ben Hebard Fuller," 76–77.

52. Bickel, *Mars Learning*, 51–52.

53. Millett, *Semper Fidelis*, 276–77.

54. Ibid., 278–80.

55. Ibid., 280–82.

56. See Jack Sweetman, *The Landing at Vera Cruz: 1914* (Annapolis, MD: Naval Institute Press, 1968).

57. See Musicant, *Banana Wars*, chaps. 1–6, for description of the events of these interventions.

58. See Daugherty, "Brigadier General Dion Williams."

59. Metcalf, "Education of Marine Officers," 19.

60. Bickel, *Mars Learning*, 69–70; Millett, *Semper Fidelis*, 184–86. For more detailed discussion of the causes of the Haitian intervention, see Hans Schmidt, *The Occupation of Haiti, 1915–1934* (New Brunswick, NJ: Rutgers University Press, 1971).

61. Bickel, *Mars Learning*, 80–81.

62. Millett, *Semper Fidelis*, 187.

63. Ibid., 186–87; Bickel, *Mars Learning*, 69–71. The amnesty program clearly gained momentum after the November destruction of Fort Riviere.

64. Millett, *Semper Fidelis*, 188–90; Bickel, *Mars Learning*, 80–87.

65. Millett, *Semper Fidelis*, 189–90, 196–210.

66. Ibid., 190–96; Bickel, *Mars Learning*, 107–27.

67. Millett, *Semper Fidelis*, 185–86, 190–92.

68. See Donovan, *United States Marine Corps*, 16–18, 24–25, for a short comment on Belleau Woods and Marine involvement in World War I. He argues that the Marines began to develop capacity for larger-unit warfare as a result of Belleau Woods but continued to focus on the "banana wars" under the leadership of World War I veterans such as John Lejeune. See also Bickel, *Mars Learning*, 54–55.

69. Metcalf, "Education of Marine Officers," 48–49.

70. See Marine History website, http://www.mcu.usmc.mil/historydivision/pages/frequently_requested/EndStrength.aspx.

71. Metcalf, "Education of Marine Officers," 49–50.

72. Ibid., 48–49.

73. Ibid., 48–50.

74. Millett, *Semper Fidelis*, 243–45; Bickel, *Mars Learning*, 155.

75. Millett, *Semper Fidelis*, 247–50; Bickel, *Mars Learning*, 156–60.

76. Millett, *Semper Fidelis*, 250–60; Bickel, *Mars Learning*, 160–78.

77. Bickel, *Mars Learning*, 164–65.

78. The most detailed account of the evolution of War Plan ORANGE is Edward S. Miller, *War Plan ORANGE: The U.S. Strategy to Defeat Japan, 1897–1945* (Annapolis, MD: Naval Institute Press, 1991).

79. Millett, *Semper Fidelis*, 320–21.

80. Ibid., 322–25.

81. Ibid., 325–26.

82. Ibid., 327–28. See also Kenneth J. Clifford, *Amphibious Warfare Development in Britain and America from 1920–1940* (Laurens, NY: Edgewood, 1983), 85–92.

83. See Daugherty, "Brigadier General Dion Williams."

84. Schmidt, *Occupation of Haiti*, 202–8.

85. M. Bartlett, "Ben Hebard Fuller," 77–82.

86. Ibid., 82–86.

87. School memorandum, June 3, 1932, quoted in Bickel, *Mars Learning*, 208.

88. Anthony Frances, *History of the Marine Corps Schools* (n.p.: 1945), 39–40 (available at Marine Corps Archives, Quantico, Virginia, Marine Corps Schools History, box 1).

89. Ellis Miller, *The Marine Corps in Support of the Fleet*, bound version of the lecture, June 1, 1933; quoted in Bickel, *Mars Learning*, 208.

90. See *Basic School History*, 10–11 (Basic School History, box 1, folder 5), and Basic School Pamphlets (Marine Corps Schools, box 4, folder 37), both at Marine Corps Archives, Quantico.

91. M. Bartlett, "Ben Hebard Fuller," 86–90.

92. Bickel, *Mars Learning*, 211–21.

93. For an overview, see Richard Wheeler, *A Special Valor: The U.S. Marines and the Pacific War* (New York: Harper and Row, 1983).

94. See https://www.mcu.usmc.mil/historydivision/pages/frequently_requested/EndStrength.aspx (accessed August 21, 2014) and *Basic School History*, 22.

95. On the Marines in Korea, see Eliot Cohen and John Gooch, *Military Misfortunes: The Anatomy of Failure in War* (New York: Free Press, 1990), chap. 7.

96. Mandated by legislation at three divisions and three air wings in 1952, the Corps has consistently had an end strength of one hundred seventy thousand or more since World War II, with the exception of the three years 1948–50. The Third Marine Division had been stationed on Okinawa since the mid-1950s.

97. "Ambassadors in green" was a term in common use for the Marine Corps in the 1960s, similar in tone to "State Department troops." It is also the title of a monograph about Marine involvement in Vietnam. See Tom Bartlett, *Ambassadors in Green* (Washington, DC: Leatherneck Association, 1971).

98. See William B. Quandt, "Lebanon, 1958," in Barry M. Blechman and Stephen S. Kaplan, eds., *Force without War* (Washington, DC: Brookings Institution, 1978), for the Marines in Lebanon, and the chapter "Dominican Republic, 1964" in Musicant, *Banana Wars*, for the Marines (as well as some Army Airborne troops) in the Dominican Republic.

99. Not that the amphibious subculture would give up entirely, launching operations in the Mediterranean in the 1960s in an attempt to find a bigger role in NATO for the Corps. The first, known as Operation Steel Pike I, included over twenty thousand Marines in an exercise in Spanish waters.

5. A Family of Regiments

1. Public schools, also called independent schools, are privately funded schools that are generally associated with the upper class and the aspiring middle class.

2. Cathy Downes, *Special Trust and Confidence: The Making of an Officer* (London: Frank Cass, 1991), 40–41.

3. K. M. MacDonald, "The Persistence of an Elite: The Case of British Army Officer Cadets," *Sociological Review*, v. 28, n. 3 (1980). Perhaps most striking of MacDonald's data is that no graduates of state schools became officers in the elite (Guards and Royal Green Jackets) infantry regiments during the period 1976–78; in contrast, roughly one out of five Sandhurst graduates from what MacDonald considers the top fourteen public schools joined one of those regiments.

4. Corelli Barnett, "The Education of Military Elites," *Journal of Contemporary History*, v. 2, n. 3 (July 1967); Karl Demeter, *The German Officer Corps in Society and State, 1650–1945*, trans. Angus Malcolm (New York: Praeger, 1965); Gordon Craig, *The Politics of the Prussian Army, 1640–1945* (London: Oxford University Press, 1955).

5. Correlli Barnett, *Britain and Her Army, 1509–1970* (New York: William Morrow, 1970), 3–20, esp. 16–17.

6. Ibid., 21–56.

7. Ibid., 79–110; Ian Gentles, *The New Model Army in England, Ireland, and Scotland, 1645–1653* (Oxford: Blackwell, 1991).

8. Barnett, *Britain and Her Army*, 111–66, quotation on 166.

9. See ibid., 178; and Alan Shepperd, *Sandhurst: The Royal Military Academy Sandhurst and Its Predecessors* (London: Country Life Books, 1980), 11–12.

10. Barnett, *Britain and Her Army*, 175–76, quotation on 175.

11. Ibid., 213–25. Barbara Tuchman, *The March of Folly: From Troy to Vietnam* (New York: Random House, 1985), 127–232, provides a concise summary of the political events that led to the problem Barnett finds insoluble by force.

12. Barnett, *Britain and Her Army*, 236–43; Shepperd, *Sandhurst*, 22–24.

13. Shepperd, *Sandhurst*, 22.

14. Ibid., 26–29.

15. Ibid., 29–31.

16. Barnett, *Britain and Her Army*, 257–71; see also Gordon Corrigan, *Wellington: A Military Life* (London: Hambledon and London, 2001).

17. Richard Holmes, *Wellington: The Iron Duke* (London: HarperCollins, 2002), 39–50.

18. Barnett, *Britain and Her Army*, 270–71.

19. Neville Thompson, *Wellington after Waterloo* (London: Routledge, 1986), 138.

20. Barnett, *Britain and Her Army*, 282.

21. Shepperd, *Sandhurst*, 41–44.

22. Barnett, *Britain and Her Army*, 279–82.

23. Ibid., 274–79.

24. Ibid., 279; John Sweetman, *War and Administration: The Significance of the Crimean War for the British Army* (Edinburgh: Scottish Academic Press, 1984), 16–17.

25. The phrase is from Sweetman, *War and Administration*, 15.

26. See Trevor Royle, *Crimea: The Great Crimean War, 1854–1856* (New York: St. Martin's Press, 2000), for an overview of the war, and Sweetman, *War and Administration*, 41–77, for specifics on transport and supply problems.

27. This account draws heavily on Cecil Woodham-Smith, *The Reason Why* (New York: McGraw-Hill, 1953).

28. Ibid., 223–34.

29. Ibid., 235–49.

30. Ibid., 258–66; Barnett, *Britain and Her Army*, 285–89.

31. See Woodham-Smith, *The Reason Why*, 1–47, 96–99, 154–60, for biographical details of the three.

32. Ibid., 185–86.

33. Ibid., 185.

34. See James McLiver Roy, *"Old Take Care": The Story of Field Marshall Sir Colin Campbell, Lord Clyde* (Glasgow: J. M. Roy, 1987), for a modern biography of Campbell.

35. See Woodham-Smith, *The Reason Why*, 215–18. Campbell also provided good advice to Lucan in the early phase of the battle; see 213.

36. Shepperd, *Sandhurst*, 60–61.

37. Ian Worthington, "Antecedent Education and Officer Recruitment: The Origins and Early Development of the Public School–Army Relationship," *Military Affairs*, v. 41, n. 4 (December 1977): 185.

38. T. A. Heathcote, *Mutiny and Insurgency in India, 1857–1858: The British Army in a Bloody Civil War* (Barnsley, UK: Pen and Sword Books, 2007), 48.

39. Ibid., 154–74.

40. Ibid., 174–75, quotation on 174.

41. Ibid., 175–80, quotation on 180.

42. Ibid., 192–98.

43. Ibid., 204–5.

44. Ibid., 211–13.

45. Ibid., 212.

46. Shepperd, *Sandhurst*, 59–61, quotation on 61.

47. Stephen M. Miller, *Volunteers on the Veldt: Britain's Citizen-Soldiers and the South African War, 1899–1902* (Norman: University of Oklahoma Press, 2007), 24–29.

48. See Thomas Gallagher, "British Military Thinking and the Coming of the Franco-Prussian War," *Military Affairs*, v. 39, n. 1 (February 1975).

49. See Shepperd, *Sandhurst*, 77, and Gallagher, "British Military Thinking," 19. Note that Peel's immediate successor in 1867, Sir John Pakington, accomplished little in the way of reform and was quickly supplanted by Cardwell in 1868.

50. Barnett, *Britain and Her Army*, 297–98, 304.

51. Ibid., 307–8; Gallagher, "British Military Thinking," 20; Shepperd, *Sandhurst*, 77–78.

52. Barnett, *Britain and Her Army*, 308.

53. Ibid., 306–7; Miller, *Volunteers on the Veldt*, 24–25.

54. Gallagher, "British Military Thinking," 19.

55. Barnett, *Britain and Her Army*, 309–10; Gallagher, "British Military Thinking," 21.

56. Shepperd, *Sandhurst*, 77–79.

57. Ibid., 81–83.

58. Ibid., 91–92.

59. Ibid., 92–95; John Keegan, "Regimental Ideology," in *War, Economy, and the Military Mind*, ed. Geoffrey Best and Andrew Wheatcroft (London: Croom Helm, 1976), 9.

60. Barnett, *Britain and Her Army*, 313–14; Keegan, "Regimental Ideology," 8–9.

61. Nigel Collett, *The Butcher of Amritsar: General Reginald Dyer* (London: Hambledon, 2005), 25; Shepperd, *Sandhurst*, 95.

62. See Keegan, "Regimental Ideology," 4–7, and Downes, *Special Trust*, 55–56.

63. Keegan, "Regimental Ideology," 9–12; Heathcote, *Mutiny and Insurgency*, 212–13; Dennis Barker, *Soldiering On: An Unofficial Portrait of the British Army* (London: Andre Deutsch, 1981), 98–104.

64. Barker, *Soldiering On*, 101, 104.

65. For example, the expedition to Sikkim in 1861; see Alistair Lamb, *British India and Tibet, 1766–1910* (London: Routledge, 1986), 79–87.

66. Barker, *Soldiering On*, 29, 45–47.

67. See M. G. Venugopalan, "Police and Political Parties: The Politician-Police-Criminal Nexus," in *Policing India in the New Millennium*, ed. P. J. Alexander (New Delhi: Allied, 2002), 95.

68. See appendix 1 in Brian Bond, ed., *Victorian Military Campaigns* (London: Tom Donovan, 1994).

69. Halik Kochanski, *Sir Garnet Wolseley: Victorian Hero* (London: Hambledon, 1999), 33–52.

70. See Charles Crosthwaite, *The Pacification of Burma* (Whitefish, MT: Kessinger, 2008), a reprint of a 1912 study.

71. Barnett, *Britain and Her Army*, 313–22; Hew Strachan, *The Politics of the British Army* (New York: Oxford University Press, 1997), 92–96.

72. On Wolseley in the Ashanti campaign, see John Keegan, "The Ashanti Campaign, 1873–1874," in Bond, *Victorian Military Campaigns*. Roberts began his career in the East India Company's army, and his first assignment was to an indigenous artillery battery; see Frederick Roberts, *Forty-one Years in India, From Subaltern to Commander-in-Chief* (New York: Macmillan, 1901), 3.

73. Harold E. Raugh, *The Victorians at War, 1815–1914* (Santa Barbara, CA: ABC-Clio, 2004), 105–6.

74. Kochanski, *Sir Garnet Wolseley*, 218–23, quotation from 223.

75. Raugh, *Victorians at War*, 49–50.

76. Thomas Pakenham, *The Boer War* (London: Cardinal, 1991; originally published 1979), 1–9, 94–97, 105. Buller, who actually knew Boers, was one of the few British who expected the war to be difficult.

77. Ibid., 125–32.

78. Ibid., 133–59.

79. Ibid., 201–41.

80. Ibid., 241–44.

81. Miller, *Volunteers on the Veldt*, 55–62.

82. Pakenham, *Boer War*, 300–307, 371–75, 432–58.

83. See Collett, *Butcher of Amritsar*, 37–39, and Crosthwaite, *Pacification of Burma*.

84. Pakenham, *Boer War*, 440–41, 452–53, 473. Buller had worked with the Boers and knew many personally, in contrast to both Roberts and Kitchener.

85. Ibid., 484–500.

86. Ibid., 534–36, quotation on 536.

87. Ibid., 493–502, 536–48.

88. Ibid., 542, 547–48, 571, quotation on 548.

89. Ibid., 548, 566–67, quotation on 567.

90. Ibid., 549–50, 561, 571.

91. Ibid., 563–71.

92. Miller, *Volunteers on the Veldt*, 58–59; Barnett, *Britain and Her Army*, 342–43.

93. Raugh, *Victorians at War*, 231.

94. Barnett, *Britain and Her Army*, 342–43; Shepperd, *Sandhurst*, 101–4.

95. Barnett, *Britain and Her Army*, 355–59.

96. See Harry Hendrick, "Children and Social Policies," in *Child Welfare and Social Policy*, ed. Harry Hendrick (Bristol, UK: Policy Press, 2005), 37–38; Paul Beashel and John Taylor, "History of Sport," in Beashel and Taylor, *Advanced Studies in Physical Education and Sport* (Cheltenham,

UK: Nelson Taylor, 1999), 317–18; and Kathleen Jones, *The Making of Social Policy in Britain*, 3rd ed. (London: Continuum, 2006), 62–67.

97. See the essays in David French and Brian Holden Reid, eds., *The British General Staff: Reform and Innovation, 1890–1939* (New York: Routledge, 2002), especially William Philpott, "The General Staff and the Paradoxes of Continental War"; Timothy Moreman, "Lord Kitchener, the General Staff and the Army of India, 1902–14"; and Ian F. W. Beckett, "'Selection by Disparagement': Lord Esher, the General Staff and the Politics of Command, 1904–1914."

98. Barnett, *Britain and Her Army*, 363–64.

99. Ibid., 364; Peter Dennis, *The Territorial Army, 1906–1940* (Wolfeboro, NH: Boydell and Brewer, 1987), 7–8.

100. Dennis, *Territorial Army*, 8–12.

101. Barnett, *Britain and Her Army*, 364–66; Dennis, *Territorial Army*, 13–17.

102. Shepperd, *Sandhurst*, 104–13.

103. Ibid., 109, 113.

104. Ian Worthington, "Socialization, Militarization and Officer Recruiting: The Development of the Officers Training Corps," *Military Affairs*, v. 43, n. 2 (April 1979).

105. Ibid., 92–94.

106. Barnett, *Britain and Her Army*, 372.

107. See David Lomas, *Mons 1914: The BEF's Tactical Triumph* (New York: Osprey, 1997), and John Terraine, *Mons: The Retreat to Victory* (Hertfordshire, UK: Wordsworth, 2002; originally published 1960), 53–98.

108. Terraine, *Mons*, 99–199.

109. There is an immense historiography on the war; for an overview, see Michael Howard, *The First World War* (New York: Oxford University Press, 2002).

110. See J. M. Bourne, *Britain and the Great War, 1914–1918* (New York: Routledge, 1989), and Elizabeth Greenhlagh, *Victory through Coalition: Britain and France during the First World War* (Cambridge: Cambridge University Press, 2009).

111. Gordon Corrigan, *Sepoys in the Trenches: The Indian Corps on the Western Front, 1914–15* (Stroud, UK: Tempus, 2006).

112. See Michael Ramsey, *Command and Cohesion: The Citizen Soldier and Minor Tactics in the British Army, 1870–1918* (Westport, CT: Praeger, 2002); Timothy Lupfer, *The Dynamics of Doctrine: The Change in German Tactical Doctrine during the First World War* (Leavenworth: Combat Studies Institute, 1981); Paddy Griffith, *Battle Tactics of the Western Front: The British Army's Art of Attack, 1916–1918* (New Haven, CT: Yale University Press, 1996).

113. Barnett, *Britain and Her Army*, 410.

114. Shepperd, *Sandhurst*, 130.

115. Dennis, *Territorial Army*, 38–85.

116. Eric Heginbotham, "The British and American Armies in World War II: Explaining Variations in Organizational Learning Patterns" (working paper, MIT Defense and Arms Control Studies, February 1996), compares the U.S. Army and the British Army, arguing that the U.S. Army was better able to "learn" in World War II. David Glantz and Jonathan House, *When Titans Clashed: How the Red Army Stopped Hitler* (Lawrence: University Press of Kansas, 1998), describes how another "continental" army, the Red Army, effectively adjusted to the demands of the war.

117. Shepperd, *Sandhurst*, 158–60.

118. Certain specialists such as doctors and chaplains take an abbreviated course; these officers are explicitly second-class citizens, and the course is accordingly nicknamed the "Vicars and Tarts course." http://www.army.mod.uk/training_education/24485.aspx (accessed August 20, 2014).

119. George Flynn, *Conscription and Democracy: The Draft in France, Great Britain, and the United States* (Westport, CT: Greenwood Press, 2002), 65–68.

120. See Raffi Gregorian, *The British Army, the Gurkhas, and Cold War Strategy in the Far East, 1947–1954* (New York: Palgrave, 2002), for discussion of the early post-Partition history of the Gurkhas.

121. Gavin Mortimer, *Stirling's Men: The Inside History of the SAS in World War II* (London: Weidenfeld and Nicolson, 2004).

122. Anthony Kemp, *The SAS: The Savage Wars of Peace, 1947 to the Present* (London: J. Murray, 1994).

123. See Delves's biography at http://www.olivegroup.com/about_advisors.htm and discussion in parliamentary questions at http://www.publications.parliament.uk/pa/cm200607 /cmhansrd/cm070604/text/70604w0039.htm (both accessed June 12, 2009).

6. "A Nasty, Untidy Mess"

1. This summary draws from George Herring, *America's Longest War: The United States and Vietnam, 1950–1975*, 4th ed. (New York: McGraw, 2001), and William Duiker, *The Communist Road to Power in Vietnam*, 2nd ed. (Boulder, CO: Westview Press, 1996).

2. "Counterinsurgency Doctrine," National Security Action Memorandum 182, August 24, 1962 (hereafter cited as NSAM 182).

3. For a more general overview of the evolution of U.S. Army COIN doctrine, see Richard Downie, *Learning from Conflict: The U.S. Military in Vietnam, El Salvador, and the Drug War* (Westport, CT: Praeger, 1998), esp. 47–60; and Andrew Krepinevich, *The Army and Vietnam* (Baltimore, MD: Johns Hopkins University Press, 1986), 38–42.

4. NSAM 182, 6–8 (emphasis in original).

5. Ibid., 12–13.

6. Jeffrey Michaels, "Managing Global Counterinsurgency: The Special Group (CI), 1962–1966," *Journal of Strategic Studies*, v. 35, n. 1 (2012).

7. Kevin Ruane, *War and Revolution in Vietnam, 1930–1975* (New York: Routledge, 1998), 56.

8. U.S. Army, FM 31-16, *Counterguerrilla Operations* (hereafter cited as FM 31-16), February 1963, 3.

9. U.S. Army, FM 100-5, *Field Service Regulations—Operations* (hereafter cited as FM 100-5), February 1962, 137.

10. Ibid., 139–40.

11. FM 31-16, February 1963, 38. All of chapter 4 of the manual is dedicated to police operations and population control.

12. Ibid., 49–60.

13. U.S. Marine Corps, *Operations against Guerrilla Forces*, FMFM-21 (hereafter cited as FMFM-21), August 1962, 17, and FM 31-16, February 1963, 92, both use this phrase. FM 100-5, February 1962, 147–48, also discusses the importance of intelligence for COIN.

14. FM 31-16, February 1963, 92.

15. FM 100-5, February 1962, 147.

16. FMFM-21, August 1962, 2–3.

17. Ibid., 72.

18. FMFM-21, 14.

19. FMFM-21, 16.

20. FMFM-21, 31.

21. FMFM-21, 32.

22. FMFM-21, 17.

23. Decker was Army Chief of Staff from 1960 to 1962, Wheeler from 1962 to 1964. Both quoted in Krepinevich, *The Army and Vietnam*, 37.

24. Maxwell Taylor, "Terms of Reference for the Senior United States Military Commander in Vietnam," memorandum for Secretary of Defense McNamara, January 12, 1962; available in *Foreign Relations of the United States, 1961–1963* (hereafter cited as *FRUS*), vol. 2, *Vietnam 1962*, document 17, http://www.state.gov/www/about_state/history/vol_ii_1961-63/index.html. This wording differs slightly from the terms approved at the January 3, 1962, Palm Beach conference. However, it is clear in the orders establishing COMUSMACV in February that Taylor's was the view that prevailed. See *FRUS*, vol. 2, documents 9, 18, and 53.

25. *FRUS*, vol. 2, documents 19, 25, 36, 40, and 52.

26. Maxwell Taylor, Letter to President Kennedy, November 3, 1961; available in *FRUS*, vol. 1, *Vietnam 1961*, document 210, http://www.state.gov/www/about_state/history/vol_i_1961 /index.html.

27. Roger Hilsman, Memorandum for the Record, January 2, 1963, in *FRUS*, vol. 3, *Vietnam, January–August 1963*, document 1, http://www.state.gov/r/pa/ho/frus/kennedyjf/iii/.

28. See, inter alia, Krepinevich, *The Army and Vietnam*, 56–66; U.S. Army, *A Program for the Pacification and Long Term Development of South Vietnam*, March 1966 (hereafter cited as PROVN), 102; and Chester Cooper et al., *The American Experience with Pacification in Vietnam*, vol. 1 (Alexandria, VA: Institute for Defense Analyses, 1972), 13–14.

29. Thomas L. Ahern Jr., *CIA and Rural Pacification in South Vietnam* (Washington, DC: Center for the Study of Intelligence, 2001), 44 (declassified 2006).

30. This account of CIDG relies on ibid., 44–62; Francis J. Kelly, *U.S. Army Special Forces, 1961– 1971* (Washington, DC: Center of Military History, 1973), 20–33; and *U.S. Army Special Forces Participation in the CIDG Program Vietnam, 1957–1970* (Houston, TX: Radix, 1996), 83–124. The latter is a reprint of a declassified Fifth Special Forces Group history written by the group headquarters staff. Kelly appears to have relied on this history, so the two sources are not independent. See also John Prados, *Lost Crusader: The Secret Wars of CIA Director William Colby* (Oxford: Oxford University Press, 2003), 83–88; Shelby Stanton, *Green Berets at War: U.S. Army Special Forces in Southeast Asia, 1956–1975* (New York: Dell, 1985); Christopher Ives, *U.S. Special Forces and Counterinsurgency in Vietnam: Military Innovation and Institutional Failure, 1961–1963* (New York: Routledge, 2007); and Gerald C. Hickey, *Free in the Forest: Ethnohistory of the Vietnamese Central Highlands, 1954–1976* (New Haven, CT: Yale University Press, 1982), 73–89.

31. Colby had worked hard to cultivate his relationship with Nhu. See Thomas Ahern, *CIA and the House of Ngo: Covert Action in South Vietnam, 1954–1963* (Washington, DC: Center for the Study of Intelligence, 2000), 135–36 (declassified 2009). Colby's own description of his relationship to Nhu is discussed in William Colby with James McCargar, *Lost Victory: A First-hand Account of America's Sixteen-Year Involvement in Vietnam* (New York: Contemporary Books, 1989), 31–35, 89–90.

32. Ahern, *CIA and Rural Pacification*, 64–71; U.S. Army Special Forces Participation, 85–88; and Kelly, *U.S. Army Special Forces*, 33–34.

33. Kelly, *U.S. Army Special Forces*, 28.

34. Ahern, *CIA and Rural Pacification*, 57; U.S. Army Special Forces Participation, 85–89; Kelly, *U.S. Army Special Forces*, 26–29. Ahern lists twenty-four ODAs operational in November 1962, while U.S. Army Special Forces Participation lists twenty-six—this could be because two of the ODAs were at the Nha Trang base rather than in the field.

35. U.S. Army Special Forces Participation, 88–91.

36. Ahern, *CIA and Rural Pacification*, 97–99.

37. Ibid., 98–110.

38. Kelly, *U.S. Army Special Forces*, 37–41.

39. U.S. Army Special Forces Participation, 92–93.

40. Kelly, *U.S. Army Special Forces*, 33–34.

41. U.S. Army Special Forces Participation, 92.

42. Ibid., 236.

43. Richard Shultz, *The Secret War against Hanoi: Kennedy's and Johnson's Use of Spies, Saboteurs, and Covert Warriors in North Vietnam* (New York: HarperCollins, 1999), 41–70.

44. Ibid., 66–68, 206–33.

45. Kelly, *U.S. Army Special Forces*, chaps. 3, 5, and 6.

46. Ahern, *CIA and Rural Pacification*, 121–60, quotation on 141.

47. Robert Whitlow, *U.S. Marines in Vietnam: The Advisory and Combat Assistance Era, 1954–1964* (Washington, DC: History and Museums Division, United States Marine Corps, 1977), 15–39.

48. Ibid., 47.

49. Ibid., 55–85.

50. Ibid., 144.

51. Ibid., 39.

52. Before its official neutralization in 1962, Laos was viewed as more likely than South Vietnam to fall to communism, prompting contingency planning for a U.S. intervention, though no one in the U.S. government, civilian or military, believed this a good idea.

53. Whitlow, *U.S. Marines in Vietnam: Advisory and Combat Assistance*, 39–41.

54. Ibid., 41–42.

55. PROVN, 76–77.

56. Ibid., 61, 66.

57. Ibid., 2-47–2-50.

58. See William Gibbons, *The U.S. Government and the Vietnam War: Executive and Legislative Roles and Relationships*, pt. 4 (Princeton, NJ: Princeton University Press, 1995), 201–12; and Lewis Sorley, "To Change a War: General Harold K. Johnson and the PROVN Study," *Parameters*, v. 28, n. 1 (Spring 1998), for the history of PROVN and reactions to it. General (ret.) Volney Warner, who as a midcareer officer was one of the authors of PROVN, confirmed the various reactions to the study via e-mail (January 4, 2007). For a somewhat different perspective, see Andrew Birtle, "PROVN, Westmoreland, and the Historians: A Reappraisal," *Journal of Military History*, v. 72, n. 4 (October 2008).

59. Quoted in Krepinevich, *The Army and Vietnam*, 197.

60. Quoted in James P. Harrison, *The Endless War* (New York: Columbia University Press, 1989), 256.

61. Quoted in Neil Sheehan, *A Bright Shining Lie: John Paul Vann and America in Vietnam* (New York: Random House, 1988), 501.

62. Quoted in ibid., 619.

63. Harrison, *Endless War*, 256.

64. Robert Scales, *Firepower in Limited War* (Novato, CA: Presidio Press, 1994), 84.

65. Ibid., 141.

66. Krepinevich, *The Army and Vietnam*, 168–69; Russell W. Glenn, *Reading Athena's Dance Card: Men against Fire in Vietnam* (Annapolis, MD: Naval Institute Press, 2000), 10–11. For a more detailed account of the Ia Drang battles, see Harold G. Moore and Joseph L. Galloway, *We Were Soldiers Once . . . and Young: Ia Drang—The Battle That Changed the War in Vietnam* (New York: Random House, 1992).

67. Bernard Rogers, *Cedar Falls–Junction City: A Turning Point* (Washington, DC: Center of Center of Military History, 1974), 8–12.

68. Ibid., 16–24, 83–90; Bernard C. Nalty, ed., *The Vietnam War: The History of America's Conflict in Southeast Asia* (London: Salamander Books, 1998), 172–75. The Army historian Andrew Birtle notes that the Army never totally eschewed small-unit operations. See Andrew Birtle, *U.S. Army Counterinsurgency and Contingency Operations Doctrine, 1942–1972* (Washington, DC: Center of Military History, 2006), 368–72.

69. See discussion in Gregory Daddis, *No Sure Victory: Measuring U.S. Army Effectiveness and Progress in the Vietnam War* (New York: Oxford University Press, 2011).

70. Jeffrey Record, 84.

71. Sheehan, *Bright Shining Lie*, 636; Jack Shulimson and Charles Johnson, *U.S. Marines in Vietnam: The Landing and Buildup, 1965* (Washington, DC: History and Museums Division, Headquarters, USMC, 1978), 115–16.

72. Sheehan, *Bright Shining Lie*, 287–88; Krepinevich, *The Army and Vietnam*, 196–205.

73. See Robert Komer, *Organization and Management of the New Model Pacification Program* (Santa Monica, CA: RAND, 1970); and Richard Hunt, *Pacification: The American Struggle for Vietnam's Hearts and Minds* (Boulder, CO: Westview Press, 1995), 99–120.

74. Shultz, 232–37.

75. United States Army Vietnam, "Long Range Patrol Conference Summary," September 26, 1968, 48 (available at the Texas Tech Vietnam Archive, Lubbock, TX). Recondo was apparently an amalgam of the words "reconnaissance," "commando," and "doughboy."

76. Ibid.

77. Ibid., 7.

78. Ibid., 14–15.

79. Shultz, 275–80.

80. Ibid., 72.

81. See Kelly, *U.S. Army Special Forces*, iv.

82. Quoted in Shulimson and Johnson, *U.S. Marines in Vietnam: Landing and Buildup*, 38.

83. Both quoted in ibid., 39.

84. Ibid., 46.

85. Ibid., 133.

86. *Basic School History*, iv (available at Marine Corps Archives, Quantico, Basic School History, box 1, folder 5).

87. Shulimson and Johnson, *U.S. Marines in Vietnam: Landing and Buildup*, 135.

88. Ibid., 138, as is Walt quotation.

89. Ibid., 142–43.

90. Ibid., 143–44.

91. Robert J. Hanyok, *Spartans in Darkness: American SIGINT and the Indochina War, 1945–1975* (Fort Meade, MD: Center for Cryptologic History, 2002), chapter 7 (declassified 2007–8). For a more detailed account of STARLITE, see Otto J. Lehrack, *The First Battle: Operation Starlite and the Beginning of the Blood Debt in Vietnam* (Havertown, PA: Casemate, 2004).

92. See, for example, Letter, Krulak to Paul Nitze, July 17, 1966, Marine Corps Historical Center, Krulak Papers, Box 1; and Jack Shulimson, *U.S. Marines in Vietnam: 1966; An Expanding War* (Washington, DC: History and Museums Division, Headquarters Marine Corps, 1982), 14, 216.

93. *Basic School History*, 22.

94. Ibid., 30–31. The curriculum was deemed mostly adequate, though more map reading was added, as small-unit patrols relied heavily on this skill.

95. Chieu Hoi Division, Military Assistance Command CORDS, "The Kit Carson Scout Program, 1966–1968," January 18, 1968, 1–2 (available in the Ogden Williams Collection, Texas Tech Vietnam Archive).

96. Ibid., 5.

97. See *U.S. Marine Corps Civil Affairs in I Corps Republic of South Vietnam, April 1966–April 1967* (Washington, DC: Historical Division, Headquarters, U.S. Marine Corps, 1970), 15–17 (available at the Texas Tech Vietnam Archive); George W. Allen, *None So Blind: A Personal Account of the Intelligence Failure in Vietnam* (Chicago: Ivan R. Dee, 2001), 220–22; and Anders Sweetland, *Item Analysis of the HES (Hamlet Evaluation System)* (Santa Monica, CA: RAND, 1968), 1.

98. On CAP, see F. J. "Bing" West Jr., *The Village*, rev. ed. (New York: Simon and Schuster, 2003); Al Hemingway, *Our War Was Different: Marine Combined Action Platoons in Vietnam* (Annapolis, MD: Naval Institute Press, 1994); Michael E. Petersen, *Combined Action Platoons: The U.S. Marines' Other War in Vietnam* (Westport, CT: Praeger, 1989); and Brooks R. Brewington, "Combined Action Platoons: A Strategy for Peace Enforcement" (thesis, Marine Command and Staff College, 1996).

99. Michael A. Hennessy, *Strategy in Vietnam: The Marines and Revolutionary Warfare in I Corps, 1965–1972* (Westport, CT: Praeger, 1997), 94, 131.

100. Willard Pearson, *The War in the Northern Provinces, 1966–1968* (Washington, DC: Center of Military History, 1975), 6–7.

101. Ibid., 9; Hennessy, *Strategy in Vietnam*, 94.

102. Jack Shulimson, "The Marine War: III MAF in Vietnam, 1965–1971" (paper presented at Texas Tech Vietnam Center symposium, Lubbock, TX 1996), 3. The quote is from Brigadier General Lowell E. English. English was the assistant division commander for the Third Marine Division and, as West notes in *The Village*, had rejected the option of removing one of the first CAP units from its village following an attack by a main force insurgent unit. See West, *The Village*, 131.

103. Marine Corps Training and Education Command Historical End Strength data available from author.

104. Allan Millet and Jack Shulimson, *Commandants of the Marine Corps* (Annapolis, MD: Naval Institute Press, 2004), 378–79.

105. Quoted in Graham A. Cosmas and Terrence R. Murray, *U.S. Marines in Vietnam: Vietnamization and Redeployment, 1970–1971* (Washington, DC: History and Museums Division, Headquarters, U.S. Marine Corps, 1986), 344. Huff was also notable for being the first African American sergeant major in the Marine Corps in a time of increasing racial discord within the Corps. His observation is confirmed by discussions with other Marine officers who joined during the late Vietnam period.

106. See Gary Telfer, Lane Rogers, and V. Keith Fleming, *U.S. Marines in Vietnam: Fighting the North Vietnamese, 1967* (Washington, DC: History and Museums Division, Headquarters, U.S. Marine Corps, 1984), 9–24.

107. Hennessy, *Strategy in Vietnam*, 123–24.

108. Ibid., 111.

109. Ibid., 118.

110. Jack Shulimson, Leonard A. Blasiol, Charles R. Smith, and David A. Dawson, *U.S. Marines in Vietnam: The Defining Year, 1968* (Washington, DC: History and Museums Division Headquarters, U.S. Marine Corps, 1997), 13.

111. Pearson, *War in the Northern Provinces*, 13–16.

112. Ibid., 15–18.

113. Ibid., 18–19; James J. Wirtz, *The Tet Offensive: Intelligence Failure in War* (Ithaca, NY: Cornell University Press, 1991), 143.

114. Shulimson et al., *U.S. Marines in Vietnam: Defining Year*, 258–61; Hanyok, *Spartans in Darkness*, 320–23.

115. Shulimson et al., *U.S. Marines in Vietnam: Defining Year*, 265–68, 273–75. See also John Prados and Ray Stubbe, *Valley of Decision: The Siege of Khe Sanh* (Annapolis, MD: Naval Institute Press, 1991).

116. Shulimson et al., *U.S. Marines in Vietnam: Defining Year*, 471–77.

117. Ibid., 261–64.

118. Pearson, *War in the Northern Provinces*, 66.

119. Erik Villard, *The Tet Offensive Battles of Quang Tri City and Hue* (Washington, DC: Center of Military History, 2008), 12–25; Shulimson et al., *U.S. Marines in Vietnam: Defining Year*, 133–37.

120. Villard, *Tet Offensive Battles*, 25–78; Shulimson et al., *U.S. Marines in Vietnam: Defining Year*, 173–223.

121. See Gibbons, *U.S. Government and the Vietnam War*, pt. 4, pp. 22, 303, 549, 685–86, for Russell's feelings on the war, and pp. 595, 597–99, 802–3 for Rivers's.

122. See ibid., 220–21, for comments by Rivers and Russell. These comments were echoed by such Republican leaders as Representative Gerald Ford and Senator Leverett Saltonstall. See ibid., 800 for Ford and 220 for Saltonstall.

123. Deborah D. Avant, *Political Institutions and Military Change: Lessons from Peripheral Wars* (Ithaca, NY: Cornell University Press, 1994), 73.

124. FM 100-5, September 1968, 13-1.

125. FM 31-16, March 1967, 7–8.

126. FM 100-5, September 1968, 13-2.

127. FM 31-6, March 1967, 32–33.

128. Ibid., 36.

129. U.S. Marine Corps, *Counterinsurgency Operations*, FMFM 8-2 (hereafter FMFM 8-2), December 1967, 28; FM 100-5, September 1968, 13-5.

130. Headquarters, Military Assistance Command Vietnam, *Handbook for Military Support of Pacification*, February 1968, 1.

131. See FMFM 8-2, December 1967, 3.

132. Ibid., 28.

133. Ibid., 72–74.

134. See Lewis Sorley, *A Better War: The Unexamined Victories and Final Tragedy of America's Last Years in Vietnam* (New York: Harcourt, Brace, 1999), for a positive treatment of Abrams's time as COMUSMACV.

135. Ibid. See also Mark Moyar, *Phoenix and the Birds of Prey: The CIA's Secret Campaign to Destroy the Vietcong* (Annapolis, MD: Naval Institute Press, 1997); and William Colby, *Lost Victory: A Firsthand Account of America's Sixteen Year Involvement in Vietnam* (Chicago: Contemporary Books, 1989).

136. For evidence of Abrams's frustration with subordinates' attitudes toward his "better war," see *Vietnam Chronicles: The Abrams Tapes, 1968–1972*, ed. Lewis Sorley (Lubbock: Texas Tech University Press, 2004), 116–17, 285–86. For other comments that Abrams was unable to effect change, see Krepinevich, *The Army and Vietnam*, 252–57; Cincinnatus [Cecil Currey], *Self-Destruction: The Disintegration and Decay of the United States Army during the Vietnam Era* (New York: W. W. Norton, 1981), 125; and Brian Jenkins, *The Unchangeable War* (Santa Monica, CA: RAND, 1972).

137. Both quotations from Hunt, *Pacification* 213.

138. Richard Stewart, ed., *American Military History*, vol. 2, *The United States Army in a Global Era, 1917–2003* (Washington, DC: Center of Military History, 2005), 348.

139. Robert J. Graham, "Vietnam: An Infantryman's View of Our Failure," *Military Affairs*, v. 48, n. 3 (July 1984): 135.

140. Ibid., 134.

141. John Hawkins, "The Costs of Artillery: Eliminating Harassment and Interdiction Fire during the Vietnam War," *Journal of Military History*, v. 70, n. 1 (January 2006).

142. Quoted in Hunt, *Pacification*, 213.

143. Julian Ewell and Ira Hunt, *Sharpening the Combat Edge: The Use of Analysis to Reinforce Military Judgment* (Washington, DC: Center of Military History, 1974), 78.

144. Ibid., 160

145. Ibid., 180–81, quotation from 181.

146. On SPEEDY EXPRESS, see Kevin Buckley, "Pacification's Deadly Price," *Newsweek*, June 19, 1972; Hunt, *Pacification*, 189; Nick Turse, *Kill Anything That Moves: The Real American War in Vietnam* (New York: Metropolitan Books, 2013), chap. 6; and David Hackworth, *Steel My Soldiers' Hearts* (New York: Touchstone, 2002), 370. Hackworth was a battalion commander in the Ninth Infantry Division during SPEEDY EXPRESS.

147. Julian Ewell, "Impressions of a Division Commander in Vietnam," September 11, 1969, 5 (available from the Defense Technical Information Center). Ewell does claim that the Ninth emphasized small-unit action, but that is belied by other comments he makes elsewhere in the document.

148. Ibid., 12.

149. See Hunt, *Pacification*, 320n23; Buckley.

150. Birtle, *U.S. Army Counterinsurgency*, 367–68, quotation on 367.

151. Sorley, *Vietnam Chronicles*, 212–13. Emphasis and parentheticals in original. Mildren was deputy commanding general, U.S. Army Vietnam.

152. Hunt, *Pacification*, 231–32; quotation from 232.

153. Ibid., 233.

154. Shulimson et al., *U.S. Marines in Vietnam: Defining Year*, 607–8.

155. Ibid., 619.

156. Ibid., 623.

157. Ibid., 625.

158. Pearson, *War in the Northern Provinces*, 74.

159. Shulimson et al., *U.S. Marines in Vietnam: Defining Year*, 623.

160. Ibid., 625.

161. Ibid.

162. Fleet Marine Force Pacific, *Operations of U.S. Marine Forces Vietnam, September 1969*, iii.

163. Ibid., 2–3.

164. Hunt, *Pacification*, 227–28.

165. *Operations of U.S. Marine Forces Vietnam, September 1969*, 10–16.

166. Ibid., 23–24; III Marine Amphibious Force, *Fact Sheet on the Combined Action Force*, March 1970, 2 (available at the Texas Tech Vietnam Archive); Hennessy, *Strategy in Vietnam*, 161.

167. *Operations of U.S. Marine Forces Vietnam, September 1969*, v.

168. *Fact Sheet on the Combined Action Force*, 1.

169. Fleet Marine Force Pacific, *Operations of U.S. Marine Forces Vietnam, May and June 1971*, 5–7; Hennessy, *Strategy in Vietnam*, 162.

170. https://www.mcu.usmc.mil/historydivision/pages/frequently_requested/End Strength.aspx (accessed August 20, 2014).

171. Millet and Shulimson, *Commandants of the Marine Corps*, 406–8.

172. For an analysis of Army change in Vietnam that emphasizes organizational culture and principal-agent theory in contrasting the adoption of airmobility with counterinsurgency, see Adam Stulberg and Michael Salomone, *Managing Defense Transformation: Agency, Culture and Service Change* (Burlington, VT: Ashgate, 2007), chap. 6.

7. A Natural Experiment in I Corps, 1966–68

1. See map in Jonathan Schell, *The Real War: The Classic Reporting on the Vietnam War* (New York: Pantheon, 1987), 189.

2. Ibid., 195–97; interview with Major Edward Tipshus, U.S. Marine Corps History and Museums Division Oral History Project, January 12, 1966 (available at the Texas Tech Vietnam Archive). Tipshus had served as an artillery adviser to the ARVN division in Quang Ngai in 1964.

3. Jack Shulimson and Charles Johnson, *U.S. Marines in Vietnam: The Landing and Buildup, 1965* (Washington, DC: History and Museums Division, Headquarters, USMC, 1978), 138.

4. Ibid.

5. Edward Murphy, *Semper Fi: Vietnam, from Da Nang to the DMZ Marine Corps Campaigns, 1965–1975* (New York: Random House), 45.

6. See David Ott, *Field Artillery, 1954–1973* (Washington, DC: Center of Military History, 1975), 98–101.

7. Murphy, *Semper Fi*, 45–46.

8. Ibid., 46; Headquarters, Third Marine Division, "Commander's Analysis, Techniques Utilized and Lessons Learned: Operation Double Eagle I and II," 4, 9–10 (available in the U.S. Marine Corps History Division Vietnam War Documents Collection, Texas Tech Vietnam Archive). Double Eagle II was a redeployment of the forces used in Double Eagle to Quang Nam Province immediately after Double Eagle ended.

9. Murphy, *Semper Fi*, 47–48.

10. Headquarters, Third Marine Division, "Commander's Analysis, Techniques Utilized and Lessons Learned," 1.

11. See Fleet Marine Force Pacific, Western Pacific Situation Report, May 12, 1967, section 2 (C), which notes that Task Force Oregon initiated Operation MALHEUR in the same area previously covered in Double Eagle I (available in OP Malheur folder, U.S. Marine Corps History Division Vietnam War Documents Collection, Texas Tech Vietnam Archive).

12. *Operations of the III Marine Amphibious Force Vietnam*, February 1966, 10, 15. Most Marine small-unit operations were much smaller than a company, generally ranging from a four-man fire team to a platoon. This and all other cited *Operations of the III Marine Amphibious Force Vietnam* records are available in the Operations of U.S. Marine Forces, Vietnam folder, U.S. Marine Corps History Division Vietnam War Documents Collection, Texas Tech Vietnam Archive.

13. *Operations of the III Marine Amphibious Force Vietnam*, March 1966, 11–16.

14. Ibid., 9.

15. *Operations of the III Marine Amphibious Force Vietnam*, April 1966, 11–17.

16. Ibid., 9.

17. Table 6 is derived from the following sources: *Operations of the III Marine Amphibious Force Vietnam*, May 1966, 11–17; *Operations of the III Marine Amphibious Force Vietnam*, June 1966, 11, 13; *Operations of the III Marine Amphibious Force Vietnam*, July 1966, 7, 17; *Operations of the III Marine Amphibious Force Vietnam*, August 1966, 21, 32; *Operations of the III Marine Amphibious Force Vietnam*, September 1966, 6, 12–13, 16; *Operations of the III Marine Amphibious Force Vietnam*, October 1966, 20, 34; *Operations of the III Marine Amphibious Force Vietnam*, November 1966, 14, 17; *Operations of the III Marine Amphibious Force Vietnam*, December 1966, 20, 28.

18. F. J. "Bing" West Jr., *The Village*, rev. ed. (New York: Simon and Schuster, 2003), 14.

19. Murphy, *Semper Fi*, 98.

20. Ibid., 98–99.

21. Ibid., 100.

22. Ibid., 99; *Operations of the III Marine Amphibious Force Vietnam*, January 1967, 11; *Operations of the III Marine Amphibious Force Vietnam*, February 1967, 22.

23. Murphy, *Semper Fi*, 99–100.

24. Ibid., 101.

25. Ibid.; *Operations of the III Marine Amphibious Force Vietnam*, March 1967, 16. Revolutionary Development teams were Vietnamese cadres intended to live in villages and develop progovernment sentiments. They had some self-defense capability but were easily overwhelmed by even modest insurgent forces.

26. *Operations of the III Marine Amphibious Force Vietnam*, January 1967, 20.

27. *Operations of the III Marine Amphibious Force Vietnam*, February 1967, 28; *Operations of the III Marine Amphibious Force Vietnam*, March 1967, 27.

28. See West, *The Village*, 42–43.

29. "Operational Report—Lessons Learned, Headquarters, Americal Division Artillery, Period Ending 31 January 1970," April 21, 1970, 8 (available in the Glenn Helm Collection, Texas Tech Vietnam Archive).

30. *Operations of the III Marine Amphibious Force Vietnam*, January 1967, 13.

31. *Operations of the III Marine Amphibious Force Vietnam*, December 1966, 58.

32. Fleet Marine Force Pacific Situation Report, May 12, 1967, section C. Unless otherwise noted, all cited operational records on Malheur are available in the OP Malheur folder, U.S. Marine Corps History Division Vietnam War Documents Collection, Texas Tech Vietnam Archive.

33. Ibid.; Commander, Military Assistance Command Vietnam Report, June 8, 1967, section B.

34. These numbers are calculated from Fleet Marine Force Pacific Situation Reports for nineteen days between May 11 and June 5. The total and average are likely understatements, as at least one day for which contact was listed as "moderate" and artillery was used does not list a total number of rounds. See Fleet Marine Force Pacific Situation Report, May 29, 1967, section 6 (A). All are available in the OP Malheur folder, U.S. Marine Corps History Division Vietnam War Documents Collection, Texas Tech Vietnam Archive.

35. Fleet Marine Force Pacific Situation Report, June 5, 1967, section 6 (A) and (B).

36. Schell, *Real War*, 216–20; numbers from 219.

37. Fleet Marine Force Pacific Situation Report, June 10, 1967, section (A); Fleet Marine Force Pacific Situation Report, August 2, 1967, section 8 (A). Unless otherwise noted, all cited operational records on Malheur II are available in the OP Malheur II folder, U.S. Marine Corps History Division Vietnam War Documents Collection, Texas Tech Vietnam Archive.

38. This information is derived from forty-eight Fleet Marine Force Pacific Situation Reports from June 10 to August 2.

39. Commander, Military Assistance Command Vietnam Report, July 31, 1967, section C.

40. Fleet Marine Force Pacific Situation Report, July 17, 1967, section 6.

41. Combat After Action Report, Operation HOOD RIVER, Headquarters, First Brigade, 101st Airborne Division, December 11, 1967, 19–20, quotation on 19 (available from the Defense Technical Information Center).

42. This is based on counts from nine Fleet Marine Force Pacific Situation Reports from August 1 to August 11, 1967, available in the OP Hood River Folder, U.S. Marine Corps History Division Vietnam War Documents Collection, Texas Tech Vietnam Archive. The discrepancy is likely due to the after-action report counting only rounds expended by the brigade's organic artillery, whereas the situation reports include artillery from all sources, such as TF Oregon's division artillery.

43. Commander, Military Assistance Command Vietnam Report, August 11, 1967, available in the OP Hood River folder, U.S. Marine Corps History Division Vietnam War Documents Collection, Texas Tech Vietnam Archive.

44. Schell, *Real War*, 263.

45. Ibid., 248–49.

46. The Marines averaged about ten thousand refugees a month for five provinces in 1966. The Army was generating about twelve thousand a month in one province.

47. Schell, *Real War*, 240, 244.

48. Robert O'Melia, "The Refugees of Duc Pho," 3, 5–6, http://www.historynet.com/the-refugees-of-duc-pho.htm.

49. *Operations of the III Marine Amphibious Force Vietnam*, October 1967, 39.

50. Ibid.

51. See *Report of the Department of the Army Review of the Preliminary Investigations into the My Lai Incident* (hereafter *Peers Report*, after principal investigator Lieutenant General William Peers), March 1970, 3-11–3-12; and Headquarters, Fourth Battalion, Third Infantry, "After Action Report (Operation Muscatine)," June 20, 1968, 1 (available from author).

52. *Peers Report*, 3-11–3-12; Headquarters, Fourth Battalion, Third Infantry, "After Action Report (Operation Muscatine)," June 20, 1968, 26.

53. Headquarters, Fourth Battalion, Third Infantry, "After Action Report (Operation Muscatine)," June 20, 1968, 1–2, quotation on 1.

54. "Americal Division Artillery Field Standing Operating Procedures," December 1, 1967, A-4-2 (available in the My Lai Collection, Texas Tech Vietnam Archive).

55. West, *The Village*, 280–81, 325–28, 332.

56. Shulimson and Johnson, *U.S. Marines in Vietnam*, 85.

57. Ibid., 84.

8. Out of Africa

1. John Nagl, *Learning to Eat Soup with a Knife: Counterinsurgency Lessons from Malaya and Vietnam* (Chicago: University of Chicago Press, 2005).

2. Robert Cassidy, *Counterinsurgency and the Global War on Terror: Military Culture and Irregular War* (Westport, CT: Praeger Security International, 2006), 90.

3. For an overview of Malaya, see Robert Komer, *The Malayan Emergency in Retrospect: Organization of a Successful Counterinsurgency Effort* (Santa Monica, CA: RAND, 1972).

4. See Nigel Pavitt, *Kenya: A Country in the Making, 1880–1940* (New York: W. W. Norton, 2008), and Wunyabari Maloba, *Mau Mau and Kenya: An Analysis of a Peasant Revolt* (Bloomington: Indiana University Press, 1998), 1–35.

5. David Anderson, *Histories of the Hanged: The Dirty War in Kenya and the End of Empire* (New York: W. W. Norton, 2005), 9–53.

6. David Gordon, *Decolonization and the State in Kenya* (Boulder, CO: Westview Press, 1986), 85–108.

7. Gordon, *Decolonization*, 113–14.

8. Anderson, *Histories of the Hanged*, 28–41.

9. Maloba, *Mau Mau and Kenya*, 99–113.

10. Daniel Branch, *Defeating Mau Mau, Creating Kenya: Counterinsurgency, Civil War, and Decolonization* (New York: Cambridge University Press, 2009), 35–46.

11. Anderson, *Histories of the Hanged*, 41–53.

12. Ibid., 54–62.

13. Ibid., 62–69; Anthony Clayton, *Counterinsurgency in Kenya: A Study of Military Operations against Mau Mau* (Nairobi: Transafrica, 1976), 21.

14. Quotation from Anderson, *Histories of the Hanged*, 239; see also ibid., 85, and Frank Kitson, *Gangs and Counter-gangs* (London: Barrie and Rockcliff, 1960), 11.

15. Anderson, *Histories of the Hanged*, 76, 85; Clayton, *Counterinsurgency in Kenya*, 44–45.

16. Clayton, *Counterinsurgency in Kenya*, 45–46; Anderson, *Histories of the Hanged*, 239–43. For clarity, Home Guard will be used throughout this chapter.

17. Anderson, *Histories of the Hanged*, 239.

18. Ibid., 84–86, 111–18.

19. Ibid., 235–38; Clayton, *Counterinsurgency in Kenya*, 27–28.

20. Anderson, *Histories of the Hanged*, 35–38, 181–90.

21. Ibid., 190–92.

22. Ibid., 118–39.

23. Ibid., 179–80; Clayton, *Counterinsurgency in Kenya*, 5–6; Huw Bennett, *Fighting the Mau Mau: The British Army and Counter-insurgency in the Kenya Emergency* (New York: Cambridge University Press, 2013), 17–18.

24. UK National Archives record WO 276/411, "Anti Mau Mau Policy Directives," January 1–June 30, 1953, 5–7, quotation on 7 (London, UK).

25. Ibid., 8, emphasis in original.

26. Clayton, *Counterinsurgency in Kenya*, 23–24; Bennett, *Fighting the Mau Mau*, 15–16.

27. ATOM went through three editions: 1952, 1954, and 1958. A copy of the 1952 edition is available at the Tameside Local Studies and Archives, Tameside, UK, document MR3/26/163.

28. WO 279/241, *The Conduct of Anti-Terrorist Operations in Malaya* (1958), chap. 3, pp. 1–4.

29. Ibid., chaps. 5, 7, and 8.

30. Ibid., chap. 4.

31. Ibid., chap. 3, pp. 14–15.

32. Ibid., chap. 14.

33. Clayton, *Counterinsurgency in Kenya*, 6–7; Bennett, *Fighting the Mau Mau*, 11–12, 19–20.

34. Anderson, *Histories of the Hanged*, 180; Clayton, *Counterinsurgency in Kenya*, 7–8.

35. David Percox, "British Counter-insurgency in Kenya, 1952–1956: Extension of Internal Security Policy or Prelude to Decolonisation?," *Small Wars and Insurgencies*, v. 9, n. 3 (Winter 1998): 48.

36. Quoted in Clayton, *Counterinsurgency in Kenya*, 7n13.

37. Quoted in Anderson, *Histories of the Hanged*, 85.

38. Quoted from ibid., 260.

39. Clayton, *Counterinsurgency in Kenya*, 7–8.

40. Ibid., 10–11. Quotations from Anderson, *Histories of the Hanged*, 269.

41. Kitson, *Gangs and Counter-gangs*, 11–13.

42. Clayton, *Counterinsurgency in Kenya*, 8–9; Bennett, *Fighting the Mau Mau*, 50–52.

43. Clayton, *Counterinsurgency in Kenya*, 9–10.

44. Ibid., 38–42; Bennett, *Fighting the Mau Mau*, 109–23; Anderson, *Histories of the Hanged*, 257–60.

45. Anderson, *Histories of the Hanged*, 262–63, 391; Clayton, *Counterinsurgency in Kenya*, 24–25. The Buffs rotated out in November 1953, replaced by the Royal Bucks.

46. WO 276/409, "Appreciation of Operation Buttercup, Fort Hall District," July 10, 1953, 1–2.

47. WO 32/21902, "Erskine to Chief of Imperial General Staff (CIGS)," July 23, 1953.

48. WO 276/460, "Instructions in Creating Specialist Forces to Combat Mau Mau," November 25, 1954, 1.

49. WO 32/21902, "Erskine to CIGS," July 7, 1953, 2.

50. WO 276/437, "39 INF BDE Jock Scott OP Instructions," November 24, 1954, 9–10.

51. Bennett, *Fighting the Mau Mau*, 129.

52. Anderson, *Histories of the Hanged*, 263; Clayton, *Counterinsurgency in Kenya*, 24. See also Alan Waters, "The Cost of Air Support in Counter-insurgency Operations: The Case of Mau Mau in Kenya," *Military Affairs*, v. 37, n. 3 (October 1973).

53. WO 32/21902, "Erskine to Chief of Imperial General Staff (CIGS)," July 23, 1953.

54. Jonathan B. A. Bailey, *Field Artillery and Firepower* (Annapolis, MD: Naval Institute Press, 2003), 364.

55. CO 822/790, "Organization of the Intelligence Service in Kenya"; CO 882/445, "Reorganization of Intelligence Services," March 4, 1953; Bennett, *Fighting the Mau Mau*, 54–56; Christopher Andrew, *Defend the Realm: The Authorized History of MI5* (New York: Alfred A. Knopf, 2009), 456–57.

56. Clayton, *Counterinsurgency in Kenya*, 33–36; Kitson, *Gangs and Counter-gangs*, 18–19.

57. Kitson, *Gangs and Counter-gangs*, 1–2. See also Frank Kitson, *Bunch of Five* (London: Faber and Faber, 1977).

58. Kitson, *Gangs and Counter-gangs*, 17; Anderson, *Histories of the Hanged*, 241. Kitson was initially disappointed because not much overt activity was taking place in Kiambu, yet later

realized that "virtually everything that happened in Kiambu or Thika had ramifications in Nairobi." Kitson, *Gangs and Counter-gangs*, 51.

59. Kitson, *Gangs and Counter-gangs*, 19, 28–29.

60. Ibid., 29.

61. Ibid., 39–43, quotation on 40.

62. WO 276/437, "39 INF BDE Operating Instructions," January 13, 1954.

63. WO 32/21902, "Erskine to CIGS," June 14, 1953, 3.

64. WO 32/21902, "Erskine to CIGS," July 7, 1953, 2.

65. Branch, *Defeating Mau Mau*, 72.

66. See ibid., 66–92.

67. Anderson, *Histories of the Hanged*, 273; Clayton, *Counterinsurgency in Kenya*, 25.

68. Anderson, *Histories of the Hanged*, 232–34, 273–77; Clayton, *Counterinsurgency in Kenya*, 34; Maloba, *Mau Mau and Kenya*, 84–85.

69. Bennett, *Fighting the Mau Mau*, 24, 139. The preparations for Overdraft are described in WO 32/21902, "GHQ East Africa Operating Instruction 17," March 27, 1954.

70. Kitson, *Gangs and Counter-gangs*, 73–104, 170; Anderson, *Histories of the Hanged*, 284–86; Clayton, *Counterinsurgency in Kenya*, 35; Bennett, *Fighting the Mau Mau*, 152–53; Maloba, *Mau Mau and Kenya*, 94–96.

71. Bennett, *Fighting the Mau Mau*, 153–58; WO 32/21902, "Emergency Directive Number 14," December 6, 1954.

72. Anderson, *Histories of the Hanged*, 200–211; Clayton, *Counterinsurgency in Kenya*, 25–26; Kitson, *Gangs and Counter-gangs*, 78–82; Maloba, *Mau Mau and Kenya*, 86–87, 124–25.

73. WO 236/18, "The Kenya Emergency, June 1953–May 1955," 20.

74. Anderson, *Histories of the Hanged*, 201–4; Clayton, *Counterinsurgency in Kenya*, 25; Maloba, *Mau Mau and Kenya*, 86–87. The number of detainees varies in other sources. The numbers given are over 20,000 in Anderson, *Histories of the Hanged*, 16,500 in Clayton, and 30,000 in Maloba. Clayton's number appears to be Erskine's number for those sent to detention camps, while Maloba seems to use the number of those initially screened. Anderson's number may include those detained in follow-up operations after ANVIL ended.

75. Anderson, *Histories of the Hanged*, 212–14, 220–24.

76. WO 32/21902, "Governor [Baring] to Secretary of State for the Colonies [Lennox-Boyd]," October 21, 1955, 1.

77. Anderson, *Histories of the Hanged*, 268, 294–95; Branch, *Defeating Mau Mau*, 107–10; Bennett, *Fighting the Mau Mau*, 222–24; Clayton, *Counterinsurgency in Kenya*, 26–27; Maloba, *Mau Mau and Kenya*, 90–91.

78. Anderson, *Histories of the Hanged*, 268–69.

79. Ibid., 214–16; Kitson, *Gangs and Counter-gangs*, 140–42. Kitson was present at the battle, but the numbers of combatants he gives, based on initial estimates, are incorrect.

80. WO 276/545, *A Handbook on Anti–Mau Mau Operations* (n.p.: 1954). See also discussion in Ian F. W. Beckett, *Modern Insurgencies and Counter-insurgencies: Guerrillas and Their Opponents since 1750* (London: Routledge, 2001), 103.

81. WO 276/545, *Handbook on Anti–Mau Mau Operations*, chap. 3.

82. Ibid., chaps. 4, 8, and 9.

83. Ibid., 80–81.

84. Anderson, *Histories of the Hanged*, 269; Clayton, *Counterinsurgency in Kenya*, 27–28.

85. Clayton, *Counterinsurgency in Kenya*, 28–30, quotation on 30; Maloba, *Mau Mau and Kenya*, 94; Bennett, *Fighting the Mau Mau*, 140–42; Anderson, *Histories of the Hanged*, 269–71, 392. On the reorganization of the Home Guard, see WO 236/18, "The Kenya Emergency, June 1953–May 1955," 33–34; and FCO 141/6187, "Future of Director, Kikuyu Guard," July 17, 1954.

86. Anderson, *Histories of the Hanged*, 269–70, 391–92.

87. Oxford Biography, http://www.oxforddnb.com/view/article/31335 (accessed August 20, 2014).

88. Percox, "British Counter-insurgency in Kenya," 88–89; WO 236/20, "The Kenya Emergency, May 1955–November 1956," 4. The latter is Lathbury's end of tour campaign history.

89. WO 236/20, "The Kenya Emergency, May 1955–November 1956," 13.

90. Soldiers of Gloucestershire Museum, http://www.glosters.org.uk/textonly_timeline/7 (accessed March 21, 2013).

91. Frank Furedi, *Colonial Wars and the Politics of Third World Nationalism* (London: I. B. Tauris, 1994), 182–83, quotation on 183.

92. See WO 276/184, "Operations Dante and Beatrice"; Kitson, *Gangs and Counter-gangs*, 190–96; Kitson, *Bunch of Five*, 50–53.

93. Kitson, *Gangs and Counter-gangs*, 195–96; Kitson, *Bunch of Five*, 52–53.

94. WO 236/20, "The Kenya Emergency, May 1955–November 1956," 12.

95. Percox, "British Counter-insurgency in Kenya," 88–89.

96. WO 236/20, "The Kenya Emergency, May 1955–November 1956," 17; Kitson, *Gangs and Counter-gangs*, 186–88, 208–9; Maloba, *Mau Mau and Kenya*, 94–96. See also Ian Henderson with Phillip Goodhart, *Man Hunt in Kenya* (New York: Doubleday, 1958).

97. Percox, "British Counter-insurgency in Kenya," 89; Maloba, *Mau Mau and Kenya*, 96.

98. Percox, "British Counter-insurgency in Kenya," 89; Anderson, *Histories of the Hanged*, 286–87.

99. Percox, "British Counter-insurgency in Kenya," 89; Maloba, *Mau Mau and Kenya*, 96; quotation in Percox.

100. See Henderson, *Man Hunt in Kenya*; Percox, "British Counter-insurgency in Kenya," 89–90; Anderson, *Histories of the Hanged*, 288.

101. WO 236/20, "The Kenya Emergency, May 1955–November 1956," 15.

102. Henderson, *Man Hunt in Kenya*, 30.

9. Counterinsurgency in the Land of Two Rivers

1. Unfortunately, none of these personnel can be identified by name. Unclassified briefings are cited by title and date where possible.

2. Through contracts with the RAND Corporation, I served in two different military organizations. The first was with a joint task force, Task Force-134/Detention Operations, which enabled travel to U.S. Army, U.S. Marine Corps, British, and U.S. special operations forces facilities in Baghdad, Anbar, Diyala, and Basrah provinces. The second was with Multinational Force–West, the Marine Corps senior command responsible for Anbar Province, which enabled interaction with U.S. Marine, U.S. Army, and U.S. special operations forces. Finally, in December 2009, I was in Baghdad, Erbil, and Kirkuk as a consultant to International Crisis Group, which allowed interaction with U.S. Army and U.S. Army Special Forces personnel.

3. For a series of personal vignettes on this time, see James Kitfield, *Prodigal Soldiers* (Washington, DC: Brassey's, 1995).

4. Inter alia, see Gregg Herken, *Counsels of War* (New York: Oxford University Press, 1987), and William Burr, "The Nixon Administration, the 'Horror Strategy,' and the Search for Limited Nuclear Options, 1969–1972: Prelude to the Schlesinger Doctrine," *Journal of Cold War Studies*, v. 7, n. 3 (Summer 2005).

5. See Paul Herbert, *Deciding What Has to Be Done: General William E. DuPuy and the 1976 Edition of FM 100-5, Operations* (Fort Leavenworth, KS: Combat Studies Institute, U.S. Army Command and General Staff College, 1988).

6. On this period in the Army, see Herbert, *Deciding What Has to Be Done*; Ingo Trauschweizer, *The Cold War Army: Building Deterrence for Limited War* (Lawrence: University Press of Kansas, 2008); Richard Lock-Pullan, "'An Inward-Looking Time': The United States Army, 1973–1976," *Journal of Military History*, v. 67, n. 2 (April 2003); and John L. Romjue, *From Active Defense to AirLand Battle: The Development of Army Doctrine, 1973–1982* (Fort Monroe, VA: Historical Office, U.S. Army Training and Doctrine Command, 1984).

7. For a contemporaneous view of the change, see Zeb Bradford and Frederic Joseph Brown, *The United States Army in Transition* (Beverly Hills, CA: Sage, 1973). For later assessments, see Suzanne Christine Nielsen, "Preparing for War: The Dynamics of Peacetime Military Reform" (PhD diss., Harvard University, 2003), and Colin Jackson, "From Conservatism to Revolutionary Intoxication: The U.S. Army in the Second Interwar Period," in *Creation without Destruc-*

tion: The Revolution in Military Affairs and the U.S. Military during the Second Interwar Period, ed. Harvey Sapolsky, Benjamin Friedman, and Brendan Green (New York: Routledge, 2009).

8. See Rick Atkinson, *Crusade: The Untold Story of the Persian Gulf War* (Boston: Houghton Mifflin, 1993), and Michael Gordon and Bernard Trainor, *The Generals' War: The Inside Story of the Conflict in the Gulf* (Boston: Back Bay Books, 1995).

9. In an unpublished manuscript entitled "The Evolution of Land Warfare," Barry Posen describes the Army in this period as being a new military format, which he refers to as the "thorough exploitation of science and technology" due to its adoption of high-technology methods of training as well as improved equipment.

10. Sean Maloney, "Fire Brigade or Tocsin? NATO's ACE Mobile Force, Flexible Response, and the Cold War," *Journal of Strategic Studies*, v. 27, n. 4 (December 2004); Barry Posen, "Inadvertent Nuclear War? Escalation and NATO's Northern Flank," *International Security*, v. 7, n. 2 (Fall 1982); Linton Brooks, "Naval Power and National Security: The Case for the Maritime Strategy," *International Security*, v. 11, n. 2 (Autumn 1986).

11. See *A Discussion of the Rapid Deployment Force with Lieutenant General P. X. Kelley* (Washington, DC: American Enterprise Institute, 1980).

12. Dennis Beal, "The M1A1 Tank: Its Role in the Marine Corps" (Marine Corps Command and Staff College paper, 1991).

13. T. X. Hammes, "Insurgency: The Forgotten Threat," *Marine Corps Gazette*, v. 72, n. 3 (March 1988); Eric Nyberg, "Insurgency: The Unsolved Mystery" (Marine Corps Command and Staff College paper, 1991).

14. Molly Moore, "Marine Commandant Striving for Leaner, Meaner Fighting Machine," *Los Angeles Times*, February 5, 1989.

15. See, for example, Charles Krulak, "Commandant's Planning Guidance Frag Order," *Marine Corps Gazette*, v. 81, n. 10 (October 1997).

16. Charles Krulak, "The Strategic Corporal: Leadership in the Three Block War," *Marine Corps Gazette*, v. 83, n. 1 (January 1999).

17. See Linda Robinson, *Masters of Chaos: The Secret History of the Special Forces* (New York: PublicAffairs, 2004), 38–40; and William Meara, *Contra Cross* (Annapolis, MD: Naval Institute Press, 2006), 12–72.

18. On this period, see Steven Emerson, *Secret Warriors: Inside the Covert Military Operations of the Reagan Era* (New York: Putnam, 1988).

19. Milt Bearden and James Risen, *The Main Enemy: The Inside Story of the CIA's Final Showdown with the KGB* (New York: Random House, 2003).

20. Thomas K. Adams, *US Special Operations Forces in Action: The Challenge of Unconventional Warfare* (New York: Frank Cass, 1998), 210; Susan L. Marquis, *Unconventional Warfare: Rebuilding US Special Operations Forces* (Washington, DC: Brookings Institution, 1997), 203–4.

21. Robinson, *Masters of Chaos*, 136–90.

22. See David Tucker and Christopher J. Lamb, *United States Special Operations Forces* (New York: Columbia University Press, 2007); Sean Naylor, "Support Grows for Standing Up an Unconventional Warfare Command," *Armed Forces Journal*, November 2007; and Colin Jackson and Austin Long, "The Fifth Service: The Rise of Special Operations Command," in Sapolsky, Friedman, and Green, *U.S. Military Innovation since the Cold War*.

23. Charles Briscoe, Richard Kiper, James Schoder, and Kalev Sepp, *Weapon of Choice: US Army Special Forces in Afghanistan* (Fort Leavenworth, KS: Combat Studies Institute Press, 2003).

24. Joint Special Operations Task Force–Philippines overview briefing, February 2008.

25. See Carl Schulze, *The British Army of the Rhine* (London: Windrow and Greene, 1995), and Correlli Barnett, *Britain and Her Army, 1509–1970* (New York: William Morrow, 1970), 483–93.

26. See J. Bowyer Bell, *The Irish Troubles: A Generation of Violence, 1967–1992* (New York: St. Martin's, 1993), and Thomas Mockaitis, *British Counterinsurgency in the Post-Imperial Era* (New York: Manchester University Press, 1995), 96–132.

27. See Mockaitis, 107–8, and Adam Fresco, "Old School Policing Leads to Return of the Supergrass," *Times* (London), December 29, 2008.

28. Mockaitis, *British Counterinsurgency*, 107–8.

29. Ibid., 103–4.

30. Ibid., 102–3.

31. Ibid., 72–95; John Akehurst, *We Won a War: The Campaign in Oman, 1965–1975* (Salisbury, UK: Michael Russell, 1982).

32. Mockaitis, *British Counterinsurgency*, 108–10.

33. Bernard Trainor and Michael Gordon, *Cobra II: The Inside Story of the Invasion and Occupation of Iraq* (New York: Vintage Books, 2005), is perhaps the best overview. See also Stephen Biddle, "Speed Kills? Reassessing the Role of Speed, Precision, and Situation Awareness in the Fall of Saddam," *Journal of Strategic Studies*, v. 30, n. 1 (February 2007). For a brigade-level view, see David Zucchino, *Thunder Run: The Armored Strike to Capture Baghdad* (New York: Atlantic Monthly Press, 2004).

34. See, inter alia, George Packer, *The Assassin's Gate: America in Iraq* (New York: Farrar, Straus and Giroux, 2005), Rajiv Chandrasekaran, *Imperial Life in the Emerald City: Inside Iraq's Green Zone* (New York: Alfred A. Knopf, 2006), and James Dobbins et al., *Occupying Iraq: A History of the Coalition Provisional Authority* (Santa Monica, CA: RAND, 2009).

35. For a more detailed treatment of Army counterinsurgency doctrine between Vietnam and Iraq, see David Fitzgerald, *Learning to Forget: U.S. Army Counterinsurgency Doctrine and Practice from Vietnam to Iraq* (Stanford, CA: Stanford University Press, 2013).

36. U.S. Department of the Army, Field Manual 3-07, *Stability and Support Operations*, February 2003, p. 2–3. The format for FM numbering can be confusing—it is chapter and then page number within chapter, so 2–3 is not the first and second pages of the manual. Rather it is the third page in chapter 2.

37. Ibid., pp. 2-15, 3-4.

38. Ibid., pp. 3-4–3-7.

39. U.S. Department of the Army, Field Manual–Interim 3-07.22, *Counterinsurgency Operations*, October 2004, p. 1-3.

40. Ibid., pp. 4-2 to 4-5.

41. Ibid., pp. 2-10–2-13.

42. Ibid., p. 3-10.

43. Ibid., pp. 3-9, 3-11–3-14.

44. Thomas Ricks, *Fiasco: The American Military Adventure in Iraq* (New York: Penguin, 2006), 232–33.

45. Dexter Fillkins, "The Fall of the Warrior King," *New York Times Magazine*, October 23, 2005.

46. See also Thomas Ricks, "It Looked Weird and Felt Wrong," *Washington Post*, July 24, 2005.

47. Patrecia Slayden Hollis, "Division Operations across the Spectrum: Combat to SOSO in Iraq," *Field Artillery* (March–June 2004), x; brackets in original.

48. Ibid., xi; brackets in original.

49. Ibid., xi–xii; brackets in original.

50. Ricks, *Fiasco*, 233.

51. Hollis, "Division Operations," xii.

52. Ricks, *Fiasco*, 233–38.

53. Dexter Filkins, "The Fall of the Warrior King," quotation on 2. Sassaman's own version of events is different; see Nathan Sassaman and Joe Layden, *Warrior King: The Triumph and Betrayal of an American Commander in Iraq* (New York: St. Martin's/Griffin, 2008).

54. Ricks, *Fiasco*, 138–40.

55. Ibid., 140–42.

56. See John R. Ballard, *Fighting for Fallujah: A New Dawn for Iraq* (Westport, CT: Praeger, 2006), 5–6.

57. Ibid., 11–12; Eric Schmitt, "Test in a Tinderbox," *New York Times*, April 28, 2004.

58. Both operations are described in "Iraqi, Coalition Forces Catch Suspects with Munitions," *American Forces Press Service*, November 17, 2005.

59. *Final Report of the Independent Panel to Review DoD Detention Operations* (hereafter Schlesinger Report) (Washington, DC: Department of Defense: August 2004), 29.

60. Author observations and discussions while working in detention operations, August 2007–January 2008.

61. Schlesinger Report, 11.

62. Robert Burns, "Battalion to Secure Iraq Prison Population," Associated Press, August 17, 2005.

63. Transcript of Donald Rumsfeld on *Fox News Sunday*, http://www.foxnews.com/story/0,2933,101956,00.html.

64. Edward Epstein, "Success in Afghan War Hard to Gauge," *San Francisco Chronicle*, March 23, 2002.

65. Joseph Giordono and Lisa Burgess, "Insurgent 'Body Count' Records Released," *Stars and Stripes*, October 1, 2007.

66. Julian Barnes, "War by the Numbers," *U.S. News and World Report*, July 10, 2005.

67. See Michael Gordon, "101st Scores Success in Northern Iraq," *New York Times*, September 4, 2003.

68. Ricks, *Fiasco*, 229.

69. See Kayla Williams, *Love My Rifle More Than You: Young and Female in the U.S. Army* (New York: W. W. Norton, 2006).

70. Author visited Third ACR at Fort Carson in December 2004, shortly before its deployment. See also Thomas Ricks, "The Lessons of Counterinsurgency," *Washington Post*, February 16, 2006.

71. George Packer, "The Lesson of Tal Afar," *New Yorker*, April 10, 2006; David R. McCone, Wilbur J. Scott, and George R. Mastroianni, "The 3rd ACR in Tal'Afar: Challenges and Adaptations" (U.S. Army War Strategic Studies Institute paper, January 8, 2008).

72. Robert Chamberlin, "Finding the Flow: Shadow Economies, Ethnic Networks, and Counterinsurgency," *Military Review*, v. 88, n. 5 (September–October 2008).

73. See Trainor and Gordon, *Cobra II*, and Bing West, *The March Up: Taking Baghdad with the United States Marines* (New York: Bantam, 2004).

74. See Carter Malkasian, "Signaling Resolve, Democratization, and the First Battle of Fallujah," *Journal of Strategic Studies*, v. 29, n. 3 (June 2006).

75. See Malkasian, "Signaling Resolve," and Hannah Allam, "Fallujah's Real Boss: Omar the Electrician," Knight Ridder Newspapers, November 22, 2004.

76. See Malkasian, "Signaling Resolve"; Matt Matthews, "Operation AL FAJR: A Study in Army and Marine Corps Joint Operations," Long War Occasional Paper 20 (Fort Leavenworth, KS: Combat Studies Institute Press, 2006); and Bing West, *No True Glory: A Frontline Account of the Battle for Fallujah* (New York: Bantam, 2005).

77. Austin Long, "The Anbar Awakening," *Survival*, v. 50, n. 2 (March/April 2008); John A. McCary, "The Anbar Awakening: An Alliance of Incentives," *Washington Quarterly*, v. 32, n. 1 (January 2009).

78. Ellen Nickmeyer and Jonathan Finer, "Insurgents Assert Control over Town Near Syrian Border," *Washington Post*, September 6, 2005; Carter Malkasian, "A Thin Blue Line in the Sand," *Democracy*, n. 5 (Summer 2007); Carter Malkasian, "Did the Coalition Need More Forces in Iraq?," *Joint Forces Quarterly*, n. 46 (Summer 2007).

79. See Malkasian, "Did the Coalition Need More Forces in Iraq?"; and John Ward Anderson, "U.S. Widens Offensive in Far Western Iraq," *Washington Post*, November 15, 2005.

80. See "State of the Insurgency in al-Anbar," I MEF G2 intelligence report, August 17, 2006, http://www.washingtonpost.com/wp-dyn/content/article/2007/02/02/AR2007020201197.html; Toby Harnden, "US Army Admits Iraqis Outnumber Foreign Fighters as Its Main Enemy," *Daily Telegraph*, December 3, 2005; and Multinational Force–Iraq press briefing, "Tearing Down al-Qaida in Iraq," December 2006.

81. Robinson, *Masters of Chaos*, 191–340, provides an extensive overview. See also see Michael Tucker and Charles Faddis, *Operation Hotel California: The Clandestine War inside Iraq* (Guilford, CT: Lyons Press, 2008).

82. Combined Joint Task Force–Arabian Peninsula overview briefing, February 2007.

83. This task force was generically known as OCF-I (Other Coalition Forces Iraq) and carried a three-number designation that changed from time to time. In 2008, according to a public statement by Chairman of the Joint Chiefs of Staff Michael Mullen, this designation was Task Force 714. See Mullen transcript, June 10, 2008, http://www.airforce-magazine.com/DWG/Documents/2008/061008mullen.pdf.

84. See, for example, Ann Scott Tyson, "In a Volatile Region of Iraq, US Military Takes Two Paths," *Washington Post*, September 15, 2006; and Bruce Pirnie and Edward O'Connell, *Counterinsurgency in Iraq (2003–2006)* (Santa Monica, CA: RAND, 2008).

85. James Gavrilis, "The Mayor of Ar Rutbah," *Foreign Policy* (November/December 2005).

86. Donald P. Wright, Timothy R. Reese, et al., *On Point II: Transition to the New Campaign—The United States Army in Operation IRAQI FREEDOM, May 2003–January 2005* (Fort Leavenworth, KS: Combat Studies Institute Press, 2008), chap. 11; Combined Joint Task Force–Arabian Peninsula overview briefing, n.d.

87. Some missions were undertaken by SEALs; over time the SEALs came to be responsible principally for Anbar Province. This began in roughly 2006; by mid-2008 the CJSOTF task force in Anbar was all SEALs.

88. See Robinson, *Masters of Chaos*, 291–94.

89. See MNF-I Memo 11-1, Annex R, MNF-I Uniform Wear, Appearance, Conduct and Standards (September 2008). The author observed CJSOTF-AP personnel on operations out of uniform on several occasions in 2008 and 2009.

90. *Army Field Manual*, vol. 1, *Combined Arms Operations: Part 10, Counterinsurgency Operations* (2001).

91. Ibid., A-1-1.

92. Ibid., B-6-1.

93. Ibid., B-3-2, B-3-4, chap. 7.

94. Tom Dunn, "First British-Iraqi Police Patrols Begin," April 13, 2003, http://news.bbc.co.uk/2/hi/uk_news/2944603.stm; David Ucko and Robert Egnell, *Counterinsurgency in Crisis: Britain and the Challenges of Modern Warfare* (New York: Columbia University Press, 2013), 50–60.

95. See BBC News, "British Military Police Killed in Iraq," June 24, 2003, http://news.bbc.co.uk/2/hi/middle_east/3017332.stm; "UK Troops Attacked in Basra," August 9, 2003, http://news.bbc.co.uk/2/hi/middle_east/3137779.stm; and "British Soldier Killed in Basra," *The Guardian*, August 14, 2003.

96. BBC News, "UK Troops Clash with Basra Gunmen," May 8, 2004, http://news.bbc.co.uk/2/hi/middle_east/3695787.stm; Ucko and Egnell, *Counterinsurgency in Crisis*, 58–61.

97. Michael Knights and Ed Williams, "The Calm before the Storm: The British Experience in Southern Iraq," Washington Institute for Near-East Policy, Policy Focus 66 (February 2007), 8, 20–21; Ucko and Egnell, *Counterinsurgency in Crisis*, 58–61.

98. Ibid., 25.

99. Ibid., 22.

100. On intelligence presence, see Mahan Abedin, "Britain, Iran Playing with Iraqi Shi'ite Fire," *Asia Times*, October 1, 2005.

101. See Knights and Williams, "Calm before the Storm," 30; and Adrian Blomfield and Thomas Harding, "Troops Free SAS Men from Jail," *Daily Telegraph*, September 21, 2005.

102. It is possible, perhaps even likely, that these soldiers were from another British special operations unit, the Special Reconnaissance Regiment, which focuses on intelligence collection.

103. Blomfield and Harding, "Troops Free SAS Men."

104. See Mark Urban, *Task Force Black: The Explosive True Story of the SAS and the Secret War in Iraq* (London: Little, Brown, 2010); Sean Naylor, "SpecOps Unit Nearly Nabs Zarqawi," *Army Times* (online version), April 28, 2006; and Sean Naylor, "More Than Door Kickers," *Armed Forces Journal*, March 2006.

105. Nigel Aylwin-Foster, "Changing the Army for Counterinsurgency Operations," *Military Review*, v. 85, n. 6 (November–December 2005).

106. Kevin Benson, "OIF IV: A Planner's Reply to Brigadier Aylwin-Foster," *Military Review*, v. 86, n. 2 (March–April 2006), 61, makes specific reference to the September 2005 British raid on the Basra jail.

107. Rod Thornton, "British Counterinsurgency Operations in Iraq," in House of Commons Defence Committee, *Iraq: An Initial Assessment of Post-conflict Operations*, Sixth Report of Session 2004–5, v. 2:141–42, quotation on 141.

108. Thomas Ricks, "U.S. Counterinsurgency Academy Giving Officers a New Mind-Set," *Washington Post*, February 21, 2006.

109. Multinational Force Iraq, *MNF-I Counterinsurgency Handbook*, May 2006, 9–19, 30–37.

110. Ibid., 20–29, 59–63.

111. Ibid., 38–52.

112. Ibid., 64–70.

113. Brian Bennett and Al Jallam, "How Operation Swarmer Fizzled," *Time*, March 17, 2006.

114. For subsequent examples of continuing insecurity around Samarra, see MNF-I press release, "Coalition Forces Discover Sizable Caches South of Samarra," December 26, 2006; and MNF-I press release, "Iraqi Police Find Bomb Near Golden Mosque in Samarra," December 12, 2006.

115. MNF-I weekly press briefing, March 23, 2006.

116. Multinational Force–Iraq press briefing, "Tearing Down al-Qaida in Iraq," December 2006.

117. See Eliot Cohen, Conrad Crane, Jan Horvath, and John Nagl, "Principles, Imperatives, and Paradoxes of Counterinsurgency," *Military Review*, v. 86, n. 2 (March–April 2006).

118. U.S. Department of the Army and U.S. Marine Corps, Field Manual 3-24 / Fleet Marine Force Manual 3-24, *Counterinsurgency*, final draft, June 2006.

119. Ibid., pp. 2-2–2-3.

120. Ibid., pp. 2-9–2-13.

121. Ibid., p. 3-1.

122. Compare ibid., draft chapter 3 and appendix B, to U.S. Department of the Army and U.S. Marine Corps, Field Manual 3-24/Marine Corps Warfighting Publication 3-33.5, *Counterinsurgency*, December 2006, chapter 3.

123. Joint press conference, Major General William Caldwell, MNF-I spokesman, and Dr. Ali al-Dabbagh, government of Iraq spokesman, May 23, 2007.

124. Ann Scott Tyson, "Troops at Baghdad Outposts Seek Safety in Fortifications," *Washington Post*, May 8, 2007.

125. Julian Barnes, "U.S. Troops Close, but So Far," *Los Angeles Times*, July 8, 2007.

126. Ibid., 2.

127. James Russell, *Innovation, Transformation, and War: Counterinsurgency Operations in Anbar and Ninewa Provinces, Iraq, 2005–2007* (Stanford, CA: Stanford University Press), 94–133.

128. "Start of 'Arrowhead Ripper' Highlights Iraq Operations," American Forces Press Service, June 19, 2007.

129. "Lightning Hammer Disrupts Terrorists in Iraq's Diyala Province," American Forces Press Service, August 24, 2007.

130. "Operation Lightning Hammer II Expands Pursuit of al-Qaeda," Multi-National Division–North press release, September 6, 2007.

131. For example, a year after Arrowhead Ripper, the governor of Diyala was almost assassinated outside the Governance Center of Baqubah even as Iraqi forces conducted another major operation to secure the province. See "Suicide Bomber Kills 1, Injures 9 in Baqubah," Multi-National Division–North press release, August 12, 2008.

132. Author interviews, November 27–28, 2007, FOB Warhorse, Diyala Province, Iraq.

133. Walter Pincus, "U.S. Holds 18,000 Detainees in Iraq," *Washington Post*, April 15, 2007.

134. Thom Shanker, "With Troop Rise, Iraqi Detainees Soar in Number," *New York Times*, August 24, 2007.

135. Giordono and Burgess, "Insurgent 'Body Count' Records Released."

136. Dale Andrade, *Surging South of Baghdad: The 3rd Infantry Division and Task Force Marne in Iraq, 2007–2008* (Washington, DC: Center of Military History, 2010), 180–90.

137. Ibid., 123–61.

138. Ibid., 155–56.

139. Fred Baker, "Al Qaeda Fighters Flee Cities, Head for Desert or out of Iraq," American Forces Press Service, February 11, 2008; "Multi-National Corps–Iraq Commences Phantom Phoenix," Multi-National Corps–Iraq press release, January 8, 2008.

140. Campbell Robertson, "Iraqi Army Seeks Out Insurgents and Arms in Diyala, Backed by U.S. Forces," *New York Times*, July 30, 2008; MNF-I briefing with Major General Mohammed al-Askari and Brigadier General David Perkins, August 13, 2008.

141. Andrade, *Surging South of Baghdad*, 308–26, quotation on 317.

142. Ibid., 318–19.

143. See "State of the Insurgency in al-Anbar"; Multinational Force–Iraq press briefing, "Tearing Down al-Qaida in Iraq," December 2006; "Iraqi Rebels Turn on Qaeda in Western City," Reuters, January 23, 2006; and Jonathan Finer and Ellen Nickmeyer, "Sunni Leaders Attacked in Iraq," *Washington Post*, August 19, 2005.

144. Conversations with Marines stationed in Ramadi from February to September 2006.

145. McCary, "Anbar Awakening"; Malkasian, "Thin Blue Line"; Greg Jaffe, "Tribal Connections: How Courting Sheiks Slowed Violence in Iraq," *Wall Street Journal*, August 8, 2007; Mark Kukis, "Turning Iraq's Tribes against Al-Qaeda," *Time*, December 26, 2006.

146. Thomas R. Searle, "Tribal Engagement in Al Anbar Province: The Critical Role of Special Operations Forces," *Joint Forces Quarterly*, n. 50 (Summer 2008); Ann Scott Tyson, "In a Volatile Region of Iraq, US Military Takes Two Paths," *Washington Post*, September 15, 2006; Dick Couch, *The Sheriff of Ramadi: Navy SEALs and the Winning of al-Anbar* (Annapolis, MD: Naval Institute Press, 2008), 76; Stephen Manning, "CIA Chief: Military Strikes Offer Lessons," *USA Today*, September 17, 2008.

147. "State of the Insurgency in al-Anbar."

148. Matthew C. Armstrong, "A Friend in the Desert," *Winchester Star*, April 8, 2008; and Pamela Hess, "Building Security in Barwanah," two-part article from *United Press International Security and Terrorism*, February 27 and March 2, 2007.

149. For MacFarland's version of the origin of the Awakening, see Niel Smith and Sean MacFarland, "Anbar Awakens: The Tipping Point," *Military Review* (March–April 2008); and Russell, *Innovation, Transformation, and War*.

150. Tina Sussman, "Slain Sheik a Stark Contrast to His Brother," *Los Angeles Times*, October 13, 2007.

151. Sudarsan Raghavan, "In Fallujah, Peace through Brute Strength," *Washington Post*, March 24, 2008.

152. Author observation, Fallujah, Iraq, May–August 2008.

153. Ibid.

154. This arrangement was very clearly the case in both Regimental Combat Team 5 (RCT 5) and Regimental Combat Team 1 (RCT 1) in 2008, though there were variations. In RCT 5 in western Anbar, the regimental commander, supported by the S-2A (regimental targeting officer), conducted many of the engagements. In RCT 1 in eastern Anbar, the S-2 conducted more engagements himself.

155. Based on briefings, this was certainly the model for Third Battalion, Eighth Marines in 2006.

156. See, for example, reporting on the area around Karmah-Sam Dagher, "Tribal Rivalries Persist as Iraqis Seek Local Posts," *New York Times*, January 19, 2009; Achilles Tsantarliotis, "Karmah Sheikhs Committed to Progression," *Regimental Combat Team 1* blog, October 10, 2008, http://fearless1stmarines.vox.com/library/post/karmah-sheiks-committed-to-progression .html?_c=feed-atom.

157. Sam Dagher, "How Fragile Is Baghdad's Calm?," *Christian Science Monitor*, November 27, 2007.

158. Charles Crain, "Iraq's New Job Insecurity," *Time*, December 24, 2007.

159. See, for example, Multinational Corps–Iraq press release, "Iraqi Special Operations Forces Engage, Kill 22 in Basra," March 30, 2008.

160. Author observation, Iraq, August 2007–January 2008.

161. See Jed Babbin, "Robin Sage," *National Review Online*, November 20, 2003, http://www .nationalreview.com/babbin/babbin200311200838.asp; and Sean Naylor, "Special Forces Expands," *Army Times*, August 11, 2008.

162. Author conversations with Special Forces personnel from 2007 to 2009.

163. See, for example, Hy S. Rothstein, *Afghanistan and the Troubled Future of Unconventional Warfare* (Annapolis, MD: Naval Institute Press, 2006), 175–78. Author conversations with Special Forces personnel from 2007 to 2009 produced a variety of similar anecdotes.

164. See Mark Oliver, "Two More Held over Iraq 'Abuse' Video," *The Guardian*, February 14, 2006; BBC, "Iraqis Resume Ties with British," May 7, 2006, http://news.bbc.co.uk/2/hi/middle_east/4982930.stm; and Jason Burke and Ned Temko, "British Soldiers Die as Helicopter Is Shot Down," *The Guardian*, May 7, 2006.

165. Anne Penketh, "State of Emergency in Basra Threatens British Withdrawal," *The Independent*, June 1, 2006.

166. Richard Norton-Taylor, "General Warns of Rising Levels of Violence in Basra," *The Guardian*, June 21, 2006.

167. MNF-I press release, "Iraqis Control First Province," July 14, 2006.

168. MNF-I press release, "Iraqis Take Control in Dhi Qar," September 22, 2006.

169. Damien McElroy, "3,000 British Troops Try to Tame Basra," *Daily Telegraph*, September 28, 2006.

170. Raymond Whitaker, "Operation Sinbad: Mission Failure Casts Doubt on Entire British Presence in Iraq," *The Independent*, October 8, 2006. See also Ucko and Egnell, *Counterinsurgency in Crisis*, 61–63.

171. BBC, "UK Troops Storm Iraqi Police HQ," December 25, 2006, http://news.bbc.co.uk/2/hi/uk_news/6208535.stm.

172. Richard Beeston, "British Soldier Shot in the Chest during Routine Patrol in Basra," *Times* (London), February 10, 2007.

173. MNF-I press release, "Maysan Security Now in Iraqi Hands," April 27, 2007.

174. BBC News, "Troops Withdraw from Basra Base," August 26, 2007, http://news.bbc.co.uk/2/hi/uk_news/6964736.stm.

175. See Martin Fletcher, "Basra Celebrates British Withdrawal," *Times* (London), September 3, 2007; and BBC News, "Troops Withdraw from Basra Base."

176. See BBC News, "UK Troops to Be Cut to 2,500," October 8, 2007, http://news.bbc.co.uk/2/hi/uk_news/politics/7034010.stm; and MNF-I press release, "Ceremony Marks Iraqi Control," December 16, 2007. The author visited Basra airfield several times between September and December 2007; observations there and at Camp Bucca to the south confirm the view that the British withdrawal was little short of a retreat. See also Ucko and Egnell, *Counterinsurgency in Crisis*, 63–68.

177. See James Glanz, "Iraqi Army's Assault on Militias in Basra Stalls," *New York Times*, March 27, 2008; MNF-I press release, "Iraq Special Operations Forces Engage, Kill 22 in Basra," March 29, 2008; and BBC News, "British Army Joins Basra Fighting," March 29, 2008, http://news.bbc.co.uk/2/hi/in_depth/7320696.stm.

178. James Glanz and Alissa Rubin, "Iraqi Army Takes Last Basra Areas from Sadr Force," *New York Times*, April 20, 2008.

179. John Burn and Michael Gordon, "U.S. Says Iran Helped Iraqis Kill Five G.I.'s," *New York Times*, July 3, 2007; Jim Garamone, "Iran Arming, Training, Directing Terror Groups in Iraq, U.S. Official Says," American Forces Press Service, July 2, 2007.

180. Deborah Haynes, "General Petraeus Hails SAS after Iraq Success over al-Qaeda Car Bombers," *The Guardian*, August 11, 2008.

181. Richard Norton-Taylor, "SAS Soldier Killed in Iraq Gunfight," *The Guardian*, March 27, 2008.

182. BBC News, "Browne Meets Residents of Basra," May 22, 2008, http://news.bbc.co.uk/2/hi/uk_news/7415625.stm.

183. BBC News, "Hutton Hails UK Progress in Iraq," October 21, 2008, http://news.bbc.co.uk/2/hi/uk_news/7681233.stm; Simon Hoggart, "Tea and Dates in Basra," *The Guardian*, October 29, 2008.

10. Counterinsurgency in Afghanistan, 2003–11

1. On this initial period, see Gary Schroen, *First In: An Insider's Account of How the CIA Spearheaded the War on Terror in Afghanistan* (New York: Ballantine Books, 2005); Gary Berntsen and Ralph Pezzullo, *Jawbreaker: The Attack on Bin Laden and Al Qaeda* (New York: Crown, 2005); Henry A. Crumpton, "Intelligence and War: Afghanistan 2001–2002," in *Transforming U.S. Intelligence*, ed. Jennifer E. Sims and Burton Gerber (Washington, DC: Georgetown University Press, 2005); Charles Briscoe, Richard Kiper, James Schoder, and Kalev Sepp, *Weapon of Choice: US Army Special Forces in Afghanistan* (Fort Leavenworth, KS: Combat Studies Institute Press, 2003); Dalton Fury, *Kill Bin Laden: A Delta Force Commander's Account of the Hunt for the World's Most Dangerous Man* (New York: St. Martin's, 2008); and Sean Naylor, *Not a Good Day to Die: The Untold Story of Operation Anaconda* (New York: Berkley Books, 2005).

2. Stephen Biddle, "Allies, Airpower, and Modern Warfare: The Afghan Model in Afghanistan and Iraq," *International Security*, v. 30, n. 3 (Winter 2005–6); Peter Krause, "The Last Good Chance: A Reassessment of U.S. Operations at Tora Bora," *Security Studies*, v. 17, n. 4 (October 2008).

3. Antonio Giustozzi, *Koran, Kalashnikov, and Laptop: The Neo-Taliban Insurgency in Afghanistan* (New York: Columbia University Press, 2008); Seth Jones, *Counterinsurgency in Afghanistan* (Santa Monica, CA: RAND, 2008).

4. David Barno, "Fighting 'the Other War': Counterinsurgency Strategy in Afghanistan, 2003–2005," *Military Review* (September–October 2007).

5. Hooman Peimani, "Mission Impossible for the Afghan Army," *Asia Times*, July 26, 2003; Voice of America, "Up to 100 Afghan Militants Killed in Operation 'Mountain Viper,'" September 5, 2003, http://www.voanews.com/content/a-13-a-2003-09-05-25-up-67475047/386245.html; Voice of America, "15 Suspected Taleban [*sic*] Fighters Killed in Afghanistan Clashes," September 15, 2003, http://www.voanews.com/content/a-13-a-2003-09-15-25-15-67321742/381859.html.

6. Jacob Caldwell, "'Diablo' Weakens Taliban Mountain Stronghold," Army News Service, June 28, 2005.

7. "Coalition Launches 'Operation Mountain Lion' in Afghanistan," American Forces Press Service, April 12, 2006.

8. Declan Walsh, "U.S.-Led Troops Launch Largest Assault on Taliban since 2001," *The Guardian*, June 15, 2006; Carolyn Trias-DeRyder, "Operation Mountain Thrust," *Army Logistician* (January–February 2008).

9. Jacob Caldwell, "Company Works to Flush Out Taliban during 'Rock Avalanche,'" Armed Forces Press Service, October 31, 2007.

10. International Security Assistance Force press release, "ANSF, ISAF Completing Operation Mountain Fire," July 16, 2009.

11. Voice of America, "U.S. Will Have 140,000 Troops in Iraq at End of 'Surge,'" February 25, 2008, http://www.voanews.com/content/a-13-2008-02-25-voa60/404913.html.

12. Author visited the COIN Academy in July 2009.

13. Don Huvane, "High School Reopens in Afghanistan's Nangarhar Province," American Forces Press Service, March 29, 2006; Trista Talton, "Marine Spec Ops Commander Relieved," *Marine Corps Times*, April 11, 2007; 22nd MEU official website, http://www.22ndmeu.marines.mil/UnitHome/History.aspx.

14. Jerry Meyerle, Megan Katt, James Gavrilis, *On the Ground in Afghanistan: Counterinsurgency in Practice* (Quantico, VA: Marine Corps University Press / Center for Naval Analyses, 2012), 30.

15. Julian Borger and Ewen MacAskill, "US Marines Pour into Helmand in Biggest Offensive against Taliban for Five Years," *The Guardian*, July 2, 2009.

16. Marine Expeditionary Brigade press release, "Marines Launch Operation Khanjar in Southern Afghanistan," July 2, 2009.

17. Noah Shachtman, "Firepower Trumps 'Soft Power' in This Afghan Town," *Wired: Danger Room*, http://www.wired.com/dangerroom/2009/09/tweets-are-comi-2/.

18. The story of Garmser is described at length in Carter Malkasian, *War Comes to Garmser: Thirty Years of Conflict on the Afghan Frontier* (New York: Oxford University Press, 2013).

19. Meyerle et al., *On the Ground*, 37–38.

20. Ibid., 40.

21. See Adrian Bogart, *One Valley at a Time* (Hurlburt Field, FL: Joint Special Operations University, 2006).

22. Ibid., 58.

23. Ibid., 60–66.

24. Meyerle et al., *On the Ground*, 95–96.

25. For an extended discussion of one Special Forces team's deployment with ANCOP in 2010, see Kevin Maurer, *Gentleman Bastards: On the Ground with America's Elite Special Forces* (New York: Berkley Books, 2012).

26. Kate Clark, "War without Accountability: The CIA, Special Forces and Plans for Afghanistan's Future," Afghan Analysts Network, February 2012.

27. Jules Cavendish, "Revealed: Afghan Chief Accused of Campaign of Terror Is on US Payroll," *The Independent*, March 18, 2011; ISAF press release, "Afghan Police Protect PRT from Roadside Bomb," January 2013.

28. This discussion of local defense in Afghanistan draws heavily on the author's field research and experience with the local defense effort in June 2010, January 2011, June–August 2011, and May–August 2013; along with Dan Madden, "The Evolution of Precision Counterinsurgency: A History of Village Stability Operations and the Afghan Local Police," Headquarters Combined Forces Special Operations Component Command–Afghanistan, June 2011. See also Linda Robinson, *One Hundred Victories: Special Ops and the Future of American Warfare* (New York: PublicAffairs, 2013), and Austin Long et al., *Locals Rule: Historical Lessons for Creating Local Defense Forces for Afghanistan and Beyond* (Santa Monica, CA: RAND, 2012).

29. NATO Training Mission–Afghanistan, "Afghanistan Local Police Update"; David Cloud and Laura King, "Afghan Police Units Tangled in Criminal Activity," *Los Angeles Times*, May 14, 2012.

30. Unless otherwise noted, this section is drawn from author observations and conversations with U.S. personnel, Afghan personnel, and interpreters in Khakrez district in June 2010, January 2011, and July 2011.

31. Richard Norton-Taylor, "Mission Unaccomplished," *The Guardian*, June 20, 2002.

32. See Ministry of Defence press release, "Gurkhas Train Afghan Police," February 12, 2009; and "Ministry of Defence Operations in Afghanistan, http://www.operations.mod.uk /afghanistan/forces.htm.

33. Foreign and Commonwealth Office, "Afghanistan: Paper on UK PRT Experience," http://www.fco.gov.uk/resources/en/pdf/pdf13/fco_fpr_afghan_prt.

34. *Provincial Reconstruction Teams in Afghanistan: An Interagency Assessment* (Washington, DC: United States Agency for International Development, 2006), 10. The assessment was conducted by a joint USAID, State Department, and military (Joint Center for Operational Analysis) team.

35. Nick Grono, testimony before the UK International Development Committee, House of Commons, December 13, 2005.

36. See James Fergusson, *A Million Bullets: The Real Story of the British Army in Afghanistan* (New York: Bantam, 2008) and U.S. Army Corps of Engineers, *GWOT Reconstruction Report*, August 6, 2007.

37. David Ucko and Robert Egnell, *Counterinsurgency in Crisis: Britain and the Challenges of Modern Warfare* (New York: Columbia University Press, 2013), 76–84.

38. See ibid., 84–88; Fergusson, *A Million Bullets*; James Meek, "In Their Minds, All They Want to Do Is Kill English Soldiers," *The Guardian*, October 14, 2006; Defence Committee, House of Commons, Thirteenth Report, 2006–2007 session, chap. 3, "UK Operations in Southern Afghanistan."

39. Ministry of Defence press release, "UK Troops Redeploy from Musa Qala as Afghan Government Hands Security to Local Elders," October 18, 2006; Defence Committee, "UK Operations in Southern Afghanistan"; Jason Burke, "Taliban Town Seizure Throws Afghan Policy into Disarray," *The Observer*, February 4, 2007.

40. See Meyerle et al., *On the Ground*, 118; Thomas Harding and Tom Coghlan, "Britain in Secret Talks with the Taliban," *Telegraph* (UK), December 26, 2007; and Tom Coghlan, "Key Tribal Leader on Verge of Deserting Taliban," *Telegraph* (UK), October 29, 2007.

41. See Theo Farrell, "Improving in War: Military Adaptation and the British in Helmand Province, Afghanistan, 2006–2009," *Journal of Strategic Studies*, v. 33, n. 4 (2010).

42. Ministry of Defence press release, "ISAF Troops Launch Major Afghan Offensive," April 10, 2007; Ministry of Defence press release, "On the Heels of Achilles," May 3, 2007.

43. Ministry of Defence press release, "U.K.-Led Operation Helps ISAF Take Control in Northern Helmand," May 31, 2007; Ministry of Defence press release, " 'Vikings' Lead the Way in Sangin Clearance Operation," July 5, 2007.

44. Ministry of Defence press release, "British and Afghan Forces Launch New Offensive against the Taliban," July 26, 2007; Ministry of Defence press release, "Warrior Debuts in Helmand Offensive," September 21, 2007.

45. Meyerle et al., *On the Ground*, 119–21; Ministry of Defence press release, " 'Time Is Now Right' for Retaking Musa Qaleh—Browne," December 9, 2007; Mark Townsend, "Fierce Battle Rages for Taliban Stronghold," *The Observer*, December 9, 2007; Ministry of Defence press release, "Gurkhas Fight for Security in Musa Qaleh," November 25, 2008.

46. Ministry of Defence press release, "British Troops and ANA in Apache-Backed Operation," June 4, 2008; Ministry of Defence press release, "British Troops Complete Operation to Deliver Vital Power Turbine," September 2, 2008.

47. Ministry of Defence press release, "2 PARA Tough It Out in Helmand's 'Green Zone,' " August 13, 2008; Ministry of Defence press release, "Pashty-Speaking Paras: The Face of the British Army in Helmand," August 19, 2008; David Pratt, "Target: The Taliban," *Sunday Herald* (UK), January 25, 2009. For a deeper treatment of the 2006–7 fighting, see Fergusson, *A Million Bullets*.

48. Ministry of Defence press release, "Marines Shatter 'Illusion of Enemy Safe Haven,' " March 26, 2009; Ministry of Defence press release, "Black Watch Conduct First Major Afghan Operation," May 1, 2009; Ministry of Defence press release, "Fusiliers and Afghan Soldiers Clear Taliban Stronghold," June 2, 2009.

49. See Ministry of Defence press release, "On Patrol with the Welsh Guards in Helmand," June 3, 2009; and BBC News, "Helmand Day Three—Inches and Plate Spinning," March 13, 2009, http://news.bbc.co.uk/2/hi/uk_news/7942269.stm.

50. Ministry of Defence press release, "3 SCOTS Launch Massive Air Assault," June 23, 2009; Jon Boone, "The Battle for Babaji: A Fight for Hearts and Minds in Afghanistan but None Are to Be Found," *The Guardian*, June 24, 2009; Ministry of Defence press release, "U.K., U.S. and Afghan Commanders Unite as Taliban Flee," July 10, 2009; Ministry of Defence press release, "Helicopter Assault Starts Latest Phase of Attack on Taliban," July 20, 2009; Ministry of Defence press release, "Armoured Thrust Clears Final Taliban from 'Panther's Claw,' " July 27, 2009.

51. Farrell, "Improving in War," 582.

Index

Note: The letters *t* and *n* indicate that the entry refers to a page's table or note, respectively.